The Right to Housing in Law and Society

From the very first negotiations of the International Covenant on Economic, Social and Cultural Rights half a century ago to the present day, socio-economic rights have often been regarded as less enforceable than civil and political rights. The right to adequate housing, even though protecting one of the most basic needs of human beings, has not escaped this classification. Despite its strong foundations in international, regional and domestic legislation, many people are still deprived of one or more of the different key elements that comprise adequate housing.

How, then, can international human rights theory and case law be developed into effective vehicles at the domestic level? Rather than focusing merely on possibilities for individualized relief through the court system, *The Right to Housing in Law and Society* looks into more effective socio-economic rights realization by addressing both conceptual and practical stumbling blocks that hinder a more structural progress at the national level. The Flemish and Belgian housing legislation and policy are used to highlight the problems and illustrate the pathways here presented.

While first and foremost legal in its approach, the book also offers a more sociological perspective on the functioning of the right to housing in practice. It shows the latest state of knowledge on the topic and will be of interest to researchers, academics, policymakers and students in the fields of international socio-economic rights law and human rights law more generally.

Nico Moons is Doctor of Law at the University of Antwerp, Belgium.

Routledge Research in Human Rights Law

Available titles in this series include:

The Positive Obligations of the State under the European Convention of Human Rights
Dimitris Xenos

International Human Rights Law and Domestic Violence
The Effectiveness of International Human Rights Law
Ronagh McQuigg

The Right to Religious Freedom in International Law
Between Group Rights and Individual Rights
Anat Scolnicov

The Right to Development in International Law
The Case of Pakistan
Khurshid Iqbal

Global Health and Human Rights
Legal and Philosophical Perspectives
John Harrington and Maria Stuttaford

Human Rights, Constitutional Law and Belonging
The Right to Equal Belonging in Democratic Society
Elena Drymiotou

Dignity, Degrading Treatment and Torture in Human Rights Law
The Ends of Article 3 of the European Convention on Human Rights
Elaine Webster

The Right to Housing in Law and Society
Nico Moons

https://www.routledge.com/Routledge-Research-in-Human-Rights-Law/book-series/HUMRIGHTSLAW

The Right to Housing in Law and Society

Nico Moons

Routledge
Taylor & Francis Group
LONDON AND NEW YORK

First published 2018 by Routledge

2 Park Square, Milton Park, Abingdon, Oxfordshire OX14 4RN
52 Vanderbilt Avenue, New York, NY 10017

Routledge is an imprint of the Taylor & Francis Group, an informa business

First issued in paperback 2020

Library of Congress Cataloging-in-Publication Data
Names: Moons, Nico, author.
Title: The right to housing in law and society / Nico Moons.
Description: New York, NY : Routledge, 2018. |
Series: Routledge research in human rights law | Includes bibliographical references and index.
Identifiers: LCCN 2017060229| ISBN 9781138093270 (hardback) |
ISBN 9781351605625 (web pdf) | ISBN 9781351605618 (epub) |
ISBN 9781351605601 (mobipocket)
Subjects: LCSH: Right to housing.
Classification: LCC K3550. M66 2018 | DDC 344/.063635—dc23
LC record available at https://lccn.loc.gov/2017060229

ISBN: 978-1-138-09327-0 (hbk)
ISBN: 978-0-367-59043-7 (pbk)

Typeset in Galliard
by Keystroke, Neville Lodge, Tettenhall, Wolverhampton

Contents

Acknowledgments

This book is an adaptation of my PhD thesis, which I defended at the University of Antwerp, on 18 November 2016. Neither this book nor the thesis would have seen the light of day without the assistance and support of colleagues, family and friends. Specific gratitude goes to my supervisors, prof. dr. Bernard Hubeau and prof. dr. Wouter Vandenhole. They helped me grow as a researcher and were always there to answer my relevant and less relevant questions. I would like to thank them not only for sharing their expertise, but also for providing me with the freedom and trust to pursue and develop my own ideas and theories.

In addition, I wish to thank the distinguished members of my PhD jury for their time, recommendations and expressed interest in my work: prof. dr. Padraic Kenna (National University of Ireland, Galway), prof. dr. Nicolas Bernard (Saint-Louis University Brussels, Belgium), prof. dr. Danielle Dierckx and prof. dr. Jan Velaers (both from the University of Antwerp).

Lastly, I would like to express my deepest gratitude to Sophia and my parents Lutje and Dirk, whose unconditional love, support, understanding and patience have been an indispensable source of motivation.

Nico Moons
Antwerp, Belgium
November 2017

Introduction

1. International Acknowledgment of the Importance of Housing

This book delves into questions concerning the effectiveness of the right to adequate housing. By doing so, it discusses a right to one of the most basic needs of human beings. For many households, the cost of housing (together with food and water) is not only a considerable share of their budget expenditure; it is also their primary concern. This is especially the case with regard to people who have trouble making ends meet.[1] In extreme cases, they run a severe risk of being evicted or having to live on the streets.[2] But adequate housing is more than mere protection from the elements, more than a roof above one's head.[3] Not only can a subpar housing situation have a negative impact on a person's health, but it can also influence people's performances (work, school) and be a burden on one's social life.[4] Adequate housing also affects our self-image and is an outward sign of status. For all these reasons, having decent accommodation at one's disposal is a fundamental necessity to

1 L. VAN THIELEN and B. STORMS, *Het maximum uit het minimum halen. Overlevingsstrategieën van mensen die moeten rondkomen met een te beperkt inkomen*, Geel, CEBUD, 2013, 43; E. KEMPSON, A. BRYSON and K. ROWLINGSON, *Hard times? How poor families make ends meet*, London, Policy Studies Institute, 1994, 305 pages.

2 G. VAN MENXEL, H. BLOW and A. DE WACKER, "Thuisloosheid schaadt de gezondheid", in J. VRANKEN, G. CAMPAERT, K. DE BOYSER and D. DIERCKX (eds.), *Armoede en sociale uitsluiting. Jaarboek 2007,* Leuven, Acco, 2007, 221–239.

3 For more views on the concept of home, see e.g. L. FOX, *Conceptualising home. Theories, laws and policies,* Oxford, Hart Publishing, 2007, 131–180; R.M. RAKOFF, "Ideology in everyday life: the meaning of the home", *Politics and Society* 1977, vol. 7, no. 1, 85–104; G. TESTER and A.H. WINGFIELD, "Moving past picket fences: the meaning of 'home' for public housing residents", *Sociological Forum* 2013, vol. 28, no. 1, 70–83.

4 R.G. BRATT, M.E. STONE and C.W. HARTMAN, "Why a right to housing is needed and makes sense", in R.B. BRATT, M.E. STONE and C.W. HARTMAN (eds.), *A right to housing. Foundation for a new social agenda*, Philadelphia, Temple University Press, 2006, 2–3; G. CAMPAERT, "De onderkant van de woonmarkt", in J. VRANKEN, G. CAMPAERT, K. DE BOYSER and D. DIERCKX (eds.), *Armoede en sociale uitsluiting. Jaarboek 2007,* Leuven, Acco, (99) 99.

be able to achieve one's full potential as a human being.[5] It is the epicenter of one's personal, family and community life and is therefore the central setting that allows us to fully enjoy all other human rights.

In short, the impact of adequate housing on life in general is difficult to underestimate. Accordingly, most countries worldwide have acknowledged the need for at least a right to housing on paper, incorporating it into their constitution or elsewhere.[6] For a long time, the international community has formally acknowledged its importance by incorporating housing into covenants and charters as a fundamental right too. A common starting point for such an overview is obviously the Universal Declaration of Human Rights. Article 25 (1) of the Declaration recognizes the necessity of housing as part of everyone's right to an adequate standard of living:

> Everyone has the right to a standard of living adequate for the health and well-being of himself and of his family, including food, clothing, housing and medical care and necessary social services, and the right to security in the event of unemployment, sickness, disability, widowhood, old age or other lack of livelihood in circumstances beyond his control.

This principle was later translated into law in article 11 (1) of the International Covenant on Economic, Social and Cultural Rights (ICESCR):

> The States Parties to the present Covenant recognize the right of everyone to an adequate standard of living for himself and his family, including adequate food, clothing and housing, and to the continuous improvement of living conditions [. . .]

The content of the right to housing has been further specified in General Comment no. 4 of the UN Committee on Economic, Social and Cultural Rights (CESCR). It enumerates seven fundamental elements of adequate housing: legal security of tenure; availability of services, materials, facilities and infrastructure; affordability; habitability; accessibility; location; and cultural adequacy.[7] Legal security of tenure was later discussed more extensively in General Comment no. 7 on forced evictions. In addition to the ICESCR,

5 T. BYRNE and D.P. CULHANE, "The right to housing: an effective means for addressing homelessness?", *Univ. of Pennsylvania Journal of Law and Social Change* 2011, vol. 14, (379) 381; C. HARTMAN, "The case for a right to housing", *Housing Policy Debate* 1998, vol. 9, no. 2, (223) 228–229.

6 M. OREN, R. ALTERMAN and Y. ZILBERSHATS, "Housing rights in constitutional legislation: a conceptual classification", in P. KENNA (ed.), *Contemporary housing issues in a globalized world*, Farnham, Ashgate, 2014, 141–158.

7 UN Committee on Economic, Social and Cultural Rights (CESCR), *General Comment No. 4: The right to adequate housing (art. 11 (1) of the Covenant)*, 13 December 1991, par. 8 (hereafter General Comment No. 4).

several other core conventions on human rights also feature the right to housing in a more subject-specific context.[8,9]

The right to housing is widely protected at the regional level as well. Regional human rights systems worldwide have recognized the right to housing. Considering the discussion of European jurisprudence later in this research and the use of the Belgian/Flemish context as illustration, we will confine ourselves to European legislation.[10] Here, the fundamental right is recognized by law in both the Council of Europe and the European Union. While some rights protected by the European Convention on Human Rights (ECHR) can be tied in with aspects of the right to housing (infra, part II), the ECHR concerns civil and political rights. For an explicit right to housing within the context of the Council of Europe, one must look at article 31 of the Revised European Social Charter (RESC):

> With a view to ensuring the effective exercise of the right to housing, the Parties undertake to take measures designed:
>
> 1. to promote access to housing of an adequate standard;
> 2. to prevent and reduce homelessness with a view to its gradual elimination;
> 3. to make the price of housing accessible to those without adequate resources.

In addition, the RESC mentions housing as an essential element in different contexts: persons with disabilities (article 15), family life (article 16), elderly persons (article 23) and protection against poverty (article 30).

Finally, and also most recently, the European Union has included a right to housing assistance in article 34 of its Charter of Fundamental Rights:

> In order to combat social exclusion and poverty, the Union recognizes and respects the right to social and housing assistance so as to ensure a decent existence for all those who lack sufficient resources, in accordance with the rules laid down by Union law and national laws and practices.

8 Article 14 International Convention on the Elimination of all Forms of Racial Discrimination; Article 14 (2)(h) of the Convention on the Elimination of all Forms of Discrimination against Women (CEDAW); Article 27 of the Convention on the Rights of the Child (CRC).

9 In August 1994, Special Rapporteur on Adequate Housing Rajindar Sachar even proposed a draft International Convention on Housing Rights: UN Sub-Commission on Prevention of Discrimination and Protection of Minorities, *The right to adequate housing. Second Progress Report submitted by Mr. Rajindar Sachar, Special Rapporteur*, 21 June 1994, E/CN.4/Sub.2/1994/20.

10 The right to housing has, of course, been protected in other regional human rights systems. For more information, see: J. HOHMANN, *The right to housing. Law, concepts, possibilities*, Oxford, Hart Publishing, 2013, 75–91.

Since the entry into force of the Lisbon Treaty in 2009, the Charter of Fundamental Rights of the European Union has become binding upon the national governments. As we will see further on, the provision has so far had little impact. The EU Charter remains nonetheless another testament of the undisputed consensus concerning the importance of protecting housing as a fundamental right.

2. Approach and Aims of the Book

Despite the widespread recognition of housing as a fundamental right in international and national law, the main elements of what constitutes adequate housing according to the CESCR remain anything but guaranteed for a lot of people. In part, this is still due to the fact that socio-economic rights like the right to housing belong to the so-called second generation of human rights. In contrast to civil and political rights, their enforceability is perceived as much less evident as they ought to be "only" realized progressively. We will return to this matter more extensively further down the line, but in practice this leaves states that have, for example, ratified the ICESCR a very large margin of appreciation with regard to the realization of this right. If a state goes a step further and acknowledges the right to housing in its own constitution, it will usually be interpreted as having no direct effect. Its main function is then still an instructive one, instructing the competent legislator(s) to take measures to concretize the right.

From a legal perspective, this places emphasis primarily on the sufficiency of efforts taken by governments and draws attention away from the question whether the right itself is effectively realized.[11] This book addresses what an effective realization of the right to housing entails and uses international human rights law to explore ways to ensure that the focus at the domestic level is directed more at making further progress. It does so by looking into a selection of stumbling blocks, essential concepts and legal options that have not always been given due attention or have not yet been fully developed in this context but could nonetheless have an impact on or contribute to the full realization of this fundamental right on the national plane.

In the first of three parts, we start with a broader outlook on the issue at hand. We zoom in on what impacts the effectiveness of housing rights law from a more sociological perspective. This highlights the influences that are external to the content and legal effects of the legislation itself but which should equally be taken into consideration for housing law and policy-making. Specific attention is also given to the role of human dignity, a concept often connected to and used in the context of human rights and socio-economic rights law in particular. What does it bring to the table in a legal context? Can it provide

11 Ibid., 131–133.

extra protection for the right to housing? Does dignity not add an extra dimension to what adequate housing entails and therefore provide a certain guidance as to the recommendable direction of housing policies?

In Parts II and III, the focus shifts to more legal options and proposals to trigger or compel a state to protect and fulfill the right to housing. First, we take a look at what (quasi-) jurisprudence of the European Court of Human Rights, the European Committee of Social Rights and, to a lesser extent, the European Court of Justice tells us. Rather than elaborating on individual claims themselves, the focus lies on what a government can, cannot and must do in the context of the right to housing. We have chosen not to discuss all relevant decisions and judgments of these institutions under a different heading, but rather to show their interrelation, either directly by referencing one another or more indirectly by content. This illustrates how one is or could be influenced by the other, working together towards a more thorough protection of the right to housing. We also explore the possibility and impact of a potential collective complaint to the European Committee of Social Rights with regard to a state's general housing situation and policy. What is a likely outcome and would it enhance the state's obligation to pursue progress?

Finally, Part III departs from the simple question of how we can develop the right to housing into a stronger obligation for the national government. In an attempt to answer that question, Chapter 4 deals with the longstanding distinction between obligations of means and obligations of result. It discusses the problems the application of this dichotomy has created over time and how it might not be the most appropriate distinction to make in order to improve the right to housing. Instead, we will introduce the term "result-oriented obligation". In order to concretize this concept, Chapter 5 draws on international human rights law and explores the concepts of progressive realization and retrogressive measures and their potential contribution. This analysis finally leads into the development of our own proposal in Chapter 6. It starts from the question whether progress has been made rather than whether housing rights protection has not decreased or sufficient efforts have been taken. It ultimately aims to incentivize the adoption of measures that are directed towards attaining the full realization of the right to housing.

Each of the three parts of the book tries to contribute to the right to housing in its own specific way. The perspective shifts from the scope and content of the fundamental right, the enforceability through European (quasi-)jurisprudence to more structural modifications to strengthen housing legislation and policy. What they all have in common, however, is that they build on concepts and options that have thus far been insufficiently elaborated on as possible gateways for the improvement of the right to adequate housing on the domestic level. How can concepts such as human dignity, obligations of result and progressive realization or, for example, the collective complaints procedure before the European Committee of Social Rights be legitimate stepping stones towards a more effective right to housing?

3. The Belgian and Flemish Right to Housing as Illustration

Before we proceed, it is important to mention that throughout the book the Belgian and Flemish housing rights context will be used to illustrate, accentuate and concretize the theoretical content and recommendations. It will expose general areas of concern and at times provide insight in what might (not) work in terms of achieving further progress within the context of the fundamental right under scrutiny. While our findings would obviously apply to Belgium and Flanders in particular, the book aims to evoke questions and provide options that are relevant and valid for any state protecting housing rights, especially those that have ratified the ICESCR and/or have incorporated the right to housing into their constitution. By tackling issues concerning the (lack of) enforceability of socio-economic rights, its progressive realization or the effectiveness of law to attain this objective, we will elaborate on issues that are in essence indispensable to any domestic interpretation and application of this fundamental right.

Against this background, the aim of the book is clearly not to offer an exhaustive analysis of Belgian and Flemish housing legislation and policies. Whenever necessary for an optimal understanding of the text, specific issues will be briefly elaborated on *ad hoc*. For now it suffices to mention the two most relevant pieces of legislation.

First, there is the recognition of the right to adequate housing in article 23 of the Belgian Constitution, amidst a list of other socio-economic rights. The provision reads as follows:

> Everyone has the right to lead a life in keeping with human dignity.
> To this end, the law, federate laws and rules referred to in article 134 guarantee economic, social and cultural rights, taking into account corresponding obligations, and determine the conditions for exercising them.
>
> These rights include among others:
> [. . .] 4° the right to adequate housing.

It is often stated that the rights guaranteed in article 23 of the Belgian Constitution and therefore the right to adequate housing have no direct effect. Not only can we deduce this from the adopted text drafted by the Senate,[12]

12 Explanatory Memorandum of the proposal by Mr. Stroobant and Mr. Taminiaux, *Parl. St.* Senaat BZ 1991–92, no. 100–2/3°, 11; Report on behalf of the Commission for the review of the Constitution and the reform of the institutions released by Mr. Arts and Ms. Nelis, *Parl.St.* Senaat BZ 1991–92, no.100–2/4°, 84–91.

but it is also a recurrent principle (or at least a starting point) according to the legal doctrine.[13] Several judgments by higher and lower courts have clearly stated accordingly as well.[14]

In practice, article 23 does have some legal consequences. In cases where the relevant legislation includes vague and open legal norms that can be interpreted in different ways, the judge will, for example, be obliged to opt for an interpretation in conformity with the Constitution.[15] In addition to that, a judge will often invoke the constitutional right to housing when balancing the interests of landlord and tenant (e.g. cases concerning rent arrears, evictions).[16] Article 23 is then used as an extra – albeit not necessarily decisive – argument backing the interests of the tenant.

Above all, article 23 of the Constitution instructs the competent legislators to further concretize and guarantee the right to adequate housing. Since Belgium is a federal state and housing has been a regional competence since 1980,[17] the most important housing legislation comes from the three regions:

13 E.g. A. ALEN, J. CLEMENT, W. PAS, P. PEETERS and J. VAN NIEUWENHOVE, "Het federale België in de gecoördineerde Grondwet van 17 februari 1994, *RW* 1993–94, (1345) 1346; M. VERDUSSEN and A. NOËL, "Les droits fondamentaux et la réforme constitutionnelle de 1993", *APT* 1994, (127) 131.

14 Council of State 3 July 1995, no. 54.196, Beerts, *TBP* 1996, 118–119; Council of State 24 March 2005, no. 142.620, 3.2.3; Peace Court Verviers 30 June 2000, *Echos log.* 2000, note L. THOLOMÉ; Court of Appeal Antwerpen (6th Chamber) 28 June 2005, RW 2007–08, no. 33, 1374; Court of Appeal Luik (12th Chamber) 9 January 2015, *JLMB* 2015, no. 23, 1076; Peace Court Leuven 16 April 1996, *T. Huur* 1996, 80, note C. VAN DER ELST.

15 J. VANDE LANOTTE and G. GOEDERTIER, *Overzicht publiekrecht*, Brugge, Die Keure, 2008, 429–431; Court of Cassation 20 April 1950, *Arr.Cass.* 1950, 517; Peace Court Marche-en-Famenne 21 February 1995, *JLMB* 1995 (summary), 1301, note M. COPPETIERS; M. JAMOULLE, "L'article 23 de la Constitution belge dans ses relations avec les droits fondamentaux, le droit au travail et la sécurité sociale", in G. VAN LIMBERGHEN and K. SALOMEZ (eds.), *Sociale grondrechten als bakens voor een vernieuwd sociaal recht – Liber amicorum professor Maxime Stroobant*, Gent, Mys & Breesch, 2001, (121) 146; Peace Court Halle 11 April 2007, *T. Huur* 2008, no. 4, 212–214; Peace Court Grâce-Hollogne 1 October 1999, *JLMB* 2000, 900; Peace Court Antwerpen (2nd Chamber) 23 December 2014, *RW* 2015–16, no. 3, 119.

16 M. DAMBRE, "De (relatieve) doorwerking van het grondrecht op wonen in de rechtspraktijk, inzonderheid in de jurisprudentie in België", in B. HUBEAU and R. DE LANGE (eds.), *Het grondrecht op wonen. De grondwettelijk erkenning van het recht op huisvesting in België en Nederland*, Antwerpen, Maklu, 1995, 105–112; A. VANDEBURIE, *L'article 23 de la Constitution. Coquille vide ou boîte aux trésors?*, Brussel, La Charte, 2008, 128–129; Peace Court Grâce-Hollogne 27 March 2001, *Echos log.* 2002, no. 1, 26; Peace Court Roeselare 1 March 1996, *RW* 1997–98, 1504; Peace Court Elsene (2nd Chamber) 27 April 1994, *T.Vred.* 1997, 122, note B. HUBEAU; Peace Court Elsene (2nd Chamber) 3 December 1997, *Act.jur.baux* 1998, 57; Voorz. Rb. Namen 11 May 1994, *Dr.Q.M.* 1995, no. 7, 54, note J. FIERENS; Peace Court Elsene 6 March 1995, *TBBR* 1996, 296, note B. HUBEAU.

17 Art. 6, §1 IV Special law 8 August 1980 for the reform of institutions, *BS* 15 August 1980.

Flanders, Wallonia and Brussels-Capital. This has been further established with the most recent state reform in 2014, when the contractual relationship between tenant and landlord was transferred to the regional level too.[18]

Just as the other regions, Flanders has utilized its long-acquired housing competences to develop a Housing Code, a "constitution" on housing as one might call it.[19] As the most important provision, article 3 of the Flemish Housing Code specifies (the protection of) the right to housing in article 23 of the Belgian Constitution as follows:

> Everyone has a right to decent housing.
> To this end, the disposition of housing adjusted to one's personal needs, of good quality, in a decent living environment, for an affordable price and with housing security has to be promoted.

One might notice that the key elements of adequate housing described by the Flemish Housing Code and explained more comprehensively in the explanatory memorandum[20] are very similar to those set out by the CESCR. It also contains the disposition/availability of housing for everyone, how housing should be accessible and therefore adjusted to the needs and possibilities of the residents, the quality of housing, its affordability and the security of tenure. This makes the Flemish Housing Code a very convenient mechanism to draw national parallels with international human rights law.

Bibliography

ALEN, A., CLEMENT, J., PAS, W., PEETERS, P. and VAN NIEUWENHOVE, J., "Het federale België in de gecoördineerde Grondwet van 17 februari 1994", *RW* 1993–94, 1345–1360.

BRATT, R.G., STONE, M.E. and HARTMAN, C.W., "Why a right to housing is needed and makes sense", in BRATT, R.G., STONE, M.E. and HARTMAN, C.W. (eds.), *A right to housing. Foundation for a new social agenda*, Philadelphia, Temple University Press, 2006, 1–19.

BYRNE, T. and CULHANE, D.P., "The right to housing: an effective means for addressing homelessness?", *Univ. of Pennsylvania Journal of Law and Social Change* 2011, vol. 14, 379–391.

18 Art. 15, Special law 6 January 2014 concerning the sixth state reform, *BS* 31 January 2014 juncto article 6, §1 IV, Special law 8 August 1980 for the reform of institutions, *BS* 15 August 1980; B. HUBEAU and D. VERMEIR, *Regionalisering van de federale huurwetgeving*, Leuven, Steunpunt Wonen, 2013, 118 pages.

19 Decree Flemish Government of 15 July 1997 concerning the Flemish Housing Code, *BS* 19 August 1997.

20 Explanatory Memorandum to the draft of Decree concerning the Flemish Housing Code, *Parl. St.* Vl. Parl. 1996–97, no. 654/1, 11.

CAMPAERT, G., "De onderkant van de woonmarkt", in VRANKEN, J., CAMPAERT, G., DE BOYSER, K. and DIERCKX, D. (eds.), *Armoede en sociale uitsluiting. Jaarboek 2007*, Leuven, Acco, 2007, 99–111.

DAMBRE, M., "De (relatieve) doorwerking van het grondrecht op wonen in de rechtspraktijk, inzonderheid in de jurisprudentie in België", in HUBEAU, B. and DE LANGE, R. (eds.), *Het grondrecht op wonen. De grondwettelijk erkenning van het recht op huisvesting in België en Nederland*, Antwerpen, Maklu, 1995, 105–112.

FOX, L., *Conceptualising home. Theories, laws and policies*, Oxford, Hart Publishing, 2007, 551 pages.

HARTMAN, C., "The case for a right to housing", *Housing Policy Debate* 1998, vol. 9, no. 2, 223–246.

HOHMANN, J., *The right to housing. Law, concepts, possibilities*, Oxford, Hart Publishing, 2013, 75–91.

HUBEAU, B. and VERMEIR, D., *Regionalisering van de federale huurwetgeving*, Leuven, Steunpunt Wonen, 2013, 118 pages.

JAMOULLE, M., "L'article 23 de la Constitution belge dans ses relations avec les droits fondamentaux, le droit au travail et la sécurité sociale", in VAN LIMBERGHEN, G. and SALOMEZ, K. (eds.), *Sociale grondrechten als bakens voor een vernieuwd sociaal recht – Liber amicorum professor Maxime Stroobant*, Gent, Mys & Breesch, 2001, 121–147.

KEMPSON, E., BRYSON, A. and ROWLINGSON, K., *Hard times? How poor families make ends meet*, London, Policy Studies Institute, 1994, 305 pages.

OREN, M., ALTERMAN, R. and ZILBERSHATS, Y., "Housing rights in constitutional legislation: a conceptual classification", in KENNA, P. (ed.), *Contemporary housing issues in a globalized world*, Farnham, Ashgate, 2014, 141–158.

RAKOFF, R.M., "Ideology in everyday life: the meaning of the home", *Politics and Society* 1977, vol. 7, no. 1, 85–104.

TESTER, G. and WINGFIELD, A.H., "Moving past picket fences: the meaning of 'home' for public housing residents", *Sociological Forum* 2013, vol. 28, no. 1, 70–83.

VANDEBURIE, A., *L'article 23 de la Constitution. Coquille vide ou boîte aux trésors?*, Brussel, La Charte, 2008, 266 pages.

VANDE LANOTTE, J. and GOEDERTIER, G., *Overzicht publiekrecht*, Brugge, Die Keure, 2008, 1576 pages.

VAN MENXEL, G., BLOW, H. and DE WACKER, A., "Thuisloosheid schaadt de gezondheid", in VRANKEN, J., CAMPAERT, G., DE BOYSER, K. and DIERCKX, D. (eds.), *Armoede en sociale uitsluiting. Jaarboek 2007*, Leuven, Acco, 2007, 221–239.

VAN THIELEN, L. and STORMS, B., *Het maximum uit het minimum halen. Overlevingsstrategieën van mensen die moeten rondkomen met een te beperkt inkomen*, Geel, CEBUD, 2013.

VERDUSSEN, M. and NOËL, A., "Les droits fondamentaux et la réforme constitutionnelle de 1993", *APT* 1994, 127–143.

Part I

An Effective Right to Housing: Beyond Legal-Technical Issues

Whereas Part II and III discuss and explore more legal-technical ways to try to strengthen housing rights obligations at the domestic level, we will first take a look at a couple of aspects that should be taken into account when aspiring for a (more) effective right to housing. In Chapter 1 we do so by tackling a concept often used in international as well as national socio-economic rights law: human dignity. Despite its popularity, there are a lot of questions with regard to both its meaning and its potential role in a legal context. If dignity is indeed taken as an important and perhaps useful concept, what implications does that have for how to protect, configure and realize the right to housing? Chapter 2 proceeds further with the question of what an effective right to housing entails, but here it does so by approaching the matter at hand from a more socio-legal perspective. It explores the top-down and bottom-up influences that (can) have an impact on the effectiveness of housing rights in society.[1]

1 See also N. MOONS, "Tenant vs. owner: deriving access to justice from the right to housing", *RdW* 2015, vol. 36, no. 3, (99) 104–109.

1 Human Dignity: A Guiding Principle for a Stronger Right to Housing?

What role is there for an essentially non-legal concept in the bigger picture of realizing the right to housing? Is it first of all recommendable to use a vague[1] and interdisciplinary[2] term like human dignity for the protection of fundamental rights? These are some of the questions this chapter will discuss. We will start close to the concept itself. What does it traditionally mean and how has it been used in a legal context? We will see how human rights law (as well as article 23 of the Belgian Constitution for that matter) have given human dignity multiple functions. Next, we look at the added value as well as the deficiencies of the concept and propose what in our opinion are the essential aspects of what we by then call social dignity that should have to be taken into account in the pursuit of a more effective right to housing. It is on the basis of this interpretation that we will then look at a couple of housing-related issues (housing security, property vs. tenancy, social housing) and how the concept could be a guiding principle in this context.

1. Exploring the Content of Human Dignity and Its Use in a Human Rights Context

A. History of the Concept

According to the Oxford English Dictionary, dignity means "the quality of being worthy or honorable". It refers to a person's status, position or rank.

1 A. SEN, *Vrijheid is vooruitgang*, Amsterdam, Contact, 2000, 144–156 At the Hobart-conference in Tasmania (2004) a group of interdisciplinary scientists discussed the concept of human dignity, but did not come to a substantive conclusion beyond some generally accepted platitudes; I. CASIER, A. BAUWENS, W. DISTELMANS and S. SNACKEN, "Over het concept menselijke waardigheid", in K. RAES, W. DEBEUCKELAERE, S. GUTWIRTH and M. LAMBRECHTS (eds.), *Ontmoetingen met Koen Raes*, Brugge, die Keure, 2012, (85) 87.

2 For an impressive overview of different interpretations of human dignity, see: M. DÜWELL, J. BRAARVIG, R. BRONSWORD and D. MIETH (eds.), *The Cambridge handbook of human dignity. Interdisciplinary perspectives*, Cambridge, Cambridge University Press, 2014.

This definition still reflects the classical Roman conception of *dignitas hominis*, a notion that was ascribed to those people that possessed a certain title or quality within a hierarchically structured society, a characteristic of great men, those meriting special honor or distinction.[3]

This interpretation shows obvious differences with the predominant contemporary philosophical ideas of human dignity. It has obtained an absolute and intrinsic character that belongs to every human being regardless of his or her social position. Some authors believe that the current notion of human dignity is "the product of a different history that ran parallel to the (classical Roman) origins",[4] while others argue that the *dignitas* conception has simply transformed into a more egalitarian conception and that the respect and status once reserved only for the chosen few has expanded to humanity in its entirety.[5]

It is open for discussion as to where the exact roots of the more modern interpretation of human dignity can be found. One could go all the way back to Cicero,[6] but he does seem to focus more on distinguishing human beings from animals than on acknowledging the universal character of the concept. This universality is present in the Judeo-Christian notion of dignity, but this traditional conception obviously remains deeply hierarchical (i.e. the relation between God and man).[7] In the Middle Ages, these combined ideas were developed into natural law theory by Christian philosophers such as Thomas Aquinas.[8] By the late fifteenth century, Pico della Mirandola, in his *Oration on the Dignity of Man*, recognized dignity as the ability of human beings to choose what they want to be. Although the underlying reason for this free choice was still assigned to God,[9] Pico was an important figure in broadening the philosophical scope of human dignity.[10]

3 N. JACOBSON, "Dignity and health: a review", *Social Science & Medicine* 2007, vol. 62, (292) 293.

4 L.R. BARROSO, "Here, there and everywhere: human dignity in contemporary law and in the transnational discourse", *Boston College International & Comparative Law Review* 2012, vol. 35, (331) 335; Other authors following this strand of thinking: C. McCRUDDEN, "Human dignity and judicial interpretation of human rights", *EJIL* 2008, vol. 19, no. 4, (655) 657; T. IGLESIAS, "Bedrock Truths and the Dignity of the Individual", *Logos* 2001, vol. 4, 144; D. BEYLEVELD and R. BROWNSWORD, "Human dignity, human rights and human genetics", *Modern Law Review* 1998, (661) 666–667.

5 J. WALDRON, "Dignity, rights and responsibilities", *New York University Public Law and Legal Theory Research Paper Series* 2010, Working paper no. 10–83, 11–12; E.K. WHITE, "There is no such thing as a right to human dignity: a reply to Conor O'Mahony", *Int'l. J. Const. L.* 2012, vol. 10 (2), 575–584.

6 McCRUDDEN (n 4) 657.

7 Ibid., 19.

8 E. GRANT, "Dignity and equality", *HRLR* 2007, vol. 7, no. 2, (299) 304.

9 R.D. GLENSY, "The right to dignity", *Columbia Human Rights Law Review* 2011, (65) 74–75.

10 McCRUDDEN (n 4) 659; J. FIERENS, "La dignité humaine comme concept juridique", *JT* 2002, no. 22, (577) 577–578.

Nonetheless, a specifically person-based idea of human dignity was only first developed during the Enlightenment. Probably the most prominent contributor to the relevant discussion was Immanuel Kant. He distinguished human beings from material objects and other living creatures by stating that both have a different value:

> A human being regarded as a person [. . .] is exalted above any price; for as a person he is not to be valued merely as a means to the ends of others or even to his own ends, but as an end in himself.[11]

Human beings possess an absolute intrinsic and incomparable value by virtue of their shared humanity: dignity. It is a value without any equivalence and thus cannot be traded, substituted or replaced.[12] In his view, human dignity is endowed on every human being because he has the capacity as a rational agent for reason and autonomy.[13] It is inviolable, constant, inalienable, unconditional and equal for all human beings.[14]

B. Human Dignity in a Human Rights Context

1) First Function: A Foundation for Human Rights

While interpretations might have evolved and changed over time, Kant is still frequently regarded as the father of the modern, universal interpretation of human dignity as an inherent worth equal in all people.[15] This particular

11 I. KANT, *Groundwork for the Metaphysics of Morals*, as translated by A.W. WOOD, New Haven, Yale University Press, 2002, 434–435.

12 GLENSY (n 9) 76; A. WOOD, "Human dignity, right and the realm of ends", *Acta Juridica* 2008, (47) 49–52.

13 M.A. LUTZ, "Centering social economics on human dignity", *Review of Social Economy* 1995, vol. 53, no. 2, (171) 173; M. WHITE, "Kantian dignity and social economics", *Forum for Social Economics* 2003, vol. 32, no. 2, (1) 2.

14 A. BARBOSA DA SILVA, "Autonomy, dignity and integrity in health care ethics – a moral philosophical perspective", in H. SINDING AASEN, R. HALVORSEN and A. BARBOSA DA SILVA (eds.), *Human rights, dignity and autonomy in health care and social services: Nordic perspectives*, Antwerp, Intersentia, 2009, (13) 22.

15 O. SCHACHTER, "Human dignity as a normative concept", *The American Journal of International Law* 1983, vol. 77, no. 4, 848–854; H.C. KELMAN, "The conditions, criteria and dialectics of human dignity: a transnational perspective", *International Studies Quarterly* 1977, vol. 21, no. 3, (529) 531; R.E. HOWARD and J. DONNELLY, "Human dignity, human rights and political regimes", *The American Political Science Review* 1986, vol. 80, no. 3, (801) 802; BARBOSA DA SILVA (n 14) 51. There are, of course, also authors denying the inherent character of human dignity, e.g. B. MORRIS, "The dignity of man", *Ethics* 1946, vol. 57, no. 1, (57) 63–64; P. SINGER, *Applied Ethics*, London, Oxford University Press, 1986, 264 pages.; D.J. MATTSON and S.G. CLARK, "Human dignity in concept and practice", *Policy Sciences* 2011, vol. 44, (303) 305; JACOBSON (n 3) 294.

aspect of his basic conception of human dignity is also noticeable in the international human rights discourse[16] and particularly provides a significant philosophical underpinning for the Universal Declaration of Human Rights: "Whereas recognition of the inherent dignity and of the equal and inalienable rights of all members of the human family is the foundation of freedom, justice and peace in the world".[17] Here it serves as a symbolic and theoretical basis for human rights in the absence of any other grounds for consensus.[18] This relationship is even more clearly described in the preambles of the subsequent International Covenants on Economic, Social and Cultural Rights (ICESCR) on the one hand and on Civil and Political Rights (ICCPR) on the other, "recognizing that these rights derive from the inherent dignity of the human person".[19] It was repeated along the same lines in the Vienna Declaration made at the World Conference on Human Rights in 1993, which says that "all human rights derive from the dignity and worth inherent in the human person".[20]

Within the Organization of American States (OAS), this link between dignity and both of the "generations" of human rights was explicitly stated in the Additional Protocol to the Convention in the area of Economic, Social and Cultural Rights (more commonly known as the Protocol of San Salvador): "Considering the close relationship that exists between economic, social and

16 V.B. MONSALVE and J.A. ROMÁN, "Tensions of human dignity: conceptualization and application to international human rights law", *IJHR* 2009, vol. 6, no. 11, (39) 41; G. HAARSCHER, "Le droit de mener une vie conforme à la dignité humaine", in R. ERGEC (ed.), *Les droits économiques, sociaux et culturels dans la Constitution: actes du colloque tenu les 21 et 22 décembre 1994*, Brussel, Bruylant, 1995, (133) 134; S. PAREKH, "Resisting 'dull and torpid' assent: returning to the debate over the foundations of human rights", *Human Rights Quarterly 2007*, vol. 29, (763) 763; S.J. KERSTEIN, "Kantian dignity: a critique", in M. DÜWELL, J. BRAARVIG, R. BRONSWORD and D. MIETH (eds.), *The Cambridge handbook of human dignity. Interdisciplinary perspectives*, Cambridge, Cambridge University Press, 2014, (220) 224.

17 Preamble and art. 1 Universal Declaration of Human Rights; Y. ARIELI, "On the Necessary and Sufficient Conditions for the Emergence of the Doctrine of the Dignity of Man and His Rights", in D. KRETZMER and E.KLEIN (eds.), *The Concept of Human Dignity in Human Rights Discourse*, The Hague, Kluwer, 2002, (1) 7; GRANT (n 8) 304–305; G. HUGHES, "The concept of dignity in the Universal Declaration of Human Rights", *Journal of Religious Ethics* 2011, (1) 3; P.B. CLITEUR and R.G.T. VAN WISSEN, "De menselijke waardigheid als grondslag voor mensenrechten: een beschouwing over het werk van Kant en Schopenhauer in relatie tot de filosofische reflective over mensenrechten", in G.A. VAN DER LIST (ed.), *De Rechten van de Mens*, Den Haag, Teldersstichting, 1998, (25) 32 and 34.

18 J. MORSINK, *The Universal Declaration of Human Rights. Origins, Drafting and Intent*, Philadelphia, University of Pennsylvania Press, 1999, 39–42; D. SHULTZINER, "Human Dignity – Functions and Meanings", *Global Jurist Topics* 2003, vol. 5, (1) 5.

19 Preambles to the ICESCR and ICCPR.

20 Preamble UN General Assembly, World Conference on Human Rights, *Vienna Declaration and Programme of Action*, 25 June 1993, A/CONF 157/23.

cultural rights, and civil and political rights, in that the different categories of rights constitute an indivisible whole based on the recognition of the dignity of the human person [. . .]"[21] Consequently, human dignity in this context forms the foundation of both civil and political rights as well as economic, social and cultural rights. In short, Gewirth adequately describes the relationship between human dignity and human rights as follows: "Human rights are based upon or derivative from human dignity. It is because humans have dignity that they have human rights."[22]

Interestingly, neither the European Convention on Human Rights (ECHR)[23] nor the European Social Charter (ESC) themselves use (inherent) dignity as the foundation for the fundamental rights they protect.[24] Their (quasi-)judicial bodies on the other hand have made similar statements. The European Committee of Social Rights has, for example, said that "human dignity is the fundamental value and indeed the core of positive European human rights law – whether under the ESC or under the European Convention on Human Rights".[25] In comparison, though, to the UN Covenants, for example, these applications of dignity are already closer to the concept's second function in human rights law.[26]

2) Second Function: A Value/Right to Protect and Guarantee

Human dignity has not been confined to the foundational meaning.[27] A fair number of constitutions and jurisdictions make reference to an actual right to dignity. Even if not always explicitly worded as such, dignity is described as a value that needs to be legally respected and protected.[28] European human

21 Preamble Add. Prot. to the American Convention on Human Rights in the Area of Economic, Social and Cultural Rights "Protocol of San Salvador", 17 November 1988.

22 A. GEWIRTH, "Human Dignity as the Basis of Rights", in M. MEYER and W. PARENT (eds.), *The Constitution of Rights: Human Dignity*, Ithaca, Cornell University Press, 1992, (1) 10.

23 That is, if we only take the Convention itself into consideration. The preamble to Protocol no. 13 to the Convention concerning the abolition of the death penalty does refer to inherent dignity.

24 J. ZAJADLO, "Human dignity and human rights", in R. HANSKI and M. SUSKI (eds.), *An introduction to the international protection of human rights: a textbook*, Turku, Institute for Human Rights, Abo Akademi University, 1999, (15) 21–22.

25 ECSR 8 September 2004, no. 14/2003, International Federation of Human Rights Leagues (FIDH)/France, par. 31.

26 The same can be said about the use of human dignity in the EU Charter of Fundamental Rights (preamble vs. art. 1, 25 and 31).

27 R. BUITENWEG, *Recht op een menswaardig bestaan. Een humanistieke reflectie op sociaal-economische mensenrechten*, Utrecht, de Graaff, 2001, 96.

28 As such, it deviates from the Kantian notion of inviolable dignity, independent of the external world, see: M. NUSSBAUM, "Human dignity and political entitlements", in President's Council on Bioethics (ed.), *Human dignity and bioethics: essays commissioned by the President's Council on Bioethics*, Washington, 2008, (351) 355–357.

rights jurisprudence is also more familiar with this application of dignity.[29] This conception is, however, irreconcilable with dignity construed as a value inherent in all human beings or as the foundational principle of all human rights.[30] It "reverses the more commonly accepted order of things by suggesting that dignity is founded on the enjoyment of human rights rather than that human rights are founded on the inherent dignity of every human being".[31] Article 23 of the Belgian Constitution shows the same pattern: in order for people to live in human dignity, the enlisted socio-economic rights must be guaranteed.[32] The provision can be considered incompatible with the first function because of the contradictory "right" to dignity.

If dignity is indeed an inherent feature of the human being, a right to dignity does not make much sense, since it is impossible to lose it or to be denied it, unlike the human rights norms it has triggered itself. In other words, such a notion is existentially contradictory with a foundational, inherent conception of dignity.[33] O'Mahoney concludes from this conundrum that it would be better "to confine the use of human dignity as a legal concept to that role [i.e. as a foundational principle] and not to additionally recognize a right to dignity or to lead a dignified life".[34] As we will see in the next paragraph, there are indeed reasons for not using dignity in a rights context. However, since it is exactly this form of dignity that constitutions often use and most legal scholars write about when discussing the subject, we prefer not to neglect it,

29 E.g. ECtHR 28 September 2015, no. 23380/09, Bouyid/Belgium, par. 90; ECtHR 21 January 2011, no. 30696/09, M.S.S./Belgium and Greece, par. 221, 233 and 253; ECSR 18 October 2006, no. 31/2005, ERRC/ Bulgaria, par. 51 and 56; ECSR 5 December 2007, no. 33/2006, ATD Fourth World/France, par. 163; With regard to the European Court of Justice, see also ECJ 9 October 2001, no. C-377/98, Netherlands/ Parliament and Council, par. 70: "*It is for the Court of Justice (. . .) to ensure that the fundamental right to human dignity and integrity is observed*"; For more information on the use of dignity in European jurisprudence, see: L. BURGORGUE-LARSEN (ed.), *La dignité saisie par les juges en Europe*, Brussel, Bruylant, 2010.

30 J. DAVIS, "Doing justice to dignity in the criminal law", in J. MALPAS and N. LICKISS (eds.), *Perspectives on human dignity: a conversation*, Dordrecht, Springer, 2007, (169) 177; G. DEN HARTOGH, "Is human dignity the ground of human rights?" in M. DÜWELL, J. BRAARVIG, R. BRONSWORD and D. MIETH (eds.), *The Cambridge handbook of human dignity. Interdisciplinary perspectives*, Cambridge, Cambridge University Press, 2014, (200) 200; M. DÜWELL, "Human dignity: concepts, discussions, philosophical perspectives", in M. DÜWELL et al. (eds.), *The Cambridge handbook of human dignity. Interdisciplinary perspectives*, Cambridge, Cambridge University Press, 2014, (23) 42–43.

31 C. O'MAHONEY, "There is no such thing as a right to dignity", *Int'l. J. Const. L.* 2012, vol. 10, no. 2, (551) 562.

32 A. VANDEBURIE, *L'article 23 de la Constitution. Coquille vide ou boîte aux trésors?*, Brussel, La Charte, 2008, 162.

33 A. GEWIRTH, *Self-fulfillment*, Princeton, Princeton University Press, 1998, 163; BARROSO (n 4) 357; MATTSON (n 15) 306; O'MAHONEY (n 31) 562–563.

34 O'MAHONEY (n 31) 562.

but rather to speak of a different type of dignity, a social dignity. In contrast to the somewhat transcendent nature of the classical meaning of human dignity, social dignity envisions a right to live a dignified everyday life.[35] We will elaborate further on this concept later in this chapter.

In the constitutional tradition, human dignity is at least as popular as a social notion (social dignity) than as a transcendent value. The explicit proclamation of a right to dignity, however, as is the case in article 23 of the Belgian Constitution, is rather exceptional. Human dignity is often regarded as something that needs to be respected and protected through the realization of human rights.[36] This does not mean that dignity as an inherent and/or foundational principle has no place left in constitutions and legal orders. The Polish Constitution, for example, predicates that "the inherent and inalienable dignity of the person shall constitute a source of freedoms and rights of persons and citizens",[37] while the Canadian Supreme Court has said that "the dignity of the individual is a fundamental value underlying both the common law and the Charter".[38] The South African Constitution dictates that "everyone has inherent dignity".[39] However, in illustration of the double meaning of dignity, this sentence continues by declaring that everyone also has "the right to have their dignity respected and protected".[40] In a similar vein, the South African Constitutional Court has stated that "dignity is not only a value fundamental to our Constitution, it is a justiciable and enforceable right that must be respected and protected".[41] In Germany, this dual meaning has triggered a longstanding debate among German scholars on the constitutional status of human dignity,[42] while the French Constitutional Council has used human dignity (which does not appear in the French Constitution as such) differently

35 M. LEVINET, "Dignité contre dignité. L'épilogue de l'affaire du 'lancer de nains' devant le Comité des droits de l'homme des Nations Unies", *RTDH* 2003, (1024) 1034.

36 E.g. art.1 Charter of Fundamental Rights of the European Union: "Human dignity is inviolable. It must be respected and protected"; art. 19 Finnish Constitution; art. 7 Swiss Constitution; art. 3 Italian Constitution; art. 13 Portuguese Constitution.

37 Art. 30 Polish Constitution.

38 Supreme Court (Canada) 2 February 1995, no. 23581, R./S. (R.J.), [1995] 1 S.C.R, 605; For more on the Canadian perspective on human dignity in light of the equality guarantee, see: D. ROBITAILLE, "De gerechtelijke opvatting over armoede in Canada: onveranderlijke maatschappelijke positie of gewoon een kwestie van wil?", in Steunpunt tot Bestrijding van Armoede, Bestaansonzekerheid en Sociale Uitsluiting, *Armoede-Waardigheid-Mensenrechten*, Brussel, 2008, 95–104.

39 Section 10 South African Constitution.

40 Section 10 South African Constitution; GRANT (n 8) 310.

41 Constitutional Court (South Africa) 7 June 2000, CCT 35/99, Dawood et al./Minister of Home Affairs et al.

42 C. ENDERS, "A right to have rights – The German Constitutional concept of human dignity", *NUJS Law Review* 2010, (253) 255; McCRUDDEN (n 4) 681.

in the first two cases in which it discussed the matter.[43] The same duality is still noticeable in the Belgian context. Regardless of the legislator's socially inspired intentions for the use of dignity,[44] scholars still make occasional mention of "inherent dignity"[45] and dignity as the basis for socio economic rights or even for *all* human rights.[46] It is thus evident that both applications still exist side by side and are used interchangeably by courts of even the same country. Human dignity manages to be both source and purpose of fundamental rights.

C. *The Added Value and Pitfalls of Using Human Dignity*

1) *As an Equivalent of Decent or Adequate Housing*

Although human dignity has obviously evolved into a frequently used legal principle, a comprehensive definition or even an attempt at circumscribing the scope of human dignity is often missing in both legislation as well as jurisdiction. Not only is it a vague concept, but it is also a relative concept, both culturally and politically, which gives way to a wide variety of interpretations.[47] One can find an illustration of that very problem in the *Omega* judgment by the European Court of Justice. Here, the Court implicitly stated that different perceptions of human dignity could exist even between European jurisdictions.[48]

Belgian housing legislation remains tacit about the exact meaning of dignity too. Within the framework of the Belgian right to housing, the concept has scarcely been further elaborated on in regional legislation. Article 3 of the Flemish Housing Code and article 2 of the Walloon Housing Code provide certain aspects that are regarded as an essential part of the right to housing in conformity with human dignity, such as "good quality" and "affordable price". Although one could argue that such descriptions merely shift the interpretative dilemma from human dignity to other notions, they are less vague, rooted

43 Conseil Constitutionnel (France) 27 July 1994, no. 94-343/344 DC (classic use of human dignity); Conseil Constitutionnel (France) 19 January 1995, no. 94-359 DC (social notion of dignity).

44 For example, by referring to the use of dignity in the OCMW law as an indication for its constitutional use.

45 W. PAS and J. VAN NIEUWENHOVE, "Het recht een menswaardig leven te leiden", in ICM (ed.), *Jaarboek Mensenrechten 1994*, Antwerpen, Maklu, 1995, (113) 123.

46 M. VERDUSSEN and A. NOËL, "Les droits fondamentaux et la réforme constitutionnelle de 1993", *APT* 1994, (127) 1994; E. BREMS and J. VRIELINK, *Menselijke waardigheid in de Nederlandse Grondwet? Voorstudie ten behoeve van de Staatscommissie Grondwet (2009)*, Alphen aan den Rijn, Kluwer, 2010, 23; VANDEBURIE (n 32) 160.

47 W. BRUGGER, "Human rights norms in ethical perspective", *German Yearbook of International Law* 1982 vol. 25, (113) 132; HOWARD (n 15) 801–802; KELMAN (n 15) 544; FIERENS (n 10) 581; M.Y.K. LEE, "Universal Human Dignity: some reflections in the Asian Context", *Asian Journal of Comparative Law* 2008, vol. 3, no. 1, (1) 30.

48 ECJ 14 October 2004, no. C-36/02, Omega.

more firmly in everyday life and are thus easier for a judge to apply. Of course, one could then pose the question of what the added value is of using such a heavily loaded term like human dignity, if it is used merely as a synonym for decent housing (or decent other socio-economic provisions protected by the ICESCR for that matter).

2) As an Open-ended Norm for Courts and Other Institutions

A. A DRIVING FORCE FOR OTHER RIGHTS

Despite the fact that human dignity can be equated with the more specific socio-economic rights at first sight, one could argue that the concept of human dignity still holds an extra significance, an additional value.[49] The combination of both the considerable philosophical weight and the vagueness of a concept such as human dignity enables judges, in theory at least, to use it as a basis for developing new rights. Human dignity certainly has the ability to lend itself to interpretations beyond the basic content of already existing rights. It can be used as a catalyst for other rights. In Belgium, courts have, for example judged that shutting down the energy and water supply constitutes a violation of one's (right to) human dignity.[50] As Fierens points out, human dignity can be "un instrument à la disposition de juge lui permettant d'écarter le jeu habituel des règles au nom d'un principe supérieur" [an instrument that allows a judge to broaden the usual rules of the game in the name of a superior principle].[51] In these specific cases, however, it is highly questionable whether this decision really needed the input of dignity, given the fact that water and energy supply are already mentioned as quality criteria in both the Flemish[52] and the Walloon Housing Code,[53] and the judges could just as easily have concluded on a violation of the right to decent housing in particular. This brings us back to the argument against the extended application of dignity when used as an equivalent of decent housing.

B. THE OTHER SIDE OF THE COIN: A RACE TO THE BOTTOM?

The previous paragraph showed us that a large margin of interpretation can lead to a broad interpretation. Evidently, the opposite is also very much a

49 HUGHES (n 17) 7–8.
50 Kort Ged. Rb. Charleroi 19 January 2000, *TBBR* 2000, 590, note J. FIERENS; Vred. Moeskroen 24 May 2004, *TBBR* 2008, no. 5, 273, note A. VANDEBURIE; Court of Appeal Brussel 24 December 1992, *Iuvis* 1994, 203, note P. BOUWENS; Vred. Fontaine-l'Evêque 15 October 2009.
51 J. FIERENS, La dignité humaine, limite à l'application de l'exception d'inexécution, *TBBR* 2000, (594) 598.
52 Art. 5 Flemish Housing Code.
53 Art. 3 Walloon Housing Code.

possibility. The judiciary can apply the concept as a restriction on restrictions on the right to housing. In other words, courts sometimes use dignity as a limit to possible constraints on fundamental rights imposed by legislative measures.[54] Considering the open character of this concept, however, when human dignity is applied as an ultimate limit to these restrictions, courts may draw up a concept that might be narrower than the fundamental rights it was set out to represent. With a vague and malleable concept like human dignity, this appears to be possible. Consequently, dignity runs the risk of being severely limited, while it was intended as the ultimate goal for realizing these fundamental rights.[55] This use could potentially lower its aspirations to that of a *minimum minimorum*.

These observations are not only relevant to the judiciary. Other public institutions can also be in a position to apply the concept. In Belgium this is the case with regard to the Public Centers for Social Welfare (OCMW). When an individual applies for public assistance, this municipal public institution will have to investigate on a case-by-case basis whether this assistance is necessary to live a life in dignity in accordance with article 1 of the 1976 OCMW law.[56]

Even though all OCMWs share this same legal basis, they are free to pursue their own policies and to interpret human dignity in their own way. Since we are already dealing with a very vague concept, there is only agreement on some general conditions such as being able to feed oneself, having a place to stay or having access to healthcare. In 2006, one out of four OCMWs did not even have a standardized set of formal or informal norms for the assessment of financial support.[57] This autonomy has thus created some serious discrepancies between different municipalities in similar situations. In other words, the chances of an assistance seeker receiving assistance depend partly on the municipality where this person resides.[58] It has been documented repeatedly that such differences occur even within the same OCMW.[59] In its

54 E.g. Constitutional Court 20 October 2004, no. 160/2004; Constitutional Court 10 July 2008, no. 101/2008, B.33.2.

55 BREMS (n 46) 34.

56 W. RAUWS, "Niet de ver-van-mijn-bed-show: sociale grondrechten en de praktijk", in W. VAN EECKHOUTTE and M. RIGAUX (eds.), *Sociaal recht: niets dan uitdagingen*, Gent, Mys & Breesch, 1996, (793) 798.

57 N. VAN MECHELEN and. K. BOGAERTS, *Aanvullende steun in Vlaamse OCMW's*, Antwerpen, Centrum voor Sociaal Beleid, 2008.

58 D. CUYPERS and B. DE VOS, "De menselijke waardigheid en de arbeidsgerechten", *TSR* 1999, (495) 535.

59 K. BEYNS et al., *Menswaardig leven. Een onderzoek binnen de Kempense OCMW's*, Geel, Katholieke Hogeschool Kempen, 2008; B. STORMS et al., "Ook getest op mensen. Referentiebudgetten als maatstaf voor de doeltreffendheid van de sociale bescherming", in L. WILLY, P. ISABELLE, J. VRANKEN and R. VAN ROSSEM (eds.), *Armoede en Sociale Uitsluiting. Jaarboek 2013*, Leuven, Acco, 2013, 267–287; J. VRANKEN, "Het OCMW: dertig jaren op weg naar een recht op maatschappelijke dienstverlening", in J. VRANKEN, K. DE BOYSER and D. DIERCKX (eds.), *Armoede en Sociale Uitsluiting.*

book for new OCMW council members (2013), the Flemish government also touches upon this ambiguity, but merely as a consequence of local autonomy:

> What human dignity exactly entails is open to interpretation and depends on the spirit of the times, the culture and the ideology. Although the financial resources should not play a part in determining how human dignity is interpreted, yet we observe that in harsh financial and economic times this is a factor in the decision-making process.[60] [Translated]

We notice in particular the reference to ideology. This raises an interesting question: to what extent is human dignity politically malleable? How much influence does the council for public welfare exercise on what dignity entails through the party politics of its members?[61] Although working towards more harmonization and standardization is certainly recommended, this should be approached with the utmost care, because such a process may well result in an interpretation of human dignity as a "lowest common denominator".[62]

C. SUBJECTIVE VS. OBJECTIVE DIGNITY

For some authors, the role of the courts is too prominent in interpreting dignity. Although one could argue that the use of open legal norms is inevitable to accommodate evolution in society, they question the monopolistic position that judges acquire in this debate and the broad judicial freedom of interpretation on the matter.[63] More precisely, they warn against what is called a "*gouvernement des juges*".[64] Lee goes as far as saying that "[dignity's] lack of

Jaarboek 2005, Leuven, Acco, 2006, (151) 159; Steunpunt tot bestrijding van armoede, bestaansonzekerheid en sociale uitsluiting, *Recht op maatschappelijke dienstverlening: 10 jaar na het algemeen verslag over de armoede*, 2005, 6–7.

60 Agentschap Binnenlands Bestuur, *Startersboek OCMW-raadsleden*, 2013, 13.

61 VRANKEN (n 59) 160.

62 Steunpunt tot bestrijding van armoede, bestaansonzekerheid en sociale uitsluiting, *Recht op maatschappelijke dienstverlening: 10 jaar na het algemeen verslag over de armoede*, 2005, 7.

63 M. MAHLMANN, "The Basic Law at 60 – Human Dignity and the Culture of Republicanism", *German Law Journal* 2010, vol. 11, no. 1, (9) 11; GLENSY (n 9) 76; WOOD (n 12) 138.

64 S. HENNETTE-VAUCHEZ, "When ambivalent principles prevail. Leads for explaining Western legal orders' infatuation with the human dignity principle", *EUI Working Papers Law* 2007, 18 pages.; P. MARTENS, "Encore la dignité humaine: réflexions d'un juge sur la promotion par les juges d'une norme suspecte", in X. (ed.), *Les Droits de l'homme au seuil du troisième millénaire : mélanges en hommage à Pierre Lambert*, Brussel, Bruylant, 2000, (561) 568: "Le juge puise dans le mystère d'une notion métaphysique et éthique pour y trouver l'instrument de son jugement. Il ne se réfère plus à la loi, ni même à la Constitution puisque le principe sur lequel il se fonde est pré-juridique ou

precision often leads judges to introduce their own moral standards amid competing claims of rights each of which has a plausible case of human dignity violation".[65] The most cited and criticized (but by no means only[66]) case in that regard is the *Wackenheim* case. Manuel Wackenheim suffered from human growth hormone deficiency. He participated in a rather bizarre form of public entertainment: a dwarf-tossing competition. Authorities decided to ban the competition on the basis of human dignity and the consequential violation of public order. Although he consented to the whole ritual and claimed to be happy on both a professional (gathered an monthly income of 20.000 FF) and a personal level (he had friends and ambitions for the first time in his life), both the French Conseil d'État[67] and the UN Human Rights Committee[68] sided against Wackenheim.

We are thus presented with two different views on human dignity, two subcategories which we will call subjective and objective dignity respectively. While subjective dignity encompasses what we as individuals regard as pertaining to our personal human dignity, objective dignity is more of a perceived dignity – what society beholds as human dignity.[69] A highly individual interpretation today may become a prevailing thought or principle in the future and become part of the "objective dignity".[70] Nevertheless, objective dignity raises two serious questions.

First, we might argue about how objective this dignity can be (in the hands of a judge)?[71] What is the basis for a judge to be able to determine what is good

supraconstitutionel. [. . .] La notion est si vague, son contenu si indécelable qu'en l'inscrivant dans un texte normatif, le constituant donne une véritable délégation constitutionelle au juge".

65 LEE (n 47) 1–33.

66 This is not the only case where the individually perceived dignity of a person is overruled by a different interpretation of dignity by the court, e.g. Court of Appeal Antwerp 30 September 1997, *RW* 1997–98, 749–750 (case of the SM-judge); ECtHR 29 April 2002, no. 2346/02, Pretty/UK, par. 53 and 65; Constitutional Court (Germany) 15 December 1981, no. C232.79, BVerfGE 64, 274 (Peep-show case): the court found that a striptease performed by a woman in some sort of cage, who gradually becomes more visible when the audience pays more, violated human dignity; Administrative Court of Appeal (France) 9 June 1998, no. 95PA03104, (Senanayake case): although a Jehovah's witness declined a blood transfusion on the basis of human dignity, the doctors still performed the procedure when the person's health deteriorated, upon which the Court decided that human dignity is not synonymous with autonomous freedom and the doctor's obligation to save lives therefore took precedence over the will of the patient.

67 Conseil d'État (France) 27 October 1995, no. 136727, concl. Frydman.

68 UN Human Rights Committee, *Manuel Wackenheim v. France*, 15 July 2002, no. 854/1999, UN Doc. CCPR/C/75/D/854/1999.

69 FIERENS (n 10) 580.

70 In our opinion, Julia Davis aptly refers to human dignity in the context of the Wackenheim case as morally important, but factually imprecise: DAVIS (n 30) 177–178.

71 Let alone the cultural relevance of a concept like dignity; for more on this subject see: J. DONNELLY, "Human rights and human dignity: an analytic critique of non-western

for someone and other people alike?[72] Do these questions go too far in that they actually criticize the core task of the judiciary itself? After all, law applies quite a lot of other open notions: public order, democratic society, reasonableness, good manners, etc.[73] There is nonetheless a certain tension between both subcategories of subjective and objective dignity. In the socio-economic field, this tension is eminently at stake in the *Gosselin* decision by the Canadian Supreme Court.[74] In this case, a complaint was lodged against the Quebec government which provided those who were single, unemployed and under the age of 30 with only Can$170 per month in social assistance (only one-third of the regular benefits). This could only be augmented through participation in employability programs. A small majority of the Supreme Court did not find a violation of the "equality rights" of section 15 of the Canadian Charter of Rights and Freedoms. They held that human dignity was not violated by these regulations because a reasonable person would have perceived the government's positive motives, namely to promote long-term employability of young people. In her dissenting opinion, Justice L'Heureux-Dubé claims that instead of focusing on the actual experiences of the applicant (i.e. subjective dignity), the majority focuses on the introduction of an objective element (i.e. objective dignity), a "reasonable person", which turns out to be no more than the government's own perception of its policy aims.[75] In contrast, L'Heureux-Dubé considers the possible physical and psychological threats of such a legislative scheme for individuals and concludes that they could indeed perceive that their dignity had been threatened.[76]

The second, more general, question concerns the relationship between objective dignity (or what it is perceived to be) and the individual's own sense of dignity. Some authors advocate a more subjective approach, stating that "human dignity seems constantly oriented to enhancing the dominant values of the community regardless of the individual's choices",[77] while it is in fact

conceptions of human rights", *The American Political Science Review* 1982, vol. 76, no. 2, 303–316.

72 P. CAROZZA, "Human dignity and judicial interpretation of human rights: a reply", *EJIL* 2008, vol. 19, no. 5, (931) 944; McCRUDDEN (n 4) 705–707.

73 J. FIERENS, "Existe-t-il un principe général du droit du respect de la dignité humaine" (note under Court of Cassation 18 November 2013), *RCJB* 2015, no. 4, (358) 376.

74 Supreme Court (Canada) 19 December 2002, no. 27418, Gosselin/Quebec (Attorney General), [2002] 4 S.C.R. 429.

75 S. FREDMAN, "Providing Equality: Substantive Equality and the Positive Duty to Provide", *S. Afr. J. on Hum. Rts.* 2005, vol. 21, (163) 177.

76 G. BRODSKY, "Gosselin v. Quebec (Attorney General): Autonomy with a Vengeance", *Canadian Journal of Women and the Law* 2004, vol. 15, 194–213; S. LIEBENBERG, "The value of human dignity in interpreting socio-economic rights", *S. Afr. J. on Hum. Rts.* 2005, vol. 21, (1) 18–20.

77 M.R. MARELLA, "A New Perspective on Human Dignity: European Contract Law, Social Dignity and the Retreat of the Welfare State", in S. GRUNDMANN (ed.), *Constitutional Values and European Contract Law*, The Netherlands, Kluwer, 2008, (123) 130.

this subjective experience that forms the focal point of dignity.[78] When applied to *Wackenheim*, this means that no imperatives should have to be imposed on this person's free choice to be part of a dwarf-tossing competition, certainly given the fact that this does not affect any other individual's free will.[79] But does this also imply that a measure that obliges homeless people, who clearly live in conditions contrary to "objective human dignity", to accept help and temporary shelter is contrary to human dignity when this goes directly against their own wishes?[80] This criticism on the judicial interpretation of human dignity is often based on the argument of autonomy. As Feldman says:

> [T]his paternalistic approach (by the judiciary) is allied to a form of legal moralism which treats autonomy as an aspect of human dignity but one which can be overridden by reference to the need to maintain respect for the dignity of whole human societies and the human race. [. . .] Human dignity becomes a ground for interfering with human autonomy.[81]

A fierce defender of autonomy in the context of dignity is Kant himself. According to him, dignity and autonomy are of a complementary nature. When a person's autonomy is restricted, his dignity will be violated and vice versa.[82] Consequently, the majority of Kant scholars believe that his concept of human dignity justifies the enforcement of only negative rights,[83] rights not to interfere with one's life. Although we concur that autonomy is indeed an important aspect of dignity, we oppose such a one-sided notion of the concept and give a much broader interpretation to what social dignity is.

2. Social Dignity

In the previous paragraphs we have seen how, in the context of the right to housing, the concept of human dignity tends to merge with the idea of decent housing and how its open-endedness has the potential to establish a very restrictive interpretation. Since it raises more questions than it solves and thereby creates a certain level of preventable legal insecurity, we argue that its conceptual added value as a dispute settlement or administrative criterion is at the very least questionable. At the same time we cannot deny how dignity

78 MATTSON (n 15) 309.
79 ENDERS (n 42) 261.
80 This is not a mere hypothetical situation. In the winter of 2010, for example, such an emergency ordinance was promulgated by the major of Amsterdam.
81 D. FELDMAN, "Human Dignity as a Legal Value: part 1", *Pub. L.* 1999, (682) 702.
82 J. RABKIN, "What can we learn about human dignity from international law?", *Harvard Journal of Law & Public Policy* 2003, vol. 27, no. 1, 145–168; BARBOSA DA SILVA (n 14) 24; J. RAZ, *The authority of law*, Oxford, Clarendon Press, 1979, 221.
83 WHITE (n 13) 6.

takes center stage and performs an important role in human rights law and socio-economic rights law in particular. It is only logical for the purposes of law- and policy-making that we elaborate on the meaning of such a right to social dignity.

We have explained earlier that we use the term "social dignity" instead of "human dignity" because it serves as a way to distinguish the use of the concept as a value or right worthy of protection from its application as an inherent characteristic of all human beings validating the protection of human rights. We should clarify first, however, that our choice of the word "social" as used here in social dignity should be understood neither as the exact opposite of a personal or individually perceived dignity nor as a concept that is engaged only in socio-economic rights (which thereby consolidates or emphasizes the classical dichotomy of human rights). Rather, it should be interpreted *sensu lato*, as being able to develop as a full member of society. As such, the word social acquires a relational value.[84] While a vital feature, dignity is not just a question of legal or material conditions. As interconnected beings, our sense of self-worth, autonomy and freedom is also impacted by the perception of others and society at large. In that connection, it is just as important to constitute positive relationships in which people can empower themselves as they wish to.

A. Conceptualization in the Context of Social Justice

1) Autonomy and Wellbeing

Based on how dignity is regularly incorporated as the aim of the right to housing, our broad interpretation concerns more than only a minimum standard or, as sometimes proclaimed, a minimum core, more than just a socio-economic safety net.[85] It takes into account the legal-philosophical concerns and underpinnings that have, for example, also formed the basis for the distinction between objective versus subjective dignity. In more concrete terms, social dignity encompasses wellbeing as well as autonomy and freedom.[86]

84 S. LIEBENBERG, "The value of human dignity in interpreting socio-economic rights", in A.J. VAN DER WALT (ed.), *Theories of social and economic justice*, Stellenbosch, Sun Press, 2005, (141) 149–152.

85 G. MAES, *De afdwingbaarheid van sociale grondrechten*, Antwerpen, Intersentia, 2003, 409–411, 414 and 451.

86 K. RAES, *Controversiële rechtsfiguren. Rechtsfilosofische excursies over de relaties tussen ethiek en recht*, Gent, Academia Press, 2001, 340; A. GEWIRTH, *Reason and morality*, Chicago, University of Chicago Press, 1978, 52–62 and 210–248: Alan Gewirth refers to these two aspects as necessary goods for agency (i.e. voluntary and purposeful human action), from which he derives human dignity; see also: M. PETRUSEK, "Human capacities and the problem of universally equal dignity: two philosophical test cases and a theistic response", *Journal of Moral Theology* 2016, vol. 5, no. 1, (37) 43–45.

We consider the latter features to both precede and follow from the former. It pertains to the autonomy to achieve wellbeing or what one wishes to attain in general and the freedom one acquires as a consequence of that wellbeing at the same time. When combined, a right to social dignity can be said to entail a right to personal development, to be able to fully participate in society. Social dignity thus goes beyond basic means of subsistence and satisfactory material conditions, even though those are still a major component of it. It includes, to quote Marella, "a set of conditions that make a person a fully participating member of society".[87]

The aspects of wellbeing/social welfare and autonomy/freedom are traditionally linked respectively with socio-economic rights on the one hand and civil and political rights on the other.[88] Yet freedom is definitely not a monopoly of civil and political rights. Academic literature has repeatedly mentioned that without a certain amount of material needs, unfortunate people will *de facto* also be deprived of their individual freedom and autonomy.[89, 90] Similarly, the South African Constitutional Court stated in its famous *Grootboom* decision that "there can be no doubt that human dignity, freedom and equality [. . .] are denied [to] those who have no food, clothing or shelter".[91] Former President of the United States Franklin D. Roosevelt argued back in 1941 in the same vein that "true individual freedom cannot exist without economic security and independence. Necessitous men are not free men".[92] Consequently, both socio-economic wellbeing and autonomy

87 MARELLA (n 77) 126 and 133.

88 T.H. MARSHALL, *Class, citizenship and social development*, Chicago, University of Chicago Press, 1977, 78–79.

89 H. SHUE, *Basic rights*, Princeton, Princeton University Press, 1980, 23–26; KELMAN (n 15) 533–535; LUTZ (n 13) 188; B.A. ANDREASSEN, A.G. SMITH and H. STOKKE, "Compliance with economic and social human rights: realistic evaluations and monitoring in the light of immediate obligations", in A. EIDE and B. HAGTVET (eds.), *Human Rights in Perspective: a Global Assessment*, Oxford, Oxford University Press 1992, (252) 260; J. RAWLS, *A theory of justice*, Cambridge, Harvard University Press, 1971, 62 and 92; BUITENWEG (n 27) 102; P. KING, "Housing as a freedom right", *Housing Studies* 2003, vol. 18, no. 5, 661–672; J. RAZ, *The morality of freedom*, Oxford, Clarendon Press, 1986, 155.

90 With regard to housing in particular, it has been said that an acceptable standard is a necessary condition of full membership of society; see: MARSHALL (n 88) 70; D. MILLER, "Democracy and social justice", *British Journal of Political Science* 1978, vol. 8, 1–19.

91 Constitutional Court (South Africa) 4 October 2000, CCT 11/00, Government of the Republic of South Africa et al./Grootboom et al., par. 23.

92 F.D. ROOSEVELT, *The four freedoms*, speech delivered on 6 January 1941; A. EIDE, "Economic, social and cultural rights as human rights", in A. EIDE, C. KRAUSE and A. ROSAS (eds.), *Economic, social and cultural rights*, Dordrecht, Martinus Nijhoff Publishers, 2001, (9) 15; C. ALBISA and J. SCHULTZ, "The United States", in

are not only indispensable for social dignity but also interdependent concepts.[93] And considering that socio-economic rights pursue socio-economic wellbeing, these rights are just as necessary to enable everyone to obtain the autonomy envisioned and pursue their conception of a good life.[94]

In the end, both generations of human rights play their part to achieve that goal. Effective socio-economic rights will help to create the conditions to be able to fully exercise the classic fundamental rights,[95] while the intensity of socio-economic needs does not diminish the urgency to realize civil and political freedoms either.[96] Against that background it is regrettable that the Belgian Constitution approaches social dignity exclusively from the socio-economic viewpoint.[97] The Commission of Professors, appointed to assist the Federal Government to elaborate on a coordinated version of the Constitution back in 1992, had nonetheless suggested placing "human dignity" at the very beginning of Title II of the Constitution ("Belgians and their rights").[98] The Commission proclaimed:

> [A] dignified life [. . .] encompasses all values of freedom, equality and solidarity [. . .]. This concept does not only open the door for social, economic and cultural rights, but in reality forms the synthesis of all fundamental rights. For example, a life in dignity also postulates protection of privacy. [Translated]

M. LANGFORD (ed.), *Social rights jurisprudence. Emerging trends in international and comparative law*, Cambridge, Cambridge University Press, 2009, 232.

93 C. FABRE, *Social rights under the Constitution: government and the decent life*, Oxford, Oxford University Press, 2000, 13 and 18–19.

94 F.M.C. VLEMMINX and H.R.B.M. KUMMELING, "Algemene situering van de sociale grondrechten in de Nederlandse rechtsorde", in B. HUBEAU and R. DE LANGE (eds.), *Het Grondrecht op wonen. De grondwettelijke erkenning van het recht op huisvesting in Nederland en België*, Antwerpen, Maklu, 1995, (13) 15–16; RAES (n 86) 344–345.

95 N. CHANDHOKE, "Thinking through social and economic rights", in D.A. BELL and J.-M. COICAUD (eds.), *Ethics in action: the ethical challenges of international human rights nongovernmental organizations*, Cambridge, Cambridge University Press, 2007, (181) 193–194; H.J.L.M. VAN DE LUYTGAARDEN, "Sociale grondrechten "gerenoveerd": het rechtskarakter van sociale grondrechten vanuit juridiseringsperspectief", in A.R.J. GROOT and H.J.L.M. VAN DE LUYTGAARDEN (eds.), *Zonder meer recht*, Zwolle, Tjeenk Willink, 1993, (149) 171–172; J. WALDRON, *Liberal rights*, Cambridge, Cambridge University Press 1993, 276.

96 MARSHALL (n 88) 7; A. SEN, *Vrijheid is vooruitgang*, Amsterdam, Contact, 2000, 144–156; K. RAES and G. COENE, "Sociale grondrechten als voorwaarden voor een gelijke handelingsvrijheid", *Welzijnsgids* 2009, no. 72, (25) 46.

97 VANDEBURIE (n 32) 154–156; Constitutional Court 26 April 2007, no. 66/2007, B.10.3.

98 *Parl.St.* Kamer, 1992–93, no. 1092/1; *Parl.St.* Senaat, BZ 1991–92, no. 100–46/5°.

In the context of the given interpretation of social dignity, this different layout would have made more sense. It encompasses the need for both types of fundamental rights to fully realize one's capabilities.[99]

Some have interpreted the freedom that stems from socio-economic rights as positive freedom and have drawn a distinction with the abstinence of governmental interference that characterizes negative freedom.[100] Others have phrased it differently and have distinguished liberty from the worth of liberty. In that interpretation, socio-economic rights are only geared towards increasing the worth of liberty offered by the classic fundamental rights in the first place.[101] In essence, both distinctions depart from the idea that the first and second generation of human rights establish freedom respectively in a direct and indirect manner, which once again emphasizes the gap between both types of fundamental rights. Moreover, it takes away from the fact that in our interpretation wellbeing remains a full-fledged aspect of social dignity in its own right. We do not interpret it as *only* a condition for autonomy.[102] We concur with Fabre in that it is not the only justification for socio-economic rights and that we should not fail to account for legislation and policies aimed primarily at simply establishing socio-economic security.[103] Providing housing to the homeless is, for example, not just prompted by the idea that without a home they will not be able to enjoy freedom to its full extent. It also simply protects them from suffering. As a consequence, even though wellbeing is an important factor in enabling freedom, we consider it just as much to be an independent aspect of social dignity.

Translated to housing legislation and policies, this means that not each and every measure taken must be primarily occupied in creating more autonomy. But when dignity is indeed given a central place in socio-economic and housing rights protection, it does, of course, mean that the idea of freedom and personal development should be generally present throughout the policies that try to effectively realize the right to housing.[104]

99 K. RIMANQUE, "Synthese: de betekenis van de sociale grondrechten", in ICM (ed.), *Jaarboek Mensenrechten 1994*, Antwerpen, Maklu, 1995, (179) 181.

100 I. BERLIN, *Four essays on liberty*, Oxford, Oxford University Press, 1964; R.P. VAN EXTER, *Het internationale aspect der grondrechten*, Vlaardingen, Drukkerij Van Dooren, 1955, 32, 37–38 and 41–44.

101 RAWLS (n 89) 204–205; G.M. VAN ASPEREN, *Het bedachte leven*, Amsterdam, Boom Uitgevers, 1993, 111; see also J. WALDRON, "Socioeconomic rights and theories of justice", *Public Law Research Paper no. 10–79*, 2010, 19.

102 E.g. RAZ (n 89) 288–320; A. GEWIRTH, *The community of rights*, Chicago, University of Chicago Press, 1996, 12; For more on how housing is not just a purpose in and of itself anymore, no longer a mere basic requirement, but a means for self-creation and self-fulfillment, see also D. CLAPHAM, *The meaning of housing. A pathways approach*, Cambridge, Policy Press, 2005.

103 FABRE (n 93) 13 and 20.

104 E. LANCKSWEERDT, "Het concept menselijke waardigheid als motor voor de verdere ontwikkeling van recht en rechtspraktijk", *TBP* 2013, vol. 9, (534) 536–537.

2) Connection to Capabilities?

Our conception of social dignity envisions concerns for wellbeing as well as autonomy and the capability of people to develop as they wish. These characteristics create at first sight a logical connection to Amartya Sen's capability approach.[105] Sen combines the same concerns and looks at what people are actually able to be and do. It is in this context equally important to refer to Martha Nussbaum, who took the capabilities approach more concretely into the heartland of human rights law.[106] As a matter of fact, she applied the concept of human dignity as the basis for her list of entitlements that every society should strive to guarantee to its members.[107]

In order to see what the distinguishing features are, we must first take a look at the content of this approach. Capability refers to the set of valuable functionings that a person has effective access to. These human functionings are states of being and doing, such as having shelter.[108] A person's capability then represents the freedom to choose what he/she perceives as a valuable functioning.[109] Sen describes the relevant concepts as follows: "Functionings are [. . .] different aspects of living conditions. Capabilities, in contrast, are notions of freedom, in the positive sense: what real opportunities you have regarding the life you may lead."[110]

Of course, the protagonists of the approach acknowledge that the necessary capabilities are not always at one's disposal. The approach therefore targets the creation of conditions that endows all citizens with opportunities with regard to their preferred life path.[111] It concerns the real opportunities (as against

105 This concept was first developed in A. SEN, "Equality of what?", *The Tanner Lecture on Human Values* 1980, vol. 1, 197–220.

106 M. NUSSBAUM, *Creating capabilities: the human development approach*, Cambridge, Harvard University Press, 2011, 33–34.

107 At its core, Alan Gewirth's moral theory shows significant similarities with Nussbaum's capability theory of justice. Both focus on whether a person is able to pursue his goals and both attach in that context considerable importance to wellbeing and positive rights, see: R. CLAASSEN and M. DÜWELL, "The foundations of capability theory: comparing Nussbaum and Gewirth", *Ethic Theory and Moral Practice* 2013, vol. 16, no. 3, (493) 502.

108 A. SEN, "Capability and well-being, in M. NUSSBAUM and A. SEN (eds.), *The quality of Life*, Oxford, Clarendon Press, 1993, (30) 31.

109 A. SEN, *Rationality and freedom*, Cambridge, Harvard University Press, 2002, 586.

110 A. SEN, *The standard of living*, Cambridge, Cambridge University Press, 1987, 36.

111 J.M. ALEXANDER, "Capabilities, human rights and moral pluralism", *The International Journal of Human Rights* 2004, vol. 8, no. 3, 3–4; P. VAN DIJK and G.J.H. VAN HOOF, *De Europese Conventie in theorie en praktijk,* Nijmegen, Ars Aequi Libri, 1982, 547; W. CASSIERS, "Les droits sociaux en quête d'effectivité", in V. VAN DER PLANCKE (ed.), *Les droits sociaux fondamentaux dans la lutte contre la pauvreté,* Brussel, Die Keure, 2012, (288) 303–305; RAES (n 96) 39; D. BILCHITZ, "Poverty and Fundamental Rights: The Justification and Enforcement of Socio-Economic Rights", Oxford, Oxford University Press, 2007, 11–14; S. LIEBENBERG,

formal opportunities) of people to be, do and achieve what they desire to. This can justify a selective approach to welfare (or in our case housing policy), but not one that should automatically be means-tested.[112] The central question is not as much what a person does, but rather what this person is in a position to do.[113] That is the central element to freedom in Sen's approach.

The conundrum created by this approach is where exactly one should draw the line between being in a position to achieve certain aspired functionings and not being capable of doing so. In an attempt to address this question, Nussbaum provides us with a list of functional capabilities necessary for human flourishing.[114] Capabilities such as life, bodily health and bodily integrity, but also control over one's material environment and even play can definitely be used as a justification for a right to housing[115], one that even appears to cover more than merely a right to basic shelter.[116] After all, adequate housing enables us to increase our capabilities by allowing us to rest, clean ourselves, work, provide space for personal and social relations, stimulate creativity, participate in politics, etc.[117]

It remains difficult to deduce an adequate standard of housing (and the scope of a right thereto) from this list of capabilities. In that regard, an important difference in rationale between our point of view and the capability theory exists. The capability approach is a basis for a theory of social justice, by way of which (certain) human rights or at the very least their core could be

Socio-economic rights. Adjudication under a transformative constitution, Claremont, Juta, 2010, 10.

112 BILCHITZ (n 111) 178; M. GARRIDO GÓMEZ, "Rights Guarantees, Equality and Social Rights", in J. MOTMANS, D. CUYPERS, P. MEIER, D. MORTELMANS and P. ZANONI (eds.), *Equal is not Enough: Challenging Differences and Inequalities in Contemporary Societies*, 2012, (17) 19; RAES (n 96) 40; A. SEN, "Elements of a theory of human rights", *Philosophy and Public Affairs* 2004, vol. 23, no. 4, (315) 332: As such, we argue that a capabilities approach would, for example, support a system of social housing distribution where people with the greatest housing need are given priority over those who are simply next on the waiting list, as is currently still more established for social rental agencies than social housing companies.

113 M. NUSSBAUM, *Women and human development: the capabilities approach*, Cambridge, Cambridge University Press, 2000, 70–74 and 88; A. SEN, "Human rights and capabilities", *Journal of Human Development* 2005, vol. 6, no. 2, (151) 153–154.

114 NUSSBAUM (n 106) 33–34; for another attempt at a capabilities list that also provides clear connections to a right to housing, see: P. VIZARD and T. BURCHARDT, *Developing a capability list: final recommendations of the equalities review steering group on measurement*, London, Centre for Analysis of Social Exclusion, 2007, 6.

115 C. McNAUGHTON NICHOLLS, "Housing, homelessness and capabilities", *Housing, Theory and Society* 2010, vol. 27, no. 1, (23) 30–36; S. FITZPATRICK, B. BENGTSSON and B. WATTS, "Rights to housing: reviewing the terrain and exploring a way forward", *Housing, Theory and Society* 2014, vol. 31, no. 4, (447) 451.

116 KING (n 89) 669.

117 G.F. EVANGELISTA, "Poverty, homelessness and freedom: an approach to the capabilities theory", *European Journal of Homelessness* 2010, vol. 4, (189) 193.

justified. Given the opportunity-based nature of the capability approach, though (as opposed to a more outcome-based one), the scope of fundamental rights could potentially be perceived as fairly limited. As a consequence, the capability approach obviously does not impose an obligation with regard to the realization of specific goals or the maximization of wellbeing.[118]

Our research on the other hand departs from already existing and functional human rights law, from an already established (higher) level of protection. In that context it is legally determined what aspects of housing must be protected and fulfilled and that the state must realize them progressively. The maximization of wellbeing and the attainment of specific goals are therefore automatically part of the fabric of our research, which expands beyond what one might envision as just in the context of a capability approach. One could describe our starting point as a very maximalist approach to capabilities, departing from a right to housing aimed at the realization of all aspects of adequate housing that could contribute to being autonomous, to being able to develop as one pleases.

With these differences firmly in the back of our mind, our conception of social dignity remains as the capability theory concerned with freedom. In Sen's approach, though, capability actually represents freedom and as such offers an interpretation of freedom that can be virtually equated with the ability to achieve a life one values living rather than the freedom that might flow from adequate housing.[119] He thereby distinguishes his approach from, for example, Rawls' theory of social justice, which describes so-called primary goods as a means to this freedom.[120] Both of these aspects of freedom relate to our conception of social dignity as set out earlier. Translated to our research topic, it raises questions as to the factual opportunities to apply housing rights to their full extent as well as how housing is able to establish autonomy. Considering the important place and proverbial weight given to dignity and a right thereto, we will take a more concrete look with regard to these questions and how our conception of dignity can be connected to current housing legislation and policies shortly.

3) A Different Voice on Social Justice

Before we continue with some applications of social dignity on the right to housing, though, we should point out that there are also diverging theories of social justice (and autonomy for that matter) and that some (more libertarian)

118 CLAASSEN (n 107) 502.

119 K. MENON, "Justice", in R. BHARGAVA and A. ACHARYA (eds.), *Political theory: an introduction*, Delhi, Pearson, 2008, (74) 83; A. SEN, "Human rights and capabilities", *Journal of Human Development* 2005, vol. 6, no. 2, (151) 153–154.

120 RAWLS (n 89) 75–80; see also S. FREEMAN, *Rawls*, London, Routledge, 2007, 90–91.

of them give leeway to a more hostile perspective on socio-economic rights.[121] Perhaps the best-known proponent of that approach is Robert Nozick.[122] While he does not neglect socio-economic needs and suffering, he is of the opinion that people cannot be forced in their positive responsibilities towards others. Their right to property is in that regard considered an inviolable right. This means that measures such as the obligation that rests upon building operators to reserve a certain quota of houses for social housing purposes would be unacceptable. As a matter of fact, state intervention in the housing market must automatically be condemned as a violation of individual rights, regardless of whether such intervention would be beneficial in terms of utility.[123] Nozick deems the entitlements that socio-economic rights create in general to restrict the freedom of other individuals because the cost for realizing these rights will ultimately be recovered from other people's property. In other words, his conception of autonomy is very differently construed than ours. That does not mean that a libertarian perspective is entirely void of the concept of equality; it is only differently construed. More specifically, it concerns an equal respect for everyone in that no one should be given advantages. This idea goes hand in hand with the argument that too much paternalism will hinder personal engagement, that any other approach will reinforce the status of dependency and take away incentives to social improvement, thereby limiting autonomous choice and personal responsibility.[124] For these reasons, a state should not actively intervene for reasons of social redistribution.[125] People's liberties should not be traded off for the sake of the socio-economic wellbeing of the weaker people in society.[126]

We do not agree with the idea that every interference in a person's life should be seen as a violation of one's liberties. As Griffin made clear, a tax that does not hinder a person to pursue or live a valuable life does not destroy this person's liberty. One might find it unjust or disproportionate, but it does not limit someone's capabilities when living comfortably above minimum levels.[127] This argument, though, is not very convincing from a libertarian viewpoint.

121 WALDRON (n 101) 2; T.R. MACHAN and D.B. RASMUSSEN (eds.), *Liberty for the twenty-first century*, Lanham, Rowman & Littlefield Publishers, 1995.

122 R. NOZICK, *Anarchy, state and utopia*, New York, Basic Books, 1974.

123 Ibid., 150–153.

124 P. SPICKER, "The rights of the poor: conceptual issues", in P. ROBSON and A. KJONSTAD (eds.), *Poverty and the law*, Oxford, Hart Publishing, 2001, 13; P. DE BEER, J. VAN DER MEER and P. PEKELHARING, *Gelijk. De noodzakelijke terugkeer van een klassiek ideaal*, Amsterdam, Van Gennep/De Balie, 2006, 181; R.L. KIDDER, *Connecting law and society*, New Jersey, Prentice-Hall, 1983, 137; LIEBENBERG (n 111) 147.

125 W. KYMLICKA, *Contemporary political philosophy: an introduction*, Oxford, Clarendon Press, 1990, 97.

126 NOZICK (n 122) 166–172.

127 J. J. GRIFFIN, "Welfare rights", *The Journal of Ethics* 2000, vol. 1–2, (27) 39.

There, freedom is very much focused on freedom from coercion imposed by the state. It is, in other words, of little relevance whether one is still capable of personal development after his contributions to the state. But freedom can also be perceived as freedom not only from but also in and through or by means of the state.[128] A better question to ask, then, is why deprivation of socio-economic needs is not also perceived as a restriction on people's freedom.[129] Does this not hinder them in exercising their freedom? Deprivation can just as well be described as the presence of coercion.[130]

Additionally, there is also a more practical argument in response to this individualistic approach to social justice. If having to pay taxes to the state is an infringement of the right to property, then it would obviously be purposeful having to pay as little as possible. Yet that view does not take into account that poverty and social inequality might in fact be more expensive for a society than the scenario in which there is more social equality.[131] It has, for example, been said that inequality leads to an increase in crime rates which raises imprisonment costs.[132] While these are not expenses in the context of socio-economic entitlements, they will inevitably have to be paid for by the public.

B. Social Dignity in the Right to Housing

Admittedly, dignity as interpreted here remains a difficult multifaceted concept. This conceptualization definitely opens up its meaning beyond a mere standard for housing quality and prevents it from being a convenient but vague *deus ex machina* whenever a decision requires some extra backing. But considering its comprehensive meaning, more than a concept apt for housing rights jurisprudence, it should provide direction for law- and policy-making. Against the background of our interpretation of social dignity, we now pose the question of what the implications are for some housing-related issues and policies, especially with regard to the element of autonomy. This selection of issues below relates to both aspects of autonomy we have distinguished, as the ability to enjoy the right to housing and the freedom adequate housing creates. In that regard, we take a look at how the social housing system relates to these concerns, the provision of social legal aid and the arguments it raises in favor or against a property-driven housing policy.

128 N. BOBBIO, *The age of rights*, Cambridge, Polity Press, 1995, 18.

129 In the words of Raz, "an autonomous agent is one who is not always struggling to maintain the minimum conditions of a worthwhile life". In that regard, government can encourage the creation of the conditions for such a life; see: RAZ (n 89) 155 and 297.

130 BUITENWEG (n 27) 352–354.

131 A. GLYN and D. MILIBAND (eds.), *Paying for inequality. The economic cost of social injustice*, London, Rivers Oram, 1994.

132 R.H. McADAMS, "The economic costs of inequality", *John M. Olin Program in Law & Economics working paper no.* 370, 2007.

1) Housing First

We start, though, by briefly mentioning a copybook example of a project that neatly fits the concept of social dignity: Housing First. Originally developed in the United States in the 1990s, Housing First has a particularly simple yet for a long time neglected starting point. It is first and foremost preoccupied with providing homeless people quick access to secure and permanent independent housing.[133] This means that housing is not made dependent upon having a regular job and that no prior commitment to treatment is necessary for those with psychiatric problems or addictions. Support in different shapes and forms may, of course, be necessary and should be available, but Housing First rests on the belief that it is beneficial to separate housing from guidance and not to have those people go through a classic staircase model where in a way they have to earn permanent housing step by step.[134] Ultimately, Housing First aims to establish wellbeing and autonomy first in order to provide homeless people with the opportunity to empowerment.[135]

After several different forms were adopted across the EU,[136] the Housing First Belgium project was set in motion in 2013 and operates in the five largest cities. According to an evaluation presented at the Housing First conference of 9 June 2016, the project has been a success up to now. We should mention, however, that none of these projects ought to be considered Housing First *sensu stricto*. In Antwerp, for example, empty social housing is used only as temporary housing for the chronically homeless.[137] Yet the paradigm shift that appears to take place in the direction of at least more of a 'housing-led' policy (also supported by the Flemish action plan on poverty reduction) can only be welcomed. As we will see in Part III, a more prominent focus on stable, permanent housing for homeless people also saves the government a considerable amount of money in the long run.[138]

133 N. PLEACE, *Housing First*, DIHAL, 2012, 3.

134 I. PANNECOUCKE and P. DE DECKER, *Housing first: een alternatief voor de woonladder?*, Leuven, Steunpunt Wonen, 2014, 3–6 and 8.

135 Housing First is in other words a capabilities informed framework: McNAUGHTON NICHOLLS (n 115) 37–38.

136 E.g. H. TAINIO and P. FREDIKSSON, "The Finnish homelessness strategy: from a 'staircase' model to a 'housing first' approach to tackling long-term homelessness", *European Journal of Homelessness* 2009, vol. 3, 181–199; N. HOUARD, "The French homelessness strategy: reforming temporary accommodation, and access to housing to deliver 'Housing First': continuum or clean break", *European Journal of Homelessness* 2011, vol. 5, no. 2, 83–98; V. BUSCH-GEERTSEMA, "Housing First Europe – results of a European social experimentation project", *European Journal of Homelessness* 2014, vol. 8, no. 1, 13–28.

137 FLEMISH HOUSING COUNCIL, *Dak- en thuisloosheid in Vlaanderen: pistes voor een meer woongericht beleid*, 24 March 2016, no. 2016/04, 31.

138 E. DEMAERSCHALK, "Dakloosheid kost handenvol geld. Housing First als goedkoper alternatief", *Alert* 2014, vol. 40, no. 5, 16–24.

2) Social Legal Aid

People who live in adequate housing will be better placed to develop themselves as they wish. Measures that aim to provide people with such socio-economic security will therefore enhance their autonomy indirectly. But there are more influences than only the material content of the socio-economic measures itself – for example, the importance of clear-cut legislation, the weaker position of tenants, etc. They reveal how it is one thing for a right to housing to exist, but often a whole different matter to be able to properly apply and enforce it. The former alone does not guarantee the essential assets necessary for personal development. As such, we stress the importance of being free from practical hindrances to be able to attain one's aspired level of wellbeing.

If we were to apply a strict capability approach, the earlier-mentioned conundrum would creep up once again. At what point does a person have the opportunity to overcome these influences? When is he/she adequately positioned to do so? Approaching it from an established right to social dignity as we do, however, a different, more positive question arises: what can be done to enhance that sense of autonomy? In that regard, we can only encourage initiatives that provide the necessary legal aid to those persons in need of it and thereby at the same time contribute to their active participation in society. It emphasizes how our interpretation of autonomy is not one of essential independency. One does not exclude the other.[139] Rather, it is a reminder of the relational nature of our conception of dignity.

In Flanders, different specific housing legal aid institutions are already in place. Tenant unions originally developed out of more general law shops, which found themselves predominantly occupied with rental law issues anyway. In accordance with the Flemish Housing Code, tenant unions can now be officially recognized and funded by the Flemish government.[140] They are appointed to contribute to the realization of the right to housing and to protect in particular the interests of the most vulnerable families and single persons on the private housing market. This mission and the tasks it brings with it are described more extensively in a 2006 decision by the Flemish government.[141]

Tenant unions have a wide array of functions, but their core task revolves around providing information and legal aid to both private and social tenants. This information can concern an explanation of legal provisions, procedures or

139 R. DE BRABANDER, *Wie wil er nou niet zelfredzaam zijn? De mythe van zelfredzaamheid*, Antwerpen, Garant, 2014, 86–91.

140 Article 56 and 58 Flemish Housing Code; T. VANDROMME and B. HUBEAU, "Algemene schets van de huisvestingssector en het huisvestingsrecht", in X. (ed.), *Het onroerend goed in de praktijk*, Mechelen, Kluwer, 2015, VII.A-1–VII.A.3-11, (351) 378.

141 Article 2 Decision Flemish Government 6 February 2004 concerning the stipulation of the conditions for the recognition and subsidization of social rental agencies, *BS* 16 March 2004.

institutions, as long as it is tenancy-related. They also investigate the lawfulness of a situation or dispute and propose resolution patterns. In order to request such advice, the tenant will have to pay a yearly fee of €12–17, depending on which province they live in. In order to lower possible barriers further, organizations and local governments can also subscribe collectively. When, for example, an OCMW enters into such a subscription, they can provide people who have tenancy problems with more specific advice coming straight from the tenant union or even refer them directly to one, all without it costing their clients any money at all. Furthermore, tenant unions cooperate with the Flemish translation phone service in order to provide the same opportunities to this weaker group of non-native speakers too.

As an additional service, tenant unions can engage in communication with the concerned landlord or other parties involved. In exceptional cases, they will go even further and actually assist and/or represent a member in court procedures or mediation. Furthermore, they also try to put their mark on housing policies by, for example, actively participating in housing councils. Last but certainly not least, tenant unions have an important preventive function as well. By holding educational sessions in schools, for resident groups and advisors from different organizations, they engage themselves in trying to tackle tenancy problems at their root.[142]

The tenant unions in Flanders reside under a coordination structure also institutionalized by the Flemish Housing Code.[143] The Platform for Tenants is responsible for the collaboration with and support of all tenant unions in Flanders. It assists the tenant unions in the realization of their missions and looks after their interests in consultations with the relevant governments. As an illustration of this, the Platform occasionally also lodges complaints before court, even up to the Constitutional Court.[144]

Housing shops provide a different channel through which to pose questions and from which to receive information and advice with regard to housing and housing subsidies. In contrast to the tenant unions, their services are not confined to tenancy problems. The concept has found its way under the guise of several different names and practices, but they all have the same main objective: to support and orientate people in their search for adequate housing.[145] They do so in a characteristically personal and integrated manner. This means that, when useful, a housing shop will make an analysis of a

142 J. GOORDEN, J. MERTENS et al., "De sociale rechtshulp in kaart gebracht", in J. GOORDEN and J. MERTENS (eds.), *Recht op recht. Sociale rechtshulp en sociaaljuridische dienstverlening in Vlaanderen*, Mechelen, Kluwer, 2011, (47) 83–86.

143 Art. 57 Flemish Housing Code.

144 E.g. Council of State 18 February 2003, no. 222.544, *RW* 2013–14, no. 39, 1533, note B. HUBEAU and T. VANDROMME; Constitutional Court 5 March 2015, no. 24/2015; Constitutional Court 10 July 2008, no. 101/2008; Summary Procedure Court of First Instance Gent 30 October 2003, *T. App.* 2004, no. 3, 18.

145 GOORDEN (n 142) 89–91.

household's situation (housing-related and beyond) and propose a custom-made plan to overcome the potential problems. In other instances it will be appropriate to refer cases to better-placed services such as the tenant unions, but sometimes they do mediate renting matters themselves or even lodge complaints against the refusal of subsidies. Finally, housing shops also try to put their mark on (local) housing policies.[146]

In contrast to the tenant unions which are organized by province, housing shops predominantly operate as part of cities and municipalities, public authorities from which they also receive their funding. With their local character and personal approach, housing shops aim to be easily accessible to everyone with housing questions. Unfortunately, however, their services are said not to (or insufficiently) reach those who could use their assistance most (homeless people, squatters, etc.). If we want these organizations to fully achieve what they set out, which is to make the right to housing a capability for personal development not only in theory but also in practice, it is important to get a better understanding of why these apparent barriers still exist and what can be done to overcome them.

3) Property as a Primary Concern

A. THE RIGHT TO HOUSING AS A RIGHT TO PROPERTY

In Part II of this book we will see that the European Court of Human Rights utilizes the right to property (article 1 of the First Protocol to the ECHR) in such a way that it can have an influence on the right to housing and domestic housing policies. Even tenants can have their interests protected by this provision. But, of course, both rights are not the same.[147] No matter how broad the interpretation of possession may be (i.e. a legitimate expectation of something), the right to property does not envision everyone acquiring property as is the case with adequate housing and the fundamental right thereto.

That does not take away from the fact that governments are often focused on promoting the acquisition of property. Over the years, many countries have generally been shown to favor fiscal benefits with regard to home ownership.[148]

146 S. GIBENS and B. HUBEAU, "Legal aid and housing issues", in B. HUBEAU and A. TERLOUW (eds.), *Legal aid in the Low Countries*, Antwerpen, Intersentia, 2014, (141) 147.

147 UN Office of the High Commissioner for Human Rights, *The Right to Adequate Housing. Fact sheet no. 21*, 7–8; P. KENNA, "Housing rights: positive duties and enforceable rights at the European Court of Human Rights", *E.H.R.L.R.* 2008, no. 2, (193) 198–199.

148 F. FIGARI, A. PAULUS, H. SUTHERLAND, P. TSAKLOGLOU, G. VERBIST and F. ZANTOMIO, "Removing home ownership bias in taxation: the distributional effects of including net imputed rent in taxable income", *Fiscal Studies* 2016, vol. 37;

But while most European governments did not pursue home ownership as a primary objective until the 1970s and 1980s,[149] Belgium has a longstanding history of a property-driven housing policy. It dates all the way back to the end of the nineteenth century. The first Housing Act was drafted in 1889 and laid the foundation for the system of fiscal benefits for home owners. After responsibility for housing policy was transferred to the regions, a budgetary shift became visible to the social rental sector, a shift which could potentially re-establish itself now that the regions have become responsible for private rental legislation and tax benefits for homeowners as well.[150] Still, however, the Flemish government has over the years retained its primary goal of supporting private home ownership.[151] This is not all that surprising given the consensus that seems to exist on this topic across the entire political spectrum.[152]

According to Verbist, even the Constitutional Court has hinted at the idea that the right to housing is first and foremost a right to home ownership.[153] In a case that contested social tenants' right to buy the social dwelling they live in, the court decided that in light of the constitutional right to housing the assessment of the legislators concerning the general interest had to be respected. Yet the court did not stop there. By considering that the legislator found itself in the position to argue that the previous regulation (by which the social housing companies could decide whether or not to sell their property) did not sufficiently respond to the aims of its housing policy,[154] Verbist sees the court implicitly recognizing the right to housing as a right to home ownership. By extension he argues that, following this judgment, housing without a right to property is apparently inadequate.[155]

S.C. BOURASSA and W.G. GRIGSBY, "Income tax concessions for owner-occupied housing", *Housing Policy Debate* 2000, vol. 11, no. 3, 521–546; H. TER RELE and G. VAN STEEN, "Measuring housing subsidies: distortionary and distributional effects in the Netherlands", *Fiscal Studies* 2003, vol. 24, no. 3, 317–339.

149 D. CONLEY and B. GIFFORD, "Home ownership, social insurance, and the welfare state", *Sociological Forum* 2006, vol. 21, no. 1, (55) 60; J. DOLING and R. RONALD, "Home ownership and asset-based welfare", *Journal of Housing and the Built Environment* 2010, vol. 25, no. 2, 165–173.

150 S. WINTERS, "Are there grounds for housing allowances in Flanders (Belgium)?", *European Journal of Housing Policy* 2005, vol. 5, no. 2, (167) 168–170.

151 V. GEURTS and L. GOOSSENS, "Home ownership and social inequality in Belgium", in K. KURZ and H.P. BLOSFELD (eds.), *Home ownership and social inequality in comparative perspective*, Stanford, Stanford University Press, 2004, (79) 82.

152 P. DE DECKER, *Eigen woning: geldmachine of pensioensparen?*, Antwerpen, Garant, 2013, 9–10 and 41–43.

153 S. VERBIST, "Impliceert het recht op behoorlijke huisvesting een recht op eigendom" (note under Constitutional Court 7 March 2007, no. 33/2007), *RABG* 2007, no. 16, 1103–1109.

154 Constitutional Court 7 March 2007, no. 33/2007, B.5.4.

155 VERBIST (n 153) 1107–1108.

Regardless of whether one is supportive of this reading of the judgment, the longstanding focus on property-based welfare has not missed its effect on the composition of the housing market. The home ownership rate in Flanders climbed to about 75 percent in 2005 before decreasing slightly over the following years to 70.5 percent by 2013. That slight decrease, however, appears to be related to demographic changes more than to any drop in preference or fundamental change in political focus. The impact also seems to be confined to the two lowest income quintiles, an observation which we will return to later.[156]

That all said, the following question now arises: on the basis of our conception of social dignity and with autonomy as a component of it, should home ownership indeed be pursued in the context of the right to housing as the most important housing policy option?[157]

B. HOME OWNERSHIP AS THE PINNACLE OF AUTONOMY

1. The Benefits of Home Ownership in the Balance Housing has been described as a means for self-creation and self-fulfillment, a safe space for the construction and maintenance of personal identity.[158] Many relate these features exclusively to home ownership.[159] Ownership of property is said to enhance social citizenship and political participation, spread wealth and equality, and be the foundation for social stability and democracy.[160] It is often equated with the characteristics of dignity, autonomy and liberty (which for non-owners are then much more difficult to establish[161]) and therefore justifies specific protection by the state.[162] This perspective on the connection between dignity,

156 K. HEYLEN, *Grote woononderzoek 2013. Deel 2. Deelmarkten, woonkosten en betaalbaarheid,* Leuven, Steunpunt Wonen, 2015, Leuven, Steunpunt Wonen, 10.

157 B. CLAESSENS, E. VLERICK and P. DE DECKER, *Op zoek naar de betekenis van wonen. Een verkennend literatuuronderzoek*, Heverlee, Steunpunt Ruimte en Wonen, 2009, 25.

158 CLAPHAM (n 102).

159 Saunders, for example, one of the most prominent academic supporters of home ownership as a source of individual rewards, describes home ownership as "an emotional expression of autonomy, security, or personal identity"; see: P. SAUNDERS, *A nation of homeowners*, London, Unwin Hyman, 1990, 39; C. ROSE, "Property as a keystone right?", *Notre Dame Law Review* 1995, vol. 71, (329) 358; S. SMITH, "The essential qualities of home", *Journal of Environmental Psychology* 1994, vol. 14, no. 1, 31–46.

160 D.B. BARROS, "Home as a legal concept", *Santa Clara Law Review* 2006, vol. 46, (255) 300–305; L. UNDERKUFFLER, *The idea of property: its meaning and power*, Oxford, Oxford University Press, 2003, 138.

161 D. ROSENDORF, "Homelessness and the uses of theory: an analysis of economic and personality theories of property in the context of voting rights and squatting rights", *University of Miami Law Review* 1990, (701) 710.

162 M.J. RADIN, "Property and personhood", *Stanford Law Review* 1982, vol. 34, (957).

freedom and home ownership finds its roots in the ideas of Kant and Hegel,[163] the latter claiming that private property "is something everyone needs in order to develop his freedom and individuality".[164]

These more academic considerations are reflected in the preferences of citizens across first world countries.[165] Some have proposed that this aspiration for home ownership has been influenced by the socio-cultural portrayal of ownership, backed by government rhetoric.[166] Kemeny, for example, believes that tenure systems are a cause rather than a product of tenure preferences.[167] Regardless of the composition of the national housing market or the promotion of home ownership, however, people traditionally prefer to acquire their own property.[168] Take, for example, Sweden, a country where home ownership has not been promoted to the same extent as in many other countries and which is ahead of the pack when it comes to tenant protection.[169] Still the outcome remains the same. Swedish households show a preference for owner-occupied housing as well.[170]

163 M. SIGRON, *Legitimate expectations under article 1 of Protocol no. 1 to the European Convention on Human Rights*, Antwerpen, Intersentia, 2014, 23–25.

164 J. WALDRON, *The right to private property*, Oxford, Oxford University Press, 1990, 351.

165 A preference for home ownership is present in all European countries discussed in M. ELSINGA, P. DE DECKER, N. TELLER and J. TOUSSAINT (eds.), *Home ownership beyond asset and security. Perceptions of housing related security and insecurity in eight European countries*, Amsterdam, IOS Press, 2007; A. VASSENDEN, "Homeownership and symbolic boundaries: exclusion of disadvantaged non-homeowners in the homeowner nation of Norway", *Housing Studies* 2014, vol. 29, no. 6, 760–780 (Norway); R.M. RAKOFF, "Ideology in everyday life: the meaning of the house", *Politics and Society* 1977, vol. 7, (85) 100 (United States); L. HOLDSWORTH, "Sole voices: experiences of non-homeowning sole mother renters", *Journal of Family Studies* 2011, vol. 17, no. 1, 59–70 (Australia); A. DUPUIS and D.C. THORNS, "Home, home ownership and the search for ontological security", *The Sociological Review* 1998, vol. 46, no. 1, 24–47 (New Zealand).

166 R. LAWRENCE, "Deciphering home: an integrative historical perspective" in D. BENJAMIN (ed.), *The home: words, interpretations, meanings and environments*, Aldershot, Ashgate, 1995, 60.

167 J. KEMENY, *The myth of home ownership: public versus private choices in housing tenure*, London, Routledge, 1981, 63.

168 Even a housing market crisis does not seem to push public opinion into a definitive different direction; see: H. RUONAVAARA and P. NAUMANEN, "Finland: trust, risk-taking and scepticism", in ELSINGA, P. DE DECKER, N. TELLER and J. TOUSSAINT (eds.), *Home ownership beyond asset and security. Perceptions of housing related security and insecurity in eight European countries*, Amsterdam, IOS Press, 2007, (67) 77–78; SAUNDERS (n 159) 69 and 80.

169 D. ANDREWS, A. CALDERA SÁNCHEZ and A. JOHANSSON, *Housing markets and structural policies in OECD countries*, OECD Economics Department Working Papers no. 836, 47–49.

170 E. ANDERSSON, P. NAUMANEN, H. RUONAVAARA and B. TURNER, "Housing, socio-economic security and risks. A qualitative comparison of household attitudes in

More generally speaking, renting is seen as a negative choice that one is forced to make due to financial or unforeseen personal circumstances rather than as a positive choice. When asked about this, people usually refer to several reasons that can be linked to autonomy and freedom, or at least their perceptions on it. On the basis of their arguments, we distinguish financial, material and subjective autonomy.

From a financial standpoint, the main argument seems to be universally agreed upon. The advantage connected to acquiring property is that money is spent efficiently. In comparison, paying rent to a landlord is widely interpreted as *de facto* throwing money away.[171] One could potentially reap financial benefits from rising house prices (even though that appears to be less probable in the case of low-income households[172]), but that possibility is not the advantage we should focus on in the context of autonomy. Even regardless of whether the value of one's property increases or decreases, home ownership is still regarded as a good financial investment simply because it creates financial freedom (over time).[173] In that regard, the very prospect of fully acquired home ownership appears to overshadow the fact that one is usually still dependent upon financial institutions for several years and even decades due to mortgage debts, a period during which financial difficulties could potentially occur. Still it is, of course, true that once this mortgage is paid off, home owners are able to live rent-free and gather additional income (imputed rent) after retirement. With the social welfare state and old-age pensions under significant financial pressure, however, the political support for home ownership might exist not only to promote this financial aspect of autonomy, but also as a means to remove some of the financial burden away from the state and to cut back on social expenses.[174]

Finland and Sweden", *European Journal of Housing Policy 2007*, vol. 7, no. 2, (151) 168.

171 DE DECKER (n 152) 66, 71 and 126; ELSINGA (n 165) 79 (Finland), 182 (the Netherlands) and 269 (United Kingdom); C. GURNEY, "Lowering the drawbridge: a case study of analogy and metaphor in the social construction of home ownership", *Urban Studies* 1999, vol. 36, (1706) 1716.

172 J. DOLING and B. STAFFORD, *Home ownership: the diversity of experience*, Aldershot, Gower, 1989; G. McCARTHY, S. VAN ZANDT and W. ROHE, *The economic benefits and costs of homeownership. A critical assessment of the research*, Arlington, Research Institute for Housing America, 2001, 18.

173 G. McCARTHY, S. VAN ZANDT and W. ROHE, *The economic benefits and costs of homeownership. A critical assessment of the research*, Arlington, Research Institute for Housing America, 2001, 18; M. HAFFNER, *Appel voor de dorst. Vermogen van ouderen op de woningmarkt*, Utrecht, NETHUR, 2005; J. DOLING and M. ELSINGA, *Demographic change and housing wealth: homeowners, pensions and asset-based welfare in Europe*, Dordrecht, Springer, 2013, 105 and 107.

174 F.G. CASTLES, "The really big trade-off: home ownership and the welfare state in the new world and the old", *Acta Politica* 1998, vol. 33, no. 1, (5) 8; P. DE DECKER and V. GEURTS, "Belgium" in J. DOLING and J. FORD (eds.), *Globalisation and home*

A second advantage of home ownership that people connect to the term "autonomy" concerns the idea of freedom from external control by a landlord. On the one hand, it means that you can do as you like with the property, shape your home to your preferences and needs, and through that build and maintain personal identity, uncompromised by possible conditions set in a rental agreement.[175] On the other hand, this material control has a sense of security associated with it. It has been emphasized that an amount of certainty about the home, of being in control of (not) moving is vital to one's ability to develop.[176] It might even be the most indispensable element of a right to housing, as a basis upon which to build a life and fully participate in society.[177] As such it is also critical for our conception of social dignity. Owners are in that sense not subjected to the uncertainty that the landlord might want to sell his property or move into the dwelling himself (or his family), unlike tenants who would then be forced to search for a new place to call home.[178]

Private rent law in most countries, of course, will provide tenants with a certain degree of protection against eviction and insecurity of tenure more generally. The ease with which a landlord is legally able to exercise his power to evict , however, not be the only thing that matters. Important also is the mere capacity to do so – the possibility that this might happen.[179] In that sense, both *de iure* and *de facto* security play their role in the perception of home ownership and tenancy.[180]

ownership. Experiences in eight member states of the European Union, Delft, Housing and Urban Policy Studies, DUP Science, 2003, 23–24; P. DE DECKER and C. DEWILDE, "Home ownership and asset-based welfare: the case of Belgium", *Journal of Housing and the Built Environment* 2010, vol. 25, (243) 250–253.

175 DE DECKER (n 152) 65–66; VASSENDEN (n 165) 769–770.

176 S.J. BRIGHT and N. HOPKINS, "Home, meaning and identity: learning from the English model of shared ownership housing", *Theory and Society* 2011, vol. 28, no. 4, (377) 287.

177 S. LECKIE, "Where it matters most: making international housing rights meaningful at the national level", in S. LECKIE (ed.), *National perspectives on housing rights*, The Hague, Martinus Nijhoff Publishers, 2003, (3) 35; D.H. BELL, "Providing security of tenure for residential tenants: good faith as a limitation on the landlord's right to terminate", *Ga. L. Rev.* 1985, vol. 19, (483) 532; Some authors have claimed, though, that the significance has been exaggerated: M. BALL, *The UK private rented sector as a source of affordable accommodation*, York, Joseph Rowntree Foundation, 2010, 15; J. RUGG and D. RHODES, *The private rented sector: its contribution and potential*, York, Centre for Housing Policy, 2008.

178 H. RUONAVAARA, "Types and forms of housing tenure, toward solving the comparison/translation problem", *Scandinavian Housing and Planning Research* 1993, vol. 10, (3) 12.

179 S. LUKES, *Power: a radical view*, Basingstoke, Palgrave Macmillan, 2005, 12; J.-L. VAN GELDER, "What tenure security? The case for a tripartite view", *Land Use Policy* 2010, vol. 27, (449) 451.

180 S. FITZPATRICK and H. PAWSON, "Ending security of tenure for social renters: transitioning to 'ambulance service' social housing", *Housing Studies* 2014, vol. 29, no. 5, (597) 603–604.

It is not only the preference of the landlord that influences security of tenure. Other elements of the right to housing such as affordability can have an impact too.[181] The difference is that affordability problems can affect the degree of security for (mortgage-paying) owners also. This has become all the more visible following the economic crisis. In Spain, 350,000 foreclosures occurred between 2007 and 2012, with 159 evictions a day in 2012 and still 95 a day two years later.[182] The Belgian mortgage market has been spared such dramatic figures, but it has been reported that ever more Belgian home owners are incapable of paying off their mortgage debts on time. It can reasonably be suspected that households facing (considerable) mortgage arrears seem unlikely to derive the same feelings of freedom or identity that still seem to be exclusively associated with home ownership.[183]

Finally, there is subjective autonomy. It should be clear by now that the previous arguments in favor of home ownership are not entirely objective anyway, but what we allude to here is the status that is linked to this form of tenure.[184] People (not only home owners) tend to make positive connotations to home ownership, while renting often has a stigma attached to it.[185] Owning a home is in that regard interpreted as the result of being a hard worker and a responsible human being. It is something to be proud of, something that has an impact on one's self-esteem. People who rent their home, on the other hand, are widely perceived as poorer, less civic-minded and less successful,[186] especially if they have passed the age of 30.[187] This is even more the case in regard to social tenants.[188]

Whether or not these connotations hold little truth, we cannot dismiss these perceptions considering the relational nature of dignity that we explained

181 Think, for example, also of a dwelling of severely insufficient quality, which can also lead to a forced eviction.

182 UN General Assembly, *Report of the Special Rapporteur on adequate housing as a component of the right to an adequate standard of living*, 10 August 2012, A/67/150, 10.

183 C. GURNEY, *The meaning of home in the decade of owner occupation: towards an experiential perspective*, Bristol, School of Advanced Urban Studies, 1990, 8.

184 J. HOHMANN, *The right to housing. Law, concepts, possibilities*, Oxford, Hart Publishing, 2013, 175; J. FORD, R. BURROWS and S. NETTLETON, *Home-ownership in a risk society*, Bristol, The Policy Press, 2001, 148–149; S. MALLETT, "Understanding home: a critical review of the literature", *The Sociological Review* 2004, vol. 52, no. 1, (62) 66.

185 C. GURNEY, "Pride and prejudice: discourses of normalization in public and private accounts of home ownership", *Housing Studies* 1999, vol. 14, (163) 165.

186 W.M. ROHE and W.A. STEGMAN, "The effects of homeownership: on the self-esteem, perceived control and life satisfaction of low-income people", *Journal of the American Planning Association* 1994, vol. 60, no. 2, 173–184; E. SCANLON, *Home ownership and its impacts: implications for housing policy for low-income families*, Center for Social Development, Washington University, 1996, 7–9; L. FOX, *Conceptualising home. Theories, laws and policies,* Oxford, Hart Publishing, 2007, 173.

187 B. MEEUS and P. DE DECKER, *De geest van Suburbia*, Antwerpen, Garant, 2013, 302.

188 FITZPATRICK (n 180) 600.

earlier; our sense of freedom is also impacted by the perception of society. That perception, however, appears to be somewhat malleable. In contrast to the general preference for home ownership which as we said is not influenced by the composition of the housing market or the extent of tenant protection, the latter influence appears to be able to play a role with regard to the general attitude towards and the status of renting.[189] In the Netherlands, Sweden and Germany, renting is seen as an Tacceptable alternative rather than a temporary solution or a last resort. Considering that on average they provide stronger legal protection for tenants (also through some form of rent control[190]), it is interesting to see that the connotation society usually makes with regard to renting is largely absent in these countries.[191]

2. Justifying a Property-Driven Policy We come to the main question: does (a right to) social dignity encourage or at least justify the promotion of home ownership? We will argue that some of the proclaimed advantages of home ownership that are connected to an interpretation of autonomy are not always as clear-cut or exclusive. Consequently, the question arises as to whether all the advantages described above are actually advantages that should be pursued in the context of social dignity.

I. (PERCEPTION OF) HOUSING SECURITY Back in 1998, Murie argued that "certain attributes of the tenure (i.e. owner-occupation) have been increasingly identified as if they were inherent to it and were the underlying reason for its promotion".[192] Along the same lines, we believe that part of the autonomy that is now often attributed to home ownership in particular could also be provided to tenants. In order to enhance this autonomy, thereby taking into account that housing security is seen as an important feature for personal development, it would be an option to increase legal security of tenure through a comprehensive system of rent control and/or a more "pro-tenant" bias in rental contract regulation.

189 VASSENDEN (n 165) 778.

190 M. HAFFNER, M. ELSINGA and J. HOEKSTRA, "Rent regulation: the balance between private landlords and tenants in six European countries", *European Journal of Housing Policy* 2008, vol. 8, no. 2, (217) 224–225 and 228–229.

191 ANDERSSON (n 170) 159--160 and 168–169; G. TEGEDER and I. HELBRECHT, "Germany: home ownership, a Janus-faced advantage in time of welfare restructuring", in M. ELSINGA, P. DE DECKER, N. TELLER and J. TOUSSAINT (eds.), *Home ownership beyond asset and security. Perceptions of housing related security and insecurity in eight European countries*, Amsterdam, IOS Press, 2007, 128; VAN GELDER (n 179) 453.

192 A. MURIE, "Secure and contented citizens? Home ownership in Britain" in A. MARSH and D. MULLINS (eds.), *Housing and public policy: citizenship, choice and control*, Buckingham, Open University Press, 1998, (79) 82; see also K. HULSE and V. MILLIGAN, "Secure occupancy: a new framework for analyzing security in rental housing", *Housing Studies* 2014, vol. 29, no. 5, (638) 639 and 642–644.

With regard to the former, it would be possible to establish a system of rent prices on the basis of objective parameters. If that would put too much of a strain on landlords, tenants could alternatively be given the opportunity to question the reasonableness of the rental price or a maximum limit could be set to prevent abuses.[193] While some countries already apply certain derivatives of these systems (e.g. Sweden,[194] Denmark,[195] the Netherlands,[196] Germany[197]), Belgian rent law only regulates the rent price by assuring its continuity throughout the term of the contract. The price itself is freely negotiated by the contracting parties and can be subjected to yearly increases made in accordance with the health index.

From a more general perspective, the level of housing security protection offered by private rental law obviously varies widely from country to country as well. The OECD has stated that Belgian contract regulations are neutral, in favor of neither tenant nor landlord.[198] In comparison to other OECD countries, it thereby ranks slightly below the middle of the pack in terms of housing security for private tenants.[199] At the same time, though, private rent agreements are considered to have a duration of nine years,[200] which is fairly

193 M. DAMBRE, *De huurprijs. Analyse van de financiële verbintenissen van de huurder en onderzoek naar de mogelijkheid tot objectivering van de woninghuurprijzen*, Brugge, Die Keure, 2009, 344 and 361.

194 TENLAW, *National Report for Sweden,* 2015, 78: In Sweden, rents are determined via collective bargaining between tenants unions and the property federations. It should be established at a reasonable amount, which is considered not to be palpably higher (+/– 5%) than the rent for units of equivalent utility value. Before 2011, the municipal housing companies had a normative role for all rents, since their prices set the ceiling for the rents in equivalent private landlord dwellings;

195 FEANTSA, *The role of housing in pathways into and out of homelessness*, 2008, 28: For privately rented buildings constructed before 1991, the rent is set in proportion to running costs. Landlords can also pass on a capital charge (between 7 and 14%), calculated on the basis of the value of the house. There is also a rent control board to see whether the conditions abide by law.

196 S. WINTERS, *Huurprijzen en richthuurprijzen. Deel I: literatuurstudie over richthuurprijzen*, Leuven, Steunpunt Ruimte en Wonen, 2012, 11–12: The rental price regulation in the Netherlands only applies for housing under the so-called liberalization limit (2015: €710.68/month). The maximum price for these accommodations is based on a point system that takes into account the characteristics of the dwelling itself and its environment. The government determines these points.

197 In Germany, reference prices are set on the basis of the '*mietspiegel*', a database on all rental contracts from a certain area over the past four years containing reference prices for similar dwellings: M. ELSINGA, M. HAFFNER, J. HOEKSTRA, P. VANDENBROUCKE, E. BUYST and S. WINTERS, *Beleid voor de private huur: een vergelijking van zes landen*, Brussel, Departement RWO-Woonbeleid, 2007, 40–41.

198 C. CUERPO, S. KALANTARYAN and P. PONTUCH, *Rental market regulation in the European Union*, Brussels, European Commission, 2014, 7–8.

199 ANDREWS (n 169) 47–49.

200 Art. 3, § 1 Housing Rent Act.

long when compared with rental agreements in other European countries.[201] That said, the majority of rental agreements in practice are still short-term and a landlord can also end long-term agreements at any time during the tenure. This is possible for personal use of the property or use by a family member to the second degree, but can also be done without mentioning any motive at all (even though this scenario requires the landlord to pay financial compensation).[202]

Certain changes to private rental law would be able to add nuance to the idea that certain autonomy and freedom traits are exclusive to home ownership. Still, it would not alter a person's preference to own his/her own home. It would be foolish to neglect the advantages that do remain connected to home ownership. But we have also mentioned earlier how there appears to be a link between more positive connotations of rented housing and the legal protection of tenants.[203] Besides the fact that renting would *de iure* become more of a full-fledged alternative for those who are not in a position to become owners,[204] greater tenancy protection might also change the perception of renting, which is also important in terms of our concept of social dignity. The only risk is that a stronger legal protection of tenants, with or without a form of rent control, could lead to a greater reluctance by owners to rent out their property. This in turn could lead to more short-term contracts or a decline in private rental housing. But while it is true that the benefits would indeed be primarily found on the side of the tenants, landlords could experience some indirect positive effects as well, from fewer switchover maintenance and search costs to increased popularity of the sector.[205]

II. CONSEQUENCES FOR THE RENTAL MARKET A second reason why we believe increased attention to the rental market is justified on the basis of our conception of dignity that also entails autonomy and freedom is that some of the discussed advantages of home ownership linked to these features are pretty far-reaching for what we perceive as indispensable for social dignity. We should not be hypocritical in denying the remaining benefits of home ownership. It would be ideal if everyone were able to acquire property without running any severe financial risks, but that is simply not realistic. What is necessary to

201 K. SCANLON, "Private renting in other countries", in K. SCANLON and B. KOCHAN (eds.), *Towards a sustainable private rented sector. The lessons from other countries*, London, LSE, 2011, (15) 31–37; HULSE (n 192) 647–648 and 650.

202 M. DAMBRE, "Woninghuur in Vlaamse handen: nieuwe kansen voor het grondrecht op behoorlijke huisvesting?", in B. HUBEAU and T. VANDROMME (eds.), *Vijftien jaar Vlaamse Wooncode. Sisyphus (on)gelukkig?*, Brugge, Die Keure, 2013, (273) 274–275.

203 See footnotes 189 and 191.

204 GEURTS (n 151) 85; P. DE DECKER, "Op weg naar een duurzaam woonbeleid? Hoe tegenwoordig blijft het verleden?" *Welzijnsgids* 2002, no. 44, (23) 36; CLAESSENS (n 157) 27.

205 HAFFNER (n 190) 219, 222 and 229–230.

experience a sense of self-fulfillment and the ability to develop, however, is in our opinion not an exclusive Hegelian feature of owner-occupancy.[206] It can be established for tenants as well, even though these housing elements are currently less attained on the private rental market.[207] From a fundamental rights perspective, a more preferential treatment of private tenants would therefore be appropriate. Freedom in the context of social dignity does therefore not encourage the government to promote home ownership in particular – at the very least not to the extent to which the Flemish government has done so over the years.

In Flanders, this distorted balance has especially manifested itself in the context of housing affordability and fiscal benefits. It has been proven that the higher-income deciles in particular have profited from the primary source of public spending, the so-called housing bonus.[208] That is not very surprising in and of itself. Measures that support home ownership are to some extent inherently asocial because a household will always have to dispose of a sizable income to consider buying property in the first place.[209] In the same vein, it has been said that Flanders has financially promoted home ownership for many households that did not need such a boost to acquire property in the first place.[210] While it has been established that the housing bonus has had a slight positive effect on the poverty risk (number of households with a disposable income below the poverty line, which is 60% of the median equivalized disposable income) and poverty gap (average shortfall of the population from the poverty line),[211] it has also – almost evidently – increased income inequality.[212] This can only be seen as an undesirable effect both in light

206 P. MARCUSE, "The ideologies of ownership and property rights" in R. PLUNZ (ed.), *Housing form and public policy in the United States*, New York, Praeger, 1980, 41; HOHMANN (n 184) 164.

207 S. WINTERS, "Belgian state reform as an opportunity to reorient Flemish housing policy", *International Journal of Housing Policy* 2013, vol. 13, no. 1, (90) 95.

208 K. HEYLEN, "Nieuwe inzichten in matteüseffect van het woonbeleid", *De Gids* 2013, (10) 14; K. HEYLEN and S. WINTERS, *De verdeling van de subsidies op vlak van wonen in Vlaanderen*, Heverlee, Steunpunt Ruimte en Wonen, 2012, 80 and 84.

209 DE DECKER (n 204) 38; Balchin even described measures that financially support home ownership as unjust, wasteful and inefficient, see: P. BALCHIN, *Housing policy: an introduction*, London, Routledge, 1995, 225.

210 GEURTS (n 151) 103; P. DE DECKER, "Not for the homeless? Housing policy in Flanders: between selectivity and legitimacy", *European Journal of Homelessness* 2011, vol. 5, no. 2, (129) 1134–1135.

211 G. VERBIST and J. VANHILLE, "Tussen huursubsidies en woonbonus: een verdelingsanalyse voor Vlaanderen", in D. DIERCKX, J. COENEN, A. VAN HAARLEM and P. RAEYMAECKERS, *Armoede en sociale uitsluiting. Jaarboek 2013*, Antwerpen, Acco 2013, (293) 299–300.

212 G. GOEYVAERTS, M. HAFFNER, K. HEYLEN, K. VAN DEN BROECK, F. VASTMANS and S. WINTERS, *Onderzoek naar de woonfiscaliteit in Vlaanderen. Deel 4 Bouwstenen en scenario's*, Leuven, CES-KU Leuven, 2014, 41.

of human rights law in general and the idea of empowerment and social dignity in particular.[213]

With housing prices rising, it has nonetheless become harder to buy property over recent years.[214] While still significantly lower than for private tenants, the proportion of owner-occupiers whose mortgage accounts for more than 30 percent of their income has increased by 10 percent between 2005 and 2013 (27.1%).[215] According to several studies, the housing bonus itself is partly to blame. Due to the low long-term price elasticity of Belgian housing stock, the mortgage tax relief has likely been passed on to higher housing prices, benefiting sellers rather than buyers and distributing welfare primarily on the property market.[216] For all these reasons it can only be welcomed that the Flemish government decided to reduce the tax benefits provided by the housing bonus following its transition to the regions.[217] That decision, however, was made out of budgetary concerns more than anything else.[218] The savings were not planned to be used for redirecting Flemish housing policy, but more specifically for creating a more fiscally neutral housing policy. The latter has nonetheless been recommended by, among others, academics, the OECD and the Special Rapporteur for housing.[219] In illustration of how this is not a (primary) concern, an additional adjustment to the housing bonus now enables borrowers to profit from the housing bonus not only with regard to their first but also their second, third . . . dwelling. This does obviously not abide by housing affordability concerns at all.

213 E.g. ECSR 7 December 2005, no. 27/2004, European Roma Rights Centre/Italy, par. 18: "the right to housing [. . .] contributes to the abolishment of socio-economic inequalities."

214 S. ZWART, *Maintaining an efficient and equitable housing market in Belgium*, OECD Economics Department Working Papers, no. 1208, Paris, OECD Publishing, 2015, 13.

215 HEYLEN (n 156) 28–29.

216 R. HELGERS and E. BUYST, *Woningprijzen: een regionaal woningprijsmodel*, Leuven, Steunpunt Wonen, 2014, 35; ANDREWS (n 169); GOEYVAERTS (n 212).

217 In 2014, the last year in which the previous conditions were applied, the cost of the housing bonus for Flanders was €1.7 billion. Since the conditions will not change retroactively, the housing bonus will remain a large expenditure for several years to come. For new loan contracts (1 January 2015), the housing bonus is cut by one-third. The deduction at the borrower's marginal tax rate was converted into a flat rate deduction of 40 percent; See S. WINTERS and K. VAN DEN BROECK, "Milestones in 25 years of housing finance in Belgium", in J. LUNDE and C. WHITEHEAD (eds.), *Milestones in European housing finance*, Oxford, Wiley-Blackwell, 2016, (75) 88–89.

218 M. HAFFNER and S. WINTERS, "Homeownership taxation in Flanders: moving towards 'optimal taxation'?", *International Journal of Housing Policy* 2015, (1) 14–15.

219 E.g. FLEMISH HOUSING COUNCIL, *Aanbodbeleid op de private huurmarkt. Bevraging van actoren en voorstellen van de Vlaamse Woonraad*, 17 December 2015, no. 2015/14, 36; ZWART (n 214) 20–21; UN General Assembly, *Report of the Special Rapporteur on adequate housing as a component of the right to an adequate standard of living*, 10 August 2012, A/67/150, 21–22; GOEYVAERTS (n 212).

It should be made clear that we do not oppose all forms of financial benefits for property owners. Yet they should be sufficiently selective as well as targeted at specific groups – for example, at older homeowners who cannot afford the necessary renovations to improve quality standards.[220] The more selective nature of social loans obviously render them as a better, more justifiable alternative, but their large and increasing cost has a negative effect on those households that cannot gather together enough capital to consider this option and are designated to the rental market. With a budget of €925 million available for social loans in 2016 and the enormous remaining cost of the housing bonus, housing affordability in Flanders is anything but tenure-neutral. In comparison, the so-called rental premium paid to people who have been waiting for social housing for more than four years costs the Flemish government a mere €14.5 million.[221]

It is against this background that we are supportive of a more general rental subsidy, distributed, for example, to everyone on the waiting list for social housing. According to financial estimations, this would still cost a government only a marginal amount in comparison with the public investments in property acquisition.[222] This is only one option. The subsidy could also be connected to housing need and distributed to households with a limited income and excessive housing costs.[223] While a decrease of fiscal benefits on property for the benefit of a more extensive rental subsidy is projected to make more losers than winners, the losses would be rather insignificant compared with the gains made by the beneficiaries.[224] It would also have a larger positive effect on the poverty risk and poverty gap than the housing bonus. On the downside, we should add that there is still some uncertainty on what the effect of such subsidies would be on rental prices.

In sum, our interpretation of social dignity, a concept founded in human rights law, neither justifies nor promotes a housing policy that is focused mainly on home ownership. We do not consider the right to housing as only a freedom right, but the elements that generate adequate housing are indeed indispensable to create that freedom. Considering that the attainment of these elements is a problem that more tenants than owner-occupiers struggle

220 WINTERS (n 207) 96.

221 Additionally and according to the Flemish Housing Council, the share of beneficiaries of rental subsidies in Flanders is significantly low (2.1%) in comparison with most other Western European countries, see: FLEMISH HOUSING COUNCIL, *Aanbodbeleid op de private huurmarkt. Bevraging van actoren en voorstellen van de Vlaamse Woonraad*, 17 December 2015, no. 2015/14, 17.

222 Report on behalf of the Commission on Housing, Poverty Policy and Equal Opportunities released by Mr. Anseeuw and Ms. Hostekint concerning the policy letter housing 2015–2016, *Parl.St.* Vl.Parl. 2015–16, no. 524–4, 28 and 39.

223 FLEMISH HOUSING COUNCIL, *Huursubsidie voor kandidaat-huurders sociale huisvestingsmaatschappijen*, 26 January 2010, no. 2010/02, 6.

224 VERBIST (n 211), 300–302.

with, a more tenure-neutral policy seems fitting. This might positively influence the perception of renting at the same time, creating a double impact on social dignity.

4) Stigmatization on the Social Rental Market

The previous sections predominantly focused on the private rental market, but there is no doubt that both nationally and internationally social housing is by far the most stigmatized by the public.[225] According to De Decker, policy makers and the media play an important role in reinforcing this image.[226] More so than other forms of tenure, the social housing market is related to social problems of different sorts, almost as a natural consequence of the high concentration of 'weaker' groups. A social tenant with rent arrears will more quickly be perceived as irresponsible, while an owner-occupier with mortgage debts is more probably seen as a victim of unfortunate circumstances. We have already alluded to the impact of a negative connotation on the relational aspect of dignity. A negative reputation can have its repercussions on self-image and magnify a person's marginality.[227] We therefore take a look at some options for social renting and the social rental sector inspired by our considerations for social dignity.

A. COMPOSITION OF THE (SOCIAL) RENTAL SECTOR

A drastic approach to counter residualization of the social rental sector could be to dismantle the social housing market constructed as a separate component of a dualist rental system. In defence of this option, we could refer back to Sweden, where, as we said earlier, the stigma with regard to renting has been much less tangible.[228] This could in part be due to what Bengtsson describes

225 A. VASSENDEN and T. LIE, "Telling others how you live – refining Goffman's stigma theory through an analysis of housing strugglers in a homeowner nation", *Symbolic Interaction* 2013, vol. 36, no. 1; FITZPATRICK (n 180) 600.

226 P. DE DECKER, "Rook zonder vuur? Fragmenten van de genese van een slechte reputatie en haar gevolgen voor de sociale huursector", in J. VRANKEN, K. DE BOYSER and D. DIERCKX (eds.), *Armoede en Uitsluiting. Jaarboek 2004*, Leuven, Acco, 2004, 207–225.

227 Ibid., 221–223.

228 The Netherlands and Germany, the two other countries we have mentioned as being not predominantly stigmatizing towards renting also have an integrated rental market. Due to allocation systems and rent regulation, however, the gap between both rental markets is larger than in Sweden. Based on: M. HAFFNER, J. HOEKSTRA, M. OXLEY and H. VAN DER HEIJDEN, "Universalistic, particularistic and middle way approaches to comparing the private rental sector", *International Journal of Housing Policy* 2010, vol. 10, no. 4, (357) 372–374; J. KEMENY, "Corporatism and housing regimes", *Housing, Theory and Society* 2006, vol. 23, no. 1, 1–18.

as a universal housing system open to everyone.[229] This does not mean that selective measures such as housing allowances to support certain households do not exist (all welfare systems are to an extent selective), but what makes it universal is the fact that the Swedish housing market is not divided into an open and a protected sector.[230] There is only one integrated rental market with non-profit municipally owned housing companies in it.[231] Due to strong tenancy and rent control regulations, not only is there equality in terms of access to housing, but the differences in housing quality and rent levels are also smaller.[232] This housing policy (or philosophy) is under serious pressure. The special position of the municipal rental housing companies has been largely abolished, not in the least due to the incompatibility with European rules on state support.[233] This is only complicated by the fact that Swedish rent regulation links private sector rents to those charged by the social sector, and unsubsidised commercial suppliers therefore have to charge sub-market rents.[234] More privatisation has become the obligatory new mantra. According to Holmqvist and Turner, the Swedish model of a non-profit sector open to all will probably come to an end, making it harder to prevent housing segregation in a structural manner.[235]

Against the specific background of UK housing policy, King also proposes the establishment of only one rental market with housing benefits for those in need of it.[236] In contrast, his plea relies on privatisation from the get-go. He gives a lot of proverbial weight to the concept of choice, which a social tenant is considered unable to exercise but would be available to all tenants once the rental market is universalized. Based on the idea that the consequences of one's choices generate responsibility, the proposition is seen as a form of real empowerment. Before continuing, we should perhaps repeat that there is actually some limited amount of choice involved in the allocation of social housing in Flanders. Flemish applicants for social housing are able to give

229 B. BENGTSSON, "Housing as a social right: implications for welfare state theory", *Scandinavian Political Studies* 2001, vol. 24, no. 4, (255) 270.

230 Ibid., 262–264 and 267–269; J. KEMENY, *From public housing to the social market: rental policy strategies in comparative perspective*, London, Routledge, 1995, 49–58.

231 H. RUONAVAARA, "Home ownership and Nordic housing policies in 'retrenchment'", in R. RONALD and M. ELSINGA (eds.), *Beyond home ownership: housing, welfare and society*, London, Routledge, 2011, (91) 97–99; ANDERSSON (n 170) 151–170.

232 J. HOEKSTRA, "Two types of rental system? An exploratory empirical test of Kemeny's rental system typology", *Urban Studies* 2009, vol. 46, no. 1, (45) 53.

233 E. HOLMQVIST and L.M. TURNER, "Swedish welfare state and housing markets: under economic and political pressure", *Journal of Housing and the Built Environment* 2014, vol. 29, (237) 241; RUONAVAARA (n 231) 103–104.

234 M. OXLEY, M. ELSINGA, M. HAFFNER and H. VAN DER HEIJDEN, "Competition and social housing in Europe", *Economic Affairs* 2008, vol. 28, no. 2, (31) 31.

235 HOLMQVIST (n 233) 249 and 251.

236 P. KING, *Choice and the end of social housing*, London, The Institute of Economic Affairs, 2006, 103–127.

preferences in relation to a couple of categories. We do admit, though, that this choice is different from the choices on the property or the private rental market.

Yet the only potential we can see for an integrated market to work effectively in the context of social dignity and the right to housing is under the condition of strong rental legislation highly protective of tenants' interests (i.e. rent control[237]), as is (was?) the case in Sweden but is only scarcely highlighted in King's approach.[238] If this was not the case, the socio-economically disadvantaged tenant could very well be constrained in his real choices once again, being subjected to the forces of the free market. How much is choice ultimately worth in the context of empowerment if the attainment of the primary elements for human flourishing, the different aspects of adequate housing, becomes much more uncertain? In Flanders, those housing elements are right now definitely better protected by social housing, with dwellings of higher quality, fewer tenants with a disproportionate housing cost and more security of tenure than on the private rental market. Not only that, but a large majority of social tenants (81.2%) are still shown to be satisfied with their dwelling, even if this number has dropped almost 8 percent in comparison with 2005.[239]

A different way to counter or prevent possible negative perception to some extent and at the same time provide something of a middle ground between either a single or a dual rental system is by way of intermediary institutions between private landlords and social tenants. In Flanders this is the task of so-called social rental agencies. In contrast to the more traditional social housing companies, who buy, build, renovate and rent out their own housing stock, social rental agencies rent houses and apartments on the private rental market and put them at the disposal of tenants at social rates, in exchange for considerable guarantees for the owners (such as assured payment of the rent, fiscal advantages, maintenance costs). Such a system first of all limits concentration or what some may call segregation of socio-economically disadvantaged groups. Owners might not be in direct relation to the sub-tenants, but for them the latter will no longer be a separate group in (or at the boundaries of) society. On the contrary, the system will actually provide them certain benefits.

With regard to the more "traditional" type of social housing, it would be possible to expand income requirements to try to create more of a social mix

237 The Swedish rent control system has been said to keep the rent level permanently below the market level, see: H. LIND, "Rent regulation: a conceptual and comparative analysis", *European Journal of Housing Policy* 2001, vol. 1, no. 1, (41) 48–49; D. CZISCHKE, "Managing social rental housing in the EU: a comparative study", *European Journal of Housing Policy* 2009, vol. 9, no. 2, (121) 128.

238 KING (n 236) 110.

239 I. PANNECOUCKE and P. DE DECKER, *Grote Woononderzoek 2013. Deel 7. Woontevredenheid en woongeschiedenis*, Leuven, Steunpunt Wonen, 2015, 10–11.

(on this occasion more particularly a socio-economic mix) and again affect the predominantly negative status of social tenants. That, of course, assumes that higher-income households will not be hindered by the negative image of social housing. Additionally, the higher-income groups are sometimes portrayed as being able to perform an exemplary role for others, thereby increasing the liveability of neighbourhoods.[240] There is, however, a lot of uncertainty about whether this is actually the case.[241] Moreover, there is the problem of the limited social housing stock, to which we will return in Chapter 3. All in all, it might be more effective to create such a social mix more organically, through smaller social housing building initiatives rather than through changing income requirements.[242]

B. PARTICIPATION IN SOCIAL HOUSING

When people feel excluded, their self-development potential can be harmed.[243] In social housing, these feelings have a bigger breeding ground. In comparison to owner-occupiers and even private tenants, social tenants are less autonomous in the sense that they are more strongly dependent upon legislation and the social housing company. For reasons of empowerment it is therefore of increased importance that social tenants are given the opportunity to participate to some extent on issues such as the housing aspects themselves, the neighbourhood or the functioning of the social housing company.[244] This idea is clearly rooted in current Flemish legislation. The Housing Code proclaims that the government can take measures aimed at the participation of involved resident groups.[245] In several decisions the Flemish government has indeed included the involvement of tenants in the assignments of both the social

240 DE DECKER (n 226) 219 and 224.

241 N. SCHUERMANS, B. MEEUS and P. DE DECKER, "Geographies of whiteness and wealth: white, middle class discourses on segregation and social mix in Flanders, Belgium", *Journal of Urban Affairs* 2014, vol. 37, no. 4, (478) 478–479 and 491; W. BERVOETS and M. LOOPMANS, *Diversiteit en discriminatie in de sociale huisvesting: een kritische benadering van "sociale mix"*, Brussel, STeR, 2010, 21–24; K. HEYLEN, K. TRATSAERT and S. WINTERS, *Leefbaarheid en de rol van toewijzing in de Vlaamse sociale huisvesting*, Brussel, Departement RWO-Woonbeleid, 2007, 15 and 17.

242 BERVOETS (n 241) 45.

243 BUITENWEG (n 27) 129.

244 M. SANTENS, "Participatie tussen emancipatie en culturele innovatie", in L. BOUDRY et al. (eds.), *Inzet, opzet, voorzet: stadsprojecten in Vlaanderen*, Brussel, Ministerie van de Vlaamse Gemeenschap, 2006, (164) 174–176; B. VANDEKERCKHOVE and G. VAN BORTEL, "Hoe ver reikt de participatieladder voor huurders in de sociale huisvesting?", in X. (ed.), *Het onroerend goed in de praktijk*, Mechelen, Kluwer, *Het onroerend goed in de* 2012, XIV.F, (173) 183.

245 Article 4, §3, 5° Flemish Housing Code.

housing companies and the social rental agencies.[246] An important actor in putting participation in the social housing system more on the map has been VIVAS, the Flemish network of and for social tenants and a partnership of local resident groups.

While the idea of participation is catching on and social housing companies are also slowly becoming more supportive of the idea, there is still a long way to go. Despite the regulation in place, there is no clear view on how participation should be operationalized. It can be organized in many different ways and can range from being properly informed over the opportunity to react to and discuss issues and proposals of and with social housing companies, to an advisory and potentially even a decision-making role.[247] On the one hand this open-endedness enables tailor-made initiatives that take into account local sensitivities, but on the other hand further concretization in law could be fruitful to establish more participation. Currently, participation is still often perceived as a favor rather than a right. The current legislation imposes an obligation to initiate deliberation with tenants in the form of tenant meetings, but this still mainly entails gathering information from and communicating to tenants, and even that component of participation is said to be insufficiently developed by legislation. It is not too surprising, then, that only some social housing companies have given social tenants a real advisory role – for example, by establishing a tenant advice council. On this basis, legal modification is to be recommended.[248]

This is not at all to say that the Flemish government has not done anything to ascertain that social housing companies take into account their existing participation-related assignments. The 2010 decision on the recognition of social housing companies has established an independent visitation commission that subjects all social housing companies to a performance assessment every four years. Interestingly, the performance field entitled "social policy" also includes tenant involvement and is thus part of the performance assessment.[249] If this is found to be insufficient by the final visitation report,

246 Article 29bis Framework Decision Social Rent; Ministerial Decision 21 December 2007 concerning the execution of a couple of provisions of the Decision by the Flemish Government of 12 October 2007 on the regulation of the social housing system in execution of title VII of the Flemish Housing Code, *BS* 18 January 2008; Decision Flemish Government 6 February 2004 determining the conditions for recognition and financing of social rental agencies, *BS* 16 March 2004.

247 E. DEBUSSCHERE, B. VANDEKERCKHOVE and G. VAN BORTEL, *Praktisch handboek: huurdersparticipatie in de sociale huisvesting*, Heverlee, Steunpunt Ruimte en Wonen, 2009, 23–27.

248 Ibid., 28–29, 42 and 45.

249 Art. 14 Decision Flemish Government 22 October 2010 concerning the determination of complementary requirements and the procedure for the recognition as social housing company and concerning the determination of the procedure for the assessment of the performances by social housing companies, *BS* 29 December 2010.

the Minister is authorized to compel the social housing company to develop and execute an improvement plan.

C. EMPOWERMENT THROUGH OBLIGATIONS

Finally, we argue that concerns for social dignity and empowerment can also be expressed in restrictions to housing rights. Some tenant obligations within this context might not only be justified because they impose a proportionate burden of responsibility upon that party, but because they actually promote personal development themselves. Probably the most prominent example in the Flemish context is the requirement for prospective tenants of social housing to illustrate willingness to learn the Dutch language. Upon assessing the measure, the Constitutional Court described its objectives as improving communication with the social landlord and other tenants, increasing self-reliance and contributing to the recognition of these persons as valuable citizens by society.[250] The court bestowed specific importance on the fact that it concerns elementary knowledge, that the language lessons are free and that the termination of the contract is only possible if non-compliance would lead to nuisance or liveability problems for other tenants.[251]

Striking a right balance between, on the one hand, trying to create more autonomy and, on the other, not to (excessively) conditionalize the core housing elements that establish social dignity in the first place can be a very delicate matter. A good illustration is how this language requirement has recently been transformed into an obligation of result. While the Constitutional Court had already explicitly prohibited this back in 2007, that judgment was based on the fact that the obligation was concretized as a condition to gain access to social housing and that a failure to comply with it could also lead to an eviction.[252] In contrast, the current modification does not do so. When a person does not pass a language test, he can only be fined.

We acknowledge that obligations and restrictions are sometimes able to contribute to personal development, but a certain wariness is in its place, and not only with regard to the effect on the realization of the core elements of the right to housing. The politically popular term of self-reliance regularly surfaces in this context.[253] This term can, of course, be applied in a positive sense, embodying the need for empowerment. But its frequent use in relation only to the socio-economically weaker groups or – translated to housing – tenants

250 Constitutional Court 10 July 2008, no. 101/2008, B.32.1–B.32.3; This reasoning has been confirmed more recently: Constitutional Court 5 March 2015, no. 24/2015, note T. VANDROMME, "Ook partner van sociale huurder moet aan voorwaarden sociale huur voldoen", *Juristenkrant* 2015, no. 317, 4.

251 Constitutional Court 10 July 2008, no. 101/2008, B.34.1–B.34.4.

252 Constitutional Court 12 July 2007, no. 104/2007, B.9.2.

253 DE BRABANDER (n 139) 86–91, 96–98 and 171–172.

on the social housing market and what they should do "in return" also creates or feeds the impression that social housing must be equated with people who are not self-reliant and should be more independent.[254] To some extent, this devalues social housing as a fully valid alternative, as a real home, even though a lot of these social tenants are not very well positioned to grow out of this situation and are actually doing pretty well to "save themselves"[255] with what little they sometimes have.

3. Conclusion

Human dignity is complex and can be interpreted in many ways. It can be a value or a right, objective or subjective and as broad or as limited as the particular situation demands. That is therefore why we are torn about its added value in (fundamental) rights jurisprudence. Considering its persistent reoccurrence in human and socio-economic rights law, as is the case in article 23 of the Belgian Constitution, we have developed our own interpretation of what we have called a right to social dignity. This term marks the difference with the interpretation of dignity as an inherent worth justifying the existence of other human rights. Social dignity contains aspects of wellbeing and autonomy/freedom, often recurring features of dignity in philosophy and social justice theories. We have argued that autonomy both precedes and follows from wellbeing. It is the freedom a person develops from living adequately, but also the freedom from circumstances that may hinder a different person from acquiring adequate housing in the first place. Add to that the unmistakable subjective/perceptional component of autonomy and not only does social dignity clearly distinguish itself from the traditional elements of adequate housing, but it also provides for a new perspective to be taken into account when discussing housing legislation and policies. As such, we have stressed the importance of legal aid as well as participation in social housing (as a sector susceptible to marginalization), but denounced the idea that a more tenure-neutral policy is inconsistent with a serious concern for the autonomy component of social dignity.

Bibliography

ALBISA, C. and SCHULTZ, J., "The United States", in LANGFORD, M. (ed.), *Social rights jurisprudence. Emerging trends in international and comparative law*, Cambridge, Cambridge University Press, 2009, 232.

ALEXANDER, J.M., "Capabilities, human rights and moral pluralism", *IJHR* 2004, vol. 8, no. 3, 451–469.

254 R. SENNETT, *Respect in a World of Inequality*, New York, Norton, 2003, 101.

255 Translation of the Dutch word "zelfredzaamheid" to which we refer with the term "self-reliance".

ANDERSSON, E., NAUMANEN, P., RUONAVAARA, H. and TURNER, B., "Housing, socio-economic security and risks. A qualitative comparison of household attitudes in Finland and Sweden", *European Journal of Housing Policy 2007*, vol. 7, no. 2, 151–172.

ANDREASSEN, B.A., SMITH, A.G. and STOKKE, H., "Compliance with economic and social human rights: realistic evaluations and monitoring in the light of immediate obligations", in EIDE, A. and HAGTVET, B. (eds.), *Human Rights in Perspective: a Global Assessment*, Oxford, Oxford University Press, 1992, 252–267.

ANDREWS, D., CALDERA SÁNCHEZ, A. and JOHANSSON, A. *Housing markets and structural policies in OECD countries*, OECD Economics Department Working Papers no. 836, 84 pages.

ARIELI, Y., "On the Necessary and Sufficient Conditions for the Emergence of the Doctrine of the Dignity of Man and His Rights", in KRETZMER, D. and KLEIN, E. (eds.), *The Concept of Human Dignity in Human Rights Discourse*, The Hague, Kluwer, 2002, 1–11.

BALCHIN, P., *Housing policy: an introduction*, London, Routledge, 1995, 492 pages.

BALL, M., *The UK private rented sector as a source of affordable accommodation*, York, Joseph Rowntree Foundation, 2010, 36 pages.

BARBOSA DA SILVA, A., "Autonomy, dignity and integrity in health care ethics – a moral philosophical perspective", in SINDING AASEN, H., HALVORSEN, R. and BARBOSA DA SILVA, A. (eds.), *Human rights, dignity and autonomy in health care and social services: Nordic perspectives*, Antwerp, Intersentia, 2009, 13–52.

BARROS, D.B., "Home as a legal concept", *Santa Clara Law Review* 2006, vol. 46, 255–306.

BARROSO, L.R., "Here, there and everywhere: human dignity in contemporary law and in the transnational discourse", *Boston College International & Comparative Law Review* 2012, vol. 35, 331–394.

BELL, D.H., "Providing security of tenure for residential tenants: good faith as a limitation on the landlord's right to terminate", *Ga. L. Rev.* 1985, vol. 19, (483) 530.

BENGTSSON, B., "Housing as a social right: implications for welfare state theory", *Scandinavian Political Studies* 2001, vol. 24, no. 4, 255–275.

BERLIN, I., *Four essays on liberty*, Oxford, Oxford University Press, 1964, 213 pages.

BERVOETS, W. and LOOPMANS, M., *Diversiteit en discriminatie in de sociale huisvesting: een kritische benadering van 'sociale mix'*, Brussel, STeR, 2010, 96 pages.

BEYLEVELD, D. and BROWNSWORD, R., "Human dignity, human rights and human genetics", *Modern Law Review* 1998, 661–680.

BEYNS, K., BRUYNDONCKX, S., SCHILDERMANS, E., VAN BEURDEN, F., VAN BRAECKEL, F. and VAN DEUN, E., *Menswaardig leven. Een onderzoek binnen de Kempense OCMW's*, Geel, Katholieke Hogeschool Kempen, 2008.

BILCHITZ, D., *Poverty and Fundamental Rights: The Justification and Enforcement of Socio-Economic Rights*, Oxford, Oxford University Press, 2007, 300 pages.

BOBBIO, N., *The age of rights*, Cambridge, Polity Press, 1995, 192 pages.

BOURASSA, S.C. and GRIGSBY, W.G., "Income tax concessions for owner-occupied housing", *Housing Policy Debate* 2000, vol. 11, no. 3, 521–546.

BREMS, E. and VRIELINK, J., *Menselijke waardigheid in de Nederlandse Grondwet? Voorstudie ten behoeve van de Staatscommissie Grondwet (2009)*, Alphen aan den Rijn, Kluwer, 2010, 72 pages.

BRIGHT, S.J. and HOPKINS, N., "Home, meaning and identity: learning from the English model of shared ownership housing", *Theory and Society* 2011, vol. 28, no. 4, 377–397.

BRODSKY, G., "Gosselin v. Quebec (Attorney General): Autonomy with a Vengeance", *Canadian Journal of Women and the Law* 2004, vol. 15, 194–213.

BRUGGER, W., "Human rights norms in ethical perspective", *German Yearbook of International Law* 1982, vol. 25, 113–137.

BUITENWEG, R., *Recht op een menswaardig bestaan. Een humanistieke reflectie op sociaal-economische mensenrechten*, Utrecht, de Graaff, 2001, 384 pages

BURGORGUE-LARSEN, L. (ed.), *La dignité saisie par les juges en Europe*, Brussel, Bruylant, 2010, 262 pages.

BUSCH-GEERTSEMA, V., "Housing First Europe – results of a European social experimentation project", *European Journal of Homelessness* 2014, vol. 8, no. 1, 13–28.

CAROZZA, P., "Human dignity and judicial interpretation of human rights: a reply", *EJIL* 2008, vol. 19, no. 5, 931–944.

CASIER, I., BAUWENS, A., DISTELMANS, W. and SNACKEN, S., "Over het concept menselijke waardigheid", in RAES, K., DEBEUCKELAERE, W., GUTWIRTH, S. and LAMBRECHTS, M. (eds.), *Ontmoetingen met Koen Raes*, Brugge, die Keure, 2012, 85–95.

CASSIERS, W., "Les droits sociaux en quête d'effectivité", in VAN DER PLANCKE, V. (ed.), *Les droits sociaux fondamentaux dans la lutte contre la pauvreté*, Brussel, Die Keure, 2012, 288–310.

CASTLES, F.G., "The really big trade-off: home ownership and the welfare state in the new world and the old", *Acta Politica* 1998, vol. 33, no. 1, 5–19.

CHANDHOKE, N., "Thinking through social and economic rights", in BELL, D.A. and COICAUD, J.-M. (eds.), *Ethics in action: the ethical challenges of international human rights nongovernmental organizations*, Cambridge, Cambridge University Press, 2007, 181–197.

CLAASSEN, R. and DÜWELL, M., "The foundations of capability theory: comparing Nussbaum and Gewirth", *Ethic Theory and Moral Practice* 2013, vol. 16, no. 3, 493–510.

CLAESSENS, B., VLERICK, E. and DE DECKER, P., *Op zoek naar de betekenis van wonen. Een verkennend literatuuronderzoek*, Heverlee, Steunpunt Ruimte en Wonen, 2009, 100 pages.

CLAPHAM, D., *The meaning of housing. A pathways approach*, Cambridge, Policy Press, 2005, 286 pages.

CLITEUR, P.B. and VAN WISSEN, R.G.T., "De menselijke waardigheid als grondslag voor mensenrechten: een beschouwing over het werk van Kant en Schopenhauer in relatie tot de filosofische reflective over mensenrechten", in VAN DER LIST, G.A. (ed.), *De Rechten van de Mens*, Den Haag, Teldersstichting, 1998, 25–42.

CONLEY, D. and GIFFORD, B., "Home ownership, social insurance, and the welfare state", *Sociological Forum* 2006, vol. 21, no. 1, 55–82.

CUERPO, C., KALANTARYAN, S. and PONTUCH, P., *Rental market regulation in the European Union*, Brussels, European Commission, 2014, 52 pages.

CUYPERS, D. and DE VOS, B., "De menselijke waardigheid en de arbeidsgerechten", *TSR* 1999, 495–560.

CZISCHKE, D., "Managing social rental housing in the EU: a comparative study", *European Journal of Housing Policy* 2009, vol. 9, no. 2, 121–151.

DAMBRE, M. "Woninghuur in Vlaamse handen: nieuwe kansen voor het grondrecht op behoorlijke huisvesting?", in HUBEAU, B. and VANDROMME, T. (eds.), *Vijftien jaar Vlaamse Wooncode. Sisyphus (on)gelukkig?*, Brugge, Die Keure, 2013, 273–282.

DAMBRE, M., *De huurprijs. Analyse van de financiële verbintenissen van de huurder en onderzoek naar de mogelijkheid tot objectivering van de woninghuurprijzen*, Brugge, Die Keure, 2009, 598 pages.

DAVIS, J. "Doing justice to dignity in the criminal law", in MALPAS, J. and LICKISS, N. (eds.), *Perspectives on human dignity: a conversation*, Dordrecht, Springer, 2007, 169–182.

DE BEER, P., VAN DER MEER, J. and PEKELHARING, P., *Gelijk. De noodzakelijke terugkeer van een klassiek ideaal*, Amsterdam, Van Gennep/De Balie, 2006, 430 pages.

DE BRABANDER, R., *Wie wil er nou niet zelfredzaam zijn? De mythe van zelfredzaamheid*, Antwerpen, Garant, 2014, 192 pages.

DEBUSSCHERE, E., VANDEKERCKHOVE, B. and VAN BORTEL, G., *Praktisch handboek: huurdersparticipatie in de sociale huisvesting*, Heverlee, Steunpunt Ruimte en Wonen, 2009, 57 pages.

DE DECKER, P., *Eigen woning: geldmachine of pensioensparen?*, Antwerpen, Garant, 2013, 208 pages.

DE DECKER, P., "Not for the homeless? Housing policy in Flanders: between selectivity and legitimacy", *European Journal of Homelessness* 2011, vol. 5, no. 2, 129–143.

DE DECKER, P. and DEWILDE, C., "Home ownership and asset-based welfare: the case of Belgium", *Journal of Housing and the Built Environment* 2010, vol. 25, 243–262.

DE DECKER, P., "Rook zonder vuur? Fragmenten van de genese van een slechte reputatie en haar gevolgen voor de sociale huursector", in VRANKEN, J., DE BOYSER, K. and DIERCKX, D. (eds.), *Armoede en Uitsluiting. Jaarboek 2004*, Leuven, Acco, 2004, 207–225.

DE DECKER, P. and GEURTS, V., "Belgium" in DOLING, J. and FORD, J. (eds.), *Globalisation and home ownership. Experiences in eight member states of the European Union*, Delft, Housing and Urban Policy Studies, DUP Science, 2003, 21–52.

DE DECKER, P., "Op weg naar een duurzaam woonbeleid? Hoe tegenwoordig blijft het verleden?" *Welzijnsgids* 2002, no. 44, 23–59.

DEMAERSCHALK, E., "Dakloosheid kost handenvol geld. Housing First als goedkoper alternatief", *Alert* 2014, vol. 40, no. 5, 16–24.

DEN HARTOGH, G., "Is human dignity the ground of human rights?" in DÜWELL, M., BRAARVIG, J., BRONSWORD, R. and MIETH, D. (eds.), *The Cambridge handbook of human dignity. Interdisciplinary perspectives*, Cambridge, Cambridge University Press, 2014, (200) 200.

DOLING, J. and ELSINGA, M., *Demographic change and housing wealth: homeowners, pensions and asset-based welfare in Europe*, Dordrecht, Springer, 2013, 149 pages.

DOLING, J. and RONALD, R., "Home ownership and asset-based welfare", *Journal of Housing and the Built Environment* 2010, vol. 25, no. 2, 165–173.

DOLING, J. and STAFFORD, B., *Home ownership: the diversity of experience*, Aldershot, Gower, 1989.

DONNELLY, J., "Human rights and human dignity: an analytic critique of non-western conceptions of human rights", *The American Political Science Review* 1982, vol. 76, no. 2, 303–316.

DUPUIS, A. and THORNS, D.C., "Home, home ownership and the search for ontological security", *The Sociological Review* 1998, vol. 46, no. 1, 24–47.

DÜWELL, M., "Human dignity: concepts, discussions, philosophical perspectives", in DÜWELL, M. et al. (eds.), *The Cambridge handbook of human dignity. Interdisciplinary perspectives*, Cambridge, Cambridge University Press, 2014, (23) 42–43.

DÜWELL, M., BRAARVIG, J., BRONSWORD, R. and MIETH, D. (eds.), *The Cambridge handbook of human dignity. Interdisciplinary perspectives*, Cambridge, Cambridge University Press, 2014, 634 pages.

EIDE, A., "Economic, social and cultural rights as human rights", in EIDE, A., KRAUSE, C. and ROSAS, A. (eds.), *Economic, social and cultural rights*, Dordrecht, Martinus Nijhoff Publishers, 2001, (9) 15.

ELSINGA, M., DE DECKER, P., TELLER, N. and TOUSSAINT, J. (eds.), *Home ownership beyond asset and security: Perceptions of housing related security and insecurity in eight European countries*, Amsterdam, IOS Press, 2007, 335 pages.

ELSINGA, M., HAFFNER, M., HOEKSTRA, J., VANDENBROUCKE, P., BUYST, E. and WINTERS, S., *Beleid voor de private huur: een vergelijking van zes landen*, Brussel, Departement RWO-Woonbeleid, 2007, 157 pages.

ENDERS, C., "A right to have rights – The German Constitutional concept of human dignity", *NUJS Law Review* 2010, 253–264.

EVANGELISTA, G.F., "Poverty, homelessness and freedom: an approach to the capabilities theory", *European Journal of Homelessness* 2010, vol. 4, 189–202.

FABRE, C., *Social rights under the Constitution: government and the decent life*, Oxford, Oxford University Press, 2000, 202 pages.

FELDMAN, D., "Human Dignity as a Legal Value: part 1", *Pub. L.* 1999, 682–702.

FIERENS, J., "Existe-t-il un principe général du droit du respect de la dignité humaine", note under Court of Cassation 18 November 2013, *RCJB* 2015, no. 4, 358–382.

FIERENS, J., "La dignité humaine comme concept juridique", *JT* 2002, no. 22, 577–582.

FIERENS, J., "La dignité humaine, limite à l'application de l'exception d'inexécution", *TBBR* 2000, 594–601.

FIGARI, F., PAULUS, A., SUTHERLAND, H., TSAKLOGLOU, P., VERBIST, G. and ZANTOMIO, F., "Removing home ownership bias in taxation: the distributional effects of including net imputed rent in taxable income", *Fiscal Studies* 2016, vol. 37.

FITZPATRICK, S., BENGTSSON, B. and WATTS, B., "Rights to housing: reviewing the terrain and exploring a way forward", *Housing, Theory and Society* 2014, vol. 31, no. 4, 447–463.

FITZPATRICK, S. and PAWSON, H., "Ending security of tenure for social renters: transitioning to 'ambulance service' social housing", *Housing Studies* 2014, vol. 29, no. 5, 597–615.

FORD, J., BURROWS, R. and NETTLETON, S., *Home-ownership in a risk society*, Bristol, The Policy Press, 2001, 205 pages.

FOX, L., *Conceptualising home. Theories, laws and policies*, Oxford, Hart Publishing, 2007, 551 pages.

FREDMAN, S., "Providing Equality: Substantive Equality and the Positive Duty to Provide", *S. Afr. J. on Hum. Rts.* 2005, vol. 21, 163–190.

FREEMAN, S., *Rawls*, London, Routledge, 2007, 576 pages

GARRIDO GÓMEZ, M., "Rights Guarantees, Equality and Social Rights", in MOTMANS, J., CUYPERS, D., MEIER, P., MORTELMANS, D. and ZANONI, P. (eds.), *Equal is not Enough: Challenging Differences and Inequalities in Contemporary Societies*, 2012, 17–23.

GEURTS, V. and GOOSSENS, L., "Home ownership and social inequality in Belgium", in KURZ, K. and BLOSFELD, H.P. (eds.), *Home ownership and social inequality in comparative perspective*, Stanford, Stanford University Press, 2004, 79–111.

GEWIRTH, A., *Self-fulfillment*, Princeton, Princeton University Press, 1998, 248 pages.

GEWIRTH, A., *The community of rights*, Chicago, University of Chicago Press, 1996, 396 pages.

GEWIRTH, A., "Human Dignity as the Basis of Rights", in MEYER, M. and PARENT, W. (eds.), *The Constitution of Rights: Human Dignity*, Ithaca, Cornell University Press, 1992, 10–28.

GEWIRTH, A., *Reason and morality*, Chicago, University of Chicago Press, 1978, 401 pages.

GIBENS, S. and HUBEAU, B., "Legal aid and housing issues", in HUBEAU, B. and TERLOUW, A. (eds.), *Legal aid in the Low Countries*, Antwerpen, Intersentia, 2014, 141–159.

GLENSY, R.D., "The right to dignity", *Columbia Human Rights Law Review* 2011, 65–142.

GLYN, A. and MILIBAND, D. (eds.), *Paying for inequality. The economic cost of social injustice*, London, Rivers Oram, 1994, 248 pages.

GOEYVAERTS, G., HAFFNER, M., HEYLEN, K., VAN DEN BROECK, K., VASTMANS, F. and WINTERS, S., *Onderzoek naar de woonfiscaliteit in Vlaanderen. Deel 4 Bouwstenen en scenario's*, Leuven, CES-KU Leuven, 2014, 117 pages.

GOORDEN, J., MERTENS, J. et al., "De sociale rechtshulp in kaart gebracht", in HUBEAU, B., GOORDEN, J. and MERTENS, J. (eds.), *Recht op recht. Sociale rechtshulp en sociaaljuridische dienstverlening in Vlaanderen*, Mechelen, Kluwer, 2011, 47–135.

GRANT, E., "Dignity and equality", *HRLR* 2007, vol. 7, no. 2, 299–329.

GRIFFIN, J. J., "Welfare rights", *The Journal of Ethics* 2000, vols. 1–2, 27–43.

GURNEY, C., "Pride and prejudice: discourses of normalization in public and private accounts of home ownership", *Housing Studies* 1999, vol. 14, 163–183.

GURNEY, C., "Lowering the drawbridge: a case study of analogy and metaphor in the social construction of home ownership", *Urban Studies* 1999, vol. 36, 1706–1722.

GURNEY, C., *The meaning of home in the decade of owner occupation: towards an experiential perspective*, Bristol, School of Advanced Urban Studies, 1990, 54 pages.

HAARSCHER, G., "Le droit de mener une vie conforme à la dignité humaine", in ERGEC, R. (ed.), *Les droits économiques, sociaux et culturels dans la Constitution: actes du colloque tenu les 21 et 22 décembre 1994*, Brussel, Bruylant, 1995, 133–144.

HAFFNER, M. and WINTERS, S., "Homeownership taxation in Flanders: moving towards 'optimal taxation'?", *International Journal of Housing Policy* 2015, 1–18.

HAFFNER, M., HOEKSTRA, J., OXLEY, M. and VAN DER HEIJDEN, H., "Universalistic, particularistic and middle way approaches to comparing the private rental sector", *International Journal of Housing Policy* 2010, vol. 10, no. 4, 357–377.

HAFFNER, M., ELSINGA, M. and HOEKSTRA, J., “Rent regulation: the balance between private landlords and tenants in six European countries”, *European Journal of Housing Policy* 2008, vol. 8, no. 2, 217–233.

HAFFNER, M., *Appel voor de dorst. Vermogen van ouderen op de woningmarkt*, Utrecht, NETHUR, 2005, 73 pages.

HELGERS, R. and BUYST, E., *Woningprijzen: een regionaal woningprijsmodel*, Leuven, Steunpunt Wonen, 2014, 51 pages.

HENNETTE-VAUCHEZ, S., “When ambivalent principles prevail. Leads for explaining Western legal orders' infatuation with the human dignity principle”, *EUI Working Papers Law* 2007, 18 pages.

HEYLEN, K., *Grote woononderzoek 2013. Deel 2. Deelmarkten, woonkosten en betaalbaarheid*, Leuven, Steunpunt Wonen, 2015, 60 pages.

HEYLEN, K., “Nieuwe inzichten in matteüseffect van het woonbeleid”, *De Gids* 2013, no. 2, 10–16.

HEYLEN, K. and WINTERS, S., *De verdeling van subsidies op vlak van wonen in Vlaanderen*, Leuven, Steunpunt Ruimte en Wonen, 2012, 95 pages.

HEYLEN, K., TRATSAERT, K. and WINTERS, S., *Leefbaarheid en de rol van toewijzing in de Vlaamse sociale huisvesting*, Brussel, Departement RWO-Woonbeleid, 2007, 47 pages.

HOEKSTRA, J., “Two types of rental system? An exploratory empirical test of Kemeny's rental system typology”, *Urban Studies* 2009, vol. 46, no. 1, 45–62.

HOHMANN, J., *The right to housing. Law, concepts, possibilities*, Oxford, Hart Publishing, 2013, 75–91.

HOLDSWORTH, L., “Sole voices: experiences of non-homeowning sole mother renters”, *Journal of Family Studies* 2011, vol. 17, no. 1, 59–70.

HOLMQVIST, E. and TURNER, L.M., “Swedish welfare state and housing markets: under economic and political pressure”, *Journal of Housing and the Built Environment* 2014, vol. 29, 237–254.

HOUARD, N., “The French homelessness strategy: reforming temporary accommodation, and access to housing to deliver ‘Housing First’: continuum or clean break”, *European Journal of Homelessness* 2011, vol. 5, no. 2, 83–98.

HOWARD, R.E. and DONNELLY, J., “Human dignity, human rights and political regimes”, *The American Political Science Review* 1986, vol. 80, no. 3, 801–817.

HUGHES, G., “The concept of dignity in the Universal Declaration of Human Rights”, *Journal of Religious Ethics* 2011, 1–24.

HULSE, K. and MILLIGAN, V., “Secure occupancy: a new framework for analyzing security in rental housing”, *Housing Studies* 2014, vol. 29, no. 5, 638–656.

IGLESIAS, T., “Bedrock Truths and the Dignity of the Individual”, *Logos* 2001, vol. 4, 114–134.

JACOBSON, N., “Dignity and health: a review”, *Social Science & Medicine* 2007, vol. 62, 292–302.

KANT, I., *Groundwork for the Metaphysics of Morals*, as translated by WOOD, A.W., New Haven, Yale University Press, 2002, 224 pages.

KELMAN, H.C., “The conditions, criteria and dialectics of human dignity: a transnational perspective”, *International Studies Quarterly* 1977, vol. 21, no. 3, 529–552.

KEMENY, J., “Corporatism and housing regimes”, *Housing, Theory and Society* 2006, vol. 23, no. 1, 1–18.

KEMENY, J., *From public housing to the social market: rental policy strategies in comparative perspective*, London, Routledge, 1995, 49–58.

KEMENY, J., *The myth of home ownership: public versus private choices in housing tenure*, London, Routledge, 1981, 196 pages.

KENNA, P., "Housing rights: positive duties and enforceable rights at the European Court of Human Rights", *E.H.R.L.R.* 2008, no. 2, (193) 193–208.

KERSTEIN, S.J., "Kantian dignity: a critique", in DÜWELL, M., BRAARVIG, J., BRONSWORD, R. and MIETH, D. (eds.), *The Cambridge handbook of human dignity. Interdisciplinary perspectives*, Cambridge, Cambridge University Press, 2014, 220–228.

KIDDER, R.L., *Connecting law and society*, New Jersey, Prentice-Hall, 1983, 286 pages.

KING, P., *Choice and the end of social housing*, London, The Institute of Economic Affairs, 2006, 103–127.

KING, P., "Housing as a freedom right", *Housing Studies* 2003, vol. 18, no. 5, 661–672.

KYMLICKA, W., *Contemporary political philosophy: an introduction*, Oxford, Clarendon Press, 1990, 342 pages.

LANCKSWEERDT, E., "Het concept menselijke waardigheid als motor voor de verdere ontwikkeling van recht en rechtspraktijk", *TBP* 2013, vol. 9, 534–538.

LAWRENCE, R., "Deciphering home: an integrative historical perspective" in BENJAMIN, D. (ed.), *The home: words, interpretations, meanings and environments*, Aldershot, Ashgate, 1995, 53–68.

LECKIE, S., "Where it matters most: making international housing rights meaningful at the national level", in LECKIE, S. (ed.), *National perspectives on housing rights*, The Hague, Martinus Nijhoff Publishers, 2003, 3–41.

LEE, M.Y.K., "Universal Human Dignity: some reflections in the Asian Context", *Asian Journal of Comparative Law* 2008, vol. 3, no. 1, 1–33.

LEVINET, M., "Dignité contre dignité. L'épilogue de l'affaire du 'lancer de nains' devant le Comité des droits de l'homme des Nations Unies", *RTDH* 2003, 1017–1042.

LIEBENBERG, S., *Socio-economic rights: Adjudication under a transformative constitution*, Claremont, Juta, 2010, 541 pages.

LIEBENBERG, S., "The value of human dignity in interpreting socio-economic rights", in VAN DER WALT, A.J. (ed.), *Theories of social and economic justice*, Stellenbosch, Sun Press, 2005, (141) 149–152.

LIEBENBERG, S., "The value of human dignity in interpreting socio-economic rights", *S. Afr. J. on Hum. Rts.* 2005, vol. 21, 1–31.

LIND, H., "Rent regulation: a conceptual and comparative analysis", *European Journal of Housing Policy* 2001, vol. 1, no. 1, 41–57.

LUKES, S., *Power: a radical view*, Basingstoke, Palgrave Macmillan, 2005, 192 pages.

LUTZ, M.A., "Centering social economics on human dignity", *Review of Social Economy* 1995, vol. 53, no. 2, 171–194.

MACHAN, T.R. and RASMUSSEN, D.B. (eds.), *Liberty for the twenty-first century*, Lanham, Rowman & Littlefield Publishers, 1995, 386 pages.

MAES, G., *De afdwingbaarheid van sociale grondrechten*, Antwerpen, Intersentia, 2003, 523 pages.

MAHLMANN, M., "The Basic Law at 60 – Human Dignity and the Culture of Republicanism", *German Law Journal* 2010, vol. 11, no. 1, 9–32.

MALLETT, S., "Understanding home: a critical review of the literature", *The Sociological Review* 2004, vol. 52, no. 1, 62–89.

MARELLA, M.R., "A New Perspective on Human Dignity: European Contract Law, Social Dignity and the Retreat of the Welfare State", in GRUNDMANN, S. (ed.), *Constitutional Values and European Contract Law*, The Netherlands, Kluwer, 2008, 123–147.

MARCUSE, P., "The ideologies of ownership and property rights" in R. PLUNZ (ed.), *Housing form and public policy in the United States*, New York, Praeger, 1980.

MARSHALL, T.H., *Class, citizenship and social development*, Chicago, University of Chicago Press, 1977, 365 pages.

MARTENS, P., "Encore la dignité humaine: réflexions d'un juge sur la promotion par les juges d'une norme suspecte", in X. (ed.), *Les Droits de l'homme au seuil du troisième millénaire : mélanges en hommage à Pierre Lambert*, Brussel, Bruylant, 2000, 561–579.

MATTSON, D.J. and CLARK, S.G., "Human dignity in concept and practice", *Policy Sciences* 2011, vol. 44, 303–319.

McADAMS, R.H., "The economic costs of inequality", *John M. Olin Program in Law & Economics working paper no. 370*, 2007, 23–41.

McCARTHY, G., VAN ZANDT, S. and ROHE, W., *The economic benefits and costs of homeownership. A critical assessment of the research*, Arlington, Research Institute for Housing America, 2001, 62 pages.

McCRUDDEN, C., "Human dignity and judicial interpretation of human rights", *EJIL* 2008, vol. 19, no. 4, 655–724.

McNAUGHTON NICHOLLS, C., "Housing, homelessness and capabilities", *Housing, Theory and Society* 2010, vol. 27, no. 1, 23–41.

MEEUS, B. and DE DECKER, P., *De geest van Suburbia*, Antwerpen, Garant, 2013, 344 pages.

MENON, K., "Justice", in BHARGAVA, R. and ACHARYA, A. (eds.), *Political theory: an introduction*, Delhi, Pearson, 2008, 74–87.

MILLER, D., "Democracy and social justice", *British Journal of Political Science* 1978, vol. 8, 1–19.

MONSALVE, V.B. and ROMÁN, J.A., "Tensions of human dignity: conceptualization and application to international human rights law", *IJHR* 2009, vol. 6, no. 11, 39–59.

MOONS, N., "Tenant vs. owner: deriving access to justice from the right to housing", *RdW* 2015, vol. 36, no. 3, 99–112.

MORSINK, J., *The Universal Declaration of Human Rights: Origins, Drafting and Intent*, Philadelphia, University of Pennsylvania Press, 1999, 396 pages.

MORRIS, B., "The dignity of man", *Ethics* 1946, vol. 57, no. 1, (57).

MURIE, A., "Secure and contented citizens? Home ownership in Britain", in MARSH, A. and MULLINS, D. (eds.), *Housing and public policy: citizenship, choice and control*, Buckingham, Open University Press, 1998, 79–98.

NOZICK, R., *Anarchy, state and utopia*, New York, Basic Books, 1974, 367 pages.

NUSSBAUM, M., *Creating capabilities: the human development approach*, Cambridge, Harvard University Press, 2011, 237 pages.

NUSSBAUM, M., "Human dignity and political entitlements", in President's Council on Bioethics (ed.), *Human dignity and bioethics: essays commissioned by the President's Council on Bioethics*, Washington, 2008, 351–380.

NUSSBAUM, M., *Women and human development: the capabilities approach,* Cambridge, Cambridge University Press, 2000, 312 pages.

O'MAHONEY, C., "There is no such thing as a right to dignity", *Int'l. J. Const. L.* 2012, vol. 10, no. 2, 551–574.

OXLEY, M., ELSINGA, M., HAFFNER, M. and VAN DER HEIJDEN, H., "Competition and social housing in Europe", *Economic Affairs* 2008, vol. 28, no. 2, 31–36.

PANNECOUCKE, I. and DE DECKER, P., *Grote Woononderzoek 2013. Deel 7. Woontevredenheid en woongeschiedenis*, Leuven, Steunpunt Wonen, 2015, 63 pages.

PANNECOUCKE, I. and DE DECKER, P., *Housing first: een alternatief voor de woonladder?*, Leuven, Steunpunt Wonen, 2014, 31 pages.

PAREKH, S., "Resisting 'dull and torpid' assent: returning to the debate over the foundations of human rights", *Human Rights Quarterly 2007*, vol. 29, 754–778.

PAS, W. and VAN NIEUWENHOVE, J., "Het recht een menswaardig leven te leiden", in ICM (ed.), *Jaarboek Mensenrechten 1994*, Antwerpen, Maklu, 1995, 113–138.

PETRUSEK, M., "Human capacities and the problem of universally equal dignity: two philosophical test cases and a theistic response", *Journal of Moral Theology* 2016, vol. 5, no. 1, 37.

PLEACE, N., *Housing First*, DIHAL, 2012, 52 pages

RABKIN, J., "What can we learn about human dignity from international law?", *Harvard Journal of Law & Public Policy* 2003, vol. 27, no. 1, 145–168.

RADIN, M.J., "Property and personhood", *Stanford Law Review* 1982, vol. 34, 957–1015.

RAES, K. and COENE, G., "Sociale grondrechten als voorwaarden voor een gelijke handelingsvrijheid", *Welzijnsgids* 2009, no. 72, 25–84.

RAES, K., *Controversiële rechtsfiguren. Rechtsfilosofische excursies over de relaties tussen ethiek en recht*, Gent, Academia Press, 2001, 458 pages.

RAKOFF, R.M., "Ideology in everyday life: the meaning of the house", *Politics and Society* 1977, vol. 7, no. 1, 85–104

RAUWS, W., "Niet de ver-van-mijn-bed-show: sociale grondrechten en de praktijk", in VAN EECKHOUTTE, W. and RIGAUX, M. (eds.), *Sociaal recht: niets dan uitdagingen*, Gent, Mys & Breesch, 1995, 793–843.

RAWLS, J., *A theory of justice*, Cambridge, Harvard University Press, 1971, 607 pages.

RAZ, J., *The morality of freedom*, Oxford, Clarendon Press, 1986, 434 pages.

RAZ, J., *The authority of law*, Oxford, Clarendon Press, 1979, 289 pages.

RIMANQUE, K., "Synthese: de betekenis van de sociale grondrechten", in ICM (ed.), *Jaarboek Mensenrechten 1994*, Antwerpen, Maklu, 1995, 179–182.

ROBITAILLE, D., "De gerechtelijke opvatting over armoede in Canada: onveranderlijke maatschappelijke positie of gewoon een kwestie van wil?", in Steunpunt tot Bestrijding van Armoede, Bestaansonzekerheid en Sociale Uitsluiting, *Armoede-Waardigheid-Mensenrechten*, Brussel, 2008, 95–104.

ROHE, W.M. and STEGMAN, W.A., "The effects of homeownership: on the self-esteem, perceived control and life satisfaction of low-income people", *Journal of the American Planning Association* 1994, vol. 60, no. 2, 173–184.

ROSE, C., "Property as a keystone right?", *Notre Dame Law Review* 1995, vol. 71, 329–365.

ROSENDORF, D., "Homelessness and the uses of theory: an analysis of economic and personality theories of property in the context of voting rights and squatting rights", *University of Miami Law Review* 1990, 701.

RUGG, J. and RHODES, D., *The private rented sector: its contribution and potential*, York, Centre for Housing Policy, 2008, 150 pages.

RUONAVAARA, H., "Home ownership and Nordic housing policies in 'retrenchment'", in RONALD, R. and ELSINGA, M. (eds.), *Beyond home ownership: housing, welfare and society*, London, Routledge, 2011, 91–107.

RUONAVAARA, H. and NAUMANEN, P., "Finland: trust, risk-taking and scepticism", in ELSINGA, M., DE DECKER, P., TELLER, N. and TOUSSAINT, J. (eds.), *Home ownership beyond asset and security: Perceptions of housing related security and insecurity in eight European countries*, Amsterdam, IOS Press, 2007, 67–100.

RUONAVAARA, H., "Types and forms of housing tenure, toward solving the comparison/translation problem", *Scandinavian Housing and Planning Research* 1993, vol. 10, 3–20.

SANTENS, M., "Participatie tussen emancipatie en culturele innovatie", in BOUDRY, L. et al. (eds.), *Inzet, opzet, voorzet: stadsprojecten in Vlaanderen*, Brussel, Ministerie van de Vlaamse Gemeenschap, 2006, 164–173.

SAUNDERS, P., *A nation of homeowners*, London, Unwin Hyman, 1990, 418 pages.

SCANLON, E., *Home ownership and its impacts: implications for housing policy for low-income families*, Center for Social Development, Washington University, 1996, 7–9.

SCANLON, K., "Private renting in other countries", in SCANLON, K. and KOCHAN, B. (eds.), *Towards a sustainable private rented sector. The lessons from other countries*, London, LSE, 2011, 15–44.

SCHACHTER, O., "Human dignity as a normative concept", *The American Journal of International Law* 1983, vol. 77, no. 4, 848–854.

SCHUERMANS, N., MEEUS, B. and DE DECKER, P., "Geographies of whiteness and wealth: white, middle class discourses on segregation and social mix in Flanders, Belgium", *Journal of Urban Affairs* 2014, vol. 37, no. 4, 478–495.

SEN, A., "Human rights and capabilities", *Journal of Human Development* 2005, vol. 6, no. 2, 151–166.

SEN, A., "Elements of a theory of human rights", *Philosophy and Public Affairs* 2004, vol. 23, no. 4, 315–356.

SEN, A., *Rationality and freedom*, Cambridge, Harvard University Press, 2002, 586 pages.

SEN, A. *Vrijheid is vooruitgang*, Amsterdam, Contact, 2000, 144–156

SEN, A., "Capability and well-being", in M. NUSSBAUM and A. SEN (eds.), *The quality of Life*, Oxford, Clarendon Press, 1993, 30–53.

SEN, A., *The standard of living*, Cambridge, Cambridge University Press, 1987, 125 pages.

SEN, A., "Equality of what?", *The Tanner Lecture on Human Values* 1980, vol. 1, 197–220.

SENNETT, R., *Respect in a World of Inequality*, New York, Norton, 2003, 304 pages.

SHUE, H., *Basic rights*, Princeton, Princeton University Press, 1980, 256 pages.

SHULTZINER, D., "Human Dignity – Functions and Meanings", *Global Jurist Topics* 2003, vol. 5, 1–23.

SIGRON, M., *Legitimate expectations under article 1 of Protocol no. 1 to the European Convention on Human Rights*, Antwerpen, Intersentia, 2014, 314 pages.

SINGER, P., *Applied Ethics*, London, Oxford University Press, 1986, 264 pages.

SMITH, S., "The essential qualities of home", *Journal of Environmental Psychology* 1994, vol. 14, no. 1, 31–46.

SPICKER, P., "The rights of the poor: conceptual issues", in ROBSON, P. and KJONSTAD, A. (eds.), *Poverty and the law*, Oxford, Hart Publishing, 2001, 3–15.

STORMS, B., PEETERS, N., CORNELIS, I., REYNAERT, J.-F., THIJS, P. and NISEN, L., "Ook getest op mensen. Referentiebudgetten als maatstaf voor de doeltreffendheid van de sociale bescherming", in WILLY, L., ISABELLE, P., VRANKEN, J. and VAN ROSSEM, R. (eds.), *Armoede en Sociale Uitsluiting. Jaarboek 2013*, Leuven, Acco, 2013, 267–287.

TAINIO, H. and FREDIKSSON, P., "The Finnish homelessness strategy: from a 'staircase' model to a 'housing first' approach to tackling long-term homelessness", *European Journal of Homelessness* 2009, vol. 3, 181–199.

TEGEDER, G. and HELBRECHT, I., "Germany: home ownership, a Janus-faced advantage in time of welfare restructuring", in ELSINGA, M., DE DECKER, P., TELLER, N. and TOUSSAINT, J. (eds.), *Home ownership beyond asset and security. Perceptions of housing related security and insecurity in eight European countries*, Amsterdam, IOS Press, 2007, 101–132.

TER RELE, H. and VAN STEEN, G., "Measuring housing subsidies: distortionary and distributional effects in the Netherlands", *Fiscal Studies* 2003, vol. 24, no. 3, 317–339.

UNDERKUFFLER, L., *The idea of property: its meaning and power*, Oxford, Oxford University Press, 2003, 163 pages.

VAN ASPEREN, G.M., *Het bedachte leven*, Amsterdam, Boom Uitgevers, 1993, 247 pages.

VANDEBURIE, A., *L'article 23 de la Constitution. Coquille vide ou boîte aux trésors?*, Brussel, La Charte, 2008, 266 pages.

VANDEKERCKHOVE, B. and VAN BORTEL, G., "Hoe ver reikt de participatieladder voor huurders in de sociale huisvesting?", in X. (ed.), *Het onroerend goed in de praktijk*, Mechelen, Kluwer, 2012, XIV.F, 173–190.

VAN DE LUYTGAARDEN, H.J.L.M., "Sociale grondrechten 'gerenoveerd': het rechtskarakter van sociale grondrechten vanuit juridiseringsperspectief", in GROOT, A.R.J. and VAN DE LUYTGAARDEN, H.J.L.M. (eds.), *Zonder meer recht*, Zwolle, Tjeenk Willink, 1993, 149–189.

VAN DIJK, P. and VAN HOOF, G.J.H., *De Europese Conventie in theorie en praktijk*, Nijmegen, Ars Aequi Libri, 1982, 720 pages.

VANDROMME, T. and HUBEAU, B., "Algemene schets van de huisvestingssector en het huisvestingsrecht", in X. (ed.), *Het onroerend goed in de praktijk*, Mechelen, Kluwer, 2015.

VAN EXTER, R.P., *Het internationale aspect der grondrechten*, Vlaardingen, Drukkerij Van Dooren, 1955, 157 pages.

VAN GELDER, J.-L., "What tenure security? The case for a tripartite view", *Land Use Policy* 2010, vol. 27, 449–456.

VAN MECHELEN, N. and BOGAERTS, K., *Aanvullende steun in Vlaamse OCMW's*, Antwerpen, Centrum voor Sociaal Beleid, 2008, 21 pages.

VASSENDEN, A., "Homeownership and symbolic boundaries: exclusion of disadvantaged non-homeowners in the homeowner nation of Norway", *Housing Studies* 2014, vol. 29, no. 6, 760–780.

VASSENDEN, A. and LIE, T., "Telling others how you live – refining Goffman's stigma theory through an analysis of housing strugglers in a homeowner nation", *Symbolic Interaction* 2013, vol. 36, no. 1, 78–98.

VERBIST, G. and VANHILLE, J., "Tussen huursubsidies en woonbonus: een verdelingsanalyse voor Vlaanderen", in DIERCKX, D., COENEN, J., VAN

HAARLEM, A. and RAEYMAECKERS, P., *Armoede en sociale uitsluiting. Jaarboek 2013*, Antwerpen, Acco, 2013, 291–306.

VERBIST, S., "Impliceert het recht op behoorlijke huisvesting een recht op eigendom" (note under Constitutional Court 7 March 2007, no. 33/2007), *RABG* 2007, no. 16, 1103–1109.

VERDUSSEN, M. and NOËL, A., "Les droits fondamentaux et la réforme constitutionnelle de 1993", *APT* 1994, 127–143.

VIZARD, P. and BURCHARDT, T., *Developing a capability list: final recommendations of the equalities review steering group on measurement*, London, Centre for Analysis of Social Exclusion, 2007, 92 pages.

VLEMMINX, F., and KUMMELING, H.R.B.M., "Algemene situering van de sociale grondrechten in de Nederlandse rechtsorde", in HUBEAU, B. and DE LANGE, R. (eds.), *Het Grondrecht op wonen. De grondwettelijke erkenning van het recht op huisvesting in Nederland en België,* Antwerpen, Maklu, 1995, 13–36.

VRANKEN, J., "Het OCMW: dertig jaren op weg naar een recht op maatschappelijke dienstverlening", in VRANKEN, J., DE BOYSER, K. and DIERCKX, D. (eds.), *Armoede en Sociale Uitsluiting. Jaarboek 2005*, Leuven, Acco, 2006, 151–164.

WALDRON, J., "Dignity, rights and responsibilities", *New York University Public Law and Legal Theory Research Paper Series* 2010, Working paper no. 10–83, 1–25.

WALDRON, J., "Socioeconomic rights and theories of justice", *Public Law Research Paper no. 10–79*, 2010, 1–30

WALDRON, J., *Liberal rights*, Cambridge, Cambridge University Press 1993, 480 pages

WALDRON, J., *The right to private property*, Oxford, Oxford University Press, 1990, 470 pages.

WHITE, E.K., "There is no such thing as a right to human dignity: a reply to Conor O'Mahony", *Int'l. J. Const. L.* 2012, vol. 10, no. 2, 575–584.

WHITE, M., "Kantian dignity and social economics", *Forum for Social Economics* 2003, vol. 32, no. 2, 1–11.

WINTERS, S., *Huurprijzen en richthuurprijzen. Deel I: literatuurstudie over richthuurprijzen*, Leuven, Steunpunt Ruimte en Wonen, 2012, 11–12.

WINTERS, S. and VAN DEN BROECK, K., "Milestones in 25 years of housing finance in Belgium", in LUNDE, J. and WHITEHEAD, C. (eds.), *Milestones in European housing finance*, Oxford, Wiley-Blackwell, 2016, 75–91.

WINTERS, S., "Belgian state reform as an opportunity to reorient Flemish housing policy", *International Journal of Housing Policy* 2013, vol. 13, no. 1, 74–82.

WINTERS, S., "Are there grounds for housing allowances in Flanders (Belgium)?", *European Journal of Housing Policy* 2005, vol. 5, no. 2, 167–185.

WOOD, A., "Human dignity, right and the realm of ends", *Acta Juridica* 2008, 47–65.

ZAJADLO, J., "Human dignity and human rights", in HANSKI, R. and SUSKI, M. (eds.), *An introduction to the international protection of human rights: a textbook*, Turku, Institute for Human Rights, Abo Akademi University, 1999, 15–24.

ZWART, S., *Maintaining an efficient and equitable housing market in Belgium*, OECD Economics Department Working Papers, no. 1208, Paris, OECD Publishing, 2015, 36 pages.

2 Socio-Legal Influences on the Effectiveness of the Right to Housing

In the previous chapter, the recurring use of human (or social) dignity in socio-economic rights law compelled us to develop an in-depth interpretation of the concept that should provide direction for law- and policy-making in the field of the right to housing. This chapter highlights how that law- and policy-making effort to improve this fundamental right is subjected to many different more sociological elements and how they can impact the effectiveness of housing rights. It is of vital importance for a legislator to take this wide array of influences into account to be able to make impactful decisions that shape, concretize and guarantee the right to housing.

1. Legal Instrumentalism and Its Criticism

The assumption of a straightforward causal link between legislation and its intended social effects is called the instrumentalist approach.[1] As the term suggests, law is then regarded as the dominant instrument to shape the behavior of individuals. It is rooted in a firm belief in the power of law. Legal instrumentalism considers a piece of legislation to be able to play the role of a social tool (or evidently an instrument) that the government can use to achieve certain (often social) goals and thereby change society.[2] In other words, this legal theory treats law as the ultimate vaccine.[3] This view arose at the end of the nineteenth century, when it became clear that hard work was not a guaranty for emancipation and wellbeing. Consequently, law was given a new additional function.[4]

With its focus on the strong causal link between rule and intended purpose, a strict instrumentalist view considers law and society to be two completely

1 J. GRIFFITHS, "De sociale werking van wetgeving", in J. GRIFFITHS and H. WEYERS (eds.), *De sociale werking van recht*, Nijmegen, Ars Aequi, 2005, (467) 471–472.
2 R. TOMASIC, *The sociology of law*, London, Sage Publications, 1985, 101 and 104; D. BLACK, *The behaviour of law*, New York, Academic Press, 1976, 120.
3 R.L. KIDDER, *Connecting law and society*, New Jersey, Prentice-Hall, 1983, 114–115.
4 R.J.S. SCHWITTERS, *Recht en samenleving in verandering*, Deventer, Kluwer, 2008, 32–33.

distinct entities. It does not regard law as a social product, intimately integrated in social processes, but as a unique social function.[5] Law stands on its own and is therefore thought of as capable of influencing behavior and society. When so much emphasis is laid on the fact that law can be used as a tool, it also implies that there is no distortion present in the relationship between law and society. It presupposes a society dominated by extensive individualism, where the smooth adaptation to a certain rule exemplifies the perfect communication between legislator and individual.[6] Considering the instrumentalist assumption of the resolving force of law, it is not too surprising that legal instrumentalism has also been described as the "primary cause of the juridification of society".[7]

While we should not underestimate the law, we should not overestimate it either.[8] The question whether law can be used as a tool for social change, or, in other words, whether law can change folkways, a basic instrumentalist assumption, cannot be answered with a simple yes or no. Although some theorists express themselves as pessimistic about the capabilities of law to alter behavior and social order,[9] their explanation and view on law does not deviate much from others who are more optimistic.[10] Both sides acknowledge that law in itself is insufficient and that there is no simple causal link between law and

5 TOMASIC (n 2) 101 and 104; BLACK (n 2) 101 and 105; M.M. FEELEY, "The concept of laws in social science: a critique and notes on an expended view", *Law & Society Review* 1975, vol. 10, (497) 501.

6 K. VAN AEKEN, "Een rechtssociologische analyse van de juridisering van de samenleving", in B. HUBEAU, S. GIBENS, S. MERCELIS, S. PARMENTIER, P. PONSAERS, K. VAN AEKEN, G. VANDE WALLE and J. VAN HOUTTE (eds.), *Dialogen tussen recht en samenleving*, Leuven, Acco, 2012, (67) 75; SCHWITTERS (n 4) 9 and 98; GRIFFITHS (n 1) 472–473.

7 VAN AEKEN (n 6) 74; S. FITZPATRICK, B. BENGTSSON and B. WATTS, "Rights to housing: reviewing the terrain and exploring a way forward", *Housing, Theory and Society* 2014, 31 (4), 447–463.

8 B. HUBEAU, "De sociale grondrechten na een decennium: hefboom of toekomstdroom in de uitsluiting van sociale uitsluiting", in J. VRANKEN, K. DE BOYSER and D. DIERCKX (eds.), *Armoede en sociale uitsluiting Jaarboek 2003*, Leuven, Acco, 2004, (369) 369 and 379; N. BERNARD and B. HUBEAU, "Poverty and fundamental social and economic rights: on the effectiveness of the right to decent housing", in D. DIERCKX, N. VAN HERCK and J. VRANKEN (eds.), *Poverty in Belgium*, Antwerpen, Acco, 2010, (195) 199.

9 E.g. W.G. SUMNER, *Folkways: a study of the sociological importance of usages, manners, customs, mores and morals*, Boston, Ginn and Company, 1906, 77; T.W. WÄLDE, "Non-conventional views on effectiveness: the holy grail of modern international lawyers: the new paradigm? A chimera? Or a brave new world in the global economy?", *Austrian Review of International & European Law* 1999, vol. 4, (164).

10 E.g. B. KUTCHINSKY, "The legal consciousness: a survey of research and opinion about law", in A. PODGORECKI, W. KAUPEN, J. VAN HOUTTE, P. VINCKE and B. KUTCHINSKY (eds.), *Knowledge and opinion about law*, London, Martin Robertson, 1973, 102; A. PODGORECKI, "Public opinion on law", in A. PODGORECKI, W. KAUPEN, J. VAN HOUTTE, P. VINCKE and B. KUTCHINSKY (eds.), *Knowledge*

society. It is this consideration that is the main point of criticism against instrumentalism. One should pay attention to the fact that law is only one factor of influence on human behavior. The possibility of legislation to play a role and to be an instrument of social change is thus not denied as such, only relativized. The criticism thus predominantly focuses not on instrumentalism as such, but on a naive interpretation of it. Not every societal problem is solved simply by initiating a new law.[11] Legal rules are directed at social beings who act in a social context, not at mere atomistic rational individuals. The influence of legislation can only be apprehended when we give the social order a prominent position.[12] Hence, it is vital to make a distinction between an instrumentalist point of view, which focuses on the effectiveness of the right itself, and a more pluralistic one, which examines the way in which the relevant right is given shape in society and the reason why it is or is not successful. We will now take a closer look at a selection of these other influences on human behavior that have to be taken into account when developing new rules or adapting older ones in the realm of the right to housing.

2. A Socio-Legal Perspective

A. Law in the Books vs. Law in Action vs. Living Law

The considerations from the last paragraph indicate not only the mutual relationship between law and society, but also that law *is* part of society.[13] These insights are frequently captured by the notions "law in action" and "living law". Although the authors that first used these terms, Roscoe Pound[14] and Eugen Ehrlich[15] respectively, were both concerned about law being a collection of mere paper rules, their approach was quite different.[16]

As a matter of fact, Pound follows the instrumentalist path by implying similarly that law is a tool of social engineering.[17] He argued that there was a

and opinion about law, London, Martin Robertson, 1973, 66. H. DE SOTO, *The other path: the invisible revolution in the third world*, New York, Basic Books, 1989, 185.

11 SCHWITTERS (n 4) 97.

12 GRIFFITHS (n 1) 473–475.

13 P. EWICK, R.A. KAGAN and A. SARAT, "Legacies of legal realism: social science, social policy and the law", in P. EWICK, R.A. KAGAN and A. SARAT (eds.), *Social science, social policy and the law*, New York, Russel Sage Foundation, 1999, (1) 6–7.

14 R. POUND, "Law in books and law in action", *American Law Review* 1910, vol. 44, no. 12, 12–36.

15 E. EHRLICH, *Grundlegung der Soziologie des Rechts*, Berlin, Duncker & Humblot, 1913, 409 pages.

16 D. NELKEN, "Law in action or living law? Back to the beginning in sociology of law", *Legal Studies* 1984, vol. 4, (157) 178.

17 S.F. MOORE, "Recht en maatschappelijke verandering: de rol van het 'semi-autonoom social veld'", in J. GRIFFITHS and H. WEYERS (eds.), *De sociale werking van recht*, Nijmegen, Ars Aequi, 2005, (177) 177; M. HERTOGH, "The living *Rechtsstaat*: a

distinction between the rules contained in legal provisions on the one hand ("law in the books") and the law produced by judges and other legal practitioners when they applied it on the other ("law in action").[18] Both "forms of law" still refer to the activities and behavior of lawmakers and law enforcers and therefore illustrate a top-down approach.[19]

In contrast, Ehrlich interprets law as the outcome of social processes and social change, from an obvious bottom-up perspective.[20] For him, the focal point of legal development can be found in society, which consists of many social associations that have their own "inner order". These inner orders predate the abstract and general rules of positive law.[21] To use Ehrlich's words, "it is the law that dominates life itself, even though it has not been printed in legal propositions".[22] "Living law" thus refers to the norms that citizens recognize as obligatory just by being a member of society and its many associations within.[23] This concept of law has been the subject of much criticism, not in the least by legal positivists such as Kelsen[24] and Hart.[25] We are also rather reluctant to call these social norms by inner orders "law". Nevertheless, the focus should not be on the definition of law. The real merits of Ehrlich's theory lay in his insights about law and society and its reciprocal relationship.[26]

As we will see in Part II, the European Court of Human Rights (ECtHR) interprets the European Convention of Human Rights as a "living instrument".

bottom-up approach to legal ideas and social reality", in W. VAN DER BURG and S. TAEKEMA (eds.), *The importance of ideals: debating their relevance in law, morality, and politics*, Brussel, P.I.E. Peter-Lang, 2004, (75) 85.

18 POUND (n 14) 15; A. BOSCH, *Citizens enforcing the law: The legal and social space for citizen's arrest*, Antwerp, Maklu, 2013, 17.

19 HERTOGH (n 17) 85–87; NELKEN (n 16) 165.

20 NELKEN (n 16) 162; M. HERTOGH, "Wat weten en vinden burgers van het recht", in M. HERTOGH and H. WEIJERS (eds.), *Het recht van onderop. Antwoorden uit de rechtssociologie*, Nijmegen, Ars Aequi, 2011, (287) 292.

21 N.O. LITTLEFIELD, "Eugen Ehrlich's fundamental principles of the sociology of law", *Maine Law Review* 1967, vol.19, (1) 3–4.

22 E. EHRLICH, *Fundamental principles of the sociology of law*, Cambridge, Harvard University Press, 1936, 493.

23 NELKEN (n 16) 175.

24 B.Z. TAMANAHA, "A vision of social-legal change: rescuing Ehrlich from 'living law'", *Law & Social Inquiry* 2011, vol. 36, no. 1, (297) 306 and 308; J.-L. HALPÉRIN, "Law in books and law in action: the problem of legal change", *Maine Law Review* 2011, vol. 64, no. 1, (45) 47–51.

25 G.J. POSTEMA, "Conformity, custom, and convergence: rethinking the efficacy of law", in M.H. KRAMER, C. GRANT, B. COLBURN and A. HATZISTAVROU (eds.), *The legacy of H.L.A. Hart. Legal, political and moral philosophy*, Oxford, Oxford University Press, 2008, (45) 47.

26 B. VAN KLINK, "Facts and norms: the unfinished debate between Eugen Ehrlich and Hans Kelsen", in M. HERTOGH (ed.), *Living Law. Reconsidering Eugen Ehrlich*, Oxford, Hart Publishing, 2009, (127) 152–153.

This means that the Court's interpretation of a Convention right can evolve over time, an interesting statement in the context of incorporating socio-economic concerns into the protection of what are essentially only civil and political rights. Based on the explanation given above, though, this statement is somewhat paradoxical. Despite the terminology used, the concept "living instrument" is interpreted in a way that resembles much more Pound's "law in action" than Ehrlich's "living law". Just like Pound,[27] the ECtHR considers that law should be interpreted in an updated, evolutionary way to retain its effectiveness,[28] whereas Ehrlich's "living law" is something quite different from the formal legal propositions on the basis of which the ECtHR makes its judgments.[29]

To summarise, while "law in action" in essence still refers to official legal rules, "living law" is oriented outside legal institutions. They are thus anything but identical.[30] As we will see, however, in the upcoming paragraphs, both concepts uncover certain things about the effectiveness of law and the right to housing in particular.

B. Equality and Dependency

1) Access to Justice

A good example of the gap that exists between 'law in the books' and 'law in action' has to do with equality.[31] Pound himself used the unequal treatment of rich and poor people with regard to the handling of crime suspects as an illustration of the distinction.[32] It is relatively easy to enact a law that creates formal equality (i.e. equality before the law). It is, however, much more difficult for law to also enhance substantive equality. Take, for example, a court process between a tenant and a landlord. It has long been said that even though tenant and landlord are equal before the law, the latter party has in practice often the advantage of having more experience (which equals knowledge as well as

27 HALPÉRIN (n 24) 61.

28 D. RIETIKER, "The principle of 'effectiveness' in the recent jurisprudence of the European Court of Human Rights: its different dimensions and its consistency with public international law – no need for the concept of treaty *sui generis*", *Nordic Journal of International Law* 2010, vol. 79, (245) 260–262.

29 TAMANAHA (n 24) 306.

30 Ehrlich uses the term "norms for decision" to encompass most of what Pound meant by 'law in the books' and law in action; see: S. NIMAGA, "Pounding on Ehrlich. Again?", in M. HERTOGH (ed.), *Living Law. Reconsidering Eugen Ehrlich*, Oxford, Hart Publishing, 2009, 157–175.

31 A. TERLOUW, "Draagt wetgeving bij aan gelijkheid?", in M. HERTOGH and H. WEIJERS (eds.), *Het recht van onderop. Antwoorden uit de rechtssociologie*, Nijmegen, Ars Aequi, 2011, (349) 351.

32 POUND (n 14) 16–18.

valuable contacts) with courts and lawyers than tenants, who are to a large extent unaware of the intricacies of the legal system.[33] Following Galanter's distinction, the party in the dominant position could then be called the repeat-player, in contrast to the one-shotter (in this case, the tenant).[34]

This rather simple distinction is particularly relevant when it concerns professional house renting companies or landlords with a lot of rented properties. But this is not necessarily characteristic of each rental market. In Flanders, only around 5 percent of the private rental market is represented by professional renting companies, whereas 64 percent of private landlords rent out just one property.[35] This definitely reshapes or at least puts in perspective the image of landlords as repeat-players. But even though many of those small private landlords may thus not be repeat-players, owners generally do have a stronger socio-economic profile than tenants. This can impact equal access to justice as well. Weaker groups in society, to which tenants more frequently belong than house owners, have to make relatively greater efforts to enforce their rights, since they are often less acquainted with law and social services than the middle or upper classes.[36] Evidently, this also pertains to financial burdens and the extent to which each party will be prepared to resign themselves to accepting the current (problematic) situation.

In order to avoid this discrepancy between equality pro forma and equality in practice, it is an open door to advocate the settlement of a rent dispute through reconciliation. The primary advantages, being free of charge and very low on administrative burdens, are elements that do favor tenants in particular. Yet the advantages are as clear as day for landlords as well, who can be persuaded by the financial benefits to take action more quickly. Between 2002 and 2008, the Belgian Judicial Code imposed that before a landlord could introduce a principal claim concerning a rent dispute, the defendant had to be called to attempt an amicable settlement.[37] Unfortunately, the measure did not reach its intended effect, for different reasons. There was disagreement in the jurisprudence and legal doctrine about the sanctions in case the preceding call for reconciliation was not complied with. Some jurisprudence did not even consider it obligatory in all circumstances.[38] Regrettably, tenants often did not show up either, rendering the procedure useless. It is primarily the latter one

33 KIDDER (n 3) 75; M. GALANTER, "De duivel schijt altijd op de grote hoop", in J. GRIFFITHS and H. WEYERS (eds.), *De sociale werking van recht*, Nijmegen, Ars Aequi, 2005, (435) 437–439.
34 GALANTER (n 33) 440.
35 S. WINTERS et al., *Wonen in Vlaanderen anno 2013. De bevindingen uit het Grote Woononderzoek 2013 gebundeld*, Antwerpen, Garant, 2015, 54.
36 HUBEAU (n 8) 381; BERNARD (n 8) 199.
37 J. NOLF, "Over de helaasheid der huurders", *Juristenkrant* 2010, no. 201, 11.
38 Peace Court Antwerpen 28 May 2013, *RW* 2003–04, 35; Peace Court Doornik (2nd Chamber) 8 March 2005, *JT* 2006, 512; Peace Court Sint-Gillis 23 September 2004, *T.Vred.* 2005, 295; Peace Court Halle, 15 September 2004, *Huur* 2005, 150.

that seems to have triggered a modification of the provision.[39] The legislator wanted to prevent unnecessary delays of the procedure and help peace courts with their already busy schedules. In its current form, the provision still prescribes that a reconciliation attempt should be made by the judge, but no longer is this part of a separate session preceding the introduction of the principal claim. The judge is obliged to see whether an agreement can be reached, but if that is not the case, he can just continue with the procedure. Again, however, a sanction in case of non-compliance is not included.[40]

The procedural barriers that are generally still more problematic to overcome for tenants than for owners are not the only things that create a wedge between housing law in the books and housing law in action. There is also a different level of dependency between tenant and landlord that can impact the effective application of the right to housing even before a conflict arises. Even though every tenant is to a certain extent dependent upon their landlord, low-income tenants have obviously fewer alternatives and are therefore tied even more strongly to their current dwelling. With that in mind, it could also prevent them from taking steps in accordance with housing legislation in an attempt to avoid any form of conflict with their letter. In other words, the larger the dependency, the more a tenant's legal status can be undermined.[41] In contrast, the landlord can have his dependency diffused among other tenants or, if that is not the case, it is at least spread among other potential tenants who could replace the current one.[42]

Against this background, it is important to search for initiatives that could prevent court procedures. With regard to housing quality, a state could, for example, establish a system of conformity certificates for the privately rented housing stock. Such a certificate would indicate that a dwelling is habitable and adequate for a period of ten years. While owners in Flanders can request such a certificate in their municipality, they are not mandatory in a way that would equal a renting permit. The municipalities do, however, have the power to make the certificate obligatory.[43] Obviously, if a (prospective) tenant could demand proof that the dwelling conforms with housing quality regulations, his rights with regard to the quality of housing would be considered complied with.

39 Law 18 June 2008 amending the Judicial Code with regard to the procedure concerning certain rental conflicts, *BS* 11 August 2008.

40 C. CAUFFMAN, "Hervorming van de verzoeningspoging bij hoofdvorderingen inzake de huur van woningen", *RW* 2008–09, no. 6, 252–254.

41 Raad voor Maatschappelijke Ontwikkeling, *Toegang tot Recht*, Den Haag, 2004, 56–58.

42 T.R. VAUGHAN, "The landlord-tenant relationship in low-income area", *Social Problems* 1968, vol. 16, no. 2, (208) 210.

43 P. DE SMEDT, "De Vlaamse Wooncode anno 2013: naar een (nog meer) integrale en slagkrachtige woonkwaliteitsbewaking?", in B. HUBEAU and T. VANDROMME (eds.), *Vijftien jaar Vlaamse Wooncode. Sisyphus (on)gelukkig?*, Brugge, Die Keure, 2013, (41) 58–64.

There are nonetheless a couple of problems with this approach. First, implementing further and more rigorous obligations for landlords creates the risk of a vicious circle. It could negatively impact their willingness to stay on or go to the private rental market with their property, which would be a blow to the private rental stock. Additionally, better quality would probably be reflected in higher prices, which would hurt the many low-income private tenants once again. Even ignoring these economic realities, if a quality certificate became mandatory, there is still a question of legal knowledge among tenants. It could very well be that the measure would bring about a stock of rented dwellings that have not been subjected to any quality assessment. The question remains whether tenants would then be sufficiently informed to apply their rights and thereby ensure that they obtain good-quality housing. In comparison, recent numbers show that only 43 percent of private tenants know about the EPC, the energy performance certificate which has been mandatory in Flanders now for more than half a decade.[44] It is obviously difficult to enforce legal obligations when you are not even aware of them in the first place. To establish such knowledge with regard to housing quality conformity certificates, the Flemish Housing Code has actually taken a step back since the Integration Decree of 2011.[45] No longer does it contain an obligation on behalf of the landlord to inform the tenant of the acquired certificate and to deliver him a copy. And yet, even if they are well informed on this matter, one can assume somewhat cynically that the weakest tenants, in a position of strong dependency and in search of affordable housing, may ultimately still engage with landlords who provide them with housing of subpar quality.

2) Landlord Preferences and Discrimination

Another example of how law in action is impacted by a factual imbalance of power and dependency concerns cases of discrimination.[46] Time and again private landlords in Flanders and elsewhere have been found to take a reluctant stance against certain groups in society.[47] With regard to the Flemish private rental market, recent numbers show that 22 percent of all landlords do not

44 WINTERS (n 35) 104.

45 Decree Flemish Government 29 April 2011 concerning the amendment of various decrees on housing, *BS* 4 May 2011; Article 7 Flemish Housing Code.

46 J. DE WITTE and I. AENDENBOOM, "Discriminatie en haatmisdrijven: individuele, maar ook collectieve schade", *De orde van de dag* 2011, vol. 54, (49) 52.

47 E.g. M. BOSCH, M.A. CARNERO and L. FARRÉ, "Information and discrimination in the rental housing market: evidence from a field experiment", *Regional Science and Urban Economics* 2010, vol. 40, 11–19; N. LAUSTER and A. EASTERBROOK, "No room for new families? A field experiment measuring rental discrimination against same-sex couples and single parents", *Social Problems* 2011, vol. 58, no. 3, 389–409; V.J. ROSCIGNO, D.L. KARAFIN and G. TESTER, "The complexities and processes of racial housing discrimination, *Social Problems* 2009, vol. 56, no. 1, 49–69 K. VAN DER

want tenants of foreign origin. No less than 36 percent of them will wait for a different potential renter when a candidate lives on an income provided by the public center of social welfare.[48] Similar figures with regard to discrimination on the private rental market have been arrived at following practical tests.[49] This tendency is additionally incentivized by the imbalance in private rental housing supply and demand and the residualization of the private rental market. A broad renting potential and a large share of socio-economically weaker tenants impact the selection methods of landlords.

Belgian and Flemish legislation obviously addresses the issue of discrimination (on the housing market). First, there is the more proactive measure that every public rental advertisement or public communication about the lease of an accommodation has to contain the rental price.[50] This at least prevents the price from magically fluctuating from one prospective tenant to another. The municipalities are authorized to determine, prosecute and punish violations, but since the majority of them has not adopted the necessary regulations, the provision has not had its intended impact.[51] More important, though, is the specific discrimination regulation itself. There are federal anti-discrimination[52] and anti-racism laws,[53] but ever since the transfer of the competence of private housing rent to the regions back in 2014, anyone who wishes to put forward a discrimination claim related to the Flemish rental market now has to invoke the Flemish equal treatment decree.[54] While similar in *ratione materiae*, the Flemish decree provides civil law sanctions instead of penal ones.

As with the federal laws,[55] the Flemish legislation does not lay the burden of proof exclusively on the victim/claimant. The victim must present facts that

BRACHT and B. VAN DE PUTTE, *Het not-in-my-property-syndroom (NIMPS). Etnische discriminatie*, Gent, Universiteit Gent, 2013.

48 WINTERS (n 35) 55.

49 K. VAN DEN BROECK and K. HEYLEN, *Discriminatie en selectie op de private huurmarkt in België*, Leuven, HIVA, 2014, 22–25 and 30–33.

50 Art. 1716 Belgian Civil Code; L. ZIV, “Bronnen van verbod op discriminatie bij particuliere huur”, in P. BRULEZ and A.-L. VERBEKE (eds.), *Knelpunten huurrecht: tien perspectieven*, Antwerpen, Intersentia, 2012, (253) 258–260.

51 On the contrary, tenants across Belgium are now unequally protected against discrimination: N. BERNARD, “La loi du 25 avril 2007 et les nouvelles dispositions en matière de bail à loyer”, *JT* 2007, (513) 514; G. INSLEGERS, “Graag een volwaardig huurbeleid voor de private huurmarkt”, in B. HUBEAU and T. VANDROMME (eds.), *Vijftien jaar Vlaamse Wooncode. Sisyphus (on)gelukkig?*, Brugge, Die Keure, 2013, (309) 312.

52 Law 10 May 2007 aimed at combating specific forms of discrimination, *BS* 30 May 2007 (hereafter Anti-discrimination law).

53 Law 10 May 2007 on the modification of the law of 30 July 1981 criminalizing certain acts inspired by racism and xenophobia, *BS* 30 May 2007 (hereafter Anti-racism law).

54 Decree 10 July 2008 concerning a framework for the Flemish equal opportunities and equal treatment policy, *BS* 23 September 2008; ZIV (n 50) 257–258.

55 Art. 28 Anti-discrimination law and art. 30 Anti-racism law; E. VOLCKAERT, “De weerslag van de anti-discriminatiewetgeving op het afsluiten van een huurovereenkomst”, *Huur* 2008, vol. 3, 107–113; N. VAN LEUVEN, “De antidiscriminatiewet en de

raise the suspicion of discrimination. In that case (and only then) the defendant will have to prove the opposite. Even though this has been called a reversal of the burden of proof, it is probably more accurate to speak of a distribution of that burden.[56] The Constitutional Court also picked up this nuance by establishing that it does not violate the principle of equality or the presumption of innocence.[57] Despite this distribution of the burden of proof, it often remains very difficult to demonstrate that there is a pertinent presumption of discrimination when an owner prefers not to rent someone his dwelling.[58] Since a reversal of proof is obviously no real alternative either (for reasons of presumption of innocence and principle of equality), this is a persistent hindrance for a prospective tenant's access to justice and a problem that is very hard to address appropriately.

With regard to lower-income prospective tenants in particular, a distinction between selection and (indirect) discrimination is difficult but vital. A landlord can examine whether the prospective tenant is able to pay the rent and make a decision based on his/her level of income. This falls under the heading of selection criteria. He is not allowed, though, to make a distinction based purely on the source of that income. Yet a lot of landlords are wary of prospective tenants who do not generate their income from work, and especially of those who rely for it on welfare benefits from a public institution.[59] As a result, they often adopt different selection strategies to avoid letting to this group of prospective tenants,[60] giving way to a very large grey area as to what exactly is discrimination and what is not.[61] Even if partially based on stereotypical and flawed reasoning, it is entirely understandable from a financial security point of view that owners want to prevent or at least reduce the possibility of rent arrears. It has after all been said that one out of every five private landlords has already experienced a conflict with (at least) one of their tenants about timely

huurovereenkomst", in S. STIJNS and P. WÉRY (eds.), *Antidiscriminatiewet en contracten*, Brugge, Die Keure, 2006, 111–141.

56 B. SAMYN, "De bewijslast. Rechtsleer getoetst aan tien jaar cassatierechtspraak, *P&B* 2010, (50) 67–68.

57 Constitutional Court 6 October 2004, no. 157/2004, B.82–B.86; See also Labour Court Mechelen 16 March 2006, *RW* 2007–08, no. 11, 445.

58 Court of Appeal Gent (13th Chamber) 30 November 2005, *RW* 2006–07, no. 4, 144, note J. KUSTERS.

59 J. VERSTRAETE and P. DE DECKER, "Discriminatie van financieel kwetsbare huishoudens op de private huurmarkt in België", in D. DIERCKX, J. COENE and P. RAEYMAECKERS (eds.), *Armoede en sociale uitsluiting. Jaarboek 2014*, Leuven, Acco, 2014, (110) 116–117.

60 Ibid., 119–124.

61 M. LOOPMANS et al., "Onderzoek van de private huisvestingsmarkt in België in het kader van de Diversiteitsbarometer, in Interfederaal Gelijkekansencentrum (UNIA) (ed.), *Diversiteitsbarometer huisvesting*, Brussel, Interfederaal Gelijkekansencentrum, 2014, (134) 156.

rent payments.[62] A popular recurring argument is therefore that an owner should be able to choose freely what he wants to do with his property. But if public opinion does not seem to take a stance against refusing a group of prospective tenants who are generally perceived as being less solvent, the difficult legal assessment as to when exactly discrimination is in play is not the only problem. Such conduct is then considered normal in and by society, which could in turn withhold this group of prospective tenants from seeking justice via legal institutions. Along with the difficulty of providing sufficient evidence, the burdens of a judicial process and the somewhat irrelevant result of a successful outcome (it provides no solution for the applicant's housing search or problems), this is just another influence on a victim's willingness to report alleged discriminatory behavior.[63]

C. Semi-Autonomous Social Fields

Semi-autonomous social fields (SASF) are groups of people that share certain rules of conduct and maintain them by way of social control.[64] These rules develop in any group where people act in an oriented way. And considering that people are actors dependent on and linked with one another, SASFs are everywhere: from families to hospitals, from book clubs to political parties.[65] To a considerable extent, they reflect Ehrlich's "inner orders", yet without these rules being interpreted as law in itself. Nonetheless, SASFs also create norms by which the people of these groups feel obliged. Changes in society must therefore not automatically be traced back to legislative efforts only. An adequate approach to the effectiveness of law thus also demands a bottom-up perspective, one that departs from the concrete reality of the citizen.[66] To use Griffith's words, "the influence of legislation on behavior can only be understood if the social organization takes center stage".[67] Since the social rules of an SASF are often more imbedded into a person's everyday life than legal

62 K. HEYLEN, *Grote Woononderzoek 2013: Deel 5. De private huurmarkt: vraag- en aanbodzijde*, Leuven, Steunpunt Wonen, 2015, 9.

63 N. BERNARD, "Les lois anti-discrimination et le secteur du logement (privé et social)", in C. BAYART, S. SOTTIAUX and S. VAN DROOGHENBROECK (eds.), *De nieuwe federale antidiscriminatiewetten*, Brugge, Die Keure, 2008, (797) 815; B. HUBEAU and D. VERMEIR, *Een evaluatie van het woninghuurrecht – Deel II. Bevidingen werkgroepen "Toegang, selectie en discriminatie", "Procedure en bemiddeling" en "Huurprijs", resultaten wegingsoefening en aanbevelingen expertencommissie*, Leuven, Steunpunt Wonen, 2015, 28–31 and 47–48.

64 The concept was first used by S.F. MOORE, "Law and social change: the semi-autonomous social field as an appropriate subject of study", in *Law & Society Review* 1972, vol. 7, no. 1, 720–746.

65 VAN AEKEN (n 6) 75.

66 N. HULS, *Actie en reactie. Een inleiding in de rechtssociologie*, Den Haag, Boom Juridische Uitgevers, 2008, 38–39 and 128; SCHWITTERS (n 4) 9, 84 and 97–98.

67 GRIFFITHS (n 1) 475.

rules, they can influence the compliance with and effectiveness of the law. According to Niemeijer, the success rate of a piece of legislation therefore increases as it connects more to social reality.[68]

The impact of SASFs should thus not be underestimated, as it is also visible in the context of housing. The prevailing mentality in an SASF can be the opposite of that of law or can even contradict legal rules, but it can also influence the realization of socio-economic rights positively. The French enforceable right to adequate housing, the *Droit au Logement Opposable* (DALO), has in part been the merit of civil society. In 2003, a voluntary community created a platform for the enforceable right to housing, and in the summer of 2005 the French public united after the death of 17 inadequately housed people living in converted flat buildings in Paris. Their outrage prompted a new bill on establishing an enforceable right to housing and kept the debate alive.[69]

As mentioned, however, an SASF can also share a view or approach to justice which differs from or distorts the one embedded in the legal rules. As an example, we briefly return to the topic of discrimination on the housing market. The landlord is not the only actor involved in cases of discrimination. It has been documented how real estate agencies can be involved in discriminatory treatment of potential buyers and renters as well.[70] Research figures show that this is a more common trend than one might expect. Almost 40 percent of the Flemish real estate agencies seem willing to discriminate on racial grounds, and more than 50 percent on the basis of income type.[71] Here it is also possible to speak of a prevailing mentality in a group of connected people that undermines or even contradicts legal rules, influencing the effectiveness of law and *in casu* the full realization of the accessibility of housing, one of the main aspects of the right to adequate housing.

In the context of our topic, it would be possible to consider squatters as a group that fits this category too. Without discarding the fact that some squatters have criminal motives, others break into and reside in (empty) buildings they do not possess simply because they need a roof over their head

68 B. NIEMEIJER, "Wat leren wetsevaluaties ons over de effectiviteit van wetgeving?", in M. HERTOGH and H. WEIJERS (eds.), *Het recht van onderop. Antwoorden uit de rechtssociologie*, Nijmegen, Ars Aequi, 2011, (41) 48.

69 N. PACHECO and L. SALES, "From the recognition to the justiciability of housing rights: building the future", *International Journal of Land Law & Agricultural Science* 2011, no.11, (34) 43; M. PIETERSE, "Eating socioeconomic rights: the usefulness of rights talk in alleviating social hardship revisited", *Human Rights Quarterly* 2007, vol. 29, (796) 821.

70 E.g. Court of First Instance Brussel (summary procedure) 3 June 2005, no. 05/1289/A, *T. Vreemd.* 2006, no. 1, 42, note J. KUSTERS.

71 The figures are even more significant in Brussels and Wallonia; see: VAN DEN BROECK (n 49) 54–55; HUBEAU (n 63) 14.

or, a third possibility, to make a principled point on housing policies.[72] Squatting occurs on a small basis, but in a more organized manner as well.[73] As such, it becomes not only a survival strategy, but also a way to participate in society and a form of self-empowerment, albeit one that is not only developed bottom-up but is also *contra legem*.[74]

Without romanticizing their actions too much, one could say that they illustrate how squatters value the right to housing more highly than the right to property[75] and are willing to break civil (and potentially penal) law to achieve their aims.[76] Squatters, in other words, depart from the idea that emergency breaks law and that social justice will not reach them through a rigid legal system. Consequently, they take matters into their own hands. With the exception of some (nonetheless interesting) cases before the European Court of Human Rights in which they have been the applicants (see Part II),[77] it is then no surprise that squatters can usually be found on the defendant's bench in eviction cases. The right to housing, their main point of defense, has appeared largely insufficient to prevent an eviction altogether.[78] It does not

72 G. SMAERS, "De strafbaarheid van het kraken van woningen naar Belgisch recht", *RW* 1986–87, 2193.

73 There are, for example, websites supporting and helping squatters, giving more weight to the existence of a squatter community as a semi-autonomous social field; e.g. https://krakengent.squat.net; www.squatter.org.uk; The Squatting Europe Kollective, *Squatting in Europe: radical spaces, urban struggles*, New York, Minor Compositions, 2013; J. BALL, "From individual to collective squat: economic, theory and the regulation of squatting in England and France", in P. KENNA (ed.), *Contemporary housing issues in globalized world*, Farnham, Ashgate, 2014, (227) 242–243.

74 Debruyne et al. describe it as a form of Housing First from the grassroots level: P. DEBRUYNE, S. VANDEPUTTE and S. BEUNEN, "Uit de marges van de woonpraktijk: de strijd voor het recht op wonen in de stad Gent", *Ruimte en Maatschappij* 2014, vol. 5, (1) 35–36.

75 SCHWITTERS (n 4) 10; DEBRUYNE (n 74) 17.

76 Squatting is a violation of one's right to property. The owner can therefore make a claim for the eviction of the squatters. It is possible to claim compensation for damages on the basis of art. 1382 Civil Code as well. Property is also protected by penal law, but its application is dependent upon whether parts of the property have been destroyed or damaged (art. 521, 534bis-ter and 545–546 Penal Code). Several proposals have over the years been made to make squatting itself a violation of penal law; K. DE GREVE, "Gekraakt leven – processuele actiemogelijkheden in het burgerlijk procesrecht", *Huur* 2014, no. 1, 7–20; It might be problematic, though, in accordance with the ECHR to develop legislation that enables evictions without a preceding judicial decision: T. VANDROMME, "Het kraken van panden bekeken vanuit de grondrechten, het strafrecht en het burgerlijk recht (inclusief het procesrecht)", *RW* 2014–15, no. 35, (1363) 1369–1374.

77 ECtHR 15 October 2013, Ceesay Ceesay/Spain; ECtHR 6 February 2012, A.M.B/ Spain; ECtHR 21 June 2011, no.48833/07, Orlic/Croatia; ECtHR 12 October 2010 (adm. dec.), no. 23516/08, Société Cofinfo/France.

78 E.g. Peace Court Zomergem 9 November 2012, no. 12A542, *Huur* 2013, no. 3, 153; Peace Court Waver 2 December 2010, *T.Vred.* 2012, no. 9–10, 463, note K. DE GREVE;

provide them with a justification for their actions.[79] At most, the right to housing will have a softening or corrective effect with regard to the application of other legislation. It can, for example, justify the postponement of an eviction in the middle of winter.

D. Other Influences

1) Knowledge of Law – Quality of Legislation

One of the reasons for a right not being effective is simply that people do not or insufficiently apply it because it is (reasonably) unknown. Research has repeatedly shown that tenants' knowledge of basic tenancy law is limited.[80] We have already alluded to this problem with regard to the mandatory EPC certificate. Another example is the scenario of a necessary rehousing due to serious quality defects. In that case, the Flemish Housing Code enables the tenant to claim the repayment of moving expenses and even paid rent, but since many tenants are not aware of this option, such claims are only made sporadically.[81]

This lack of knowledge is not just confined to not being aware of the existence of a certain rule. It can also relate to the lack of knowledge as to when a factual situation can warrant the application of legislation. The Flemish Housing Research of 2013 illustrates that housing occupants severely overrate the objective quality of their dwelling. While home screening revealed that 47 percent of private tenants lived in dwellings of insufficient quality, 80 percent of those people rated them as (reasonably) good.[82] In other words, tenants often do not realize that they are in a justified position to stand up for their rights. In our opinion, this scenario is just as much a question of access to justice. A housing quality deficiency might seem less problematic when a tenant does not notice or mind it, but considering that electric defects and damp problems are often recurring problems in dwellings of insufficient quality, the health and safety of that person could be in danger.

Peace Court Gent (2) 5 May 2003, no. 435/2003, *Juristenkrant* 2003, no. 79, 13 (reproduction E. BREMS); Peace Court Gent 26 December 2011, *TGR* 2012, 171.

79 E. BREMS, "Geen recht op kraken", *Juristenkrant* 2003, no. 79, 13.

80 J. VAN HOUTTE, W. VAN WAMBEKE and E. DELANOEIJE, *Rechtshulp en rechtsinformatie*, Brussel, Federale Diensten voor Wetenschappelijke, Technische en Culturele Aangelegenheden, 1995; I. PANNECOUCKE, P. DE DECKER and L. GOOSSENS, Onderzoek naar de mogelijkheden voor de integratie van de particuliere huurmarkt in het Vlaams woonbeleid, Antwerpen, OASeS, 2003, 147–149.

81 E.g. Antwerpen (12th Chamber) 23 June 2010, *Huur* 2010, no. 4, 193; T. VANDROMME, *Woningkwaliteitsbewaking in het Vlaamse Gewest*, Mechelen, Kluwer 2008, 73–74.

82 WINTERS (n 35) 52 and 58.

Generally speaking, this lack of knowledge is an element of the aforementioned underdog position of the tenant. A lack of knowledge, however, can also stem from the complexity of legislation itself. In contrast to the other influences discussed in this chapter, this one then becomes more of a top-down influence on an effective right to housing. Difficult wording and complex terminology may indeed hinder a correct and consistent application of legal measures.[83]

The complexity of legislation as an influence on its appropriate or full-fledged application is obviously not limited to the applied terminology. Let us, for example, take a look at the legal possibilities for Flemish tenants of dwellings with severe quality issues. If a dwelling does not meet the elementary conditions of safety, health and habitability, article 2, §1, 5° of the Housing Rent Act offers the tenant the choice between the execution of the necessary renovation works and the cancellation of the agreement.[84] When the tenant chooses the former option, the judge can allow a reduced rental price in anticipation of the execution of the renovation works. Either way, we are talking about a contractual sanction.

The similar housing safety, health and quality norms of article 5 of the Flemish Housing Code broaden the possibilities for tenants to protect their rights. Article 5 enables them to start an administrative procedure to have the dwelling declared unfit or uninhabitable. The regional quality norms also provide a penal law procedure to properly deal with and sanction the most persistent landlords. Considering once again the underdog position that tenants might occupy in court and the barriers that weaker groups in society experience which hinder their court journey, there is one obvious advantage to the administrative procedure for the ordinary tenant. In order to rectify housing quality deficiencies, the first step is not necessarily to take one's landlord to court, while at the same time the procedure still foresees that these tenants will be heard.

While there might be several options to draw the attention of one's landlord to his responsibilities as a landlord, this does not automatically mean that tenants know of these possibilities in general, let alone know what the consequences of each procedure are. The difference between the various procedures does, however, matter quite a lot for the everyday life of the tenant. As mentioned earlier, tenants have a choice between the execution of the necessary renovation works and the cancellation of the agreement in case of a breach of the federal Housing Rent Act. The civil law consequences, on the other hand, of an unsuitable or uninhabitable dwelling according to the Flemish housing quality norms are quite different. Considering their connection to the general interest, they are regarded as norms of public order and thus

83 NIEMEIJER (n 68) 52; V. AUBERT, "Enkele sociale functies van wetgeving", in J. GRIFFITHS (ed.), *De sociale werking van recht*, Nijmegen, Ars Aequi, 1996, (113) 121–124.

84 See also art. 1184 Civil Code.

concern a condition of validity for the rent agreement. In case of a breach of these norms, the absolute nullity of the contract theoretically follows.[85] The tenant is then not given the choice presented by the federal regulations (i.e. either execution of renovation works or annulment of the agreement), thereby possibly rendering the outcome as not the most preferable one for either tenant (in particular the low-income tenant) or landlord.[86] Fortunately, both the jurisprudence[87] and part of the legal doctrine[88] show tendencies to question the adequacy of this sanctioning system.

2) Cost–Benefit Analysis

The extent to which a piece of legislation is considered effective is also strongly connected to the question why people obey these rules. First, legislation often leans towards the (moral) convictions and habits of persons.[89] It might also be the other way around, though. A certain kind of conduct might become a habit when the relevant law is backed by threats of force for long enough.[90] Consequently, sanctions are also recognized as aspects that influence effectiveness. It would be more accurate to speak of the perception of risk, since the impact of weak or rarely carried out sanctions will be limited.[91]

Take, for example, the position of slumlords. Although the Belgian penal code ordains considerable punishments (six months to three years' detention and a fine between €500 and €25,000), the severity of those sanctions will only influence the effectiveness of law when the perpetrator believes that there is a reasonable risk that he will be caught. And here, the chances of getting caught do not necessarily outweigh the benefits. Again, the unequal relationship between the two renting parties, discussed earlier, has its impact, with the tenant being more dependent upon the landlord than the other way around.

85 B. HUBEAU and D. VERMEIR, *Regionalisering van de federale huurwetgeving*, Leuven, Steunpunt Wonen, 2013, 18–20.

86 M. DAMBRE, "Nietigheid huurcontract bij inbreuk op kwaliteitsnormen: mogelijk, wenselijk en wat zijn de gevolgen?", *TBO* 2012, no. 6, (251) 253–255: according to Dambre, the federal legislator has implicitly acknowledged that the nullity sanction can be inappropriate. By including a reference to the regional quality norms in art. 2 Housing Rent Act (Law 25 April 2007 concerning various provisions (IV), *BS* 8 May 2007), he claims that the nullity sanction should not be applied by a judge.

87 E.g. Peace Court Mol 17 September 2002, *T. Vred.* 2004, no. 1–2, 48, note M. DAMBRE; Court of First Instance Leuven (5th Chamber) 19 January 2011, *T. Vred.* 2012, no. 3–4, 187.

88 E.g. P. DE SMEDT, B. HUBEAU and E. JANSSENS, *Omzien in verwondering. Terugblik op tien jaar Vlaamse wooncode,* Brugge, Die Keure, 2007; M. DAMBRE and B. HUBEAU, *Woninghuur*, Antwerpen, Kluwer, 2002.

89 SUMNER (n 9) 77; SCHWITTERS (n 4) 82–83; KIDDER (n 3) 121–122.

90 L.M. FRIEDMAN, *The legal system. A social science perspective*, New York, Russell Sage Foundation, 1975, 124.

91 Ibid., 82–83.

Somewhat paradoxically, one of the reasons for this low perception of risk is indirectly mentioned in the relevant provision of the penal code itself. It describes a slumlord as "he who takes advantage of the vulnerable state in which a person is because of his illegal or precarious administrative status, his precarious social situation".[92] The vulnerability of the victims will frequently prevent them from taking steps against these slumlords.

On a positive note,however, figures illustrate that over the last couple of years slumlords have been convicted with more fines and more money has been collected as a consequence. In 2014 and 2015 more than ten times the amount of non-compliance penalties was collected in comparison with a couple of years earlier. These fines serve as a compulsion to repair and renovate the concerned dwelling.

As illustrated, the cost–benefit analysis to abide by a rule definitely influences compliance with law. Yet personal interest is not only an incentive to obey or infringe the law;[93] it can also render a person's behavior to be in compliance with the law without his behavior actually being a direct response to this law.[94] From the point of view of the legislator, self-interest can also be used as a factor to try to enhance the effectiveness of law. We think, for example, of financial compensations such as renovation premiums or the aforementioned system of social rental agencies. The latter is beneficial to the realization of the right to housing and at the same time invites owners to engage themselves for reasons of personal interest. It ensures that a tenant in housing needs a qualitatively sound dwelling against a reasonable rental price, while the private landlord who has signed a contract with an agency will be given certainty about the payment of the rental price (even if the sublessee has not paid), continuity of the rent (even when the dwelling is not sublet) and control over the maintenance of the dwelling in return.[95] Interviews with the owners have proven that these positive effects are definitely acknowledged and appreciated. They find it important not to be confronted with the burdens of a private rent and that is exactly what the social rental agencies has to offer them.[96, 97]

92 Art. 433 decies Penal Code.

93 FRIEDMAN (n 90) 63.

94 KIDDER (n 3) 120.

95 P. DE DECKER, E. VLERICK and M. LE ROY, "Verhuurders beoordelen sociale verhuurkantoren", in P. DE DECKER, B. MEEUS, I. PANNECOUCKE, E. SCHILLEBEECKX, J. VERSTRAETE and E. VOLCKAERT, *Woonnood in Vlaanderen. Feiten/mythen/voorstellen*, Antwerpen, Garant, 2015, (313) 315–316.

96 Ibid., 319–322.

97 The non-profit interest group for owners called United Owners is also supportive of social rental agencies: K. D'HAUWERS, "Vijftien jaar Vlaamse Wooncode: standpunt van het AES (algemeen eigenaarssyndicaat)", in B. HUBEAU and T. VANDROMME (eds.), *Vijftien jaar Vlaamse Wooncode. Sisyphus (on)gelukkig?*, Brussel, Die Keure, 2013, (295) 299.

3. Conclusion

The many examples provided throughout this chapter have illustrated how law in action is influenced by a variety of issues and how it can impact the realization of one or more aspects of the right to housing. It is clear that these influences must be taken into account if we want law to be a successful mechanism for the realization of the right to housing.

We have seen how tenants are often on the losing end of housing law in action. While there is definitely reason to plea for more rights for tenants or stronger obligations for landlords, that is not what we should take away from this chapter in the first place. Quite the contrary since we have focused here on elements that have an impact on an effective realization of the right to housing, rather than on the lack of legislation. Moreover, implementing further and more rigorous obligations for landlords creates the risk of a vicious circle. It could discourage them from going to the private rental market with their property or decrease their willingness to stay in it,[98] which would then hurt private tenants once again. This scenario is indeed plausible and can therefore not be neglected. That is also why we have discussed self-interest as a possible factor to try to enhance the effectiveness of the right to housing. For example, making the provision of affordable or good-quality housing beneficial for both parties might enhance its chances of success.

Nevertheless, since this approach walks a fine line between luring owners to the private rental market on the one hand and realizing the right to housing on the other, it requires a careful assessment. Whereas the economic reality of the housing market demands to be taken seriously as yet another influence on the impact of housing legislation, it should not allow for an erosion of the protection of this fundamental right either. From a human rights perspective, the argument of a potentially shrinking private rental market creates a difficult bargaining position. And this problem only increases when there is a significant shortage of social housing. It is therefore commendable that a measure benefits all concerned parties. At the same time, however, this argument cannot result in a situation in which landlords create certain expectations with regard to either the extent of their obligations or compensations they should receive in return. Elementary housing quality requirements, for example, should be complied with irrespective of whether compensation is in place. In that regard, we could object to the financial compensation that a Flemish owner-landlord can qualify for if he renovates his rented dwelling after it has been declared unfit by the mayor.[99] Who knows how long this underachieving landlord has benefited from rental income while providing inadequate housing, only to be

98 Ibid. 295–300; J. COLAES, "Recente wijzigingen in de Huurwet 2006–2007", *Huur* 2007, (141) 156–157.

99 Article 18 juncto article 83 Flemish Housing Code.

awarded compensation when these severe shortcomings have eventually surfaced in order to retain the rental market availability of that dwelling.

In short, influences on the effectiveness of the right to housing are ample: top-down and bottom-up, driven by the interest of a landlord and the position of a tenant, and dictated by economic interests. Taking all this into account, to actually improve/strengthen the right to housing is as vital as it is difficult.

Bibliography

AUBERT, V., "Enkele sociale functies van wetgeving", in GRIFFITHS, J. (ed.), *De sociale werking van recht*, Nijmegen, Ars Aequi, 1996, 113–135.

BALL, J., "From individual to collective squat: economic, theory and the regulation of squatting in England and France", in KENNA, P. (ed.), *Contemporary housing issues in globalized world*, Farnham, Ashgate, 2014, 227–250.

BERNARD, N. and HUBEAU, B., "Poverty and fundamental social and economic rights: on the effectiveness of the right to decent housing", in DIERCKX, D., VAN HERCK, N. and VRANKEN, J. (eds.), *Poverty in Belgium*, Antwerpen, Acco, 2010, 195–206.

BERNARD, N., "Les lois anti-discrimination et le secteur du logement (privé et social)", in BAYART, C., SOTTIAUX, S. and VAN DROOGHENBROECK, S. (eds.), *De nieuwe federale antidiscriminatiewetten*, Brugge, Die Keure, 2008, 797–843.

BERNARD, N., "La loi du 25 avril 2007 et les nouvelles dispositions en matière de bail à loyer", *JT* 2007, 513–518.

BLACK, D., *The behaviour of law*, New York, Academic Press, 1976, 203 pages.

BOSCH, A., *Citizens enforcing the law: The legal and social space for citizen's arrest*, Antwerp, Maklu, 2013, 182 pages

BOSCH, M., CARNERO, M.A. and FARRÉ, L., "Information and discrimination in the rental housing market: evidence from a field experiment", *Regional Science and Urban Economics* 2010, vol. 40, 11–19.

BREMS, E., "Geen recht op kraken", *Juristenkrant* 2003, no. 79, 13.

CAUFFMAN, C., "Hervorming van de verzoeningspoging bij hoofdvorderingen inzake de huur van woningen", *RW* 2008–09, no. 6, 252–254.

COLAES, J., "Recente wijzigingen in de Huurwet 2006–2007", *Huur* 2007, (141) 156–157.

DAMBRE, M., "Nietigheid huurcontract bij inbreuk op kwaliteitsnormen: mogelijk, wenselijk en wat zijn de gevolgen?", *TBO* 2012, no. 6, 251–256.

DAMBRE, M. and HUBEAU, B., *Woninghuur*, Antwerpen, Kluwer, 2002, 563 pages.

DEBRUYNE, P., VANDEPUTTE, S. and BEUNEN, S., "Uit de marges van de woonpraktijk: de strijd voor het recht op wonen in de stad Gent", *Ruimte en Maatschappij* 2014, vol. 5, (1) 35–36.

DE DECKER, P., VLERICK, E. and LE ROY, M, "Verhuurders beoordelen sociale verhuurkantoren", in DE DECKER, P., MEEUS, B., PANNECOUCKE, I., SCHILLEBEECKX, E., VERSTRAETE, J. and VOLCKAERT, E., *Woonnood in Vlaanderen. Feiten/mythen/voorstellen*, Antwerpen, Garant, 2015, 313–325.

DE GREVE, K., "Gekraakt leven – processuele actiemogelijkheden in het burgerlijk procesrecht", *Huur* 2014, no. 1, 7–20.

DE SMEDT, P., "De Vlaamse Wooncode anno 2013: naar een (nog meer) integrale en slagkrachtige woonkwaliteitsbewaking?", in HUBEAU, B. and VANDROMME, T.

(eds.), *Vijftien jaar Vlaamse Wooncode. Sisyphus (on)gelukkig?*, Brugge, Die Keure, 2013, 41–90.

DE SMEDT, P., HUBEAU, B. and JANSSENS, E., *Omzien in verwondering. Terugblik op tien jaar Vlaamse wooncode*, Brugge, Die Keure, 2007.

DE SOTO, H., *The other path: the invisible revolution in the third world*, New York, Basic Books, 1989, 271 pages.

DE WITTE, J. and AENDENBOOM, I., "Discriminatie en haatmisdrijven: individuele, maar ook collectieve schade", *De orde van de dag* 2011, vol. 54, 49–54.

D'HAUWERS, K., "Vijftien jaar Vlaamse Wooncode: standpunt van het AES (algemeen eigenaarssyndicaat)", in HUBEAU, B. and VANDROMME, T. (eds.), *Vijftien jaar Vlaamse Wooncode. Sisyphus (on)gelukkig?*, Brussel, Die Keure, 2013, 295–300.

EHRLICH, E., *Fundamental principles of the sociology of law*, Cambridge, Harvard University Press, 1936, 493 pages.

EHRLICH, E., *Grundlegung der Soziologie des Rechts*, Berlin, Duncker & Humblot, 1913, 409 pages

EWICK, P., KAGAN, R.A. and SARAT, A., "Legacies of legal realism: social science, social policy and the law", in EWICK, P., KAGAN, R.A. and SARAT, A. (eds.), *Social science, social policy and the law*, New York, Russel Sage Foundation, 1999, (1) 6–7.

FEELEY, M.M., "The concept of laws in social science: a critique and notes on an expended view", *Law & Society Review* 1975, vol. 10, 497–523.

FITZPATRICK, S., BENGTSSON, B. and WATTS, B., "Rights to housing: reviewing the terrain and exploring a way forward", *Housing, Theory and Society* 2014, vol. 31, no. 4, 447–463.

FRIEDMAN, L.M., *The legal system. A social science perspective*, New York, Russell Sage Foundation, 1975, 338 pages.

GALANTER, M., "De duivel schijt altijd op de grote hoop. Bespiegelingen over de grenzen van rechtshervorming", in GRIFFITHS, J. and WEYERS, H. (eds.), *De sociale werking van recht*, Nijmegen, Ars Aequi, 2005.

GRIFFITHS, J., "De sociale werking van wetgeving", in GRIFFITHS, J. and WEYERS, H. (eds.), *De sociale werking van recht*, Nijmegen, Ars Aequi, 2005, 467–505.

HALPÉRIN, J.-L., "Law in books and law in action: the problem of legal change", *Maine Law Review* 2011, vol. 64, no. 1, 45–76.

HERTOGH, M., "Wat weten en vinden burgers van het recht", in HERTOGH, M. and WEIJERS, H. (eds.), *Het recht van onderop. Antwoorden uit de rechtssociologie*, Nijmegen, Ars Aequi, 2011, 287–300.

HERTOGH, M., "The living *Rechtsstaat*: a bottom-up approach to legal ideas and social reality", in VAN DER BURG, W. and TAEKEMA, S. (eds.), *The importance of ideals: debating their relevance in law, morality, and politics*, Brussel, P.I.E. Peter-Lang, 2004, 75–95.

HEYLEN, K., *Grote Woononderzoek 2013: Deel 5. De private huurmarkt: vraag- en aanbodzijde*, Leuven, Steunpunt Wonen, 2015, 40 pages.

HUBEAU, B. and VERMEIR, D., *Een evaluatie van het woninghuurrecht – Deel II. Bevindingen werkgroepen "Toegang, selectie en discriminatie", "Procedure en bemiddeling" en "Huurprijs", resultaten wegingsoefening en aanbevelingen expertencommissie*, Leuven, Steunpunt Wonen, 2015, 255 pages.

HUBEAU, B. and VERMEIR, D., *Regionalisering van de federale huurwetgeving*, Leuven, Steunpunt Wonen, 2013, 118 pages.

HUBEAU, B., "De sociale grondrechten na een decennium: hefboom of toekomstdroom in de uitsluiting van sociale uitsluiting", in VRANKEN, J., DE BOYSER, K.

and DIERCKX, D. (eds.), *Armoede en sociale uitsluiting Jaarboek 2003*, Leuven, Acco, 2004, 369–384.

HULS, N., *Actie en reactie. Een inleiding in de rechtssociologie*, Den Haag, Boom Juridische Uitgevers, 2008, 380 pages.

INSLEGERS, G., "Graag een volwaardig huurbeleid voor de private huurmarkt", in HUBEAU, B. and VANDROMME, T. (eds.), *Vijftien jaar Vlaamse Wooncode. Sisyphus (on)gelukkig?*, Brugge, Die Keure, 2013, (309) 312.

KIDDER, R.L., *Connecting law and society*, New Jersey, Prentice-Hall, 1983, 286 pages.

KUTCHINSKY, B., "The legal consciousness: a survey of research and opinion about law", in PODGORECKI, A., KAUPEN, W., VAN HOUTTE, J., VINCKE, P. and KUTCHINSKY, B. (eds.), *Knowledge and opinion about law*, London, Martin Robertson, 1973, 101–139.

LAUSTER, N. and EASTERBROOK, A., "No room for new families? A field experiment measuring rental discrimination against same-sex couples and single parents", *Social Problems* 2011, vol. 58, no. 3, 389–409.

LITTLEFIELD, N.O., "Eugen Ehrlich's fundamental principles of the sociology of law", *Maine Law Review* 1967, vol. 19, 1–27.

LOOPMANS, M. et al., "Onderzoek van de private huisvestingsmarkt in België in het kader van de Diversiteitsbarometer, in Interfederaal Gelijkekansencentrum (UNIA) (ed.), *Diversiteitsbarometer huisvesting*, Brussel, Interfederaal Gelijkekansencentrum, 2014, 134–245.

MOORE, S.F., "Recht en maatschappelijke verandering: de rol van het 'semi-autonoom social veld'", in GRIFFITHS, J.and WEYERS, H. (eds.), *De sociale werking van recht*, Nijmegen, Ars Aequi, 2005, 177–196.

MOORE, S.F., "Law and social change: the semi-autonomous social field as an appropriate subject of study", in *Law & Society Review* 1972, vol. 7, no. 1, 720–746.

NELKEN, D., "Law in action or living law? Back to the beginning in sociology of law", *Legal Studies* 1984, vol. 4, 157–174.

NIEMEIJER, B., "Wat leren wetsevaluaties ons over de effectiviteit van wetgeving?", in HERTOGH M. and WEIJERS, H. (eds.), *Het recht van onderop. Antwoorden uit de rechtssociologie*, Nijmegen, Ars Aequi, 2011, 41–61.

NIMAGA, S., "Pounding on Ehrlich. Again?", in HERTOGH, M. (ed.), *Living Law. Reconsidering Eugen Ehrlich*, Oxford, Hart Publishing, 2009, 157–175.

NOLF, J., "Over de helaasheid der huurders", *Juristenkrant* 2010, no. 201, 11.

PACHECO, N. and SALES, L., "From the recognition to the justiciability of housing rights: building the future", *International Journal of Land Law & Agricultural Science* 2011, no. 11, 34–53.

PANNECOUCKE, I., DE DECKER, P. and GOOSSENS, L., *Onderzoek naar de mogelijkheden voor de integratie van de particuliere huurmarkt in het Vlaams woonbeleid*, Antwerpen, OASeS, 2003, 293 pages.

PIETERSE, M., "Eating socioeconomic rights: the usefulness of rights talk in alleviating social hardship revisited", *Human Rights Quarterly* 2007, vol. 29, 796–822.

PODGORECKI, A., "Public opinion on law", in PODGORECKI, A., KAUPEN, W., VAN HOUTTE, J., VINCKE, P. and KUTCHINSKY, B. (eds.), *Knowledge and opinion about law*, London, Martin Robertson, 1973, 65–100.

POSTEMA, G.J., "Conformity, custom, and convergence: rethinking the efficacy of law", in KRAMER, M.H., GRANT, C., COLBURN, B. and HATZISTAVROU, A.

(eds.), *The legacy of H.L.A. Hart. Legal, political and moral philosophy*, Oxford, Oxford University Press, 2008, 45–65.

POUND, R., "Law in books and law in action", *American Law Review* 1910, vol. 44, no. 12, 12–36.

RIETIKER, D., "The principle of 'effectiveness' in the recent jurisprudence of the European Court of Human Rights: its different dimensions and its consistency with public international law – no need for the concept of treaty *sui generis*", *Nordic Journal of International Law* 2010, vol. 79, 245–277.

ROSCIGNO, V.J., KARAFIN, D.L. and TESTER, G., "The complexities and processes of racial housing discrimination", *Social Problems* 2009, vol. 56, no. 1, 49–69.

SAMYN, B., "De bewijslast. Rechtsleer getoetst aan tien jaar cassatierechtspraak", *P&B* 2010, 50–71.

SCHWITTERS, R.J.S., *Recht en samenleving in verandering*, Deventer, Kluwer, 2008, 305 pages.

SMAERS, G., "De strafbaarheid van het kraken van woningen naar Belgisch recht", *RW* 1986–87, 2193–2218.

SUMNER, W.G., *Folkways: a study of the sociological importance of usages, manners, customs, mores and morals*, Boston, Ginn and Company, 1906, 717 pages.

TAMANAHA, B.Z., "A vision of social-legal change: rescuing Ehrlich from 'living law'", *Law & Social Inquiry* 2011, vol. 36, no. 1, 297–318.

TERLOUW, A., "Draagt wetgeving bij aan gelijkheid?", in HERTOGH, M.and WEIJERS, H. (eds.), *Het recht van onderop. Antwoorden uit de rechtssociologie*, Nijmegen, Ars Aequi, 2011, 349–370.

TOMASIC, R., *The sociology of law*, London, Sage Publications, 1985, 275 pages.

VAN AEKEN, K., "Een rechtssociologische analyse van de juridisering van de samenleving", in HUBEAU, B., GIBENS, S., MERCELIS, S., PARMENTIER, S., PONSAERS, P., VAN AEKEN, K., VANDE WALLE, G. and VAN HOUTTE, J. (eds.), *Dialogen tussen recht en samenleving*, Leuven, Acco, 2012, 67–84.

VAN DEN BROECK, K. and HEYLEN, K., *Discriminatie en selectie op de private huurmarkt in België*, Leuven, HIVA, 2014, 91 pages.

VAN DER BRACHT, K. and VAN DE PUTTE, B., *Het not-in-my-property-syndroom (NIMPS). Etnische discriminatie*, Gent, Universiteit Gent, 2013, 20 pages.

VANDROMME, T., "Het kraken van panden bekeken vanuit de grondrechten, het strafrecht en het burgerlijk recht (inclusief het procesrecht)", *RW* 2014–15, no. 35, 1363–1378.

VANDROMME, T., *Woningkwaliteitsbewaking in het Vlaamse Gewest*, Mechelen, Kluwer, 2008, 97–103.

VAN HOUTTE, J., VAN WAMBEKE, W. and DELANOEIJE, E., *Rechtshulp en rechtsinformatie*, Brussel, Federale Diensten voor Wetenschappelijke, Technische en Culturele Aangelegenheden, 1995, 160 pages.

VAN KLINK, B., "Facts and norms: the unfinished debate between Eugen Ehrlich and Hans Kelsen", in HERTOGH, M. (ed.), *Living Law. Reconsidering Eugen Ehrlich*, Oxford, Hart Publishing, 2009, 127–156.

VAN LEUVEN, N., "De antidiscriminatiewet en de huurovereenkomst", in STIJNS, S. and WÉRY, P. (eds.), *Antidiscriminatiewet en contracten*, Brugge, Die Keure, 2006, 111–141.

VAUGHAN T.R., "The landlord-tenant relationship in low-income area", *Social Problems* 1968, vol. 16, no. 2, 208–218.

VERSTRAETE J., and DE DECKER, P., "Discriminatie van financieel kwetsbare huishoudens op de private huurmarkt in België", in DIERCKX, D., COENE, J. and RAEYMAECKERS, P. (eds.), *Armoede en sociale uitsluiting. Jaarboek 2014*, Leuven, Acco, 2014, 110–126.

VOLCKAERT, E., "De weerslag van de anti-discriminatiewetgeving op het afsluiten van een huurovereenkomst", *Huur* 2008, vol. 3, 107–113.

WÄLDE, T.W., "Non-conventional views on effectiveness: the holy grail of modern international lawyers: the new paradigm? A chimera? Or a brave new world in the global economy?", *Austrian Review of International & European Law* 1999, vol. 4, 164–203.

WINTERS, S. et al., *Wonen in Vlaanderen anno 2013. De bevindingen uit het Grote Woononderzoek 2013 gebundeld*, Antwerpen, Garant, 2015, 97 pages.

ZIV, L., "Bronnen van verbod op discriminatie bij particuliere huur", in BRULEZ, P. and VERBEKE, A.-L. (eds.), *Knelpunten huurrecht: tien perspectieven*, Antwerpen, Intersentia, 2012, 253–268.

Part II

European Jurisprudence

3 The Impact of European Case Law on the Protection of (the Right to) Housing

In contrast to Part I, Parts II and III embark upon an investigation into the legal possibilities to strengthen and enforce the obligations of the state with regard to the right to housing. First, we look at what European jurisprudence is able to provide us with. For many, the word "Europe" evokes thoughts of a distant and unpopular bureaucracy. But the European (quasi-)judicial institutions in Strasbourg and even Luxembourg have clearly shown their potential as a gateway for social justice, at the very least more so than sometimes publicly perceived. It has certainly been said that Europe has significant but regularly overlooked possibilities for the right to housing and its advocates.[1] What is European jurisprudence really able to contribute with regard to imposing obligations on or at least incentivizing states to protect and fully realize the right to adequate housing? This part will provide a closer look and aims to draw connections between the case law of the three main actors at the same time: the European Court of Human Rights (ECtHR), the European Committee of Social Rights (ECSR) and to a lesser extent the European Court of Justice (ECJ).

1. Access to European Courts

A. Burdens of Admissibility

Before we plunge into the housing-related case law, it is important to mention a couple of early disclaimers. In contrast to, for example, the right to free speech, a social right like the right to housing obviously carries more weight for the weaker and marginalized persons and groups in society. Regardless of whether or not complaints before the ECtHR inspired by or linked to the right to housing can be successful, it is first and foremost necessary that those people are able to find their way to these human rights institutions. For the average

1 E.g. P. KENNA and M. JORDAN, "Housing rights in Europe: the Council of Europe leads the way", in P. KENNA (ed.), *Contemporary housing issues in globalized world*, Farnham, Ashgate, 2014, (115) 140.

tenant, however, the Council of Europe is probably as far away removed from molded bathrooms, undersized dwellings, imminent evictions and other everyday problems as it possibly could be. Even though it has been discussed more extensively earlier in this research, it feels suitable to remind the reader of the notion of one-shotters.[2] Considering the admissibility criteria that all domestic remedies (save any possible unavailable, inadequate or ineffective ones[3]) have to be exhausted, they are unlikely to litigate all the way to Europe.[4] Procedural burdens like these also make it more expensive and time-consuming to lodge a complaint. Who could blame a social tenant for spending his/her time and money on finding a suitable new home instead of contesting eviction procedures in Strasbourg? Whatever the plausibility of a successful outcome in such a case, which will be illustrated later in the chapter, we should not disregard or underestimate how these considerations have an impact on the possible role of the ECtHR for the right to housing.[5]

Unlike the European Court of Human Rights, the conditions that have to be met before a complaint will be considered admissible by the European Committee of Social Rights are much more lenient.[6] While undeniably also better placed to assess problems concerning the right to housing (under article 31 Revised European Social Charter (RESC)), the ECSR only treats collective complaints. For the purposes of this topic, the relevant claimants are then international non-governmental organizations with a consultative status at the Council of Europe and which have been registered on a list established for this purpose by the Governmental Committee.[7] State parties to the Charter can also accept other, national non-governmental organizations within their jurisdiction to formulate complaints, as long as they have particular competence

2 M. GALANTER, "Why the 'Haves' Come Out Ahead: Speculations on the Limits of Legal Change", *Law and Society Review* 1974, vol. 9, no. 1, 95–160.

3 ECtHR 6 September 1996, no. 21893/93, Akdivar/Turkey, par. 67.

4 M. SCHEININ, "Access to justice before international human rights bodies", in F. FRANCIONI (ed.), *Access to justice as a human right*, New York, Oxford University Press, 2007, 135–152.

5 For more on access to justice and the European Court of Human Rights, see: C. FORDER, "The right to legal aid according to the European Court of Human Rights: a study of the rights of undocumented persons", in B. HUBEAU and A. TERLOUW (eds.), *Legal aid in the Low Countries*, Antwerpen, Intersentia, 2014, (209) 218–225.

6 R. CHURCHILL and U. KHALIQ, "Violations of Economic, Social and Cultural Rights: The Current Use and Future Potential of the Collective Complaints Mechanism of the European Social Charter", in M.A. BADERIN and R. McCORQUODALE (eds.), *Economic, Social and Cultural Rights in Action*, Oxford University Press, Oxford, 2007, (195) 211–221; ECSR 1 July 2013 (adm. dec.), no. 86/2012 and 90/2013, FEANTSA/ The Netherlands and Conference of European Churches/The Netherlands.

7 Art. 1 Add. Prot. to the European Social Charter providing for a system of collective complaints: national and international organizations of employers and trade unions are, of course, less relevant claimants in the context of the right to housing.

in the matters governed in the Charter.[8] Thus far, however, Finland is the only signatory state to authorize national NGOs.

The impossibility for a person to lodge an individual complaint to the Committee to respond to situations of individual hardship and deprivation is obviously another disadvantage in seeking to realize one's rights.[9] That is also why there will always remain a certain attraction to the ECtHR, even though the protection of social rights will be restricted to an indirect application (infra).[10] That does not lead to the conclusion that the collective complaints mechanism is not useful; quite the contrary. It partly provides an answer to the aforementioned problem of accessibility due to the complexity of procedures. NGOs do have the power, knowledge and means (even though the latter should not be overestimated) to enforce rights, when an individual might be unable to litigate. They can address problems of victims without having to be victims themselves, since there is no such requirement. A group also has more power than an individual.[11] In the words of Langford, "collective action rights can allow marginalized groups to emerge as repeat-action litigation players rather than one-shotters; thus leveling the litigation playing field against well-organized government and corporate legal teams".[12] Additionally, collective complaints often have a preventive nature. Negative effects of legislation do not have to manifest themselves before a complaint can be made, which simplifies the assessment of progressive realization of this fundamental right.[13]

A glaring limitation to a widespread improvement of the right to housing through the recommendations of this mechanism is the number of state parties that have accepted the complaints procedure. Regrettably, only 15 of the 43 states that have ratified the RESC have done so thus far.[14] Additionally,

8 Art. 2 Add. Prot. to the European Social Charter providing for a system of collective complaints.

9 V. MANTOUVALOU and P. VOYATZIS, "The Council of Europe and the protection of human rights: a system in need of reform", in S. JOSEPH and A. McBETH (eds.), *Research Handbook on International Human Rights Law*, Cheltenham, Edward Elgar Publishing, 2010, (326) 349; H. CULLEN, "The collective complaints of the European Social Charter: interpretative methods of the European Committee of Social Rights", *HRLR* 2009, vol. 9, no. 1, (61) 66.

10 E. BREMS, "Indirect protection of social rights by the European Court of Human Rights", in D. BARAK-EREZ and A. GROSS (eds.), *Exploring social rights. Between theory and practice*, Portland, Hart Publishing, 2007, (135) 164.

11 R. BRILLAT, "De collectieve klachtenprocedure van het Europese Sociale Handvest en de strijd tegen armoede", in Steunpunt tot Bestrijding van Armoede, Bestaansonzekerheid en Sociale Uitsluiting, *Armoede-Waardigheid-Mensenrechten*, Brussel, 2008, (74) 76.

12 M. LANGFORD, "Judicial review in national courts: recognition and responsiveness", in E. RIEDEL, G. GIACCA and C. GOLAY (eds.), *Economic, social and cultural rights: Contemporary issues and challenges*, Oxford, Oxford University Press, 2014, (417) 424–425.

13 BRILLAT (n 11) 76.

14 Belgium, Bulgaria, Cyprus, Czech Republic, Finland, France, Greece, Ireland, Italy, Netherlands, Norway, Portugal, Slovenia and Sweden.

a mere nine state parties have accepted all paragraphs of article 31 on the right to adequate housing, another four at least one of its paragraphs.[15] The "à la carte" nature of the Charter combined with the fact that the right to housing is not one of the nine core rights of the RESC (of which six have to be ratified) is obviously an important factor. But even when taking this fact into account, article 31 is still the provision with the lowest acceptance rate. We will see further in the text how this problem is or can be circumvented with the application of article 16 RESC.

B. Twelfth Additional Protocol to the ECHR

In the same vein, the ratification of the Twelfth Additional Protocol to the European Convention of Human Rights could potentially also improve access to the ECtHR in the context of social rights.[16] Under this Protocol, it is no longer necessary to link a discrimination claim (article 14) with a substantive article of the ECHR. Theoretically, with the same non-exhaustive list of discrimination grounds as article 14,[17] this could open up the potential to combat social exclusion.[18] Against that background, it has been said that the *ratione materiae* of the Protocol could open up to fundamental social rights to which state parties are bound by other international instruments, such as the European Social Charter.[19] This would be hinted at by the lack of specification that the enjoyment of "any right set forth by law" should be secured without discrimination. The explanatory report on the text of the Protocol does indeed mention specifically that "law" may also cover international law.[20] The Court could obviously not examine a state's compliance

15 Andorra, Finland, France, Italy, Latvia, Lithuania, Netherlands, Norway, Portugal, Slovenia, Sweden, Turkey, Ukraine.

16 Protocol No. 12 to the Convention for the Protection of Human Rights and Fundamental Freedoms.

17 Art. 14 ECHR and art. 1 Protocol No. 12 to the Convention for the Protection of Human Rights and Fundamental Freedoms: "The enjoyment of any right set forth by law shall be secured without discrimination on any ground such as sex, race, colour, language, religion, political or other opinion, national or social origin, association with a national minority, property, birth or other status."

18 BREMS (n 10) 162–163; N. BERNARD, "Pas d'expulsion de logement sans contrôle juridictionnel – le droit au logement et la Cour Européenne des Droits de l'Homme", *RTDH* 2009, no. 79, (527) 550–551.

19 F. SUDRE, "La protection des droits sociaux par la Cour Européenne des Droits de l'Homme: un exercice de 'jurisprudence fiction'?", *RTDH* 2003, no. 55, (756) 770; F. TULKENS and S. VAN DROOGHENBROECK, "Le droit au logement dans la Convention Européenne des Droits de l'Homme. Bilan et perspectives", in N. BERNARD and C. MERTENS (eds.), *Le logement dans sa multidimensionalité. Une grande cause régionale*, Ministère de la Région wallonne, 2005, (311) 323.

20 Draft Explanatory Report to Protocol No. 12 to the Convention for the Protection of Human Rights and Fundamental Freedoms, 14 January 2000, CM(2000)53 Addendum, par. 29.

with the RESC, but it should be able to assess whether the enjoyment of a ratified provision of the European Social Charter is or is not subject to discrimination.[21] Hypothetically, the ratification of this Protocol could therefore further introduce social rights and the right to housing into the Court's jurisprudence.

Ten years after the entry into force of Protocol No. 12, however, less than half of the state parties have ratified the Protocol. The reasonably low success rate of the Protocol probably has to do with the fact that a decision regarding the non-discriminative nature of social rights can be very politically or ideologically loaded. State parties might therefore find a national court to be better placed to consider the societal context.[22] In spite of this argument, the experience the European Court has built up from repeatedly assessing the proportionality question suggests that this is not too great a task. The margin of appreciation lies at the core of a majority of its case law, including with regard to article 14. Even more so, this margin of appreciation enables the Court to be quite reticent in cases based on the Twelfth Protocol. Still, however, the case law that has applied the Protocol thus far does not appear to open up the content of the Convention in any tangible way and therefore does not provide an extra impetus to the protection of socio-economic rights.

2. Lessons from European Jurisprudence: Housing Rights Protection on Three Levels

A. *Acknowledgment of the Right to Housing by the ECtHR*

Despite its focus on civil and political rights, the European Court of Human Rights has over the years shone its light on many issues related to social and economic rights. In 1979, it stated in the *Airey* case that the European Convention on Human Rights is a "living instrument", which should be interpreted "in the light of present-day conditions" (supra, par. 92). "Whilst the Convention sets forth what are essentially civil and political rights, many of them have implications of a social or economic nature."[23] Former President of the Court, Luzius Wildhaber, has even stated that this evolutionary interpretation is fundamental to the effectiveness of the Convention system and

21 SUDRE (n 19) 775.

22 G. GOEDERTIER, "Het Twaalfde Protocol E.V.R.M.: het non-discriminatiebeginsel losgekoppeld van de in het E.V.R.M. opgenomen rechten en vrijheden", *Jaarboek Mensenrechten* 2000–2001, (71) 88.

23 ECtHR 9 October 1979, no. 6289/73, Airey/Ireland, par. 26; C. WARBRICK, "Economic and social interests and the European Convention on Human Rights", in M.A. BADERIN and R. McCORQUODALE (eds.), *Economic, Social and Cultural Rights in Action*, Oxford, Oxford University Press, 2007, (241) 245–246; I. LEIJTEN, "Meergelaagdheid en ondeelbare mensenrechten", *TBP* 2013, no. 2–3, (95) 98.

the Court's authority.[24] While it is legally accurate to say that the Convention is permeable to social rights[25] and certain aspects of socio-economic rights have been (indirectly) protected, it is important not to confuse the socio-economic implications of an effective protection of the Convention rights with the existence of a social right in the ECHR.[26] Take, for example, cases in which homosexual partners are granted the same protection as other partners with regard to housing.[27] Rather than a housing case, this is a discrimination case. A considerable bulk of the housing-related case law follows a similar pattern, dealing with housing purely factually rather than legally. In the words of Ida Elisabeth Koch, "he who is 'only' hungry, homeless or sick will go in vain to the ECtHR".[28] In spite of that the Convention has proven to be more capable than originally envisioned in protecting housing rights-related issues through a range of Convention rights.[29]

In order to avoid any misunderstanding, it is worth recalling that the Court has stressed repeatedly that it does not recognize a right to housing. In *Balakin*, the Court framed its words from the *Airey* case in a housing context and stated:

> [E]ven though there is no watertight division separating the sphere of social and economic rights from the field covered by the Convention, the Court considers that [. . .] [the right to housing] clearly belongs to the realm of socio-economic rights, which is not covered by the Convention.[30]

Much earlier, the then European Commission on Human Rights stated that while states must respect an individual's home in accordance with article 8 of the Convention, this provision "in no way imposes on a state a positive obligation to provide a home".[31] It has been said that the Convention rights

24 L. WILDHABER, "European Court of Human Rights", *C.Y.I.L.* 2002, vol. 40, (309) 310.
25 F. SUDRE, "La perméabilité de la Convention européenne des droits de l'homme aux droits sociaux", *Pouvoir et liberté. Études offertes à J. Mourgeon,* Brussel, Bruylant, 1998, 46.
26 O. DE SCHUTTER, "The protection of social rights by the European Court of Human Rights", in P. VAN DER AUWERAERT, T. DE PELSMAEKER, J. SARKIN and J. VANDE LANOTTE (eds.), *Social, economic and cultural rights. An appraisal of current European and international developments*, Antwerpen, Maklu, 2002, (207) 215.
27 ECtHR 24 July 2003, no. 40016/98, Karner/Austria; ECtHR 2 March 2010, no. 13102/02, Kozak/Poland; C.U. SCHMID and J.R. DINSE, *Towards a common core of residential tenancy law in Europe? The impact of the European Court of Human Rights on tenancy law*, 2013, 11–13.
28 I.E. KOCH, "The European Convention on Human Rights and the protection of socio-economic demands", in A. MIHR and M. GIBNEY (eds.), *The SAGE Handbook of Human Rights. Volume 2*, Los Angeles, SAGE, 2014, (673) 673.
29 S. LECKIE, "The human right to adequate housing", in A. EIDE, C. KRAUSE and A. ROSAS (eds.), *Economic, social and cultural rights*, Dordrecht, Martinus Nijhoff Publishers, 2001, (149) 159.
30 ECtHR 4 July 2013, no. 21788/06, Balakin/Russia, par. 33.
31 ECHR 21 May 1975 (adm. dec.), no. 4560/70.

do not guarantee housing "of a particular standard or at all",[32] and the Court's jurisprudence does not appear to acknowledge such a right either.[33]

State parties have been convicted for not providing social housing, but only when this had first been ordered by a national judge. Their failure to enforce domestic judgments within a reasonable time frame first and foremost brings those cases within the sphere of the right to a fair trial of article 6 and access to justice of article 13 of the Convention.[34] On this basis, the Court has decided that while a delay can be justified in certain circumstances, a lack of funds or housing cannot be cited as an acceptable excuse for not honoring a judgment.[35] This has been confirmed in a 2015 case against France, where for the first time the *Droit au Logement Opposable* was the subject of jurisprudence by the European Court of Human Rights.[36] Since the social housing ordered by the national judge had not been provided within a reasonable period of time, the Court found a violation of article 6 of the Convention. In other words, this also means that when a right to housing is made judicially enforceable at the national level, it is evidently also protected by the ECHR.

In contrast to a judicial decision, however, a mere promise of social housing by the administrative authorities, as was the case in *Balakin*, has not been deemed sufficient for a violation of the Convention rights, because such an issue was found to directly pertain to the right to housing.[37] The earlier citation of this judgment must also be understood within that context.

On this basis it seems possible to argue that the ECtHR imposes only procedural obligations. Yet the Court has also acknowledged housing as a protectable interest, not least in the context of article 8 of the Convention. This provision proclaims a right to respect private and family life including the home.[38] The peaceful enjoyment of the home has frequently been balanced against other interests of the community (often of an economic nature)[39] – for example, in cases of pollution[40] and noise disturbances.[41] But a home can also be protected autonomously on the basis of article 8 ECHR. In the

32 ECtHR 18 November 2003, no. 48758/99, Volkova/Russia.

33 ECtHR 18 January 2001, no. 27238/95, Chapman/United Kingdom, par. 99.

34 ECtHR 28 July 2009, no. 467/07, 22539/05, 17911/08 and 13136/07, Olaru and others/Moldova; ECtHR 1 July 2014, no. 29920/05 et al., Gerasimov and others/Russia; ECtHR 30 June 2005, no. 11931/03, Teteriny/Russia.

35 ECtHR 30 June 2005, no. 11931/03, Teteriny/Russia, par. 41.

36 ECtHR 9 April 2015, no. 65829/12, Tchokontio Happi/France.

37 ECtHR 4 July 2013, no. 21788/06, Balakin/Russia.

38 KOCH (n 28) 677–678.

39 P. KENNA, "Housing rights: positive duties and enforceable rights at the European Court of Human Rights", *E.H.R.L.R.* 2008, no. 2, (193) 201.

40 ECtHR 9 June 2005, no. 55723/00, Fadeyeva/Russia; ECtHR 9 December 1994, no. 16798/90, Lopez-Ostra/Spain; ECtHR 19 February 1998, no. 116/1996/735/932, Guerra and others/Italy.

41 ECtHR 8 July 2003, no. 36022/97, Hatton and others/United Kingdom; ECtHR 16 November 2004, no. 4143/02, Moreno Gómez/Spain.

Moldovan case, for example, the Court was presented with the destruction of 18 Roma houses, to which state officials had allegedly contributed. The ECtHR concluded that the applicants could no longer enjoy the use of their homes and had to live in poor, cramped conditions. It held that article 8 contains positive obligations inherent to an effective respect for private or family life and the home.[42] Considering the applicants' living conditions for the last ten years and the way they were dealt with by authorities, the Court also decided on a violation of article 3 of the Convention (inhuman or degrading treatment).[43]

In *Marzari*, the Court further elaborated on a state party's positive obligations under article 8 ECHR by arguing that while there is no guarantee "to have one's housing problems solved by the authorities, a refusal to provide assistance in this respect to an individual suffering from a severe disease might in certain circumstances raise an issue under article 8 of the Convention because of the impact on the private life of the individual".[44] Yet the closest the Court has come to recognizing a right to housing was probably in the *Yordanova* case. Not only did it consider a home to be a protectable interest in the context of article 8 ECHR and found a lack of alternative housing in case of eviction to be a weighty argument (as it has done on several occasions),[45] the Court added that for particularly vulnerable individuals, exceptional circumstances can even lead to an obligation to secure shelter.[46] Even here, however, the Court preceded this statement by repeating earlier jurisprudence that there is no right to be provided with a home and that positive obligations to house the homeless must be limited.[47]

B. Housing Rights in EU (Case) Law

While not an acknowledged right in the context of the European Convention on Human Rights, we have seen that housing has become a protectable interest. With an explicit right to housing in the Revised European Social

42 ECtHR 12 July 2005, no. 41138/98 and 64320/01, Moldovan and others/Romania, par. 93.

43 Ibid., par.110; A. BUYSE, "Destruction of housing and discrimination against Roma – developments at the ECtHR", *Housing and ESC Rights Law Quarterly* 2006, vol. 3, no. 1, (5) 5–6.

44 ECtHR 4 May 1999 (adm. dec.), no. 36448/97, Marzari/Italy; compare with ECtHR 26 June 2001 (adm. dec.), no. 39022/97, O'Rourke/United Kingdom.

45 E.g. ECtHR 9 October 2007, no. 7205/02, Stanková/Russia, par. 60; ECtHR 6 December 2011, no. 7097/10, Gladysheva/Russia, par. 96; ECtHR 24 May 2007, no. 32718/02, Tuleshov/Russia, par. 53.

46 ECtHR 24 April 2012, no. 25446/06, Yordanova and others/Bulgaria, par. 130.

47 A. REMICHE, "Yordanova and Others v. Bulgaria: the influence of the social right to adequate housing on the interpretation of the civil right to respect for one's home", *H.R.L.R.* 2012, vol. 12, no. 4, (787) 798.

Charter and a right to housing assistance (note: not a right to housing *in se*[48, 49]) to ensure a decent existence for all those who lack sufficient resources in the EU Charter of Fundamental Rights (article 34, § 3),[50] European housing-related case law has the opportunity to develop on three levels.

As with the jurisprudence of the ECtHR, however, the European Court of Justice provides only indirect protection to housing. Most of this housing-related case law is primarily concerned with the equal treatment of EU citizens and the free movement of persons, services and capital.[51] The *Kamberaj* case, the only occasion on which the ECJ has actually applied article 34, § 3 of the EU Charter thus far, also revolves around equal treatment. In this case an Albanian citizen with a permanent residence permit in Italy had not been granted the same rental subsidy as other EU citizens.[52] Housing rights concerns and the EU Charter did not play a decisive role in the judgment. Since the Court was not asked to set out the exact parameters for article 34, § 3 of the EU Charter in this particular case, it is difficult to say anything definitive about the significance of the provision on the basis of this judgment. Interestingly, however, article 34, § 3 has been said to draw on the corresponding articles (article 13, 30 and 31) of the European Social Charter.[53] Perhaps this might over time convince the European Court of Justice to look at the argumentation of the ECSR.

While the potential of the right to housing in the EU Charter of Fundamental Rights is definitely underexplored, there is also a certain limit to it. Article 51 of the Charter proclaims that the EU institutions as well as the member states implementing EU law have to recognize and respect the Charter rights, but the EU is not competent to enact rules on the right to housing. Accordingly, national law does not contain any housing rights based on EU law and domestic

48 A.P. VAN DER MEI, "The justiciability of social rights in the European Union", in F. COOMANS (ed.), *Justiciability of economic and social rights*, Antwerp, Intersentia, 2006, (389) 404.

49 In a Report on Housing and Regional Policy of 28 March 2007, the European Parliament has nonetheless taken the view that the right to adequate housing at an affordable price is indeed a fundamental right. This has actually been repeated in the context of the ECJ, albeit in an opinion of the Advocate-General. In this case, a subsidy for obtaining your own dwelling was successfully contested because the compensation was only available for housing on the German territory. See: Opinion Adv.Gen. Bot 28 June 2007, no. C-152/05, Commission/Germany, par. 87.

50 Art. 34, par.3 Charter of Fundamental Rights of the European Union, *OJ.C.* 26 October 2012, no. 326.

51 E.g. ECJ 20 January 2011, C-155/09, Commission/Greece; ECJ 11 November 2014, C-333/13, Dano/Jobcenter Leipzig; ECJ 17 January 2008, C-152/05, Commission/Germany.

52 ECJ 24 April 2012, no. C-571/10, Servet Kamberaj/ Istituto per l'Edilizia sociale della Provincia autonoma di Bolzano (IPES) and others.

53 Explanations relating to the Charter of Fundamental Rights, *OJ.C.* 14 December 2007, no. 303, 27.

housing legislation cannot be tested against article 34, § 3. The impact of the provision will therefore automatically be limited.

As the case of *Kamberaj* confirms, there are, of course, areas where EU law does apply and can at the same time affect housing rights. This is where article 34, § 3 could be able to illustrate its importance. Consumer protection is, for example, an area of EU legislation with ties to and a potential impact on the right to housing (an illustration of which will follow later this chapter). The same can be said with regard to free market regulations and their interpretation by the ECJ. In a decision addressing prejudicial questions by the Belgian Constitutional Court, the ECJ shone its light over some of the aspects that were incorporated into the Flemish Decree on Land and Real Estate. The Decree included a measure called "living in your own region" ("*wonen in eigen streek*"), requiring people who wanted to acquire grounds and buildings in certain enlisted communes to illustrate a sufficient link, be it personal or professional, with this municipality.[54] Surely, the ECJ had to test these measures against the EU freedoms in particular,[55] but decisions like this one do have an obvious impact on domestic housing legislation. What is even more interesting is how the Court clarified that limitations to free movement can be justified, accepting that housing policies can indeed be overriding reasons of general interest.[56] It thus acknowledged the importance of social housing policies. A reference to the EU Charter could have definitely been made.

Despite the described limits of the Charter, a more indirect protection of elements of the right to housing has shown its value in the context of the ECtHR. In the European Union, Charter rights could play a particularly valuable role as a social counterweight against otherwise unrestrained free market concerns.[57]

C. Shared Housing Rights Concerns

Whether the European Convention on Human Rights, the European Social Charter or EU legislation, each has been shown to have its own direct or indirect connections to the right to housing. Some housing-related circumstances, however, are connected to the ECHR, the ECSR and EU law at the same time and have therefore triggered decisions from all different levels of European jurisprudence. It is also interesting how these decisions are often formed with references to decisions in similar cases by the other (quasi-)judicial institutions.

54 Ibid., par. 52–60.
55 Art. 21, 45, 49 and 63 Treaty on the Functioning of the European Union.
56 Ibid., par. 52 and 67; see also: ECJ 1 October 2009, C-567/07, Minister voor Wonen, Wijken en Integratie/Woningstichting Sint Servatius, par. 29–30.
57 KENNA (n 1) 137 and 140.

1) Accommodation for Asylum Seekers

In the ECtHR case of *M.S.S. against Belgium and Greece*, an asylum seeker had found himself living on the streets of Greece for several months with no resources or access to essential needs. The Greek government had shown no regard to the applicant's vulnerability.[58] By implementing EU Council Directive 2003/9/EC (which has meanwhile been replaced by directive 2013/33/EU),[59] the Court judged that Greece had taken up the obligation to provide accommodation and decent material conditions to impoverished asylum seekers.[60] In this case, the Greek state had failed to do so and had violated article 3 ECHR.[61]

By mentioning Directive 2003/9/EC, a link with EU legislation is immediately established. As a matter of fact, the directive has initiated decisions by the European Court of Justice that follow the same pattern of the ECtHR in *M.S.S.* The prejudicial question in *Cimade* for example only asks whether the obligations of the directive should also be guaranteed by a member state that considers another state to have jurisdiction to examine the asylum application at hand. Yet, the positive answer appears to also be rooted in fundamental rights, referring twice to the Charter of Fundamental Rights of the European Union and the importance of human dignity to be respected and protected.[62] This is repeated in *Saciri*, a decision in response to a prejudicial question by the Labor Court of Appeal in Brussels.[63] The Court says that member states can choose to grant material reception conditions in the form of financial allowances, but they must be sufficient to ensure a dignified standard of living. This includes that financial allowances must enable them to obtain social housing, but if necessary, should even ensure their subsistence on the private rental market.[64]

The European Committee of Social Rights has also discussed several collective complaints concerning accommodation for asylum seekers and persons unlawfully present on the territory of a state party.[65] These decisions include occasional references to the *M.S.S.* case (ECtHR), Directive 2003/9/

58 ECtHR 21 January 2011, no. 30696/09, M.S.S./Belgium and Greece, par. 263.

59 Directive European Parliament and Council no. 2013/33/EU, 26 June 2013, laying down standards for the reception of applicants for international protection, *OJ L* 29 June 2013.

60 ECtHR 21 January 2011, no. 30696/09, M.S.S./Belgium and Greece, par. 250.

61 See also ECtHR 7 July 2015, no. 60125/11, V.M. and others/Belgium.

62 ECJ 27 September 2012, no. C-179/11, Cimade/Ministre de l'Intérieur, de l'Outre-mer, des Collectivités territoriales et de l'Immigration, par. 42 and 56.

63 ECJ 27 February 2014, no. C-79/13, Federaal agentschap voor de opvang van asielzoekers/Saciri and others, par. 35.

64 Ibid., par. 42.

65 E.g. ECSR 20 October 2009, no. 47/2008, Defence for Children International (DCI)/The Netherlands; ECSR 23 October 2012, no. 69/2011, DCI/Belgium; ECSR 2 July 2014, no. 86/2012, Feantsa/The Netherlands.

EC[66] and even the *Saciri* case (ECJ).[67] In contrast however to EU law and the *M.S.S.* case, which both deal with asylum seekers (i.e. with their application pending), the material scope of the relevant provisions of the RESC extends to those whose asylum claims have already been rejected.[68] Accordingly, the Committee finds that there is an obligation, both in law and practice, to provide shelter to both irregular migrant children and adults for as long as they are in a state party's jurisdiction and that all foreigners have a legal right to the satisfaction of their basic needs.[69] The Committee clarified though that this does not mean that the denial of adequate housing to those unlawfully present on the territory of the state party automatically entails a denial of these basic needs. It argued that such lasting housing could discourage people to return to their country of origin.[70]

Even though connected to different provisions focusing on different elements, which also creates different perceptions on the exact scope of obligations, the reception of asylum seekers is a good illustration of how housing rights-related concerns (in this case, temporary accommodation) can be common to both European human rights law (ECHR as well as ECSR) and European Union law.

2) *The Loss of a Home: Protection against Evictions*

According to the European Committee of Social Rights, an eviction is the deprivation of housing which a person occupied on account of insolvency or wrongful occupation.[71] As in the previous section on migration, all three levels of European jurisprudence have elaborated on such housing (or land) evictions, albeit one perhaps slightly less pronounced than the others. Unsurprisingly, the majority of eviction cases stems from the European Court of Human Rights, where the *Buckley* case is often regarded as the starting point for this important strand of human rights jurisprudence. In this case the Court expanded the meaning of "home" from article 8 to include land, caravans, etc. – basically any specific place which a party can prove a sufficient and continuous link with. Even an illegally occupied place or dwelling, whether public or private property, can be considered a home for the purposes of article 8 ECHR.[72] Consequently, interferences with these "homes" such as evictions have to be in accordance

66 ECSR 2 July 2014, no. 86/2012, Feantsa/The Netherlands, par. 27, 41–42 and 184; ECSR 23 October 2012, no. 69/2011, DCI/Belgium, par. 105.

67 ECSR 2 July 2014, no. 86/2012, Feantsa/The Netherlands, par. 42.

68 Ibid., par. 184.

69 Ibid., par. 115 and 173; ECSR 20 October 2009, no. 47/2008, DCI/the Netherlands, par. 64; ECSR 1 July 2014, no. 90/2013, Conference of European Churches (CEC)/ the Netherlands, par. 128–130

70 ECSR 20 October 2009, no. 47/2008, DCI/The Netherlands, par. 44.

71 ECSR, Conclusions 2003, vol. 2, Sweden, 655.

72 ECtHR 29 September 1996, no. 20348/92, Buckley/United Kingdom, par. 53.

with law, pursue a legitimate aim and be necessary in a democratic society. To meet this latter requirement, the Court gives state parties a large margin of appreciation. Yet, as was clarified in *Connors*, this interference should answer a "pressing social need" and be proportionate to its legitimate aim.[73] To abide by these requirements, it has been stressed time and again that procedural safeguards should have to be made available.[74]

Perhaps most iconic in this context is the case of *McCann*. Here, the Court stated "the loss of a home is a most extreme form of interference with the right to respect for the home" and that therefore the proportionality of the measure should be evaluated by an independent tribunal, still in view, of course, of the applicant's personal circumstances.[75] In doing so, it does impose certain housing security rules to be in place at the national level, even if they are again procedural in nature. This way the Court's interpretation can and has actually impacted state parties' housing legislation.[76] While the Belgian private rent legislation already held that the resolution of the contract has to be accomplished by court (art. 1184 Civil Code), *McCann* has been used in a judgment that ordered the annulment of a Flemish Housing Code provision that would enable social landlords to terminate a rental agreement without the preceding intervention of a peace judge (infra).[77] In addition, the *McCann* judgment has obtained a special place in the housing-related case law of the Constitutional Court. The court applies the judgment in its own proportionality assessments of housing legislation as an ultimate limit to the state's considerable margin of appreciation.

In spite of all this, the ECtHR once again illustrates how housing will only be indirectly protected under the Convention. The domestic legislation on evictions can still be very lenient and the result for the applicant might still be unjust; only the more objectifiable procedural safeguards can be reviewed.[78]

73 ECtHR 27 May 2004, no. 66746/01, Connors/United Kingdom, par. 81.

74 E.g. ECtHR 18 January 2001, no. 27238/95, Chapman/United Kingdom, par. 92 and 96; ECtHR 18 January 2001, no. 24882/94, Beard/United Kingdom, par. 103 and 107; ECtHR 27 May 2004, no. 66746/01, Connors/United Kingdom, par. 83–84.

75 ECtHR 13 August 2008, no. 19009/04, McCann/United Kingdom, par. 50; Repeated in e.g. ECtHR 15 January 2009, no. 28261/06, Cosic/Croatia, par. 22; ECtHR 21 September 2010, no. 37341/06, Kay and others/United Kingdom, par. 68.

76 It has had an impact on domestic legislation: M. VOLS, M. KIEHL and J. SIDOLI DEL CENO, "Human rights and protection against eviction in anti-social behaviour cases in the Netherlands and Germany", *European Journal of Comparative Law and Governance* 2015, no. 2, 156–181.

77 F. TULKENS and S. VAN DROOGHENBROECK, "Armoede en mensenrechten. De bijdrage van het Europese Hof voor de Rechten van de Mens", in Steunpunt tot Bestrijding van Armoede, Bestaansonzekerheid en Sociale Uitsluiting, *Armoede-Waardigheid-Mensenrechten*, 2008, (65) 70; Constitutional Court 10 July 2008, no. 101/208, B.23.3.

78 BERNARD (n 18) 544–545 and 549; E. DUBOUT, "La procéduralisation des obligations relatives aux droits fondamentaux substantiels par la Cour européenne de droits de l'homme", *RTDH* 2007, no. 70, (397) 402.

As we have seen, illegally occupied homes may fall under the protection of article 8 ECHR as well. With regard to the proportionality assessment, however, the illegality of that occupation is also taken into account. The Court says that those who simply squat in or on other people's property must be distinguished from others.[79] That does not mean that the ECtHR never protects illegal occupants in the context of article 8; quite the contrary. According to the Court, the proportionality principle requires that cases in which an entire community is affected over a long period of time should be treated entirely different from individual cases of removal from unlawfully occupied territory.[80] This is particularly relevant in the case of travelers. As such, the Court has stressed in the aforementioned *Yordanova* judgment that the traditional lifestyle of the applicant and the vulnerable position of travelers in general has to be taken into account.[81] Moreover, it requires that due consideration should be given to the consequences of a removal and the risk of homelessness,[82] paying attention to the specificity of social groups and their (possibly additional) needs.[83] As mentioned earlier, this ultimately leads the Court to proclaiming that an obligation to secure shelter to particularly vulnerable individuals may follow from article 8 ECHR in exceptional cases.[84] One could therefore say that the Court has added a couple of substantive touches to the other more formal and procedural safeguards that state parties were considered to comply with in the context of article 8 ECHR.[85]

While not entirely surprising considering the more progressive content of the *Yordanova* judgment itself, this was the first judgment in which the Court referred to a decision on this matter by the European Committee of Social Rights.[86] Due to the considerable number of Roma and eviction cases that are brought before the ECSR, the latter had already developed a strand of "case law" on this particular subject.[87] Identical to the ECtHR, the Committee stresses the importance of procedural safeguards and the need for legal remedies. Inspired by the Charter's right to housing, though, the Committee takes a step further and adds that authorities must also adopt measures to rehouse or financially assist persons in the case of a justified eviction.[88]

79 ECtHR 18 January 2001, no. 27238/95, Chapman/United Kingdom, par. 102; ECtHR 21 June 2011, no. 48833/07, Orlic/Croatia
80 ECtHR 24 April 2012, no. 25446/06, Yordanova and others/Russia, par. 121.
81 Ibid., par. 83.
82 Ibid., par. 126.
83 Ibid., par. 129.
84 Ibid., par. 130.
85 REMICHE (n 47) 791–793.
86 ECtHR 24 April 2012, no. 25446/06, Yordanova and others/Russia, par. 73–75.
87 M. MIKKOLA, "Housing as a human right in Europe, 2006", *European Journal of Social Security* 2008, vol. 10, no. 3, 249–294.
88 ECSR 5 December 2007, no. 39/2006, Feantsa/France, par. 86; ECSR 5 December 2007, no. 33/2006, International Movement ATD Fourth World/France, par. 78.

In the case of imminent eviction of illegal occupants, the Court has not just taken the vulnerable position of travelers into consideration. In recent years, Spanish squatters have successfully requested for the adoption of interim measures. These interim measures, described in Rule 39 of the Rules of the Court, have always been largely complied with,[89] but their binding nature has only been formally acknowledged in the 2005 case of *Mamatkulov*.[90]

On the two occasions under scrutiny, the Court instructed the Spanish government not to carry out an eviction of squatters. It added that the government should provide the Court with information on the applicant's future housing status and how violations of the Convention rights would be prevented in light of the applicant's vulnerability.[91] Although the observations submitted by the government satisfied the Court both times, it seems likely that the Court would have found a violation of article 8 had this not been the case. Even if only a temporary saving grace in practice, the decisions show that even illegal occupants are protected against evictions to the extent that state parties must at all times guarantee that safeguards are complied with and specific circumstances taken into account.

Finally, a more indirect form of protection for squatters in case of an imminent eviction has come through the Court's interpretation of article 6 ECHR. While domestic judgments on evictions must be carried out within a reasonable period of time to comply with the owner's due process rights, state parties have a margin of appreciation on this matter as well. In *Cofinfo*, the French authorities had responded to the precarious situation of the persons involved (including families and children) and had looked to rehouse them before carrying out the eviction. Persuaded by these objectives, the Court judged that the non-execution of the eviction judgment had not been the result of a fault by the administration and found their actions to be justified.[92]

What about our third branch of European jurisprudence? At first sight, there appears to be little to connect European Union law to housing evictions. In the area of consumer protection, however, the European Court of Justice has

89 H.R. GARRY, "When procedure involves matters of life and death: interim measures and the European Convention on Human Rights", *E.P.L.* 2001, vol. 7, no. 3, (399) 418.

90 ECtHR 4 February 2005, no. 46827/99 and 46951/99, Mamatkulov and Askarov/ Turkey, par. 125–129; V. KRSTICEVIC and B. GRIFFEY, "Interim measures", in M. LANGFORD, B. PORTER, R. BROWN and J. ROSSI (eds.), *The Optional Protocol to the International Covenant on Economic, Social and Cultural Rights: a commentary*, Pretoria, University Law Press, 2015, 23; On the binding character of interim measures, see also: W. VANDENHOLE, "VN-mensenrechtencomité en Mensenrechtenhof op één lijn over verplichtend karakter voorlopige maatregelen", *Juristenkrant* 2003, no. 74, 12.

91 ECtHR 28 January 2014 (adm. dec.), no.77842/12, A.M.B. and others/Spain (interim measures had been applied on 12 December 2012); ECtHR 5 November 2013, no. 62688/13, Ceesay Ceesay and others/Spain (interim measures had been applied on 15 October 2013).

92 ECtHR 12 October 2010 (adm. dec.), no. 23516/08, Société Cofinfo/France.

illustrated its concerns about this issue. In *Aziz*, the applicant had stopped paying his loan installments. Since the loan agreement had been secured by a mortgage on his family home, he was ultimately evicted. In conformity with Directive 93/13/EEC,[93] the Court argued that during national proceedings that seek to find whether a contract term is unfair, courts should be able to adopt interim measures, so that consumer protection does not preclude the prevention of the definitive and irreversible loss of the home and would automatically limit itself to the possible payment of damages.[94] The idea that the loss of a family home seriously undermines consumer rights was used in the similar but for us more interesting *Kusionova* case. Here, the European Court of Justice explicitly coupled its findings from *Aziz* with the aforementioned statements by the ECtHR on the importance of the home in *McCann*.[95] In fact, the Luxembourg Court even went a step further. It proceeded with a reference to the "right to accommodation", which it considered guaranteed by article 7 of the EU Charter of Fundamental Rights.[96] Considering that this provision is an almost perfect replica of article 8 of the European Convention on Human Rights and the ECtHR has consistently opposed that a right to housing stems from this article, the interpretation of this provision by the European Court of Justice is certainly remarkable.

D. The Right to Property: Strengthening and Weakening the Right to Housing at the Same Time

Finally, no discussion of European housing jurisprudence is complete without some elaboration on the right to property (article 1 of the First Protocol to the ECHR). This right has had a significant impact on housing rights-related case law by the European Court of Human Rights. Let us depart from the above-mentioned *Cofinfo* case. That decision, indirectly in favor of the illegal occupants, is ultimately an exception to the rule. Most evictions that are carried out late or not at all often do end up in a violation of article 6 ECHR. Not only that, but these decisions frequently contain a violation of the right to property too.[97]

93 Directive Council no. 93/13/EEC, 5 April 1993 on unfair terms in consumer contracts, *OJ.L.* 21 April 1993.

94 ECJ 14 March 2013, C-415/11, Aziz/Catalunyacaixa, par. 59 and 61.

95 ECJ 10 September 2014, C-34/13, Kusionova/SMART Capital, par. 64.

96 Ibid., par. 65.

97 ECtHR 28 July 2005, no. 55161/00, Cima/Italy; ECtHR 28 July 1999, no. 22774/93, Immobiliare Saffi/Italy; ECtHR 10 October 2013, no. 16806/11 and 61696/11, Israfilova and Agalarov/Azerbaijan; ECtHR 1 June 2006, no. 68345/01, Ciucci/Italy; F. TULKENS, "La réglementation de l'usage des biens dans l'intérêt général. La troisième norme de l'article 1er du premier Protocole de la Convention européenne des Droits de l'homme", in H. VANDENBERGHE (ed.), *Property and human rights*, Brugge, Die Keure, 2006, (61) 90.

Article 1 of the First Protocol to the ECHR is commonly applied in a way that it concerns the effective enjoyment of one's property that has been destroyed due to the actions or lack thereof by a state party.[98] At its narrow core, the right to property is in, other words, first and foremost directed at the protection of existing possessions of individuals against interference. It does not guarantee a right to acquire possession and is accordingly nothing like a right to housing.[99] Of course, this does not mean that the social function of property cannot be taken into account or that social measures can limit the right to property,[100] as is actually stipulated in the second paragraph of the relevant provision itself.[101] It does not imply either that tenants cannot lodge a complaint on the basis of article 1 Protocol No. 1. Allowing a very broad interpretation of possession, the Court held in *Stretch v United Kingdom* that 'possessions' can also include a tenant's legitimate expectation in the continuation of a tenancy.[102]

While lodged on the basis of a liberal and individualistic conception of property, allegations of unlawful or disproportionate interference with a landlord's right to property have brought about judicial decisions of a much more social nature, once again showing the permeability of the Convention to housing rights as well as the possibility for state interferences on the private rental market.[103] The first case of this kind was *James v United Kingdom*. The right of tenants under leases for a term of more than 20 years to acquire full ownership of the property was considered by the Court as a legitimate means to pursue public interest. The Court significantly states:

98 ECtHR 30 November 2004, no. 48939/99, Öneryildiz/Turkey; ECtHR 20 March 2008, no. 15339/02 et al., Budayeva and others/Russia; ECtHR 16 September 1996, no. 21893/93, Akdivar and others/Turkey.

99 TULKENS (n 19) 318–319; C. KRAUSE, "The right to property", in A. EIDE, C. KRAUSE and A. ROSAS (eds.), *Economic, social and cultural rights*, Dordrecht, Martinus Nijhoff Publishers, 2001, (191) 191.

100 J. SLUYSMANS and R. DE GRAAFF, "Ontwikkelingen in het eigendomsbegrip onder artikel 1 Eerste Protocol", *NJCM-Bulletin* 2014, vol. 39, no. 3, (255) 256 and 269; KRAUSE (n 99) 203; J. SPINKS, "De geoorloofdheid van het opleggen van eigendomsbeperkende maatregelen door de overheid", *Jura Falconis* 2004–2005, vol. 41, no. 3, (365) 390–396.

101 Art. 1, par. 2 Protocol to the Convention for the Protection of Human Rights and Fundamental Freedoms: "The preceding provisions shall not, however, in any way impair the right of a State to enforce such laws as it deems necessary to control the use of property in accordance with the general interest or to secure the payment of taxes or other contributions or penalties."

102 ECtHR 24 June 2003, no. 44277/98, Stretch/United Kingdom, par. 111; M. SIGRON, *Legitimate expectations under Article 1 of Protocol No.1 to the European Convention on Human Rights*, Antwerpen, Intersentia, 2014, 147.

103 KENNA (n 39) 198; M. SARIGIANNIDIS and I. PERVOU, "Adequate housing: seeking justiciability through the right to property", *International Journal of Human Rights and Constitutional Studies* 2013, vol. 1, no. 1, (27) 32–33.

> Modern societies consider housing of the population to be a prime social need, the regulation of which cannot entirely be left to the play of market forces. The margin of appreciation is wide enough to cover legislation aimed at securing greater social justice in the sphere of people's homes, even where such legislation interferes with existing contractual relations between private parties.[104]

Consequently, the ECtHR provides states with a rather wide margin of appreciation in implementing social policies that might result in interferences with article 1 of the First Protocol, only intervening when the national legislator's judgment of public interest is manifestly unreasonable.[105] Measures aimed at the elimination of social injustices can justify far-reaching interference in an individual's property rights. Similarly, the Court argued in *Mellacher* that the introduction of a statutory reduction in rent (which was initially freely negotiated) did not violate article 1 of Protocol No.1 to the Convention, given the wide margin of appreciation for the state.[106] The interference was thus proportionate with the aim of reducing excessive and unjustified disparities between rents for equivalent apartments. The Court also clarified that it is not for them to scrutinize whether the chosen measures are the most effective ones, responding to the applicant's argument that a genuinely social measure would have been to accord rent subsidies to the most needy.[107] Finally, the Court had also observed in the *Spadea* and *Scollo* cases that the expiration of a large number of leases within a certain period of time, combined with the concern to enable affected tenants to find new homes, can render domestic provisions suspending evictions proportionate.[108]

In 2001, Krause stated that the consequences of a rather weak right to property is actually twofold for the protection of social rights. While the application of the proportionality principle might benefit housing concerns, the extent to which social rights are also included within the broad conception of property can confine them at the same time.[109] In the years since then, many

104 ECtHR 21 February 1986, no. 8793/79, James and others/United Kingdom, par. 47

105 C.L. ROZAKIS and P. VOYATZIS, "'Le droit au respect de ses biens': une clause déclaratoire ou une 'omnibus' norme?", in H. VANDENBERGHE (ed.), *Property and human rights*, Brugge, Die Keure, 2006, (1) 23; H. VANDENBERGHE, "La privation de propriété. La deuxième norme de l'article 1er du premier protocole de la Convention européenne des Droits de l'Homme", in H. VANDENBERGHE (ed.), *Property and human rights*, Brugge, Die Keure, 2006, (29) 46 and 52.

106 ECtHR 19 December 1989, no. 10522/83 et al., Mellacher and others/Austria; LECKIE (n 29) 160.

107 ECtHR 19 December 1989, no. 10522/83 et al., Mellacher and others/Austria, par. 52.

108 ECtHR 28 September 1995, no. 12868/87, Spadea and Scalabrino/Italy, par. 31 and 38; ECtHR 28 September 1995, no. 19133/91, Scollo/Italy.

109 KRAUSE (n 99) 203.

believe that the Court has changed its lenient approach in favor of tenants for "a revival of a liberal theory of property".[110] While the interests of the landlord have been found violated because of disproportionate social measures on a number of occasions,[111] the *Hutten-Czapska* judgment (a Grand Chamber judgment), interpretable as the instigator of this "revival", is probably the most discussed one. Here, the Court elaborated on the Polish special lease system that combined restrictions on both the amount of rent chargeable and on the termination of leases.

The Grand Chamber acknowledged the difficult housing situation in Poland, but found the Rent Act to be disproportionate on the grounds that the landlord had never entered a freely negotiated lease, had lost his right to terminate the lease (unlike in *Spadea*) and that the rent levels were set below that required to cover necessary maintenance expenses (unlike in *Mellacher*).[112] In short, the Court considered the owners to carry a disproportionate burden. Most surprisingly, though, is how the Court determined that the interests of landlords (which were considered to be insufficiently taken into account) also include their entitlement to derive profit from their property.[113] Judge Zupancic dissented with this particular passage, raising the question of how deriving profit by merely owning an apartment building could be a landlord's right, let alone a human right.[114]

It is certainly true that the balance of interests has frequently tilted into the direction of the owners. In *Berger-Krall*, the applicants who invoked a violation of article 1 Protocol No.1 were tenants and not landlords.[115] They claimed that their specially protected tenancy, which allegedly constituted a possession within the meaning of the relevant provision, had been violated by an excessive increase in rent. The Court was of the opinion that this case was simply the mirror image of *Hutten-Czapska*:[116] it argued fully in line with this case but

110 T. ALLEN, "Liberalism, social democracy and the value of property under the European Convention on Human Rights", *I.C.L.Q.* 2010, (1055) 1078; see also KENNA (n 39) 199; SCHMID (n 27) 15.

111 E.g. ECtHR 24 October 2006, no. 17647/04, Edwards/Malta: ECtHR 12 June 2012, no. 13221/08 and 2139/10, Lindheim and others/Norway; ECtHR 12 June 2014, no. 14717/04, Berger-Krall and others/Slovenia; ECtHR 3 July 2014, no. 37926/05 et al., R&L, S.R.O. and others/Czech Republic; ECtHR 28 January 2014, no. 30255/09, Bittó and others/Slovakia.

112 ECtHR 19 June 2006, no. 35014/97, Hutten-Czapska/Poland, par. 224; A. KUCS, Z. SEDLOVA and L. PIERHUROVICA, "The right to housing: international, European and national perspectives", *Cuadernos Constitucionales de la Cátedra Fadrique Furi Ceriol* 2008, no. 64/65, (101) 110–111.

113 ECtHR 19 June 2006, no. 35014/97, Hutten-Czapska/Poland, par. 239; this was repeated in ECtHR 24 October 2006, no. 17647/04, Edwards/Malta.

114 Partly concurring, partly dissenting opinion by Judge Zupancic, ECtHR 19 June 2006, no. 35014/97, Hutten-Czapska/Poland.

115 ECtHR 12 June 2014, no. 14717/04, Berger-Krall and others/Slovenia.

116 Ibid., par. 202.

since the claimant was the opposite party, the Court did obviously not find a violation of article 1 Protocol No.1. Consequently, one could come to the conclusion with regard to *Berger-Krall* that the Court does not as much confine the state's margin of appreciation with regard to measures that interfere with the right to property as give considerable weight to the landlord's interests.

It is, however, difficult to say whether the Court has purposefully shifted this balance.[117] Nowhere has the Court explicitly overruled its initial principles regarding article 1 of the First Protocol, as set out in *James* and *Mellacher*. In *Hutten-Czapska*, the Grand Chamber made additional arguments on behalf of the landlord's interests, but it did not discard its earlier case law. Moreover, it explicitly distinguished the circumstances from those in *Spadea* and *Mellacher*, concluding that this earlier jurisprudence did not restrict the right to property to such a considerable extent as in the present case. In *Almeida Ferreira*, a case from 2010, the Court did not only refer to this earlier case law, but it also decided again in favor of the tenants. In this case, a domestic law protected tenants who had rented a dwelling for more than 20 years against the requisition of the property. The court found that the aim to protect a social group that the state considered in need of specific protection was proportional and did not violate the relevant provision.[118] Furthermore, the perhaps most liberal standpoint that seemed to stem from the right to property in *Hutten-Czapska*, a right to obtain profit, was categorically denied in the case of *R&L and others v. the Czech Republic*.[119] Whether or not consciously narrowing the margin of appreciation for states to make restrictions on landlord's property rights, the Court certainly considers that a limit is reached when the economic balance of the contractual exchange is manifestly disturbed.

E. Interim Conclusion

Housing is both directly and indirectly protected in European (quasi-)jurisprudence. If we take a very strict approach to the matter, case law concerning the right to housing and the substantive obligations it imposes on states is confined to the quasi-judicial decisions of the European Committee of Social Rights, whose impact and potential will be looked at more closely in the next section. However, when coupled with other rights such as articles 6 or 8 ECHR, article 1 of the First Protocol, or the free movement of persons and capital, decisions relevant (even if not always beneficial) to the right to housing can occur in any European courtroom.

117 SLUYSMANS (n 100) 269.
118 ECtHR 21 December 2010, no. 41696/07, Almeida Ferreira and Melo Ferreira/Portugal, par. 33.
119 ECtHR 3 July 2014, no. 37926/05 et al., R&L, S.R.O. and others/Czech Republic, par. 103.

Even though the EU Charter of Fundamental Rights contains a right to housing assistance, the scope of that obligation has not yet been fully explored. Since its application depends upon EU competences, its impact will probably remain limited. More interesting case law comes from the European Court of Human Rights. Due to the indirect implications of some ECHR provisions, the Court obliges states to take certain primarily procedural safeguards that fit the narrative of the right to housing at the same time. It also leaves a considerable – even if over time somewhat reduced – margin of appreciation to state parties with regard to the development of the regulation of and social protection on the housing market.

3. The Assessment of Housing Legislation and Policy through a Collective Complaint

The European Committee of Social Rights is obviously competent to assess a state parties' compliance with the right to housing in a direct way. It has done so with regard to different countries on numerous occasions, but usually targets quite specific concerns and groups of persons such as Roma or migrant children. In a more general sense, however, the ECSR is also able to review the broader housing policy and realization of the right to housing as a whole.[120] We elaborate on whether such a more general complaint could incentivize states to improve this fundamental right, perhaps even if the state in question has not yet ratified the relevant article 31 of the Social Charter. What are the conditions and parameters used by the Committee to establish (non-)compliance? And will the decision have any impact?

A. Dependency on the Ratification of Article 31 RESC

We have mentioned that no provision of the European Social Charter is accepted (both partially and in its entirety) by as few states as article 31. The Belgian state did not do so either, based on the argument that the legislation in place at the time of the ratification of the RESC could not guarantee the rights set out in article 31. This is certainly not a very strong argument. It is questionable whether the recognition of an essential fundamental right should have to be measured against the extent to which it has or has not yet been realized[121] – not least with regard to socio-economic rights in particular, because they are regarded in general as imposing progressive obligations. Ratifying this fundamental right should, in other words, have to engage a

120 ECSR 5 December 2007, no. 33/2006, International Movement ATD Fourth World/France; ECSR 5 December 2007, no. 39/2006, Feantsa/France.

121 G. INSLEGERS, "Van inroepbaarheid naar afdwingbaarheid van het recht op wonen bekeken in mensenrechtelijk perspectief", in N. BERNARD and B. HUBEAU (eds.), *Recht op wonen: naar een resultaatsverbintenis?*, Brugge, Die Keure, 2013, (253) 262.

government to take the necessary steps rather than to freeze lawmakers because of fear of possible instant findings of violations.

From an institutional perspective, the ratification process is also more complex for the Belgian state than for many other countries. Even though the sixth Belgian state reform has transferred important housing-related competences to the regions, there are still elements that are connected to the federal level (general contract law, penal law, procedural law). We are therefore dealing with a so-called mixed agreement or rather in this case a mixed treaty provision. According to the Cooperation Agreement of 1994, this type of treaty can only be ratified by the federal state with the approval of each of the competent parliaments.[122] Unsurprisingly, approval and ratification of mixed agreements take considerably more time (years, not months).[123] Still, however, considering the constitutional recognition of the right, the existence of housing codes in all three regions and the fact that plenty of time has passed by, shared approval and ultimately ratification of article 31 would only be logical.

There are, however, other viable options available to lodge complaints concerning the right to housing against states that have not (yet) ratified this provision – options that the Committee itself has eagerly turned to with respect to housing. In 2007, the Committee stated the following: "The Charter was conceived as a whole and all its provisions complement each other and overlap in part. It is impossible to draw watertight divisions between the material scope of each article or paragraph."[124] The indivisible nature of RESC rights and the strong connections between them offer the possibility to apply other relevant provisions when one is not ratified. The subject of housing is discussed in article 31, but is, for example, also touched upon in articles 16 and 30 of the Charter. The former describes the provision of housing as a necessary condition for full development of the family as a fundamental unit of society, whereas the latter predicates measures to promote effective access to housing for persons who live or risk living in a situation of social exclusion or poverty. Article 16 in particular, though different in personal and material scope, is regarded as partially overlapping with article 31.[125] The Committee considers that the

122 Cooperation Agreement 8 March 1994 between the federal government, the communities and the regions concerning the rules on concluding mixed treaties, *BS* 17 December 1996: article 2 does provide one exception in which the King can ratify a treaty without having the approval of all concerned legislative bodies; A. ALEN and K. MUYLLE, *Handboek van het Belgische Staatsrecht*, Mechelen, Kluwer, 2011, 758–761.

123 J. VELAERS, "'In foro interno et in foro externo': de international bevoegdheden van gemeenschappen en gewesten", in F. JUDO and G. GEUDENS (eds.), *Internationale betrekkingen en federalisme*, Gent, Larcier, 2006, (3) 35.

124 ECSR 26 June 2007 (adm. dec.), no. 41/2007, Mental Disability Advocacy Center (MDAC)/Bulgaria, par. 9.

125 ECSR 18 October 2006, no. 31/2005, European Roma Rights Centre (ERRC)/Bulgaria, par. 17; D. GAILIUTE, "Right to housing in the jurisprudence of the European Committee of Social Rights", *Societal Studies* 2012, vol. 4, no. 4, (1605) 1608.

explicit right to housing in article 31 does not preclude a consideration of relevant housing issues arising under article 16 and that the notions of forced eviction and adequate housing are identical under both provisions,[126] both referring to dwellings of a decent standard and suitable size and with all essential amenities.[127] The fact that a state has not ratified a right will thus not on its own render a complaint based on the subject of that right inadmissible.[128] As a result, the Committee seems to give meaning to the Convention as an all-inclusive package rather than as the originally designed *à la carte* system.[129] It is certainly well aware of the impact of its statements and the possible risk of delegitimizing the Charter, clarifying that it must ensure "that obligations are not imposed on states stemming from provisions they did not intend to accept". At the same time, however, the Committee argues that it must guard that "the essential core of accepted provisions is not amputated as a result of the fact it may contain obligations which may also result from unaccepted provisions".[130] This has been repeated and explicitly established for the right to housing in the case of the International Federation of Human Rights (FIDH) against Belgium. The Committee considered that its views on the scope of the obligations stemming from article 31 may be useful to determine the scope of the obligations with regard to the right to housing arising from both article 16 as well as article 30.[131] As a matter of fact, this statement was made in response to the Belgian government's objections to the indirect use of the non-ratified article.[132]

While the Committee's stance on article 16 appears to import the obligations of article 31, the former provision, of course, remains directed at *families* (travelers, accompanied foreign minors, adapted accommodation for highly dependent adults with disabilities, etc.).[133] The question therefore stands

126 ECSR 18 October 2006, no. 31/2005, European Roma Rights Centre (ERRC)/Bulgaria, par. 9.

127 ECSR 8 December 2004, no.15/2003, European Roma Rights Centre (ERRC)/Greece, par.24.

128 J.-F. AKANDJI-KOMBÉ, "Charte sociale européenne et procedure de reclamations collectives (1998-1er juillet 1998)", *JDE* 2008, (217) 219; N. BERNARD, "Le droit au logement dans la Charte Sociale Révisée: à propos de la condamnation de la France par le Comité Européen des Droits Sociaux", *RTDH* 2009, no. 80, (1061) 1083–1086.

129 J. HOHMANN, *The right to housing. Law, concepts, possibilities*, Oxford, Hart Publishing, 2013, 53.

130 ECSR 26 June 2007 (adm. dec.), no. 41/2007, Mental Disability Advocacy Center (MDAC)/Bulgaria, par. 9.

131 ECSR 21 March 2012, no. 62/2010, International Federation of Human Rights (FIDH)/Belgium, par. 43–46.

132 KENNA (n 1) 131–132.

133 E.g. ECSR 18 March 2013, no. 75/2011, FIDH/Belgium, par. 178–187; ECSR 23 October 2012, no. 69/2011, Defence for Children International (DCI)/Belgium, par. 142: In this case, housing for minors is also addressed under article 17 RESC.

whether a complaint targeting the imperfections of the national housing policy as a whole (eviction procedures, lacking housing quality, affordability, etc.) is also plausible on the basis of provisions other than article 31. For this we must take a first look at the leading cases regarding this type of complaint: *ATD Fourth World* and *Feantsa* against France. The French state had already ratified article 31, rendering that provision the obvious and most important basis for both complaints and decisions. Yet that did not stop the Committee from also finding violations of the overlapping articles 16 and 30 in *ATD Fourth World*. This followed from their conclusions that the poorest households were insufficiently assisted by the housing policy.[134] We therefore believe that if a collective complaint against a different state properly addressed the concerns that the current housing policy raises for poor people and family units (e.g. the relationship between serious housing quality problems and different income groups[135]), it is plausible that a similar complaint would be investigated even without the ratification of article 31. The large margin of discretion which the Committee has endowed upon itself to decide on overlapping provisions certainly seems to suggest just that.

We conclude that the ratification of article 31 might not be that much of judicial game changer for state parties that have at least ratified other relevant provisions. In that case, the admissibility of most if not all complaints related to housing rights seems plausible. While a more widespread ratification of article 31 RESC would still have a political and symbolic value at the very least, we would argue that a more important step towards a more enforceable right to housing before the European courts would be the expansion of authorized claimants to national NGOs, providing a boost to access to justice.

B. Conditions and Benchmarks Set by the ECSR

In this section, we explore the specific arguments and parameters that the ECSR has used in assessing factual circumstances on the national housing market and domestic housing legislation and policy. It sketches a rudimentary framework of situations, acts or omissions which the Committee considers to be violations of the right to housing.[136] While we should remain aware that the

134 ECSR 5 December 2007, no. 33/2006, International Movement ATD Fourth World/ France, par. 156–170.

135 Serious safety and health concerns such as a risk of CO-poisoning and moisture problems are more frequently observed in dwellings of lower income households, see: S. WINTERS et al., *Wonen in Vlaanderen anno 2013. De bevindingen uit het Grote Woononderzoek 2013 gebundeld*, Antwerpen, Garant, 2015, 69–72.

136 MIKKOLA (n 87) 36–39; BERNARD (n 128) 1070–1073; M. UHRY and T. VIARD, "De Raad van Europa pakt Frankrijk aan over het recht op huisvesting en het recht op bescherming tegen armoede", in Steunpunt tot Bestrijding van Armoede, Bestaansonzekerheid en Sociale Uitsluiting, *Armoede-Waardigheid-Mensenrechten*, 2008, (81) 86–87.

arguments and parameters that we deduct from earlier cases are not absolute, unchangeable principles by which the ECSR is bound in future decisions,[137] they do present a picture of when a state does or does not fail their obligations with regard to the European Social Charter and what would happen if a similar broad-scoped collective complaint was lodged against that state. The Belgian and particularly Flemish housing context is used as an example against which to compare these benchmarks and arguments.

The ECSR first of all provides the following list of general obligations with regard to the realization of socio-economic rights. State parties must:

a. Adopt the necessary legal, financial and operational means of ensuring steady progress towards achieving the goals laid down by the Charter;
b. Maintain meaningful statistics on needs, resources and results;
c. Undertake regular reviews of the impact of strategies adopted;
d. Establish a timetable and not defer indefinitely the deadline for achieving the objectives of each stage;
e. Pay close attention to the impact of the policies adopted on each of the categories of persons concerned, particularly the most vulnerable.[138]

In addition to that, the aforementioned decisions of *Feantsa* and *ATD Fourth World* against France in particular offer enough concrete material regarding the execution of national housing rules and policy.

A first topic that lends itself to comparison concerns the supply of affordable housing, for which governments must encourage the construction of social housing in particular.[139] While the Committee agreed that steps had been taken by the French state to improve the stock of social housing, it also noted that "even if all these objectives were achieved, [. . .] there would still be a considerable shortfall compared with needs".[140] The objective of 591,000 new social housing units did indeed not even approximate the estimated number of applications for social housing a couple of years earlier (1,640,000). In comparison, the so-called binding social objective developed by the Flemish government foresees 50,000 new social housing units by 2025.[141] Unfortunately, approximately 120,000 prospective tenants are currently registered on the waiting list. With the promise of 4,300 new social housing units by 2016, the Walloon government aimed to meet the initial objectives of 7,000 units by 2014. Nevertheless, at the beginning of 2013, almost 38,000 prospective

137 HOHMANN (n 129) 124.
138 ECSR 5 December 2007, no. 33/2006, ATD Fourth World/France, par. 60.
139 ECSR, Conclusions 2003, vol. 2, Sweden, 656.
140 ECSR 5 December 2007, no. 33/2006, ATD Fourth World/France, par. 96–98.
141 Article 4.1.2 Flemish Decree 27 March 2009 concerning Land and Housing Policy juncto art. 22 bis Flemish Housing Code; Art. 20 Draft Decree concerning the amendment of various decrees on housing.

tenants were already on the waiting list. Whether or not such a simple ratio suffices as a compelling and decisive argument on the matter, it is the one applied by the Committee. And on this basis, the ECSR could easily argue similarly vis-à-vis the Belgian state.

ATD Fourth World also received a response from the Committee to the following pressing question posed during the hearing of the case: "what is a legitimate waiting period for a household to have to its disposal a dwelling, electricity, a legally protected housing statute?"[142] According to the ECSR, the average waiting time for allocation of social housing in France is at any rate definitely too long.[143] The average of two years and four months at the time of the case is, however, still shorter than the average waiting period in Flanders, which is almost three years. The same data also reveal that this average is subject to severe differences between municipalities, ranging from 11 days to 12 years and seven months. In 2011, it was said that the average waiting period in Wallonia even amounted to five years. With respect to France, the Committee also argued that legal redress for people who had been waiting for social housing over an excessive period of time showed serious shortcomings.[144] In contrast to Belgium, however, France did already have mediation commissions in place. The Flemish region does distribute a rental premium for households that have been on the waiting list for four years (initially five),[145] but it is impossible to predict how the Committee would assess this measure. The same can be said about the access to social housing for households in the lowest income quintile. While recent numbers do show that 15 percent of the Flemish households in this income group have obtained social housing,[146] thereby topping the 5–10 percent which the Committee deemed insufficient for France,[147] it is disputable whether it would deem this a satisfactory standard.

The next line of arguments revolves around the eviction procedure. The ECSR found France in conformity with the Charter by providing a two-month period after formal notice of the eviction and suspension of evictions in winter.[148] In contrast, the Belgian Judicial Code does not go that far: it provides only one month's notice, and although this period can be extended during winter, evictions are not legally excluded during that time.[149] With regard to rehousing, on the other hand, the Committee argued that the French

142 UHRY (n 136) 83.
143 ECSR 5 December 2007, no. 33/2006, ATD Fourth World/France, par. 129.
144 ECSR 5 December 2007, no. 33/2006, ATD Fourth World/France, par. 131.
145 Art. 16 Decision Flemish Government 21 March 2014 on altering the Decision of the Flemish Government of 4 May 2012 concerning the installation of a compensation of prospective tenants, *BS* 5 May 2014.
146 K. HEYLEN, *Grote woononderzoek deel 2. Deelmarkten, woonkosten en betaalbaarheid*, Leuven, Steunpunt Wonen 2015, 9.
147 ECSR 5 December 2007, no. 33/2006, ATD Fourth World /France, par. 129.
148 Ibid., par.79.
149 Article 1344quater Belgian Judicial Code.

Anti-Exclusion Act of 1998 did not contain any guarantees. While rehousing is certainly covered much more extensively by the regional housing codes in Belgium, the question whether their guarantees reach far enough in the opinion of the Committee remains unclear.

With regard to adequate housing, France had failed to take and implement sufficient and effective measures to eradicate substandard housing. The Committee emphasized that health risks due to these substandard conditions still affected around 400,000 to 600,000 dwellings.[150] For the very first time, the Flemish Housing Research of 2013 has submitted a sample of 5,000 dwellings in Flanders to a technical screening. The results have been staggering. Despite the existence of, for example, conformity certificates, several different renovation premiums and fiscal benefits, no less than 37 percent of the Flemish housing market (circa 1 million dwellings) was found to be of inadequate quality.[151] Considering, however, that perceptions of substandard housing might differ from country to country and definitely not all defects that resulted in penalty points in the technical screening are immediate health risks, we have to be extremely careful to compare these numbers. The enduring significance of this data (which unfortunately have not been available for the other regions) makes it nonetheless likely that a hypothetical complaint would end up with a similar argument on this point.

In sum, the quasi-judicial decisions by the ECSR do provide certain parameters as to what is sufficient and what is definitely not with regard to the protection of certain elements of the right to housing. But what if articled 16, 30 or perhaps article 31 itself were ultimately found to be violated? How much influence would such a decision have? We will discuss its potential and limitations next.

C. The Value of a Decision by the ECSR

1) Legally Binding?

Régis Brillat, Executive Secretary of the European Committee for Social Rights, is clear on its wording: "Call it what you will, the fact is that the Charter is no less binding than the European Convention on Human Rights" and proceeds that "although not a court, the ECSR is a quasi-judicial body which interprets the Charter in a way that is binding on the states parties".[152]

150 ECSR 5 December 2007, no. 39/2006, Feantsa/France, par. 76.

151 L. VANDERSTRAETEN and M. RYCKEWAERT, *Grote woononderzoek 2013 deel 3. Technische woningkwaliteit*, Leuven, Steunpunt Wonen, 2015, 76.

152 R. BRILLAT, "The European Social Charter and monitoring its implementation", in N. ALIPRANTIS and I. PAPAGEORGIOU (eds.), "Social rights at European, regional and international level. Challenges for the 21st century", Brussel, Bruylant, 2010, (43) 45 and 50.

Consequently, he stipulates that states have the obligation to bring a situation in line with the RESC when a violation has been found. Later in the same publication, however, he admits that there is insufficient pressure on states to conform to the Charter.[153] In practice, this last, very true statement downgrades the previous ones.

The ECSR's conclusions on the merits are neither final nor binding as its report, which focuses solely on compliance with the RESC,[154] has to be transmitted to the Committee of Ministers for a definitive disposal of the complaint. In case of a violation, they "shall" then adopt (by a majority of two-thirds) a recommendation for the state party in question.[155] The state party must then provide information on the measures taken in response to that recommendation.[156] There has, however, been a lot of discussion about the true scope of the obligations of the Committee of Ministers.[157] Do they have to comply with the ECSR, and if so to what extent are they bound by what are essentially nothing more than declaratory decisions? Even the ECSR had to join in on the debate in response to a remark by the French state that some decisions by the Committee of Ministers differed from the ECSR.[158]

Regardless of the different interpretations, we see that the practice of providing state parties with recommendations following some kind of nonconformity with the Charter is virtually non-existent.[159] Moreover, it is generally agreed that the recommendations by the Committee of Ministers are not legally binding anyway.[160] And yet, in the aftermath of the 2014 cases of *CEC* and *Feantsa* against the Netherlands, there have been a couple of Dutch judgments in which considerable weight has been given to the Committee's decision. While these domestic judgments agree that the ECSR decisions are not directly binding, this does not mean that they deem them without any meaning. They consider them as authoritative statements that can also be used in the

153 Ibid., 53.

154 The Committee seems, for example, unqualified to award or suggest compensation or costs, see: ECSR 11 December 2001, no. 9/2000, Confédération française de l'Encadrement (CGC)/France, par. 58; ECSR 7 February 2005, no. 15/2003, ERRC/Greece, par. 57.

155 Art. 9 Add. Prot. to the European Social Charter providing for a system of collective complaints.

156 Ibid., art. 10; KUCS (n 112) 114.

157 Cf. D.J. HARRIS and J. DARCY, *The European Social Charter*, New York, Transnational Publishers, 2001, 365–367; F. SUDRE, "Le protocole additionnel à la Charte Sociale Européenne prévoyant un système de réclamations collectives", *Revue Générale de Droit International Public* 1996, vol. 100, (715) 737.

158 ECSR 30 November 2004, no. 16/2003, Confédération française de l'Encadrement CFE-CGC/France, par. 20–21.

159 The only exception is: Committee of Ministers 31 January 2001, Recommendation RecChS(2001)1 on collective complaint no. 6/1999, *Syndicat national des Professions du tourisme/France*.

160 CHURCHILL (n 6) 218.

application of articles 3 and 8 of the European Convention on Human Rights. It is clear that in practice the ECSR decisions have played a vital role in the argumentation of the Dutch courts in these cases. It has even been said that it could not be ruled out that the decisions of the ECSR can influence Dutch law with retroactive effect.[161]

Nevertheless, it is safe to say that when complaints that target the inadequacy of national housing legislation and policy as a whole would result in a violation of the RESC, there is no certainty that actual steps would be taken to address these problems. One cannot underestimate the political pressure that a decision of the Committee might cause, but the lack of legal consequences definitely remains one of the weaknesses of the complaint mechanism of the Charter. All this is influenced by the partly political nature of the whole system. However convincing the legal arguments of the ECSR may be, the Committee of Ministers will ultimately make a political decision as to the requirement of a follow-up.[162] A lot therefore depends on the political will of the Committee of Ministers, where the defendant state is also allowed to join the vote.[163]

2) Immediate Measures

With the amendments of the internal rules of procedures in 2011, the Committee has tried to improve the follow-up of its decisions through the added possibility of immediate measures (rule 36),[164] which can be requested by a party or proposed by the ECSR on its own initiative.[165] In contrast to the aforementioned interim measures of the European Court of Human Rights which are adopted before the investigation on the merits, immediate measures serve as a follow-up of the assessment. Identically, however, the purpose of such measures is to avoid the risk of a serious irreparable injury. In line with its subdued role as the little, less important sister of the more authoritative Court, the introduction of immediate measures has unfortunately not inspired a lot of jurists to write on the subject. Consequently, little has been said about the question whether or not these measures are also binding. This and similar questions did come up during a seminar organized by Housing Rights Watch in the wake of the earlier cited decisions on the merits of *CEC* and *Feantsa*

161 Central Council of Appeal 17 December 2014, no. 14-5507 WMO-VV, ECLI:NL:CRVB:2014:4178, par. 5.7; Court of First Instance Amsterdam 8 May 2015, ECLI:NL:RBAMS:2015:2651, par. 8–10 and 15.

162 CULLEN (n 9) 67.

163 CHURCHILL (n 6) 229.

164 L.J. QUESADA, Speech during a panel discussion on "Strengthening cooperation between international and regional human rights systems to mainstreaming economic, social and cultural rights", *Workshop on enhancing cooperation between United Nations and regional human rights mechanisms*, 8–9 October 2014.

165 Rule 36 of the Rules of the European Committee of Social Rights.

against the Netherlands.[166] The Committee had earlier asked for these immediate measures "through the implementation of a co-ordinated approach at national and municipal levels with a view to ensuring that their basic needs (shelter) are met".[167] Considering that the request for these measures does not go through the hands of the Committee of Ministers, it is a legitimate question whether they are actually more enforceable than the decision on the merits itself. In the same strand of reasoning it has been asked whether non-compliance with these immediate measures or irreparable damage that would result therefrom could trigger a complaint before the European Court of Human Rights, on the basis of the right to an effective remedy (article 13 ECHR). This would, of course, make both regional human rights instruments much more intertwined and once again highlight the interdependence of human rights.

In comparison with the enthusiasm for a stronger European Committee of Social Rights which is reflected in these questions, reality is (as often) much more sobering. First of all, the ECSR has made perfectly clear that immediate measures are of an exceptional nature.[168] Furthermore, on the question of the binding character of immediate measures by the Dutch Secretary of State, the advisory department of the Dutch Council of State concluded that immediate measures of the ECSR are judicially not binding, only authoritative. Its main argument relied on the fact that the decisions of the Committee were not binding either.[169] We agree that there is indeed little reason to argue *a contrario*. Interim measures, which consist more of obligations to abstain from any interference, only aim to secure the continued existence of the substantive claim of an individual, whereas immediate measures, which focus more on obligations to take action, do not. This is also illustrated by the aforementioned fact that immediate measures are ordered after the decision on the merits.[170]

Still, however, we must pose ourselves the question how this might develop over time? It is important to remember that the recognition of interim measures as binding in the context of the ECHR has also been a process of many years. Luis Jimena Quesada, President of the European Committee of Social Rights, is certainly optimistic about the immediate measures. He states that "they have already had a significant positive impact in the mass media and, above all, in

166 Housing Rights Watch Expert Seminar: Collective complaints against the Netherlands, The Hague, 14 November 2014.

167 ECSR 25 October 2013 (decision on immediate measures), no. 86/2012, Feantsa/the Netherlands; ECSR 25 October 2013 (decision on immediate measures), no. 90/2013, Conference of European Churches (CEC)/the Netherlands.

168 E.g. ECSR 25 October 2013 (decision on immediate measures), no. 86/2012, Feantsa/ the Netherlands, par. 1.

169 Adv. Council of State (NL) 13 December 2013, no. W03.13.0414/II/Vo, *Kamerstukken II 2013–14*, 29279.

170 N. BERNARD, "Des 'mesures immédiates' pour désamorcer le critère du rattachement local dans l'hébergement des sans-abri", *Housing Rights Watch* 2014, (1) 25–26.

practice through involvement of NGOs and municipalities", thereby referring to the municipalities of Utrecht, Rotterdam, Amsterdam and the Hague which have jointly declared the Committee's decision on immediate measures of great importance.[171]

3) *With a Little Help from Your Friends: Empowering Socio-Economic Rights Case Law*

Based on all of the above, it would be somewhat of an overstatement to declare that states that change domestic law in order to bring situations in line with the Charter always do so due to the legal force of the decision of the ECSR. They can, for example, also be influenced by the binding judgments of the ECtHR.[172] It is therefore important for the Committee to import principles developed by the Court whenever possible. Aware of the difference in both legal and symbolic authority, the Committee can try to use the Court's case law to compensate for the "flaws" of its mere quasi-judicial character and raise its legitimacy towards states.[173] Decisions related to the right to housing are no exception when it comes to the often applied technique of referencing ECtHR judgments. The ECSR has stated that it is "particularly concerned that its interpretation of article 31 is fully in line with the European Court of Human Rights' interpretation of the relevant provisions of the Convention".[174] More concretely, it has, for example, referred to the cases of *Buckley* and *McCann* to define "home" and to assess the access to judicial remedies in event of an eviction in line with the Court's jurisprudence.[175] The Committee has also used the interpretation of article 8 ECHR in the *Connors* case to legitimize and actually even broaden the scope of article 16 RESC.[176]

The ECSR can thus piggyback on the authority of the European Court of Human Rights by referencing the latter's judgments and thereby highlighting the indivisibility of human rights. The ECtHR itself can improve the authority of the Committee's decisions by cross-referencing as well. By doing so, it

171 QUESADA (n 164).
172 BRILLAT (n 152) 56.
173 F. BENOÎT-ROHMER, "The impact of the European Convention of Human Rights on the jurisdictionalization of the European Committee of Social Rights", in N. ALIPRANTIS and I. PAPAGEORGIOU (eds.), *Social rights at European, regional and international level. Challenges for the 21st century*, Brussel, Bruylant, 2010, (233) 235–236 and 239.
174 ECSR 5 December 2007, no. 33/2006, International Movement ATD Fourth World/ France, par. 69.
175 ECSR 21 March 2012, no. 62/2010, FIDH/Belgium, par. 32 and 71.
176 ECSR 8 December 2004, no.15/2003, ERRC/Greece, par. 19–20 and 24–25: "The implementation of article 16 as regards nomadic groups including itinerant Roma, implies that adequate stopping places be provided, in this respect article 16 contains similar obligations to article 8 of the European Convention of Human Rights"; ECtHR 27 May 2004, no. 66746/01, Connors/United Kingdom, par. 84; GAILIUTE (n 125) 1610.

validates the case law of the Committee as equally important and boosts its legitimacy.[177] In housing-related matters, however, there seems to be some reluctance by the Court to draw on the extensively developed jurisprudence based on the RESC.[178] In the *Yordanova* case discussed earlier, which involved the eviction of Roma who lived in illegally built dwellings in Bulgaria, the Court did refer to a similar case by the ECSR for the first time (*ERRC v Bulgaria*).[179] It was, however, only used as "relevant international material" and not in the assessment of the case itself. What it does, of course, illustrate is not just that article 8 of the Convention is used on its own merits in housing-related cases, but that the Court acknowledges its connection to a right to housing.[180]

In the more recent case of *Berger-Krall* against Slovenia, the Court did refer to the ECSR decision of 8 September 2009 (*Feantsa v. Slovenia*) in its actual argumentation.[181] It did not, however, use this decision in relation to the specific circumstances of the case (even though both were set against exactly the same background), but only with regard to the Committee's statement that article 31 RESC could not be interpreted as imposing an obligation of results upon states. While the Court only selected a passage from *Feantsa v Slovenia* to support the lawfulness of an interference with tenants' rights, this ECSR decision actually used an earlier ECtHR judgment (*Mellacher*) to substantiate *a contrario* that interferences are allowed to protect vulnerable tenants.[182] In other words, in this rare example of cross-referencing back and forward between Court and Committee, the Court selected argumentation from the ECSR that furthered the case for a restriction of the applicants' right to housing, while the Committee did the exact opposite with the case law of the European Court of Human Rights. The selectiveness of references can thus also negatively impact the ability of the Court's case law to increase the legitimacy of the European Social Charter system.

With regard to enhancing the importance of Committee decisions by way of referencing its argumentation, we should also reiterate that article 34 (3) EU Charter of Fundamental Rights significantly draws on the relevant provision of the RESC. Depending, of course, on the willingness of the Court of Justice, the interpretation of the content of article 34(3) could logically be drawn from the jurisprudence of the ECSR. This carries great potential to increase the importance of both institutions with regard to the right to housing. In this scenario, the European Union would then, of course, adopt a broad

177 BENOIT-ROHMER (n 173) 242.
178 KENNA (n 39) 205.
179 ECtHR 24 April 2012, no. 25446/06, Yordanova and Others/Bulgaria, par. 73; ECSR 18 October 2006, no. 31/2005, ERRC/Bulgaria.
180 REMICHE (n 47) 794.
181 ECtHR 12 June 2014, no. 14717/04, Berger-Krall and Others/Slovenia, par. 190.
182 ECSR 8 September 2009, no. 53/2008, Feantsa/Slovenia, par. 34.

interpretation of this social right, whereas the ECSR's decisions and principles would be anchored in the case law of a more established institution with binding jurisprudence that is not even only centered around just human rights, giving the Committee's considerations much more proverbial weight.

In the future, an extra influence could be lurking from beyond the European borders. With the recently established complaints mechanism of the UN Committee on Economic, Social and Cultural Rights, an additional actor joins the debate. While still pretty much in its infancy, one of the early decisions already refers to the European Court of Justice, more specifically to the aforementioned *Aziz* case.[183] It is interesting to see whether this international complaint mechanism will become an influence itself over time and whether it will borrow (more) from the housing-related European jurisprudence in the future, thereby maybe also gathering more attention for the ECSR.

Generally speaking, however, the aforementioned flaws inherent in the ECSR system have led to a sense of indifference among all relevant parties, to which we can also add the media.[184] The list of registered NGOs is still limited and the number of collective complaints is nowhere near comparable to the flood of cases before the ECtHR. Although certain institutional changes could undoubtedly be made to increase the power of the RESC, disinterest or disbelief in what the collective complaints mechanism can mean or achieve can also work as a self-fulfilling prophecy.

We therefore argue that it would be exaggerated to say that lodging a collective complaint before the ECSR is useless. Although they lack binding character, decisions by the Committee are publicized. At the very least, they are authoritative statements, which in turn can trigger bottom-up initiatives, empower civil society in their fight for more enforceable social rights and ultimately maybe trickle down (or should we say up?) into politics. The publicity generated by the guiding cases against France certainly created this kind of impetus for the proposal of the bill that ultimately became the *Droit au Logement Opposable* (DALO).[185]

4. Conclusion

This chapter has illustrated how European jurisprudence can have an effect on the protection and realization of the right to housing on the domestic level.

183 CESCR 13 October 2015, no. 2/2014, I.D.G./Spain, par. 13.6.

184 V. VAN DER PLANCKE and M. SANT'ANA, "Protection des droits sociaux fondamentaux et lutte contre la pauvreté au sein du Conseil de l'Europe", in V. VAN DER PLANCKE (ed.), *Les droits sociaux fondamentaux dans la lutte contre la pauvreté?* Brussel, Die Keure, 2012, (211) 243.

185 K. OLDS, "The role of courts in making the right to housing a reality throughout Europe: lessons from France and the Netherlands", *Wisconsin International Law Journal* 2010, vol. 28, (170) 190.

The extent to which it does so, however, is quite variable. For a judicial body judging alleged violations of a Convention that contains no right to housing, the European Court of Human Rights has surely engaged itself to discuss aspects related to housing rights through several Convention rights. We should definitely embrace its willingness to do so. Not only does the Court's jurisprudence offer solutions to individual litigation, but it indirectly sets out structural guidelines as well of what a state is or is not allowed to do with regard to, for example, interference on the private rental market/with the right to property. Despite the fact that it proclaims how specific circumstances and disadvantaged groups and persons must be taken into particular account, the Court still provides a large margin of appreciation to the state party. As a consequence, the impact on state obligations regarding the right to housing remains largely procedural. The Court has no objective to promote the realization of the right to housing as long as the procedural safeguards are in place and no disproportionate measures have been taken. It is also somewhat unclear whether that margin of appreciation is quite as broad for measures that actually protect tenants and thereby might infringe an owner's right to property.

A full-fledged right to housing is not recognized in the case law of the ECtHR. To repeat the words of Koch, he who is only homeless will go there in vain. The same is obviously true with regard to the European Court of Justice. Notwithstanding the protection of housing rights assistance in the EU Charter of Fundamental Rights, housing remains only an indirect concern in the context of the execution of competences the EU has at its disposal. In contrast, the European Committee of Social Rights *is* entitled to assess in a substantive manner a state's housing legislation and policy in the context of the protection and realization of the right to housing. Despite the low number of ratifications of article 31 RESC, other provisions provide sufficient opportunities to lodge complaints regarding this fundamental right. Yet the impact on the protection of housing rights at the domestic level remains rather limited. On the one hand, state parties are wary of allowing national NGOs to lodge complaints too, which would open up the possibility of holding domestic socio-economic rights law more under scrutiny. On the other hand, the decisions by the Committee are not legally binding. While we would argue in favor of at least an obligatory response by the state to the established violation of the Charter, we believe the legitimacy of their decisions in political circles could be also given a boost with consistent references to and, more importantly, *by* the ECtHR and the ECJ.

Bibliography

AKANDJI-KOMBÉ, J.-F., "Charte sociale européenne et procedure de reclamations collectives (1998-1er juillet 1998)", *JDE* 2008, 217–221.

ALEN, A. and MUYLLE, K., *Handboek van het Belgische Staatsrecht*, Mechelen, Kluwer, 2011, 1096 pages.

ALLEN, T., "Liberalism, social democracy and the value of property under the European Convention on Human Rights", *I.C.L.Q.* 2010, 1055–1078.

BENOÎT-ROHMER, F., "The impact of the European Convention of Human Rights on the jurisdictionalisation of the European Committee of Social Rights", in ALIPRANTIS, N. and PAPAGEORGIOU, I. (eds.), *Social rights at European, regional and international level. Challenges for the 21st century*, Brussel, Bruylant, 2010, 233–250.

BERNARD, N., "Des 'mesures immédiates' pour désamorcer le critère du rattachement local dans l'hébergement des sans-abri", *Housing Rights Watch* 2014, 26 pages.

BERNARD, N., "Pas d'expulsion de logement sans contrôle juridictionnel – le droit au logement et la Cour Européenne des Droits de l'Homme", *RTDH* 2009, no. 79, 527–552.

BERNARD, N., "Le droit au logement dans la Charte Sociale Révisée: à propos de la condamnation de la France par le Comité Européen des Droits Sociaux", *RTDH* 2009, no. 80, 1061–1089.

BREMS, E., "Indirect protection of social rights by the European Court of Human Rights", in BARAK-EREZ, D. and GROSS, A. (eds.), *Exploring social rights. Between theory and practice*, Portland, Hart Publishing, 2007, 135–167.

BRILLAT, R., "The European Social Charter and monitoring its implementation", in ALIPRANTIS, N. and PAPAGEORGIOU, I., (eds.), "Social rights at European, regional and international level. Challenges for the 21st century", Brussel, Bruylant, 2010, 43–59.

BRILLAT, R., "De collectieve klachtenprocedure van het Europese Sociale Handvest en de strijd tegen armoede", in Steunpunt tot Bestrijding van Armoede, Bestaansonzekerheid en Sociale Uitsluiting, *Armoede-Waardigheid-Mensenrechten*, Brussel, 2008, 74–80.

BUYSE, A., "Destruction of housing and discrimination against Roma – developments at the ECtHR", *Housing and ESC Rights Law Quarterly* 2006, vol. 3, no. 1, 5–6.

CHURCHILL, R. and KHALIQ, U., "Violations of Economic, Social and Cultural Rights: The Current Use and Future Potential of the Collective Complaints Mechanism of the European Social Charter", in BADERIN, M.A. and McCORQUODALE, R. (eds.), *Economic, Social and Cultural Rights in Action*, Oxford University Press, Oxford, 2007, 195–240.

CULLEN, H., "The collective complaints of the European Social Charter: interpretative methods of the European Committee of Social Rights", *HRLR* 2009, vol. 9, no. 1, 61–93.

DE SCHUTTER, O., "The protection of social rights by the European Court of Human Rights", in VAN DER AUWERAERT, P., DE PELSMAEKER, T., SARKIN, J. and VANDE LANOTTE, J. (eds.), *Social, economic and cultural rights. An appraisal of current European and international developments*, Antwerpen, Maklu, 2002, 207–239.

DUBOUT, E., "La procéduralisation des obligations relatives aux droits fondamentaux substantiels par la Cour européenne de droits de l'homme", *RTDH* 2007, no. 70, 397–425.

FORDER, C., "The right to legal aid according to the European Court of Human Rights: a study of the rights of undocumented persons", in HUBEAU, B. and TERLOUW, A. (eds.), *Legal aid in the Low Countries*, Antwerpen, Intersentia, 2014, 209–229.

GAILIUTE, D., "Right to housing in the jurisprudence of the European Committee of Social Rights", *Societal Studies* 2012, vol. 4, no. 4, 1605–1622.

GALANTER, M., "Why the 'Haves' Come Out Ahead: Speculations on the Limits of Legal Change", *Law and Society Review* 1974, vol. 9, no. 1, 95–160.

GARRY, H.R., "When procedure involves matters of life and death: interim measures and the European Convention on Human Rights", *E.P.L.* 2001, vol. 7, no. 3, 399–432.

GOEDERTIER, G., "Het Twaalfde Protocol E.V.R.M.: het non-discriminatiebeginsel losgekoppeld van de in het E.V.R.M. opgenomen rechten en vrijheden", *Jaarboek Mensenrechten* 2000–2001, 71–94.

HARRIS, D.J. and DARCY, J., *The European Social Charter*, New York, Transnational Publishers, 2001, 446 pages.

HEYLEN, K., *Grote woononderzoek 2013. Deel 2. Deelmarkten, woonkosten en betaalbaarheid,* Leuven, Steunpunt Wonen, 2015, 60 pages.

HOHMANN, J., *The right to housing. Law, concepts, possibilities*, Oxford, Hart Publishing, 2013, 75–91.

INSLEGERS, I., "Van inroepbaarheid naar afdwingbaarheid van het recht op wonen bekeken in mensenrechtelijk perspectief", in BERNARD, N. and HUBEAU, B. (eds.), *Recht op wonen: naar een resultaatsverbintenis?*, Brugge, Die Keure, 2013, 253–276.

KENNA, P. and JORDAN, M., "Housing rights in Europe: the Council of Europe leads the way", in KENNA, P. (ed.), *Contemporary housing issues in globalized world*, Farnham, Ashgate, 2014, 115–140.

KENNA, P., "Housing rights: positive duties and enforceable rights at the European Court of Human Rights", *E.H.R.L.R.* 2008, no. 2, (193) 193–208.

KOCH, I.E., "The European Convention on Human Rights and the protection of socio-economic demands", in MIHR, A. and GIBNEY, M. (eds.), *The SAGE Handbook of Human Rights. Volume 2*, Los Angeles, SAGE, 2014, 673–690.

KRAUSE, C., "The right to property", in EIDE, A., KRAUSE, C. and ROSAS, A. (eds.), *Economic, social and cultural rights*, Dordrecht, Martinus Nijhoff Publishers, 2001, 191–209.

KRSTICEVIC, V. and GRIFFEY, B., "Interim measures", in LANGFORD, M., PORTER, B., BROWN, R. and ROSSI, J. (eds.), *The Optional Protocol to the International Covenant on Economic, Social and Cultural Rights: a commentary*, Pretoria, University Law Press, 2015, 323–356.

KUCS, A. SEDLOVA, Z. and PIERHUROVICA, L., "The right to housing: international, European and national perspectives", *Cuadernos Constitucionales de la Cátedra Fadrique Furi Ceriol* 2008, no. 64/65, 101–123.

LANGFORD, M., "Judicial review in national courts: recognition and responsiveness", in RIEDEL, E., GIACCA, G. and GOLAY, C. (eds.), *Economic, social and cultural rights: Contemporary issues and challenges*, Oxford, Oxford University Press, 2014, 417–447.

LECKIE, S., "The human right to adequate housing", in EIDE, A., KRAUSE, C. and ROSAS, A. (eds.), *Economic, social and cultural rights*, Dordrecht, Martinus Nijhoff Publishers, 2001, 149–168.

LEIJTEN, I., "Meergelaagdheid en ondeelbare mensenrechten", *TBP* 2013, no. 2–3, 95–113.

MANTOUVALOU, V. and VOYATZIS, P., "The Council of Europe and the protection of human rights: a system in need of reform", in JOSEPH, S. and McBETH, A.

(eds.), *Research Handbook on International Human Rights Law*, Cheltenham, Edward Elgar Publishing, 2010, 326–352.

MIKKOLA, M., "Housing as a human right in Europe, 2006", *European Journal of Social Security* 2008, vol. 10, no. 3, 249–294.

OLDS, K., "The role of courts in making the right to housing a reality throughout Europe: lessons from France and the Netherlands", *Wisconsin International Law Journal* 2010, vol. 28, 170–199.

REMICHE, A., "Yordanova and Others v. Bulgaria: the influence of the social right to adequate housing on the interpretation of the civil right to respect for one's home", *H.R.L.R.* 2012, vol. 12, no. 4, 787–800.

ROZAKIS, C.L. and VOYATZIS, P., "'Le droit au respect de ses biens': une clause déclaratoire ou une 'omnibus' norme?", in VANDENBERGHE, H. (ed.), *Property and human rights*, Brugge, Die Keure, 2006, 1–28.

SARIGIANNIDIS, M. and PERVOU, I., "Adequate housing: seeking justiciability through the right to property", *International Journal of Human Rights and Constitutional Studies* 2013, vol. 1, no. 1, 27–40.

SCHEININ, M., "Access to justice before international human rights bodies", in FRANCIONI, F. (ed.), *Access to justice as a human right*, New York, Oxford University Press, 2007, 135–152.

SCHMID, C.U. and DINSE, J.R., *Towards a common core of residential tenancy law in Europe? The impact of the European Court of Human Rights on tenancy law*, 2013, www.jura.uni-bremen.de/lib/download.php?file=68a11d81f1.pdf&filename=WP%201_2013.pdf, 24 pages.

SIGRON, M., *Legitimate expectations under article 1 of Protocol no. 1 to the European Convention on Human Rights*, Antwerpen, Intersentia, 2014, 314 pages.

SLUYSMANS, J. and DE GRAAFF, R., "Ontwikkelingen in het eigendomsbegrip onder artikel 1 Eerste Protocol", *NJCM-Bulletin* 2014, vol. 39, no. 3, 255–271.

SPINKS, J., "De geoorloofdheid van het opleggen van eigendomsbeperkende maatregelen door de overheid", *Jura Falconis* 2004–2005, vol. 41, no. 3, 365–406.

SUDRE, F., "La protection des droits sociaux par la Cour Européenne des Droits de l'Homme: un exercice de 'jurisprudence fiction'?", *RTDH* 2003, no. 55.

SUDRE, F., "La perméabilité de la Convention européenne des droits de l'homme aux droits sociaux", *Pouvoir et liberté. Études offertes à J. Mourgeon*, Brussel, Bruylant, 1998, 46.

SUDRE, F., "Le protocole additionnel à la Charte Sociale Européenne prévoyant un système de réclamations collectives", *Revue Générale de Droit International Public* 1996, vol. 100, 715–739.

TULKENS, F. and VAN DROOGHENBROECK, S., "Armoede en mensenrechten. De bijdrage van het Europese Hof voor de Rechten van de Mens", in Steunpunt tot Bestrijding van Armoede, Bestaansonzekerheid en Sociale Uitsluiting, *Armoede-Waardigheid-Mensenrechten*, 2008, 65–73.

TULKENS, F., "La réglementation de l'usage des biens dans l'intérêt général. La troisième norme de l'article 1er du premier Protocole de la Convention européenne des Droits de l'homme", in VANDENBERGHE, H. (ed.), *Property and human rights*, Brugge, Die Keure, 2006, 61–97.

TULKENS, F. and VAN DROOGHENBROECK, S., "Le droit au logement dans la Convention Européenne des Droits de l'Homme. Bilan et perspectives", in BERNARD, N. and MERTENS, C. (eds.), *Le logement dans sa multidimensionalité. Une grande cause régionale*, Ministère de la Région wallonne, 2005, 311–323.

UHRY, M. and VIARD, T., "De Raad van Europa pakt Frankrijk aan over het recht op huisvesting en het recht op bescherming tegen armoede", in Steunpunt tot Bestrijding van Armoede, Bestaansonzekerheid en Sociale Uitsluiting, *Armoede-Waardigheid-Mensenrechten*, 2008, 81–88.

VANDENBERGHE, H., "La privation de propriété. La deuxième norme de l'article 1er du premier protocole de la Convention européenne des Droits de l'Homme", in VANDENBERGHE, H. (ed.), *Property and human rights*, Brugge, Die Keure, 2006, 29–59.

VANDENHOLE, W., "VN-mensenrechtencomité en Mensenrechtenhof op één lijn over verplichtend karakter voorlopige maatregelen", *Juristenkrant* 2003, no. 74, 12.

VAN DER MEI, A.P., "The justiciability of social rights in the European Union", in COOMANS, F. (ed.), *Justiciability of economic and social rights*, Antwerp, Intersentia, 2006, 389–408.

VAN DER PLANCKE, V. and SANT'ANA, M., "Protection des droits sociaux fondamentaux et lutte contre la pauvreté au sein du Conseil de l'Europe", in VAN DER PLANCKE, V. (ed.), *Les droits sociaux fondamentaux dans la lutte contre la pauvreté?*, Brussel, Die Keure, 2012, 211–265.

VANDERSTRAETEN, L. and RYCKEWAERT, M., *Groot woononderzoek 2013 deel 3: Technische woningkwaliteit*, Leuven, Steunpunt Wonen, 2015, 109 pages.

VELAERS, J., "'In foro interno et in foro externo': de international bevoegdheden van gemeenschappen en gewesten", in JUDO, F. and GEUDENS, G. (eds.), *Internationale betrekkingen en federalisme*, Gent, Larcier, 2006, 3–86.

VOLS, M., KIEHL, M. and SIDOLI DEL CENO, J., "Human rights and protection against eviction in anti-social behaviour cases in the Netherlands and Germany", *European Journal of Comparative Law and Governance* 2015, no. 2, 156–181.

WARBRICK, C., "Economic and social interests and the European Convention on Human Rights", in BADERIN, M.A. and McCORQUODALE, R. (eds.), *Economic, Social and Cultural Rights in Action*, Oxford, Oxford University Press, 2007, 241–256.

WILDHABER, L., "European Court of Human Rights", *C.Y.I.L.* 2002, vol. 40, 309–322.

WINTERS, S. et al., *Wonen in Vlaanderen anno 2013. De bevindingen uit het Grote Woononderzoek 2013 gebundeld*, Antwerpen, Garant, 2015, 97 pages.

Part III

Strengthening Housing Rights Obligations on the Domestic Level

Part III continues with exploring the obligations that could be imposed on states to protect and fulfill the right to adequate housing. The focus, however, shifts from what can be achieved directly or indirectly through European jurisprudence to how this fundamental right can obtain a more enforceable character at the national level.

This final part consists of three chapters that build on each other. Chapter 4 departs from the perception that socio-economic rights are less enforceable than civil and political rights and that the right to housing therefore imposes merely an obligation of means. It discusses the idea of transforming this to an obligation of result. There are, however, some serious questions and even objections to the use of such a classification of obligations with regard to the right to housing and socio-economic rights in general. In order to grasp the full extent of these complexities and its consequences on the protection of socio-economic rights, we deem it important to first take a step back and provide an in-depth analysis of the exact interpretation of these obligations. The downsides of using the obligations dichotomy as portrayed in Chapter 4 lead us to Chapters 5 and 6. Still in search of a more result-oriented right to housing at the domestic level, they explore whether progressive realization, the main concept of the International Covenant on Economic, Social and Cultural Rights (ICESCR), as well as its derivatives such as the prohibition to take retrogressive measures, could take up a (more concrete) role in this process. While Chapter 5 elaborates more theoretically about their meaning and how strictly or restrictively these obligations could or should be translated to the national level, Chapter 6 develops some more concrete proposals and recommendations on how to incorporate this idea of progressive realization more firmly and structurally into housing rights legislation and policy and trigger more result-oriented obligations.

4 From Obligation of Means to Obligation of Result?

1. Private Law

A. Origin and Meaning

Obligations of result and obligations of conduct have a longstanding history in private law. Both in national[1] as well as international[2] literature, these concepts are often attributed to French legal academic René Demogue, who first applied the distinction almost 90 years ago in the context of the burden of proof.[3] Nevertheless, obligations of means had already been introduced in a couple of Dutch publications shortly after the turn of the century.[4] Here, they were initially developed for reasons of fairness. This stemmed from situations where it might not be impossible for a debtor to achieve a certain result, but where at the same time one should not expect him to attain it.[5]

The original, private law interpretation of the distinction is unsurprisingly the most logical one. The obligation of result (*obligation de résultat*) is simply the obligation of the debtor to attain a predetermined result. The obligation of means or conduct *(obligation de moyens)* on the other hand obliges the debtor "only" to give his or her best effort to reach that result, but does not make him

1 M. STORME, *De bewijslast in het Belgisch privaatrecht*, Gent, Story-Scientia, 1962, 387–388; T. VANSWEEVELT, *De civielrechtelijke aansprakelijkheid van de geneesheer en het ziekenhuis*, Antwerpen, Maklu, 1992, 105.

2 M. PIERRAT, "De la distinction entre obligations de moyens et obligations de résultat: pile ou face?", *JT Luxembourg* 2011, no. 15, (61) 61–62; D. ALESSI, "The distinction between obligations de résultat and obligations de moyens and the enforceability of promises", *ERPL* 2005, vol. 5, (657) 659–660.

3 R. DEMOGUE, *Traité des obligations en général: Tome V*, Paris, Rousseau, 1925, 1237.

4 J.L.L. WERY, *Overmacht bij overeenkomsten*, Amsterdam, A.H. Kruyt, 1919; J.D.A. DEN TONKELAAR, *Resultaatsverbintenissen en inspanningsverbintenissen*, Zwolle, Tjeenk Willink, 1982, 1.

5 DEN TONKELAAR (n 4) 1–5; J.F. HOUWING, "Overmacht of onmogelijkheid?", *RM* 1904, 297; P.A.N. HOUWING, "De inhoud van de verbintenis en de overmacht, *WPNR* 1953, 4316–4324.

or her responsible solely on the basis of the final outcome.[6] The debtor must only act like a good housefather, or, in other words, in accordance with a thoughtful and careful person placed in the same circumstances.[7]

Obviously, this distinction offers the possibility to specify the content and scope of an agreement and can therefore also determine whether or not a debtor has complied with his responsibility.[8] Considering the cited origins for the development of the distinction, it evidently has considerable importance on the parties' burden of proof.[9] In the case of an obligation of result, the debtor can only free himself by *force majeure*.[10] With an obligation of means, on the other hand, it is the creditor who must prove non-compliance by lack of due diligence. He must demonstrate that the debtor has not acted as a *pater familias diligens*.[11] Although the burden of proof shifts from debtor to creditor depending on the qualification of the obligation, it is inaccurate to speak of a reverse *onus*. In accordance with the *actori incumbit probatio* principle, the creditor must still prove the existence and non-fulfillment of the commitment in case of an obligation of result.[12]

Considering the frequent absence of an explicit statement between the parties regarding the type of obligation, it is often the judge who will have to make a decision on the qualification. Most of the time, the aleatory character of the perceived result is then taken into account. This means that the decision depends on the extent to which the realization of the result is plausible.[13] The greater the uncertainty, the more likely it is considered to be an obligation of means, because a debtor does not want to commit himself to achieving a goal that he knows is very difficult to reach.[14]

The qualification regularly coincides with the specific nature of a certain agreement or a certain profession.[15] Professions do, however, sometimes hold both obligations of result and obligations of means. Lawyers, for example, have an obligation of result with regard to mere formal aspects of their job such as

6 P. WERY, *Droit des obligations. Vol. 1. Théorie générale du contrat*, Brussel, Larcier, 2010, 482; C. VANACKERE, "Enkele soorten verbintenissen", in J. ROODHOOFT (ed.), *Bestendig Handboek Verbintenissenrecht*, Antwerpen, Kluwer, 1998, I.2, (20) 25; L. VAN VALCKENBORGH, "De kwalificatie van een verbintenis als resultaats- of middelenverbintenis", *TBBR* 2011, vol. 5, (222) 222.

7 P. VAN OMMESLAGHE, *Droit des obligations: tome premier*, Brussel, Bruylant, 2010, 40; W. VAN GERVEN and S. COVEMAEKER, *Verbintenissenrecht*, Leuven, Acco, 2001, 28 and 239–241.

8 R. KRUITHOF, "Overzicht van rechtspraak (1974–1980)", *TPR* 1983, (495) 616.

9 VANACKERE (n 6) 25).

10 Court of Cassation 10 December 1953, *Arr. Cass.* 1954, 244; WERY (n 6) 483.

11 Court of Cassation 26 February 1962, *Pas.* 1962, I, 723; VAN GERVEN (n 7) 105–106.

12 VANSWEEVELT (n 1) 107.

13 PIERRAT (n 2) 62; VAN OMMESLAGHE (n 7) 40–41.

14 Court of Cassation 3 May 1984, *Arr. Cass.* 1983–1984, 1147–1151, concl.

15 VAN VALCKENBORGH (n 6) 223.

giving notice of appeal in due time,[16] but are not responsible for the outcome of the judgment.[17] This is, of course, somewhat different from the American point of view on advocacy, which is largely built on the idea of "no cure, no pay".[18] Furthermore, courts sometimes assess an obligation to be one of result,[19] while at other times they consider the same obligation to be one of means.[20] The obligation of a municipality to keep roads in a safe condition is a good illustration of such an inconsistency.

B. Success and Criticism

The private law distinction between obligations of result and obligations of means can only be described as a success. Extensively used in legal doctrine and frequently applied in court, the distinction has not found its way into a majority of Western and Northern European civil law codes.[21] Despite this widespread success, the concepts have not been void of criticism.[22] It has, for example, been argued that an obligation of means frequently comprises aspects that do not only require mere effort.[23] In response, we agree that there are often only a limited number of ways to work towards a certain goal in a diligent manner. It is therefore understandable that these actions or measures could also be regarded as obligations with regard to certain results or, more drastically, that the notion of obligation of means is fundamentally misconceived.[24] Nevertheless, we disagree with such criticism. The distinction is based on the obligation with regard to the intended "end result" or, in other words, the contract's purpose.[25] Performing certain actions within the realm of the agreement should thus not

16 Court of Appeal Antwerp 7 October 2002, *NJW* 2003, 493; Court of Appeal Antwerp 26 March 2006, *TBBR* 2008, 561.
17 P. DEPUYDT, "De beroepsaansprakelijkheid van de advocaat", *TBBR* 1993, 295–310; Court of Appeal Brussel 16 May 2002, *JLMB* 2003, 1673; Court of Appeal Luik 30 June 2000, *JLMB* 2005, 280.
18 R.E. KAUFMAN, M.F. DAVIS and H.M. WEGLEITNER, "The interdependence of rights: protecting the human right to housing by promoting the right to counsel", *Columbia Human Rights Law Review* 2014, vol. 45, no. 3, 772–815.
19 Peace Court Aarschot 23 October 1998, *TBBR* 1999, 148; Police Court Hoei 8 October 1985, *JL* 1985, 611.
20 Court of Cassation 6 November 2009, *TBP* 2010, 551; Court of Appeal Gent 16 April 2004, *T.Verz.* 2005, 361.
21 C. FERRON, "L'intensité de l'obligation juridique ou des obligations de diligence, de résultat et de garantie", *RDUS* 1991, (239) 240; ALESSI (n 2) 662; H. HONKA, "Harmonization of contract law through international trade: a Nordic perspective", *Tul. Eur. & Civ. L.F.* 1996, vol. 11, (111) 164–165.
22 H.C.F. SCHOORDIJK, "Inspanningsverbintenis en resultaatsverbintenis", *Bouwrecht* 1969, 65.
23 DEN TONKELAAR (n 4) 17.
24 ALESSI (n 2) 684–689. DEN TONKELAAR (n 4) 7 and 40.
25 DEN TONKELAAR (n 4) 7 and 40.

be confused with the performance connected to the contractual obligation itself.[26] The fact that, for example, a surgeon must be on time for surgery, respect hygienic procedures and apply specific tools does not in any way affect the qualification of the end result (curing the patient), as an obligation of means. If one would like to use the private law terminology for mere components of the commitment, it would be possible to speak of so-called obligations of result with regard to the means.[27]

2. Public International Law

The distinction between both types of obligations was first initiated in public international law in the context of the Draft Articles on State Responsibility (DASR) by then Special Rapporteur of the International Law Commission (ILC) Roberto Ago in the late 1970s.[28] Although the final version of the DASR no longer includes specific provisions on these obligations,[29] the commentary to the current article 12 shows that the distinction is still very much alive and relevant in international law.[30] It is therefore certainly of value to look back at the definition that was given in articles 20 and 21 DASR of the 1977 version.

According to article 21, a state has an obligation of result when it has to achieve a specific result, but still has the discretion and freedom to choose the appropriate way to reach this goal. No specific measures are, in other words, imposed internationally, or these measures only contain mere preferences. The commentaries to the concerned provision use article 2(1) of the International Covenant on Economic, Social and Cultural Rights (ICESCR) as an example of this, because it proposes the adoption of legislative measures as one of the appropriate means to progressively achieve the realization of the convention rights without limiting the state's discretion.[31] In other words, a large margin of appreciation is given to the state to accomplish what is then often some kind

26 ALESSI (n 2) 687.
27 VANSWEEVELT (n 1) 121.
28 P. GAUTIER, "On the Classification of Obligations in International Law", in H.P. HESTERMEYER, D. KÖNIG, N. MATZ-LÜCK, V. RÖBEN, A. SEIBERT-FOHR, P.-T. STOLL and S. VÖNEKY (eds.), *Coexistence, cooperation and solidarity. Liber amicorum Rüdiger Wolfrum*, Dordrecht, Martinus Nijhoff Publishers, 2012, (853) 854.
29 UN International Law Commission, *Draft Articles on Responsibility of States for Internationally Wrongful Acts*, 2001, www.un.org/ga/search/view_doc.asp?symbol=A/res/56/83.
30 UN International Law Commission, *Draft Articles on Responsibility of States for Internationally Wrongful Acts, with commentaries*, UN Doc. A/56/10, 2001, 56–57.
31 United Nations, *Sixth report on state responsibility, by Mr. Roberto Ago, Special Rapporteur – the internationally wrongful act of the state, source of international responsibility*, UN Doc. A/CN.4/302 and Yearbook of the International Law Commission 1977. Vol. II, part one, 1978, (3) 8–9.

of benchmark or imposed target[32], such as reducing homelessness to a certain level by 2020:

> A breach of an international obligation requiring the State to achieve a particular result, exists if, by the conduct adopted in exercising its freedom of choice, the State has not in fact achieved the internationally required result.[33]

In contrast to the obligation of result, the international obligation of conduct[34] compels a state to follow a specific course of action and adopt and implement defined measures.[35] In the context of the right to housing, we could think of the obligation to develop a national housing strategy.[36] Consequently, article 20 describes the non-compliance as follows:

> A breach by the State of an international obligation specifically calling for it to adopt a particular course of conduct exists simply by virtue of the adoption of a course of conduct different from that specifically required.[37]

As a matter of fact, a breach by the state of an international obligation of conduct even occurs when the set goal is effectively reached, but not in the way or by measures that were actually imposed. When, for example, child labor is non-existent in a state, this state would theoretically still violate article 10(3) ICESCR if the employment of children in circumstances that are harmful to their health is not punishable by law.[38] Evidently, this appears to have little to no relevance for human rights supervisory bodies. The absence or lack of legislation that has been imposed by human rights treaty law is highly unlikely

32 Ibid., 4 and 8–9; A.P.M. COOMANS, *De internationale bescherming van het recht op onderwijs*, Leiden, Stichting NJCM-boekerij, 1992, 28–29.

33 United Nations, *Sixth report on state responsibility, by Mr. Roberto Ago, Special Rapporteur – the internationally wrongful act of the state, source of international responsibility*, UN Doc. A/CN.4/302 and Yearbook of the International Law Commission 1977. Vol. II, part one, 1978, (3) 20.

34 In international law, obligation of conduct is more frequently used than obligation of means.

35 R. LEFEBER, *Transboundary Environmental Interference and the Origin of State Liability*, Den Haag, Kluwer, 1996, 74; United Nations, *Fourth report on state responsibility, by Mr. James Crawford, Special Rapporteur*, UN Doc. A/CN.4/498 and Yearbook of International Law Commission 2001. Volume II, part one, (1) 20.

36 S. LECKIE, "Another step towards indivisibility: identifying the key features of violations of ECOSOC rights", *HRQ* 1998, (81) 92.

37 United Nations, *Sixth report on state responsibility, by Mr. Roberto Ago, Special Rapporteur – the internationally wrongful act of the state, source of international responsibility*, UN Doc. A/CN.4/302 and Yearbook of the International Law Commission 1977. Vol.II, part one, 1978, (3) 8.

38 Ibid., 6.

to amount to a violation of that treaty when no direct victim is involved.[39] As a matter of fact, the latter is a recurrent admissibility criterion. Of course, both the universal periodic review under the auspices of the Human Rights Council and the reporting procedures by the UN treaty based committees do recognize holes in the legislative protection of human rights. The judicial consequences are then, however, confined to recommendations or issues of concern.

3. Differences between Both Approaches

Although it was clearly stated that the inspiration for the distinction in public international law came from private law, the ILC has managed to tangle up the interpretation of the concept and has to a certain extent even switched their meanings.[40] The diverging approach was even mentioned in the commentaries to that version of the DASR.[41] Remarkably, no real further thought was ever given to the possible consequences of such a conceptual development. In academic literature, the distinction has remained largely unnoticed too.[42]

Two main differences can be perceived. The first one concerns the gravity of the obligations. Since an obligation of means or conduct according to private law is only a best-efforts obligation, the obligation of result obviously comprises the heavier duty in that field of law.[43] In contrast, it is the obligation of conduct that is the more demanding obligation in public international law, as it confines the state's policy discretion to attain the set goal.[44] Considering, though, that compliance with the specific measures typical of international

39 An exception: ECtHR 22 October 1981, no. 7525/76, Dudgeon/United Kingdom.

40 P.-M. DUPUY, "Reviewing the difficulties of codification: on Ago's classification of obligations of means and obligations of result in relation to state responsibility", *EJIL* 1999, vol. 10, no. 2, (371) 376; United Nations, *Summary records of the meetings of the fifty-first session*, UN Doc. A/CN.4/SER.A/1999 and Yearbook of the International Law Commission 1999. Volume I, 48 (opinion of Mr. Al-Khasawneh).

41 United Nations, *Sixth report on state responsibility, by Mr. Roberto Ago, Special Rapporteur – the internationally wrongful act of the state, source of international responsibility*, UN Doc. A/CN.4/302 and Yearbook of the International Law Commission 1977. Vol. II, part one, 1978, (3) 8; United Nations, *Report of the International Law Commission on the work of its twenty-ninth session*, UN Doc. A/32/10 and Yearbook of the International Law Commission 1977. Vol. II, part two, 1978, 12.

42 One of the few exceptions: O. DE SCHUTTER, *Fonctions de juger et droits fondamentaux. Transformation du contrôle juridictionnel dans les ordres juridiques Américain et Européens*, Bruxelles, Bruylant, 1999, 136–139.

43 DEN TONKELAAR (n 4) 44.

44 M.E. SALOMON, *Global Responsibility for Human Rights: World Poverty and the Development of International Law*, Oxford, Oxford University Press, 2007, 133; United Nations, *Fourth report on state responsibility, by Mr. James Crawford, Special Rapporteur*, UN Doc. A/CN.4/498 and Yearbook of International Law Commission 2001. Vol. II, part one, (1) 21; DUPUY (n 40) 375–376.

obligations of conduct is in fact a result in and of itself, we argue that this type of obligation could actually be regarded as small, intermediate obligations of result according to private law.[45] These considerations are strongly reminiscent of the above-mentioned criticism on the validity of the obligation of means. The only difference here is that we are no longer talking about components of an obligation of means (private law), but about an international obligation of conduct, a full-fledged and independent obligation.

Second and strongly connected to the first difference is the basis behind the distinction.[46] In private law this is the failed result. In practice, the question as to the qualification of the obligation normally only arises on these occasions. It should not influence the debtor beforehand, since his/her intention should still be to achieve the end result of the commitment.[47] This follows quite naturally from the fact that the distinction originated in the context of the burden of proof. The distinction in international law on the other hand is primarily based on the way in which a state is expected to achieve the result.[48] Consequently, the international obligation of result strongly resembles the definition of an EU directive[49]: "A directive shall be binding, as to the result to be achieved, upon each Member State to which it is addressed, but shall leave to the national authorities the choice of form and methods."[50]

Evidently, the two different interpretations demand to be applied with the utmost care and consistency. The approaches from both fields of law should at all times be kept separately. Unsurprisingly, however, this has not always been the case. In a case between Argentina and Uruguay, the International Court of Justice initially seemed to adhere to the obligation of conduct as described in international law, proclaiming the duty to specific conduct:

> The Court considers that the obligation [. . .] prescribes the specific conduct of coordinating the necessary measures [. . .] to avoid changes to the ecological balance. An obligation to adopt regulatory or administrative

45 M.C.R. CRAVEN, *The International Covenant on Economic, Social and Cultural Rights. A perspective on its development*, Oxford, Clarendon Press, 1995, 108.

46 M. STORME (n 1) 107; J. COMBACAU, "Obligations de résultat et obligations de comportement. Quelques questions et pas de réponse", in D. BARDONNET, J. COMBACAU, M. VIRALLY and P. WEIL (eds.), *Mélanges offerts à Paul Reuter. Le droit international: unité et diversité*, Paris, Éditions A. Pedone, 1981, (181) 194: "[. . .] *que l'objectif n'ait pas été atteint, c'est sans doute une condition nécessaire à la mise en œuvre de la responsabilité*"; GAUTIER (n 28) 857.

47 ALESSI (n 2) 687.

48 COMBACAU (n 46) 194–195 and 202; ALESSI (n 2) 657–692; United Nations, *Fourth report on state responsibility, by Mr. James Crawford, Special Rapporteur*, UN Doc. A/CN.4/498 and Yearbook of International Law Commission 2001. Vol. II, part one, (1) 21.

49 GAUTIER (n 28) 855.

50 Art. 288 Treaty on the Functioning of the European Union.

> measures either individually or jointly and to enforce them is an obligation of conduct.[51]

Subsequently, however, the Court changes course and explains the obligation in a private law sense, as a best-efforts obligation:[52]

> Both parties are therefore called upon [. . .] to exercise due diligence in acting through the Commission for the necessary measures to preserve the ecological balance of the river.[53]

It is in circumstances like these that ambiguities regarding the exact scope of obligations and thus also their compliance occur. As we will see, however, the main difficulties arise in a human rights context.

4. Impact on Economic, Social and Cultural Rights and the Right to Housing

A. Obligations of Result or Conduct? According to Private or International Law?

Before proceeding with the issue under scrutiny, we deem it important to stress that economic, social and cultural rights, just as civil and political rights, actually contain both obligations of result and obligations of conduct/means. Article 6 ICESCR concerning the right to work requires, for example, that steps have to be taken to realize complete employment (international obligation of result), but also very concretely forbids forced labor (international obligation of conduct).[54] That much has even been explicitly stated in General Comment No. 3 of the Committee on Economic, Social and Cultural Rights (CESCR) on the nature of the obligations of state parties,[55] and is generally accepted in international human rights literature.[56] In practice, however, we

51 ICJ 20 April 2010, *Pulp Mills on the River Uruguay (Argentina v. Uruguay)*, www.icj-cij.org, par. 187. GAUTIER (n 28) 857.

52 GAUTIER (n 28) 857.

53 ICJ 20 April 2010, *Pulp Mills on the River Uruguay (Argentina v. Uruguay)*, www.icj-cij.org, par. 187.

54 Art. 6 ICESCR; CRAVEN (n 45) 108.

55 UN Committee of Social, Economic and Cultural Rights, *General Comment No.3: The Nature of States Parties' Obligations (art. 2, para. 1 of the Covenant)*, 14 December 1990, par. 1 (hereafter General Comment No. 3).

56 E.g. M. SEPULVEDA, *The nature of the obligations under the International Covenant on Economic, Social and Cultural Rights*, Antwerpen, Intersentia, 2003, 185–195; D. MATAS, "Economic, social and cultural rights and the role of lawyers: North American perspectives", *ICJ Review* 1985, no. 55, (123) 124; P. ALSTON and G. QUINN, "The nature and scope of states parties' obligations under the International Covenant on

notice that a dichotomy between human rights of the first and second generation is still very much present and that economic, social and cultural (ESC) rights are still perceived as having second-class status and being less enforceable.[57]

During the negotiations of what would eventually become the ICESCR back in the early 1950s, Western delegations showed considerable reluctance to make these so-called second-generation rights strong, enforceable obligations and the equivalent of civil and political rights.[58] This reticence revolved around sheer practical concerns, since the realization of ESC rights are often considered to be much more onerous and costly.[59] Consequently and similar to private law, the aleatory character of these obligations also determined the classic qualification of ESC rights. René Cassin, one of the drafters of the Universal Declaration of Human Rights, referred in this context to the private law distinction and found that ESC rights should *not* be expressed as obligations of result, but rather as obligations to take action, thereby implying obligations of means.[60] Considering that the interpretation by the ILC was still in the distant future, the distinction made by Cassin could only be interpreted in a private law sense. But even today, almost 40 years after the ILC's elaborations on the concepts, we see that the right to housing is occasionally still described as an obligation of means, especially in a domestic context.[61]

In Flanders, the preparatory works to the Housing Code are explicit: the right to housing is an obligation of means. The government should help in the realization of this right, but cannot guarantee it in absolute terms. It cannot be considered an obligation of result because the government does not, "and certainly not the Flemish government", dispose of all resources (both material

Economic, Social and Cultural Rights", *HRQ* 1987, vol. 9, no. 2, (156) 185; CRAVEN (n 45) 107–108; LECKIE (n 36) 92

57 P. O'CONNELL, *Vindicating socio-economic rights. International standards and comparative experiences*, London, Routledge, 2012, 1–2; CESCR, *Report of the open-ended working group to consider options regarding the elaboration of an optional protocol to the International Covenant on Economic, Social and Cultural Rights*, 15 March 2004, UN Doc E/CN.4/2004/44.

58 M.J. DENNIS and D.P. STEWART, "Justiciability of economic, social and cultural rights: should there be an international complaints mechanism to adjudicate the rights to food, water, housing and health?, *AJIL* 2004, vol. 98, no. 3, (462) 476–484; M.R. ISHAY, *The history of human rights*, London, University of California Press, 2004, 221–229.

59 DENNIS (n 58) 484; ALSTON (n56) 174; A. EIDE, "Economic, Social and Cultural Rights as Human Rights", in A. EIDE, C. KRAUSE and A. ROSAS (eds.), *Economic, social and cultural rights. A textbook (second revised edition)*, Dordrecht, Martinus Nijhoff Publishers, 2001, (9) 10.

60 UN Commission on Human Rights, *Summary record of the two hundred and seventieth meeting*, 14 May 1952, UN Doc. E/CN.4/SR.270, 11.

61 W. VANDENHOLE, "Recht op wonen als resultaatsverbintenis? Enkele reflecties", *Juristenkrant 2013*, no. 264, 12; F. DELPEREE, "Les droits sociaux fondamentaux et le droit belge", in M. STROOBANT (ed.), *Sociale grondrechten*, Antwerpen, Maklu, 1995, (19) 27; B. HUBEAU and A. VAN DE WIEL, "Recht op wonen als resultaatsverbintenis. Over de effectiviteit van sociale grondrechten", *TvMR* 2013, no. 3, 11–14.

and immaterial) that would require this outcome.[62] The aleatory character of the obligation illustrates its aforementioned importance for making this distinction.

On the basis, however, of a strict application of this classification, it should be possible to hold the state accountable if it does not take steps to guarantee this fundamental right. After all, an obligation of means is and remains an obligation for which the debtor in question is responsible, an enforceable duty for which the debtor can be held accountable.[63] It is not because the government has a large margin of discretion that it is hypothetically allowed not to do anything at all.[64] Back in 1995, Delpérée already argued that

> an obligation of means is not an absence of duty. When a Constitution clarifies that the law must guarantee social rights, it should not be taken as a sociological statement, but as a genuine legal obligation on the public powers [. . .] to pursue these objectives.[65] [Translated]

Yet there is clearly still some uncertainty about the possibility to lodge a successful liability claim.[66] It is almost as if the term is used in a way just to differentiate from the fact that it is not an obligation of result, that it focuses rather on the extensive freedom (policy- and resource-related) the government has at its disposal (i.e. an obligation of result according to international law) than the responsibility it should also bring along.

These previous considerations are based on the private law classification. Given, though, that human rights are part of public international law, it is not surprising that the interpretation made by the ILC has also made a considerable impact on classifying human rights obligations. The aforementioned General Comment No. 3 actually even refers to the work of the ILC as a main source.[67]

62 Explanatory Memorandum to the draft of Decree concerning the Flemish Housing Code, *Parl.St.* Vl. Parl. 1996–97, no. 654/1, 11; L. GOOSSENS, "De scheve schaats rond het recht op wonen. Bespiegelingen rond wonen na 10 jaar samenwerkingsakkoord rond armoedebeleid", in Steunpunt tot Bestrijding van Armoede, Bestaansonzekerheid en Sociale Uitsluiting, *Armoede-Waardigheid-Mensenrechten*, 2008, (147) 148.

63 Y. TRILLET, "Vers une nouvelle effectivité des droits économiques, sociaux et culturels?", *Dr.Q.M.* 2000, vol.27, (3) 9–10.

64 A. VANDEBURIE, "La mise en œuvre de droit à un logement décent de Waterloo à l'hôtel Tagawa, où sont les responsables" (note under Peace Court Brussel 14 November 2006), *TBBR* 2008, (489) 496–497.

65 DELPEREE (n 61) 27; VANDEBURIE (n 64) 495.

66 G. MAES, *De afdwingbaarheid van sociale grondrechten*, Antwerpen, Intersentia, 2003, 138; see with regard to the right to social aid: M. DISPERSYN, "Le droit à la sécurité dans l'article 23 de la Constitution", in R. ERGEC (ed.), *Les droits économiques, sociaux et culturels dans la Constitution*, Brussel, Bruylant, 1995, (193) 226: "*le citoyen ne pourra pas mettre en cause l'abstention du législateur qui n'aurait pas pris les mesures déterminant les conditions d'exercice d'un droit.*"

67 CESCR, *General Comment No. 3*, par. 1

Similarly, this distinction has again been used as a way to split civil and political rights on the one hand and economic, social and cultural rights on the other. The former category is then often labeled as obligations of conduct (the heavier obligation in international law), the latter rather as obligations of result.[68] This had sprung from the rudimentary idea that while civil and political rights mainly encompass negative obligations (obligation to respect), social and economic rights demand positive action (obligation to fulfill) and therefore also necessitate a large margin of state discretion in order to realize them, ergo only imposing obligations of result.[69]

B. A Recipe for Confusion

From the above, we can deduce that ESC rights have been called both obligations of conduct/means and obligations of result, not only because they actually entail both types of obligations, but sometimes just depending on whether the use of the concept is derived from private law or from international law. The reason why this has remained largely unnoticed probably pertains to the fact that in both fields of law these rights are linked with the "lighter" obligation. In other words, they are regarded in both formulations as having only limited enforceability. The use of one interpretation or the other possibly also depends upon the context in which the qualification is used: the judicial enforceability of an obligation or the way in which a fundamental right should be realized.

Nevertheless, we believe that this creates confusion. First because this is ambiguous in a purely terminological sense. When, for example, a judge of the European Court of Human Rights states that "social rights are usually viewed as obligations of conduct" with regard to taking steps with a view to achieve the progressive realization of these rights,[70] this deviates from General Comment No. 3, where progressive realization is considered the "principal obligation of result".[71] Did this happen consciously or is it actually a case of

68 B.A. ANDREASSEN, A.G. SMITH and H. STOKKE, "Compliance with economic and social human rights: realistic evaluations and monitoring in the light of immediate obligations", in A. EIDE and B. HAGTVET (eds.), *Human Rights in Perspective: a Global Assessment,* Oxford, 1992, (252) 256; SEPULVEDA (n 56) 185–195; MATAS (n 56) 188.

69 E.A. POSNER, "Human welfare, not human rights", *Columbia Law Review* 2008, vol. 108, (1758) 1765; B. PORTER, "Reasonableness and article 8(4)", in R. BROWN, M. LANGFORD, B. PORTER and J. ROSSI, *The Optional Protocol to the International Covenant on Economic, Social and Cultural Rights: a commentary*, Capetown, Pretoria University Law Press, 2016 (194) 196–197; EIDE (n 59) 24–25.

70 Partly concurring, partly dissenting opinion of Judge Pinto de Albuquerque, ECtHR 22 March 2012, no. 30078/06, Konstantin Markin/Russia.

71 CESCR 14 December 1990, General Comment No. 3, *The Nature of States Parties' Obligations (art. 2, para. 1 of the Covenant)*, par. 9.

what we might call "private law contamination", maybe due to the fact that the Court usually applies these obligations as private law concepts?[72, 73]

A second and more important reason for being accurate in using this typology stems from the fact that, as we have seen, the content of the cited obligations according to international law differs from the content of the obligations in private law. Moreover, they are not each other's exact opposites either. It can thus easily create ambiguities with regard to the exact scope of the obligations for states. We will illustrate this by referring to the decision of *ATD Fourth World against France* by the European Committee of Social Right[74] (see Chapter 3). On the basis of this decision, Executive Secretary of the ECSR Régis Brillat concluded, in our opinion correctly, that the classic distinction between obligations of means and obligations of result is not a satisfactory interpretation framework for understanding the Charter.[75]

We know that ATD Fourth World argued that the French state had violated articles 16, 30 and 31 of the Revised European Social Charter by not fulfilling its obligation to adequately house people who lived in situations of extreme poverty. Specifically relevant for the purposes of this chapter, however, is the argument of the French government that the right to adequate housing (art. 31) imposes only an obligation of means. That proclamation here clearly refers to the best-efforts obligation from private law.[76] In its response to the argument, the Committee agrees that the relevant provision "cannot be interpreted as imposing on states an obligation of 'results'", but also that the right must "take a practical and effective, rather than purely theoretical, form".[77] The Committee illustrates this by enlisting five measures that must be carried out in order for the situation to be in conformity with the treaty. We will return to these measures in the context of progressive realization in the next chapter.[78]

72 E.g. ECtHR 21 June 1988, no. 10126/82, Plattform "Ärtze für das Leben"/Austria, par. 34; ECtHR 25 August 2009, no. 23458/02, Giuliana & Gaggio/Italy, par. 210.

73 Another clear example of how the terminology can be mixed up: Separate Opinion of Judge Cançado Trindade, ICJ 20 July 2012, *Belgium vs. Senegal (Questions Relating to the Obligation to Prosecute or Extradite)*, www.icj-cij.org, par. 46–47.

74 ECSR 5 December 2007, no. 33/2006, International Movement ATD Fourth World/ France.

75 R. BRILLAT, "The effective implementation of the right to housing of homeless of poorly housed persons: the role of the European Social Charter", *Feantsa Magazine* 2008, no. 2, (7) 7.

76 Ibid., par. 58.

77 Ibid., par.59.

78 Ibid., par.60:

"a. adopt the necessary legal, financial and operational means of ensuring steady progress towards achieving the goals laid down by the Charter;
b. maintain meaningful statistics on needs, resources and results;
c. undertake regular reviews of the impact of the strategies adopted;
d. establish a timetable and not defer indefinitely the deadline for achieving the objectives of each stage; e. pay close attention to the impact of the policies adopted on each of the categories of persons concerned, particularly the most vulnerable."

Nonetheless, these obligations clearly reach further than the best-efforts obligation the French government had in mind when claiming that the right to housing does not impose an obligation of result. It actually obliges the state to apply imposed measures and take specific actions. In other words, the Committee interprets article 31 much more as imposing the heavier international obligation of conduct.[79] By using actual parentheses when stating that the provision in question is not an obligation of "results", the Committee unconsciously confirms the confusion surrounding the two-sided nature of the concept. Surely, the right to adequate housing might not be an obligation of result in terms of realizing adequate housing for everyone at this very moment, but it does impose smaller obligations that on their own could be interpreted as intermediate results that are enforceable and which aim at progressive realization.[80] Along the same lines, Nicolas Bernard has stated that "the traditional obligation of means should rather be understood as an obligation to gradually achieve the result" (translated).[81]

As exemplified, the muddled history of the concepts can lead to states being unsure of what exact obligations they carry, but it can also be used as an argument to try to reduce their responsibility. Considering the above, we believe that this confusion could very well have been a factor in maintaining the image of ESC rights as programmatic ideals and that it has therefore hindered the evolution of ESC rights as stronger, more enforceable human rights. Too often these rights are still interpreted as mere best-efforts obligations according to private law in order not to be held responsible by the end result, but at the same time they are coupled with the large margin of discretion typical of an international obligation of result, the less severe obligation in that field of law.

5. Towards Result-Oriented Obligations?

A. *The Right to Housing as an Obligation of Result*

In the last couple of years the idea has been raised to transform the right to housing from the current obligation of means (or at least this is what it is

79 The ECSR has repeated this approach in: ECS 19 October 2009, no. 51/2008, European Roma Rights Centre (ERRC)/France, par. 30.

80 M. UHRY and T. VIARD, "De Raad van Europa pakt Frankrijk aan over het recht op huisvesting en het recht op bescherming tegen armoede", in Steunpunt tot Bestrijding van Armoede, Bestaansonzekerheid en Sociale Uitsluiting, *Armoede-Waardigheid-Mensenrechten*, 2008, (81) 85.

81 N. BERNARD, "Le droit au logement dans la Charte Sociale Révisée: à propos de la condamnation de la France par le Comité Européen des Droits Sociaux", *RTDH* 2009, no. 80, (1061) 1078.

perceived as) to an obligation of result.[82] It was borne from the notion that the law was previously insufficiently effective, a concession that the obligation of means has failed to deliver, and, by consequence, that a switch is required to an obligation of result.

The idea of working towards an obligation of result is, of course, rather vague because the right to housing comprises much more than only one obligation by one actor. Instead, the right penetrates to different areas of law and consists of an intricate web of obligations in which various actors occur: among them legislators, mayors, social housing agencies, public centers for social welfare, but also private renters and tenants. And within this framework, several obligations of result have already been recognized. Sometimes it just depends on when exactly one considers an obligation that deals with housing in general as being connected to the fundamental right to housing. Take a normal private rental agreement managed by civil law.[83] Even though this is not directly linked to the fundamental right to housing and pertains to a strictly horizontal legal relationship, this legislation cannot be considered as being disengaged from such a fundamental rights context either. Housing rent legislation will often dictate with which elementary standards of safety, health and livability the rented property must comply.[84] This type of provision and its accompanying obligations, which often include obligations of result, are then clearly related to the fundamental right to housing too. To illustrate this, we refer to a Flemish Peace Court decision of 2012, concerning the obligation of the landlord to ensure peaceful enjoyment of the rented good, *in casu* by providing heat and water:

> [T]he landlord has failed his essential obligation of result to allow the tenant peaceful enjoyment during the term of the lease. Left without heating or hot water [. . .], Mrs. B. suffered a severe disturbance which harmed her right to housing under dignified conditions.[85]

Obligations of result have nonetheless been recognized more directly related to the Belgian constitutional right to housing as well, albeit on rare occasions. One of the few unambiguous judicial decisions regarding the type of obligation stems from the Labor Court of Nivelles. In 2005, this court emphatically imposed an obligation of result on the Public Center for Social Welfare to

82 N. BERNARD and B. HUBEAU (eds.), *Recht op wonen: naar een resultaatsverbintenis?*, Brugge, Die Keure, 2013, 308 pages; G. VAN IMPE, "L'effectivité du droit au logement: une obligation de résultat à charge des pouvoirs publics?", *Echos log.* 2012, no. 2, 39–40.

83 Art. 1708–1762bis Belgian Civil Code.

84 Art.2 Housing Rent Act.

85 Peace Court Grâce-Hollogne 25 May 2012, *JLMB* 2012, no. 40, (1917) 1921.

provide a home with respect to homeless people and people who live in unhealthy dwellings which infringe their human dignity.[86]

Consequently, the general idea to make the right to housing into an obligation of result does clearly not mean that such obligations do not yet exist in this context.[87] The idea is rather based on the notion that the right to housing could be more strongly enforced. And the way to achieve this is by having more obligations of result across the whole housing policy. But what about the obligations of result that are already in place? Do they simply not suffice to have a tangible impact on the effectiveness of this fundamental right or could it perhaps be possible that once again the complexity of the concepts leads to wrong interpretations. We will take a closer look at some obligations related to housing rights that frequently pop up in this discussion and are occasionally interpreted as imposing results.

First, references are often made to the French '*Droit au Logement Opposable*' (DALO) as a good example of how to make the right to housing an obligation of result. This tool gives homeless or inadequately housed individuals priority in the allocation – within a certain period of time – of a home suitable to their needs. The law also provides for the allocation of temporary housing. The target groups are persons who have applied for social housing but whose waiting period is exceptionally long, homeless and inadequately housed persons (including through evictions and rehousing) and persons applying for housing adapted specifically to their needs. The decision on the priority question is taken by a mediation commission. Persons who have been labeled as such then have an opportunity for recourse to the administrative courts if no housing option has been given within a certain period of time.[88] This court will then

86 Labour Court Nijvel (2nd Chamber) 8 November 2005, no. 677/N/2005, *Soc.Kron.* 2008, vol. 2, (108) 109: "Le droit au logement constitue un droit fondamental, énoncé à l'article 23 de la Constitution. Il appartient aux C.P.A.S. de garantir ce droit. Les obligations des C.P.A.S. présentent cependant des degrés différents selon la situation de la personne concernée:

A. A l'égard des personnes sans logement, ou vivant dans les conditions d'insalubrité portant gravement atteinte à la dignité humaine, le C.P.A.S. est tenu par une obligation de résultat: il doit leur trouver un logement.
B. A l'égard des personnes qui disposent d'un logement, mais qui font appel au C.P.A.S. parce que leur logement n'est plus adapté à leurs moyens financiers, à leur situation familiale ou à leur état de santé, le C.P.A.S. a une obligation de moyen: il doit mettre activement ses services à disposition de ces personnes pour les accompagner dans leurs recherches, mais elles ne disposent pas d'un droit leur permettant d'exiger du C.P.A.S. qu'il leur mette un logement à disposition."

87 VANDENHOLE (n 61) 12.

88 P. QUILICHINI, "Le droit au logement opposable", *AJDI* 2007, 364; E. SALES, "Droit constitutionnel et droit social. La dualité du 'droit au logement opposable'", *RFDC* 2009, no. 79, 601–620; R. PIASTRA, "Observations sur le droit au logement opposable", *Dalloz* 2007, 809.

oblige the prefect to rehouse this person on penalty of financial compensation. However, this non-compliance fine has to be paid not to the person in question, but to a social housing fund from the government,[89] thereby creating a vicious circle where the money goes from one specific budget line for housing to the other.[90] It is therefore debatable whether this "*droit opposable*" really imposes an obligation of result in full compliance with the concept as understood in civil law.[91]

Returning to Belgian and Flemish housing law, one of the most recognized examples of an obligation of result probably concerns the allocation of social housing. Whenever a person complies with certain admission criteria, he is entitled to it. In reality, however, there are very long waiting lists. Consequently, for many households eligible for social housing the impact of this obligation of "result" is very limited.

Another illustration is the Flemish rehousing obligation by the public government and its agencies. When a mayor decides that the occupancy of the unfit or uninhabitable dwelling has to be stopped, the Flemish Housing Code requires the mayor to try to rehouse those tenants (via the municipality, the OCMW or social housing organizations) who comply with the income and property requirements from the social rental sector. There has been some discussion in the legal doctrine on the type of obligation (result or means) that is imposed upon the mayor in cases of unsuitable, uninhabitable or overcrowded housing.[92] Most do appear to acknowledge, though, that it is an obligation of means.[93] For a mayor's rehousing obligation to amount to an obligation

89 B. LACHARME, "Reconnu hier, opposable aujourd'hui, assumé demain? Le droit au logement en France", in N. BERNARD and B. HUBEAU (eds.), *Recht op wonen: naar een resultaatsverbintenis?*, Brugge, Die Keure, 2013, (31) 40.

90 Out of discontent with this appeal procedure, some plaintiffs have (successfully) sued the state for compensation, e.g. Tribunal Administratif de Paris 17 December 2010, www.legifrance.gouv.fr.

91 L. THOLOMÉ, "Le droit au logement opposable : gadget ou véritable protection sociale?", *Echos log.* 2007, no. 2, 17–24.

92 S. LIERMAN and P.J. VAN DE WEYER, "Recente ontwikkelingen in de rechtspraak en de wetgeving over algemene bestuurlijke politiebevoegdheden van de gemeente", in X., *Recht in beweging*, Antwerpen, Maklu, 2014, 48–49; N. BERNARD, *La réception du droit au logement par la jurisprudence. Quand les juges donnent corps au droit au logement*, Brussel, Larcier, 2011, 56–63; L. THOLOMÉ, "L'article 23 de la constitution n'est pas une simple déclaration de principe", *Echos log. 2000*, no. 4, (121) 122; B. HUBEAU, "De uithuiszetting en de herhuisvesting, de Achilleshiel in het sociaal woonbeleid, ook in het Vlaamse Gewest", *PRK* 2010, vol. 14, (43) 47–48; T. VANDROMME, *Woningkwaliteitsbewaking in het Vlaamse Gewest*, Mechelen, Kluwer, 2008, 73; F. TOLLENAERE, "Uithuiszettingen, Het standpunt van de huurders", in N. BERNARD (ed.), *Les expulsions de logement/Uithuiszettingen*, Brugge, Die Keure, 2010, (161) 170; Steunpunt Armoedebestrijding, *Strijd tegen armoede. Een bijdrage aan politiek debat en politieke actie*, 2011, 33.

93 De Smedt has changed his opinion on this issue over time: P. DE SMEDT, "De woonkwaliteitsregeling in de Vlaamse Wooncode", in B. HUBEAU (ed.), *De Vlaamse*

of result in the strict sense of the word, the only valid result would be to effectively provide alternative accommodation and that otherwise the mayor in question could be held responsible. Without judging the scope of these obligations at this point, we think it is indeed clear that the Housing Code does not foresee such a broad obligation. When neither the municipality nor the relevant public center for social welfare has sufficient housing possibilities at their disposal, the mayor will have to appeal to the social housing organizations.[94] Similarly, the Walloon Housing Code states that when none of the specifically listed public housing types is available at the time,[95] the mayor should have to pass the file on to the "Société Wallonne du Logement", which will search on the territory of the entire province and will in certain cases also look at the private housing market.[96] In both scenarios, the mayor is not obliged to effectively provide rehousing. What it does, of course, mean is that mayors cannot afford not to take initiative and search for housing options, using all housing rights instruments made available by law.[97]

B. A Result-Oriented Approach

If the examples given in the previous paragraphs show us one thing, it is that the value of the obligation of result should not be overestimated. Let us first be clear that we do not deny the heavier legal-technical ramifications of the private law obligation of result compared with the obligation of means. That would be quite silly considering what we have stated at the beginning of this chapter. What we do mean, however, is that it should not be perceived as the one and only goal in order to enhance the effectiveness of the right to housing – especially not when a shortage of adequate social housing remains a pressing issue, as is the case in many countries. This will automatically compromise the impact a lot of the housing rights-related obligations of result or obligations perceived as such. As we have seen, the Belgian legal doctrine generally considers a person's legal entitlement to social housing as an obligation of result, but it can hardly be called a very effective aspect of the right to housing due to the long waiting lists.

The application of DALO also suffers from the imbalance between supply and demand. In some regions with a shortage of adequate housing, mediation commissions tend to set additional requirements for applicants of the priority

Wooncode, lokaal woonbeleid en woonkwaliteit, Brugge, Die Keure, 1999, 120; P. DE SMEDT, "Kwaliteitsbewaking in de Vlaamse Wooncode: juridische knel- en kwelpunten", in B. HUBEAU (ed.), *Vijf jaar Vlaamse Wooncode: het woonbeleid (nog) niet op kruissnelheid?*, Brugge, Die Keure, 2002, 143–144.

94 Art. 17bis Flemish Housing Code.

95 Art. 7, 8 Walloon Housing Code.

96 Art. 7, 9 Walloon Housing Code.

97 Council of State 12 February 2003, no.115/808, Leroy & Postiau; VANDROMME (n 92) 73.

status.[98] We have also said that it can be debated whether DALO really is an obligation of result *sensu stricto* due to how the compensation finds its destination in a public fund. In the aforementioned judgment of *Tchokontio Happi* by the European Court of Human Rights, the Court acknowledged that this does not suffice as an appropriate execution of the domestic judgment to provide housing.[99] Against that background, it is again difficult to speak of an obligation of result.

Regardless of the type of , though, legislation like DALO does impose strong obligations that are result-oriented, that do legally incite authorities to act and make progress in realizing the right to housing. The *Tchokontio Happi* judgment attests to this. Since the applicant had not received a housing proposal more than three years after the Paris Administrative Court had instructed the Prefect of the Île-de-France region to do so, the authorities were found not to have executed the judgment in a timely or sufficient manner.[100] The Court decided that article 6 ECHR had been violated. If not an obligation of result, the judgment surely illustrates the widespread enforceability potential of a legislative scheme like DALO.[101]

A similar conclusion can be made with regard to the rehousing obligation. While it might not be common ground to hold a mayor responsible for actual rehousing, he is responsible for performing and taking certain legally specified actions and measures in an attempt to find adequate housing. These actions then become results of themselves. Considering the above, one could say that the rehousing obligation has turned into obligations of conduct according to international law, as small, intermediate obligations of result.

It is, in other words, not because an obligation is only an obligation of means that it could not be useful or maybe even more useful. The lack of a legal obligation of result can be compensated by providing instruments that will probably lead to an effective result.[102] One should not forget that an obligation of means should also target the intended result.[103] In other words, the debate on how to make the right to housing an obligation of result should be subordinate to the question whether measures are effective and result-oriented, whatever their actual qualification might be. We therefore conclude that extensive use of this qualification hinders rather than helps the discussion on

98 LACHARME (n 89) 38–39.
99 ECtHR 9 April 2015, no. 65829/12, Tchokontio Happi/France, par. 47.
100 Ibid., par. 47–52; N. BERNARD, "Commentaire de l'arrêt Tchokontio Happi de la Cour Européenne des droits de l'homme", *Echos Log.* 2016, no. 1, (56) 58–59.
101 N. MOONS, "EHRM maakt recht op huisvesting nog meer afdwingbaar", *Juristenkrant* 2015, vol. 308, 4; BERNARD (n 100) 56–59.
102 T. VANDROMME, "Het recht op wonen: een stand van zaken", in B. HUBEAU and T. VANDROMME (eds.), *Vijftien jaar Vlaamse Wooncode. Sisyphus ongelukkig?*, Brugge, Die Keure, 2013, (17) 24.
103 VANDEBURIE (n 64) 495–496.

the effectiveness of the right to housing, and by extension other economic, social and cultural rights.

6. Conclusion

For a long time the concepts of obligations of result and obligations of conduct/means have been used in human rights law, often to distinguish civil and political rights from economic, social and cultural rights. Although a clear-cut distinction at first sight, the diverging interpretation in private law on the one hand and public international law on the other has created difficulties that have remained largely unnoticed in human rights doctrine. We have seen that the concept's complex double meaning raises questions regarding the exact scope of obligations that derive from socio-economic rights, thereby also enabling a more restrictive view on a state's responsibilities.

Additionally, the examples given in this chapter have shown us how the qualification as one type of obligation or the other is not inherently decisive for a more or less effective right to housing. We therefore argue that placing too much weight on the legal concept of the obligation of result can actually hinder the realization of this fundamental right. We believe that it is preferable for reasons of both clarity as well as enhanced enforceability, to shift our attention away from this classic qualification and rather to focus on defining clear-cut and result-oriented obligations to realize the right to housing.

Bibliography

ALESSI, D., "The distinction between obligations de résultat and obligations de moyens and the enforceability of promises", *ERPL* 2005, vol. 5, 657–692.

ALSTON, P. and QUINN, G., "The nature and scope of states parties' obligations under the International Covenant on Economic, Social and Cultural Rights", *HRQ* 1987, vol. 9, no. 2, 156–229.

ANDREASSEN, B.A., SMITH, A.G. and STOKKE, H., "Compliance with economic and social human rights: realistic evaluations and monitoring in the light of immediate obligations", in A. EIDE and B. HAGTVET (eds.), *Human Rights in Perspective: a Global Assessment*, Oxford, Oxford University Press 1992, 252–267.

BERNARD, N., "Commentaire de l'arrêt Tchokontio Happi de la Cour Européenne des droits de l'homme", *Echos Log.* 2016, no. 1, 56–59.

BERNARD, N. and HUBEAU, B. (eds.), *Recht op wonen: naar een resultaatsverbintenis?*, Brugge, Die Keure, 2013.

BERNARD, N., "Uithuiszettingen: tussen wet en praktijk", in BERNARD, N. (ed.), *Les expulsions de logement/Uithuiszettingen*, Brugge, Die Keure, 2011, 41–81.

BERNARD, N., *La réception du droit au logement par la jurisprudence. Quand les juges donnent corps au droit au logement*, Brussel, Larcier, 2011, 416 pages.

BERNARD, N., "Le droit au logement dans la Charte Sociale Révisée: à propos de la condamnation de la France par le Comité Européen des Droits Sociaux", *RTDH* 2009, no. 80, 1061–1089.

BRILLAT, R., "The effective implementation of the right to housing of homeless of poorly housed persons: the role of the European Social Charter", *Feantsa Magazine* 2008, no. 2, 7–8.

COMBACAU, J., "Obligations de résultat et obligations de comportement. Quelques questions et pas de réponse", in BARDONNET, D., COMBACAU, J., VIRALLY, J. and WEIL, P. (eds.), *Mélanges offerts à Paul Reuter. Le droit international: unité et diversité*, Parijs, Éditions A. Pedone, 1981, 181–204.

COOMANS, A.P.M., *De internationale bescherming van het recht op onderwijs*, Leiden, Stichting NJCM-boekerij, 1992.

CRAVEN, M.C.R., *The International Covenant on Economic, Social and Cultural Rights. A perspective on its development*, Oxford, Clarendon Press, 1995, 144 pages.

DELPEREE, F., "Les droits sociaux fondamentaux et le droit belge", in STROOBANT, M. (ed.), *Sociale grondrechten*, Antwerpen, Maklu, 1995, (19) 28.

DEMOGUE, R., *Traité des obligations en général: Tome V*, Paris, Rousseau, 1925.

DENNIS, M.J. and STEWART, D.P., "Justiciability of economic, social and cultural rights: should there be an international complaints mechanism to adjudicate the rights to food, water, housing and health?", *AJIL* 2004, vol. 98, no. 3, 462–515.

DEN TONKELAAR, J.D.A., *Resultaatsverbintenissen en inspanningsverbintenissen*, Zwolle, Tjeenk Willink, 1982, 95 pages.

DEPUYDT, P., "De beroepsaansprakelijkheid van de advocaat", *TBBR* 1993, 295–310;

DE SCHUTTER, O., *Fonctions de juger et droits fondamentaux. Transformation du contrôle juridictionnel dans les ordres juridiques Américain et Européens*, Bruxelles, Bruylant, 1999, 1164 pages.

DE SMEDT, P., "De woonkwaliteitsregeling in de Vlaamse Wooncode", in HUBEAU, B. (ed.), *De Vlaamse Wooncode, lokaal woonbeleid en woonkwaliteit*, Brugge, Die Keure, 1999, 120.

DE SMEDT, P. "Kwaliteitsbewaking in de Vlaamse Wooncode: juridische knel- en kwelpunten", in HUBEAU, B. (ed.), *Vijf jaar Vlaamse Wooncode: het woonbeleid (nog) niet op kruissnelheid?*, Brugge, Die Keure, 2002, 121–161.

DISPERSYN, M., "Le droit à la sécurité dans l'article 23 de la Constitution", in ERGEC, R. (ed.), *Les droits économiques, sociaux et culturels dans la Constitution*, Brussel, Bruylant, 1995, 193–230.

DUPUY, P.-M., "Reviewing the difficulties of codification: on Ago's classification of obligations of means and obligations of result in relation to state responsibility", *EJIL 1999*, vol. 10, no. 2, 371–385.

EIDE, A., "Economic, Social and Cultural Rights as Human Rights", in EIDE, A., KRAUSE, C. and ROSAS, A. (eds.), *Economic, social and cultural rights. A textbook (second revised edition)*, Dordrecht, Martinus Nijhoff Publishers, 2001, (9) 10.

FERRON, C., "L'intensité de l'obligation juridique ou des obligations de diligence, de résultat et de garantie", *RDUS* 1991, 239–246.

GAUTIER, P., "On the Classification of Obligations in International Law", in HESTERMEYER, H.P., KÖNIG, D., MATZ-LÜCK, N., RÖBEN, V., SEIBERT-FOHR, A., STOLL, P.-T. and VÖNEKY, S. (eds.), *Coexistence, cooperation and solidarity. Liber amicorum Rüdiger Wolfrum*, Dordrecht, Martinus Nijhoff Publishers, 2012, 853–879.

GOOSSENS, L., "Samenwerkingsakkoord rond armoedebeleid", in Steunpunt tot Bestrijding van Armoede, Bestaansonzekerheid en Sociale Uitsluiting, *Armoede-Waardigheid-Mensenrechten*, 2008, 208 pages

HONKA, H., "Harmonization of contract law through international trade: a Nordic perspective", *Tul. Eur. & Civ. L.F.* 1996, vol. 11, 111–184.

HOUWING, J.F., "Overmacht of onmogelijkheid?", *RM* 1904, 250–297.

HOUWING, P.A.N., "De inhoud van de verbintenis en de overmacht", *WPNR* 1953, 4316–4324.

HUBEAU, B. and VAN DE WIEL, A., "Recht op wonen als resultaatsverbintenis. Over de effectiviteit van sociale grondrechten", *TvMR* 2013, no. 3, 11–14.

HUBEAU, B., "De uithuiszetting en de herhuisvesting, de Achilleshiel in het sociaal woonbeleid, ook in het Vlaamse Gewest", *PRK* 2010, vol. 14, 43–54.

ISHAY, M.R. *The history of human rights*, London, University of California Press, 2004, 221–229.

KAUFMAN, R.E., DAVIS, M.F. and WEGLEITNER, H.M., "The interdependence of rights: protecting the human right to housing by promoting the right to counsel", *Columbia Human Rights Law Review* 2014, vol. 45, no. 3, 772–815.

KRUITHOF, R., "Overzicht van rechtspraak (1974–1980)", *TPR* 1983, 495–717.

LACHARME, B., "Reconnu hier, opposable aujourd'hui, assumé demain? Le droit au logement en France", in BERNARD, N. and HUBEAU, B. (eds.), *Recht op wonen: naar een resultaatsverbintenis?*, Brugge, Die Keure, 2013, (31) 40.

LECKIE, S., "Another step towards indivisibility: identifying the key features of violations of ECOSOC rights", *HRQ* 1998, 81–124.

LEFEBER, R., *Transboundary Environmental Interference and the Origin of State Liability*, Den Haag, Kluwer, 1996, 365.

LIERMAN, S. and VAN DE WEYER, P.J., "Recente ontwikkelingen in de rechtspraak en de wetgeving over algemene bestuurlijke politiebevoegdheden van de gemeente", in X., *Recht in beweging*, Antwerpen, Maklu, 2014, 23–50.

MAES, G., *De afdwingbaarheid van sociale grondrechten*, Antwerpen, Intersentia, 2003, 523 pages.

MATAS, D., "Economic, social and cultural rights and the role of lawyers: North American perspectives", *ICJ Review* 1985, no. 55, 123–140.

MOONS, N., "EHRM maakt recht op huisvesting nog meer afdwingbaar", *Juristenkrant* 2015, vol. 308, 4.

O'CONNELL, P., *Vindicating socio-economic rights. International standards and comparative experiences*, London, Routledge, 2012, 248 pages.

PIASTRA, R., "Observations sur le droit au logement opposable", *Dalloz* 2007, 809.

PIERRAT, M., "De la distinction entre obligations de moyens et obligations de résultat: pile ou face?", *JT Luxembourg* 2011, no. 15, 61–67.

PORTER, B., "Reasonableness and article 8(4)", in BROWN, R., LANGFORD, M., PORTER, B. and ROSSI, J., *The Optional Protocol to the International Covenant on Economic, Social and Cultural Rights: a commentary*, Capetown, Pretoria University Law Press, 2016, 194–226.

POSNER, E.A., "Human welfare, not human rights", *Columbia Law Review* 2008, vol. 108, 1758–1800.

QUILICHINI, P., "Le droit au logement opposable", *AJDI* 2007, 364–369.

SALES, E., "Droit constitutionnel et droit social. La dualité du 'droit au logement opposable'", *RFDC* 2009, no. 79, 601–620.

SALOMON, M.E., *Global Responsibility for Human Rights: World Poverty and the Development of International Law*, Oxford, Oxford University Press, 2007, 274 pages.

SEPULVEDA, M., *The nature of the obligations under the International Covenant on Economic, Social and Cultural Rights*, Antwerpen, Intersentia, 2003, 477 pages.

STORME, M., *De bewijslast in het Belgisch privaatrecht*, Gent, Story-Scientia, 1962, 475.

THOLOMÉ, L., "Le droit au logement opposable : gadget ou véritable protection sociale?", *Echos log.* 2007, no. 2, 17–24.

THOLOMÉ, L., "L'article 23 de la constitution n'est pas une simple déclaration de principe", *Echos log.* 2000, no. 4, 121–123.

TOLLENAERE, F., "Uithuiszettingen, Het standpunt van de huurders", in BERNARD, N. (ed.), *Les expulsions de logement/Uithuiszettingen*, Brugge, Die Keure, 2011, 161.

TRILLET, Y., "Vers une nouvelle effectivité des droits économiques, sociaux et culturels? ", *Dr.Q.M.* 2000, vol. 27, 3–10.

UHRY, M. and VIARD, T., "De Raad van Europa pakt Frankrijk aan over het recht op huisvesting en het recht op bescherming tegen armoede", in Steunpunt tot Bestrijding van Armoede, Bestaansonzekerheid en Sociale Uitsluiting, *Armoede-Waardigheid-Mensenrechten*, 2008, 81–88.

VANACKERE, C., "Enkele soorten verbintenissen", in ROODHOOFT, J. (ed.), *Bestendig Handboek Verbintenissenrecht*, Antwerpen, Kluwer, 1998, I.2, 1–17.

VANDEBURIE, A., "La mise en œuvre de droit à un logement décent de Waterloo à l'hôtel Tagawa, où sont les responsables" (note under Peace Court Brussel 14 November 2006), *TBBR* 2008, 489–500.

VANDENHOLE, W., "Recht op wonen als resultaatsverbintenis? Enkele reflecties", *Juristenkrant* 2013, no. 264, 12.

VANDROMME, T., "Het recht op wonen: een stand van zaken", in HUBEAU, B. and VANDROMME, T. (eds.), *Vijftien jaar Vlaamse Wooncode. Sisyphus (on)gelukkig?*, Brugge, Die Keure, 2013, 17–40.

VANDROMME, T., *Woningkwaliteitsbewaking in het Vlaamse Gewest*, Mechelen, Kluwer, 2008, 97–103.

VAN GERVEN, W. and COVEMAEKER, S., *Verbintenissenrecht*, Leuven, Acco, 2001, 919 pages.

VAN IMPE, G., "L'effectivité du droit au logement: une obligation de résultat à charge des pouvoirs publics?", *Echos log.* 2012, no. 2, 39–40.

VAN OMMESLAGHE, P., *Droit des obligations: tome premier*, Brussel, Bruylant, 2010.

VANSWEEVELT, T., *De civielrechtelijke aansprakelijkheid van de geneesheer en het ziekenhuis*, Antwerpen, Maklu, 1992, 960 pages

VAN VALCKENBORGH, L., "De kwalificatie van een verbintenis als resultaats- of middelenverbintenis", *TBBR* 2011, vol. 5, 222–231.

WERY, J.L.L., *Overmacht bij overeenkomsten*, Amsterdam, A.H. Kruyt, 1919, 140 pages.

WERY, P., *Droit des obligations. Vol. 1. Théorie générale du contrat*, Brussel, Larcier, 2010, 1056 pages.

5 Progressive Realization and Retrogressive Measures

1. Introduction

In Chapter 4, we came to the conclusion that the dichotomy between obligations of conduct or means and obligations of result is muddled with theoretical and practical difficulties. We therefore proposed to focus on adopting legal or policy measures that are result-oriented. But what does this entail? In an attempt at concretization, we notice that this necessary drive towards result is reminiscent of the basic concept of progressive realization from article 2(1) of the International Covenant on Economic, Social and Cultural Rights (ICESCR):

> Each state party to the present Covenant undertakes to take steps, individually and through international assistance and co-operation, especially economic and technical, to the maximum of its available resources, with a view to achieving progressively the full realization of the rights recognized in the present Covenant by all appropriate means, including particularly the adoption of legislative measures.

That does not mean that international human rights law has not tried to categorize this general provision as one of the aforementioned obligations (result or means) as well. General Comment No. 3 of the Committee on Economic, Social and Cultural Rights (CESCR) describes the view of achieving progressively the full realization of the rights recognized in the Covenant as an obligation of result (in its international law meaning, of course),[1] while some literature has categorized the undertaking to take steps to do so as an obligation of conduct.[2] Since the obligation to take steps still leaves a huge margin of

1 UN Committee on Economic, Social and Cultural Rights, *General Comment No. 3: The Nature of States Parties' Obligations (art. 2, para. 1 of the Covenant)*, 14 December 1990, par. 9 (hereafter General Comment No. 3).

2 M.A. BADERIN and R. McCORQUODALE, "The International Covenant on Economic, Social and Cultural Rights: Forty Years of Development", in M.A. BADERIN and R. McCORQUODALE (eds.), *Economic, Social and Cultural Rights in Action*,

appreciation, this latter argument appears to be a rather odd statement. Even the explicit reference to the adoption of legislative measures can be regarded as a mere preference or recommendation from the CESCR rather than a specific form of required conduct.[3]

In the end, it is of little importance to categorize progressive realization and article 2(1) ICESCR itself anyway. Above all, the provision is a guiding principle from which a list of specific rights-based obligations is generated in the rest of the Covenant, in other General Comments and by jurisprudence. And these more specific obligations can be obligations of conduct, obligations of result or hybrids (i.e. contain both types), all driven by the mandate of an ongoing improvement of the enjoyment of socio-economic rights.[4] It is this latter obligation, this result-oriented character, that is ultimately the essence of what progressive realization entails.

The choice for this concept as the general idea behind the ICESCR raises a number of questions: can we learn or borrow anything from the content of this international concept to possibly apply to a domestic context or to specific measures related to this fundamental right? What if we were to do so? Does it have the qualities to improve the enjoyment of socio-economic rights? This chapter (as well as the following chapter) looks in particular at the meaning of the relevant aspects of progressive realization as incorporated in article 2(1) ICESCR and the obligations it brings about for the right to housing. We will also discuss the possibility of adopting retrogressive measures and the potential and recommendable impact of such a standstill obligation.

2. The Concept of Progressive Realization under Scrutiny: From a Housing Rights Perspective

A. *Progressiveness as a Flexibility Device*

From a theoretical perspective, article 2(1) ICESCR is quite self-explanatory. A state party should take the necessary steps towards the full realization of the relevant rights in accordance with the maximum of its available resources. It has "to move as expeditiously as possible towards the realization of the rights".[5]

Oxford, Oxford University Press, 2007, (3) 12; P. ALSTON and G. QUINN, "The nature and scope of states parties' obligations under the ICESCR", *Human Rights Quarterly* 1987, (156) 165.

3 United Nations, *Report of the International Law Commission on the work of its twenty-ninth session*, UN Doc. A/32/10 and Yearbook of the International Law Commission 1977, Vol. II, part two, 1978, 20.

4 CESCR, *General Comment No.* 3, par. 1; ALSTON (n 2) 185; F. VLEMMINX, *Een nieuw profiel van de grondrechten: een analyse van de prestatieplichten ingevolge klassieke en sociale grondrechten*, Den Haag, Boom Juridische Uitgevers, 2002, 54.

5 *The Limburg Principles on the implementation of the International Covenant on Economic, Social and Cultural Rights*, as contained in Commission on Human Rights, *Note verbale dated 5 December 1986 from the Permanent Mission of the Netherlands to the United*

Taking steps should not be confined to the adoption of legal measures, but necessitate programmatic statements and policies that have the intention of realizing the full enjoyment of the relevant rights.[6] In other words, international human rights law is in theory not satisfied with mere law in the books. It is one thing to guarantee housing to every individual by law; it is another thing to give this law meaning by ensuring that sufficient housing is available. The incorporation of progressive realization into the general provision of the ICESCR rests on the earlier mentioned assumption that socio-economic rights are more onerous and costly to achieve and can therefore not be realized in a short period of time. The inclusion of this concept is thus a kind of flexibility device that allows for practical difficulties to be taken into account.[7] One of those difficulties is the availability or, more pessimistically, the scarcity of resources. There is no reason to confine this to financial resources, yet it is exactly this type that receives most attention both from jurists and from states in their arguments as to why the relevant rights have not been realized.[8] Even though departing from a different level of existing socio-economic rights protection than third world countries, resource availability is just as much a relevant factor for the most developed countries too. As part of this flexibility device, a state party also has a lot of policy freedom to work progressively towards full realization. Consequently, the CESCR does not give any preferences to one political system or policy perspective that it regards to better fit the agenda of socio-economic rights.[9] The Committee is, in other words, neutral and stresses that the realization of the rights recognized in the Covenant is possible in a wide variety of different political and economic systems.[10]

In contrast to the ICESCR, the Revised European Social Charter does not include a general clause on progressive realization.[11] In accordance, however,

Nations Office at Geneva addressed to the Centre for Human Rights ('Limburg Principles'), 8 January 1987, E/CN.4/1987/17, par. 21.

6 B.A. ANDREASSEN, A.G. SMITH and H. STOKKE, "Compliance with economic and social human rights: realistic evaluations and monitoring in the light of immediate obligations", in A. EIDE and B. HAGTVET (eds.), *Human Rights in Perspective: A Global Assessment*, Oxford, Oxford University Press, 1992, (252) 256; E.g. CESCR, *Concluding observations Canada*, E/X.12/1993/5, par. 6.

7 J. HOHMANN, *The right to housing. Law, concepts, possibilities*, Oxford, Hart Publishing, 2013, 19; CESCR, *General Comment No.* 3, par. 9.

8 For a critique on the one-sided interpretation of available resources, see: S. SKOGLY, "The requirement of using the 'maximum of available resources' for human rights realization: a question of quality as well as quantity", *HRLR* 2012, vol. 12, no. 3, 393–420.

9 Provided, of course, that it is democratic and that all human rights are thereby respected.

10 M.C.R. CRAVEN, *The International Covenant on Economic, Social and Cultural Rights. A perspective on its development*, Oxford, Clarendon Press, 1995, 123.

11 W. VANDENHOLE, "Article 26: The right to benefit from social security", in A. ALEN, J. VANDE LANOTTE, E. VERHELLEN, F. ANG, E. BERGHMANS and M. VERHEYDE (eds.), *A commentary on the United Nations Convention on the Rights of the Child*, Leiden, Martinus Nijhoff Publishers, (1) 27.

with the CESCR's use as a flexibility device, the European Committee of Social Rights (ECSR) has accepted that a state cannot be expected to give full effect to all rights immediately.[12] Against that background, the ECSR has without a doubt used the content of progressive realization in its case law, including most of the relevant aspects from the original definition in the ICESCR: "A State Party must take measures that allows it to achieve the objectives of the Charter within a reasonable time, with measurable progress and to an extent consistent with the maximum use of available resources."[13] In the *ERRC v Bulgaria* decision, the Committee repeats these words in the context of the right to housing.[14] *ATD Fourth World v France* (cited in Chapter 3) expresses, similarly to what we have mentioned in the context of article 2(1) ICESCR, that to ensure "steady progress towards achieving the goals laid down by the Charter", state parties must adopt legal, financial and operational means to do so, but also make available the resources and introduce the operational procedures necessary to give full effect to the relevant rights. Finally, in *COHRE v Italy*, the Committee held that the realization of fundamental social rights recognized by the Charter is guided by the principle of progressiveness. It even stated that this is explicitly established in the Preamble of the Charter.[15] Although we consider the latter to be a bit of a convenient *ex post* reading of the Preamble,[16] it is clear that the use of the concept of progressive realization as a flexibility device and the idea of implementing result-oriented measures is certainly present in the case law of the European Committee of Social Rights and not confined to the CESCR.

While flexibility is to a certain extent a necessary accommodation and justifies the use of progressive realization, it is important to stress that the word "progressively" has not been added to make life easy on national governments.[17] It should not in any way be interpreted as providing some sort of mechanism for states to abrogate responsibility for the implementation of socio-economic rights.[18] Yet that was exactly the fear of those who opposed the application

12 U. KHALIQ and R. CHURCHILL, "The European Committee of Social Rights", in M. LANGFORD (ed.), *Social rights jurisprudence. Emerging trends in international and comparative law*, Cambridge, University Press, 2009, (428) 434.
13 ECSR 4 November 2003, no. 13/2002, Autism Europe/France, par. 53.
14 ECSR 18 October 2006, no. 31/2005, ERRC/Bulgaria, par. 37.
15 ECSR 25 June 2010, no. 58/2009, Centre on Housing Rights and Evictions (COHRE)/ Italy, par. 27.
16 Preamble to the Revised European Social Charter: "Considering that the aim of the Council of Europe is the achievement of greater unity between its members for the purpose of safeguarding and realizing the ideals and principles which are their common heritage and of facilitating their economic and social progress, in particular by the maintenance and further realization of human rights and fundamental freedoms. [. . .]"
17 F. VLEMMINX, *Het profiel van sociale grondrechten*, Zwolle, Tjeenk Willink, 1994, 133.
18 S. LECKIE, "Another step towards indivisibility: identifying the key features of violations of ECOSOC rights", *Human Rights Quarterly* 1998, (81) 94; See also, for example: Commission on Human Rights, E/CN.4/SR.236 (1951) (Mr. Sørensen, Denmark).

of the concept during the negotiations. According to Alston and Quinn, it was indeed those states that had supported the inclusion of the obligation of progressive realization that subsequently misused the weakness of the term as evidence of the non-binding nature of socio-economic rights.[19]

B. Flexibility Does Not Equal Freedom of Obligations

1) Drittwirkung

We have stated that the Committee leaves a lot of political and economic freedom to the states in the implementation of socio-economic rights. It does not oppose the privatization of state properties, social sectors or the housing market in the context of the implementation of Covenant rights, but a state party should then in turn not expect to be exempted from its responsibility because it has taken full use of its margin of discretion and in a way outsourced (some of) its obligations. Consequently, we embark upon the concept of "*drittwirkung*" of human rights.[20] Because of its obligation to protect individuals from third parties, a state will have to adopt measures which will create obligations between those private parties, and effective ones at that. In other words, it has to take an active role to prevent and protect individuals, especially the most vulnerable and disadvantaged groups in society, against violations of socio-economic rights by private actors.[21] So when the private sector is the most important actor in providing housing, the state must ensure that the operation of the market is fair and equitable.[22] In the first instance those private parties are, of course, responsible themselves for performing according to the rules, but the state is responsible for adopting those obligations.[23] In a scenario in which a particular third party group does not abide by the obligations in general, the state should have to step up, especially when the private relationship does not lend itself to legal action or when the weaker party is ill-positioned to enforce it through court.

Translated to a national housing context, these considerations should thus also have priority when developing a housing policy that talks about enforcing

19 ALSTON (n 2) 175–179.

20 R. KÜNNEMANN, *A human rights textbook*, Heidelberg, FIAN International Secretariat, 1998, 48.

21 M. SEPULVEDA, *The nature of the obligations under the ICESCR*, Antwerpen, Intersentia, 2003, 314 and 367.

22 M.C.R. CRAVEN, "The International Covenant on Economic, Social and Cultural Rights", in R. HANSKI and M. SUKSI (eds.), *An introduction to the international protection of human rights: a textbook*, Turku, Institute for Human Rights, Abo Akademi University, 1999, (101) 110.

23 LECKIE (n 18) 111.

the private housing market.[24] Let us take a look at a more concrete example. In order to accommodate people who cannot pay their rent guarantee, Flemish banks are obliged upon request of their own clients to provide them with a loan for this guarantee.[25] The tenant is then required to reimburse the amount within a three-year period. Now evidently, if a state party decides to improve the affordability of housing by giving tenants the possibility of receiving a loan for their rental guarantee, international human rights law does not instruct it to do so by distributing such a loan directly via public services. But if the state does dedicate this task to private banks, it does bear the responsibility to ensure that sufficient obligations are in place and that they do have their effect.

As we elaborate further on our example, we notice that the legislator has not stipulated a sanction for scenarios in which a bank declines to carry out its legal obligation.[26] That means that tenants do not have the legal tools to enforce the compliance of this obligation,[27] but also that banks can have a reticent attitude towards granting this guarantee. A study conducted by the University of Ghent claims that this is exactly the case. On the basis of a practical test, it was concluded that more than 25 percent of Flemish bank branches dismiss the possibility of a bank guarantee in response to a request by mail.[28] Despite heavy criticism by the Flemish Minister of Housing concerning the methodology of the research (researchers had sent out a substantial number of e-mails to these banks requesting a guarantee but pretending to be clients and only identifying themselves by a fake surname), this percentage only relates to requests that offices rejected for reasons obviously not connected to the question of whether or not this person could be found in their customer database (e.g. "such a bank guarantee does not exist", "we cannot provide a bank guarantee for a rent guarantee", "we don't provde a bank guarantee anymore" or "it is not possible to pay off a rent guarantee by way of periodical payments and would like to redirect you to the Public Centre for Social Welfare").[29]

Despite the fact that the e-mails were not sent out by real customers, the content of these responses at the very least suggests a problem with law

24 Flemish Government, Policy Memorandum Housing, *Parl.St.* Vl. Parl. 2014–15, no. 135, 23–27.

25 Art. 10 Belgian Housing Rent Act.

26 B. HUBEAU and D. VERMEIR, *Een evaluatie van het federale woninghuurrecht. Tussentijds rapport inzake duur, opzegging, waarborg en woningkwaliteit*, Leuven, Steunpunt Wonen, 2014, 44.

27 The tenant could theoretically go to court and demand the obligatory execution, but this does not seem very likely: A. VAN OEVELEN, "Wijzigingen in het (woning)huurrecht", *RW* 2007, no. 8, (289) 305.

28 P. VERHAEGHE and K. VAN DER BRACHT, *Is de bankwaarborg wel gewaarborgd? Praktijktesten bij banken*, Gent, University of Gent, 2015, 12.

29 This information was provided by one of the authors of this research (P. Verhaeghe) as part of a written conversation we had in September 2015.

compliance. Moreover, these results follow the same pattern of earlier findings.[30] On the basis of the above, we can only conclude that steps should be taken to address these problems, whether it be by adapting the regulations for the private sector or, as repeatedly recommended by researchers,[31] poverty organizations,[32] the Flemish Housing Council[33] and in certain political circles as well,[34] by installing a central deposit fund. This fund would request payment by the tenant and procure a proof of the guarantee to the landlord. Since all communication concerning the rent deposit would go through the fund and no longer directly between the renting parties, this would prevent social exclusion. In that case that a tenant is not able to pay the amount, the fund would also lend the necessary money.[35]

2) Immediate Obligations

We come to a second aspect of how progressively working towards a result is not free of responsibilities. The immediate implications of article 2(1) ICESCR ensure that states do not avoid carrying out at least some of their most basic obligations.[36] Besides the obligation not to take retrogressive measures (which will be discussed later), General Comment No. 3 declares that, in line with the

30 Steunpunt tot bestrijding van armoede, bestaansonzekerheid en sociale uitsluiting, "Huurwaarborg: hoe werkelijk de toegang tot de huisvestingsmarkt verlagen?" in *Verslag Armoedebestrijding 2008–2009. Deel 1: Een bijdrage aan politiek debat en politieke actie*, Brussel, 2009, 35; With regard to Brussels: Brusselse Bond voor het Recht op Wonen, *Huurwaarborg: nieuwe wet werkt niet naar behoren*, 28 September 2008, www.rbdh-bbrow.be/spip.php?article961.

31 VERHAEGHE (n 28) 13; P. LEMAHIEU and E. BUYST, *Naar een centraal huurwaarborgfonds*, Leuven, Kenniscentrum voor Duurzaam Woonbeleid, 2007; N. BERNARD, "Vers un fonds centralisée (mutualisé!) de garanties locatives: balises et suggestions pour une opérationnalisation", *Les Échos du Logement* 2015, no. 3, 3–10; M. DAMBRE, *De huurprijs. Analyse van de financiële verbintenissen van de huurder en onderzoek naar de mogelijkheid tot objectivering van de woninghuurprijzen*, Brugge, Die Keure, 2009, 514–517.

32 Steunpunt tot bestrijding van armoede, bestaansonzekerheid en sociale uitsluiting (n 30) 38; Netwerk tegen Armoede, *Centraal huurwaarborgfonds geeft meer zekerheid aan huurder en verhuurder dan hogere huurwaarborg*, 29 April 2015.

33 FLEMISH HOUSING COUNCIL, *Naar een beleid ter ondersteuning van de private huurwoningmarkt*, 30 September 2010, no. 2010/11.

34 E.g. Proposal of Law (G. TURAN) concerning the adoption of a central rental guarantee fund, *Parl.St.* Senaat 2010–11, no. 5-1017/1; The proposals date back more than ten years, e.g. Proposal of Law (F. PEHLIVAN) concerning the adoption of the rental guarantee fund, *Parl.St.* Senaat 2004–05, no. 3-1308/1.

35 For more on the advantages and disadvantages of such a fund, see: HUBEAU (n 26) 50–58.

36 I. LEIJTEN, "Meergelaagdheid en ondeelbare mensenrechten", *TBP* 2013, no. 2–3, (95) 105.

1987 Limburg Principles,[37] the obligation to take steps itself applies immediately as well.[38]

Additionally, the General Comment imposes an immediate obligation to assure that the Covenant rights will be exercised without discrimination, as prescribed by articles 2(2) and 3 ICESCR.[39] This is expressed with specific regard to the right to housing in General Comment No. 4, which says that "individuals, as well as families are entitled to adequate housing regardless of age, economic status, group or other affiliation or status and other such factors".[40] As we have seen earlier in this research, however, we know that a gap definitely still exists between the legal measures of protection against discrimination and the reality on the housing market.

Furthermore, it has been argued that only the state's obligation to fulfill is actually subject to progressive realization. The obligation to respect and protect are then of immediate effect.[41] Just as the other General Comments have summed up a couple of these immediate obligations with regard to other Covenant rights, albeit in varying degrees of clarity and uniformity, General Comment No. 4 has done so too. State parties must, for example, take immediate measures to confer upon everyone legal security of tenure through legal protection against forced evictions.[42] The abstention by the government from certain practices (which is essentially the state's obligation to respect) is also listed as an immediate obligation,[43] as is the effective monitoring of the housing situation.[44] Although not explicitly referred to as having immediate effect, the composition of the text suggests that the obligation to give due priority to social groups living in unfavorable conditions[45] can be regarded as an immediate obligation as well. Finally, the adoption of a national housing

37 *The Limburg Principles on the implementation of the International Covenant on Economic, Social and Cultural Rights*, as contained in Commission on Human Rights, *Note verbale dated 5 December 1986 from the Permanent Mission of the Netherlands to the United Nations Office at Geneva addressed to the Centre for Human Rights ('Limburg Principles')*, 8 January 1987, E/CN.4/1987/17, par. 16 and 21.

38 ANDREASSEN (n 6) 256.

39 CESCR, *General Comment No. 3*, par. 8; A. CHAPMAN and S. RUSSELL, *Core obligations: building a framework for economic, social and cultural rights*, Antwerpen, Intersentia, 2002, 6.

40 CESCR, *General Comment No. 4*, par. 6.

41 M. FORMISANO PRADA, *Empowering the poor through human rights litigation*, Paris, UNESCO, 2011, 39–40; UN Office of the High Commissioner for Human Rights, *The Right to Adequate Housing. Fact sheet no. 21*, 31; E. FELNER, "Closing the 'escape hatch': a toolkit to monitor the progressive realization of economic, social and cultural rights", *Journal of Human Rights Practice* 2009, vol. 1, no. 3, (402) 403.

42 CESCR, *General Comment no. 4*, par. 8a; See also UN Office of the High Commissioner for Human Rights, *Forced Evictions. Fact Sheet no. 25*, 2014, 9.

43 CESCR, *General Comment No.4*, par.10.

44 Ibid., par.13.

45 Ibid., par.11.

strategy reflecting extensive genuine consultation with and participation by all affected parties is also hinted at as an immediate obligation.[46]

As with the approach to progressive realization, similar obligations of a more immediate nature seem to have found their way into housing rights-related decision-making of the European Committee of Social Rights. In *ATD Fourth World*, we know that the Committee stipulated the obligation to maintain meaningful statistics, undertake regular impact reviews, establish a timetable and pay particular attention to the impact of the policies on the most vulnerable.[47]

3) Minimum Core

With regard to the immediate implications of the Covenant rights, General Comment No. 3 also says that a state party must provide a minimum core. It must in other words "ensure the satisfaction of, at the very least, minimum essential levels of each of the Covenant rights".[48] This was confirmed in the 1997 Maastricht Guidelines on Violations of Economic, Social and Cultural Rights.[49] Notwithstanding the presumption of guilt on behalf of the state party, the non-fulfillment of the minimum core can still be justified. The state will then have to demonstrate that "every effort has been made to use all resources that are at its disposition in an effort to satisfy, as a matter of priority, those minimum obligations".[50] Danilo Turk, former Special Rapporteur on the Realization of Economic, Social and Cultural Rights added that this obligation stands irrespective of the level of economic development.[51] Having a development-neutral minimum core definitely makes it much more demanding for third world countries to assure compliance. In the more developed states of the first world, though, this renders the minimum core obligation more easily attainable. And since the focus is often on these more immediate implications, it can even direct attention away from housing rights problems and shortcomings that do still exist in these countries (and which they are

46 Ibid., par. 12.

47 ECSR 5 December 2007, no. 33/2006, International Movement ATD Fourth World/ France, par. 60–61.

48 CESCR, *General Comment No. 3*, par. 10; R.E. ROBERTSON, "Measuring state compliance with the obligation to devote the maximum available resources to realizing economic, social and cultural rights", *Human Rights Quarterly* 1994, (693) 701.

49 International Commission of Jurists (ICJ), "Maastricht Guidelines on Violations of Economic, Social and Cultural Rights", *HRQ* 1998, vol. 20, (691) 695, par. 9.

50 CESCR, *General Comment No. 3*, par. 10.

51 UN Sub-Commission on Prevention of Discrimination and Protection of Minorities, *The realization of Economic, Social and Cultural Rights. Second Report prepared by Mr. Danilo Türk, Special Rapporteur*, 18 July 1991, E/CN.4/Sub.2/1991/17, par. 52. For a contrasting opinion on the matter, see: VLEMMINX (n 4) 167.

obliged to address over time as well).[52] In practice, though, the Committee has applied different standards to countries of different development status in its Concluding Observations.[53]

General Comment No. 3 illustrated the minimum core with regard to the right to housing with the example that a state party should not have any significant number of individuals being deprived of basic shelter and housing. Considering the basic conception of minimum core just presented, this is a rather odd example. How could a core of a human right possibly allow for a non-significant number of persons (whatever that number may even be) to be homeless? Does a different core (*ergo* a different right) then apply to different people?

Unfortunately for us, the General Comments on housing (No. 4) and forced evictions (No. 7) did not explicitly return to, let alone clarify, the minimum core in the context of the right to housing. The early publication date of these housing-related General Comments appears to be the only reason why no core obligations were included. Ever since the CESCR's Twelfth General Comment, core obligations have consistently returned in an explicit manner and have been specified in the context of the right to food, education, work, social security, etc.[54] As a matter of fact, from General Comment No. 14 onwards, considerations on core obligations have even been dealt with under their own caption.[55] The latter General Comment, which concerns the right to the

52 I.E. KOCH, *Human rights as indivisible rights. The protection of socio-economic demands under the European Convention of Human Rights*, Leiden, Martinus Nijhoff Publishers, 2009, 285.

53 M. LANGFORD and J.A. KING, "Committee on Economic, Social and Cultural Rights", in M. LANGFORD (ed.), *Social rights jurisprudence. Emerging trends in international and comparative law*, Cambridge, Cambridge University Press, 2009, (477) 495.

54 With the exceptions of General Comments 16 and 20, which did not address a specific socio-economic right, but the right not to be discriminated in the enjoyment of economic, social and cultural rights; CESCR, *General Comment no. 12: The Right to Adequate Food (art. 11 of the Covenant)*, 12 May 1999, par. 6 and 8; CESCR, *General Comment no. 13: The Right to Education (art. 13 of the Covenant)*, 8 December 1999, par. 57.

55 CESCR, *General Comment No. 14: The Right to the Highest Attainable Standard of Health (art. 12 of the Covenant)*, 11 August 2000, par. 43–44; CESCR, *General Comment No. 15: The Right to Water (arts. 11 and 12 of the Covenant)*, 20 January 2003, par. 37; CESCR, *General Comment No. 17: The Right of Everyone to Benefit from the Protection of the Moral and Material Interests Resulting from any Scientific, Literary or Artistic Production of Which He or She is the Author (art. 15, par. 1(c) of the Covenant)*, 12 January 2006, par. 39; CESCR, *General Comment No. 18: The Right to Work (art. 6 of the Covenant)*, 6 February 2006, par. 31; CESCR, *General Comment No. 19: The right to social security (art. 9 of the Covenant)*, 4 February 2008, par. 59; CESCR, *General Comment No. 21: Right of everyone to take part in cultural life (art. 15, par. 1a of the Covenant)*, 21 December 2009, par. 55; CESCR, *Right to just and favourable conditions of work (art. 7 of the Covenant)*, Draft prepared by Virginia Bras Gomes and Renato Ribeiro Leao, 20 January 2015, par. 64.

highest attainable standard of health, does, however, explicitly mention access to basic shelter and housing as one of the core obligations.[56]

What exactly such a minimum core entails is obviously prone to at least a minimal amount of subjectivity.[57] Unsurprisingly, different approaches exist to define the minimum core (of the right to housing). One could look at the core content of the right, the normative essence.[58] It relates to the "unrelinquishable nucleus [that] is the raison d'être of the basic legal norm, essential to its definition, and surrounded by the less securely guarded elements".[59] With regard to the right to housing, Bilchitz describes its most basic feature as being free from general threats to one's survival, as one's ability to survive.[60] This is what comes to mind spontaneously when reading the CESCR's formulation of "minimum essential levels". A quite different and more subjective minimum core interpretation is a value-based core. Here, the focus is not on basic needs or necessary requirements for life, but on what is necessary to be human, based on values such as freedom, equality and – here the concept pops up again – human dignity.

Some of the legal literature has given an interpretation of the right to housing with a very broad range of elements pertaining to its minimum core. These authors consider the whole of paragraph 8 of General Comment No. 4 as minimum core guarantees.[61] This paragraph elaborates on each of the essential housing aspects that constitute adequate housing. Consequently, there are core issues with regard to habitability, security of tenure, affordability and so forth. Hohmann denounces this interpretation with specific reference to the element of availability of services, materials, facilities and infrastructure. She stated that the CESCR does not hold a failure to provide such services as an outright violation of the right to housing,[62] favoring the view that these services are long-term policy aims.[63] We agree with this criticism and argue that a minimum core for all separate housing rights-related elements would once again raise questions whether different cores apply to different people. How would this relate, for example, to the homeless, whose right to a minimum core

56 CESCR, *General Comment No. 14*, par. 43(c).

57 LEIJTEN (n 36) 107.

58 K.G. YOUNG, "The minimum core of economic and social rights: a concept in search of content", *Yale Journal of International Law* 2008, vol. 33, (113) 126–140.

59 E. ÖRÜCÜ, "The core rights and freedoms: the limits of limits", in T. CAMPBELL, D. GOLDBERG, S. McLEAN and T. MULLEN (eds.), *Human rights: from rhetoric to reality*, Oxford, Blackwell, 1986, 52.

60 D. BILCHITZ, *Poverty and fundamental rights: the justification and enforcement of socio-economic rights*, Oxford, Oxford University Press, 2007, 198.

61 UN Office of the High Commissioner for Human Rights, *The Right to Adequate Housing. Fact sheet no. 21*, 67; P. KENNA, *Housing rights and human rights*, 2005, 5–6; FORMISANO PRADA (n 41) 39–40.

62 HOHMANN (n 7) 23

63 CRAVEN (n 10) 290.

will in practice only stretch to basic shelter to survive (the night), while the proud tenants of a two-story loft could hypothetically have a minimum core right not to have mold in their bathroom? Based on this reasoning and the fact that the implementation of the ICESCR requires particular attention to the weaker people and groups in society, a limited minimum core (any other would actually be a *contradictio in terminis* anyway) reminiscent of the interpretation given by Bilchitz seems to be the better option.

But there is more to it. The CESCR has a tendency to locate the minimum core in the content of the obligations raised by the right rather than in the content of the right itself.[64] In other words, it seems ill-founded to speak in this context of a minimum core of the right to housing, while every essential housing aspect has core obligations of its own. The aforementioned example that no significant number of people should be deprived of shelter in the 25-year-old General Comment No. 3 already portrayed the core requirements of a housing policy rather than the minimum essential levels it had defined the minimum core as earlier in that same paragraph. In contrast to a minimum core comprised of both a right to shelter for the homeless and a right to a damp-free home, having core obligations for each of the right to housing components separately does certainly seem just and potentially useful, as long as the priorities are set right. But by adopting an obligations approach for the concept of minimum core, thereby expanding the core's range, the CESCR has obscured the distinction with the immediate obligations. The result is that the General Comments portray a certain degree of arbitrariness.[65] Some state explicitly that all the enlisted core obligations are immediate obligations;[66] others do not but still manage to put immediate obligations such as the duty to ensure non-discrimination, to adopt a national strategy and plan of action and/or to monitor the realization under the heading of minimum core obligations.[67]

C. Focus on Progressiveness

While it was necessary to set out the immediate implications of the ICESCR as a way to place progressive realization in its right perspective, the general thrust of this chapter is still to find ways to concretize result-oriented measures through the concept of progressive realization. Besides, these immediate effects certainly have their share of attention in human rights literature and

64 YOUNG (n 58) 117 and 154–157.
65 LANGFORD (n 53) 493–494.
66 CESCR, *General Comment No. 15*, par. 37; CESCR, *General Comment No. 17*, par. 39; CESCR, *General Comment No. 21*, par. 55.
67 E.g. CESCR, *General Comment No. 13*, par. 57; CESCR, *General Comment No. 14*, par. 43(a) and (f); CESCR, *General Comment No. 18*, par. 31(b) and (c); CESCR, *General Comment No. 19*, par. 59(b), (d) and (f).

practice already. It has even been stated that the focus on these immediate consequences has overshadowed the progressive character of socio-economic rights and the development of its content, targeting only the most flagrant, more event-based violations. This is not entirely surprising. Human rights practitioners will prefer to address breaches of immediate obligations or the minimum core, because they are more easily identifiable and assessable than obligations of a progressive nature. Considering that naming and shaming is an important method for NGOs to disclose human rights injustices, certainly when it concerns already less enforceable socio-economic rights, it is important for them to focus on more clear-cut and tangible short-term obligations to raise widespread attention.[68] While our primary focus is thus more on progressive realization itself, there is an immediate application very closely connected and (arguably) contributing to it: the prohibition of retrogressive measures.

3. Retrogressive Measures and Financial Constraints

In our pursuit of result-oriented measures, an important factor is the prohibition of retrogressive measures. Because, principally, how can a government be urged to work towards the full realization of a right if it is allowed to backtrack at random? We explore the meaning and allowable extent of retrogressive measures, but also its appropriateness. Since the principle of retrogressive measures has been recognized and regularly applied in Belgian case law, both with regard to the ICESCR and socio-economic rights in the Constitution, it offers useful insight into the possible application in a national context and the limitations and risks that go with it from a human rights perspective.

A. Origins in International Human Rights Law

As mentioned earlier, the principle that a state should generally abstain from taking retrogressive measures in the implementation of the ICESCR is one of the immediate implications of the Covenant. This manifests itself naturally as the antithesis of progressiveness, of the envisioned continuous improvement of socio-economic rights protection, explaining its said inherent nature to the idea of progressive realization.[69]

68 G. DE BECO, "The interplay between human rights and development the other way round: the emerging use of quantitative tools for measuring the progressive realization of economic, social and cultural rights", *HR&ILD* 2010, No. .2, (265) 273–274; FELNER (n 41) 407–408.

69 L. CHENWI, "Unpacking 'progressive realisation', its relation to resources, minimum core and reasonableness, and some methodological considerations for assessing compliance", *De Jure* 2013, vol. 46, no. 3, (742) 745; E. RIEDEL, G. GIACCA and C. GOLAY, "The development of economic, social, and cultural rights in international

The concept of non-retrogression was also introduced in General Comment No. 3 of the CESCR, stating that any deliberate measure of this kind "would require the most careful consideration and would need to be fully justified by reference to the totality of the rights provided for in the Covenant and in the context of the full use of the maximum of available resources".[70] The following General Comment on the right to adequate housing elaborated that if not accompanied by compensatory measures, a general decline in living and housing conditions directly attributable to policy and legislative decisions would be inconsistent with the Covenant.[71] There is a considerable difference between these descriptions. The first one concerns a measure that reduces socio-economic rights protection, whereas the latter talks about a factual decline as well. While undoubtedly convergent in some scenarios, this is certainly not always the case. A rule can be implemented with the best intentions for the protection of socio-economic rights, but indirectly create consequences that actually aggravate a situation. If a state, for example, decides to impose very strict housing quality obligations, no one would question that the idea behind it is to progressively improve housing quality. But if this were to be followed up with inspections and certificates to ensure that the obligation is goal-oriented, housing affordability could suffer in the long run, private landlords could possibly retreat from the private housing market or, even worse, a considerable number of people would have to be evicted from their home because it does not comply with quality requirements. Likewise, it is not always easy to predict whether the adoption of a rule that appears to restrict socio-economic rights protection at first sight will affect real-life conditions. Ultimately, on the basis of the consistent use of the term "measure" with regard to non-regression in the other General Comments, the examples found in the General Comment on the right to work,[72] as well as the Concluding Observations,[73] the focus of non-retrogression seems to be predominantly on the measures themselves.

law", in E. RIEDEL, G. GIACCA and C. GOLAY (eds.), *Economic, social, and cultural rights in international law: contemporary issues and challenges*, Oxford, Oxford University Press, 2014, (3) 15.

70 CESCR, *General Comment No. 3*, par. 9.

71 CESCR, *General Comment No. 4*, par. 11.

72 CESCR, *General Comment No. 18*, par. 34.

73 CESCR, *Concluding Observations New Zealand*, 31 May 2002, E/C.12/NZL/CO/3, par. 17; explicit references to retrogressive measures are quite rare. The Committee has, of course, determined deteriorating human rights conditions in other concluding observations, but it does not couple this with non-retrogression: F. COOMANS, "Reviewing implementation of social and economic rights: an assessment of the 'reasonableness' test as developed by the South African Constitutional Court", *ZaöRV* 2005, vol. 65, (167) 184.

B. Justification of Retrogressive Measures in International Human Rights Law

1) Presumption of Impermissibility

In General Comment No. 3, retrogressive measures are not regarded as *prima facie* violations of the Covenant; they merely have to be justified accordingly. In General Comment Nos. 13 through 19, however, the Committee took the position that there is a strong presumption of impermissibility of any retrogressive measures.[74] Only afterwards did it repeat the original conditions to divert from this rule with the obligatory reference to the totality of rights and the full use of maximum available resources, also adding that the state party has the burden of proving that all alternatives have been carefully considered.[75] In four of those General Comments (Nos. 14, 15, 17 and 19), the Committee has additionally stated that retrogressive measures cannot be incompatible with the core obligations.[76] Considering that there is no consensus on the content of this core, it is unclear as to when exactly a retrogressive measure would violate it.[77]

Somewhat on a side note but nonetheless illustrative of the problematic relationship between retrogression, minimum core and progressive realization, we notice that of those four General Comments, both the General Comment Nos. 14 and 15 state that the minimum core itself is also non-derogable.[78] This could be considered as a confirmation of the Maastricht Guidelines,[79] but clearly diverts from the Committee's original position in General Comment No. 3. While General Comment No. 15 already reintroduced the unavailability of resources as a justification for not fulfilling the minimum core, the other two more recent General Comments (Nos. 17 and 19) no longer characterized the

74 A. MÜLLER, "Limitations and derogations from economic, social and cultural rights", *HRLR* 2009, vol. 9, no. 4, (557) 588; A. NOLAN, "Budget analysis and economic and social rights", in E. RIEDEL, G. GIACCA and C. GOLAY (eds.), *Economic, social, and cultural rights in international law: contemporary issues and challenges*, Oxford, Oxford University Press, 2014, (369) 376.

75 CESCR, *General Comment No. 13*, par. 45.

76 CESCR, *General Comment No. 14*, par. 48; CESCR, *General Comment No. 15*, par. 42; CESCR, *General Comment No. 17*, par. 42; CESCR, *General Comment No. 19*, par. 64.

77 If applied the aforementioned maximalist approach with regard to the right to housing and included the entire paragraph 8 of General Comment No. 4 to the core or incorporate immediate obligations of respect and protect to it, a state would have a very small margin of appreciation.

78 CESCR, *General Comment No. 14*, par. 47; CESCR, *General Comment No. 15*, par. 40.

79 Maastricht Guidelines, par. 9: "minimum core obligations apply irrespective of the availability of resources of the country concerned or any other factors and difficulties"; we agree with De Schutter that this is not an accurate reading of the Committee's own position in General Comment No. 3, par. 10: O. DE SCHUTTER, "Introduction", in O. DE SCHUTTER (ed.), *Economic, social and cultural rights as human rights*, Edward Elgar Publishing, Cheltenham, 2013, (xiii) xxvii; CHENWI (n 69) 753.

core as non-derogable altogether. We therefore appear to have gone full circle with regard to the question whether the non-fulfillment of the minimum core can be justified.[80] Yet, combined with the statement in General Comments Nos. 17 and 19 that retrogressive measures cannot violate the core, it leads to the awkward conclusion that a state can justify its non-compliance with the core obligations of those rights as long as it has not realized that core yet. Beyond that point (but only then) will any measure threatening this core be held to be in violation of the Covenant. This places a burden on the better students of the international classroom and benefits the lesser ones. It serves as a first illustration of how too much focus on retrogression can easily stand in the way of the idea of progressive realization (infra).[81]

The conditions for adopting a retrogressive measure have been changing from one General Comment to the other. The most comprehensive specification of the conditions was provided by the General Comment on the right to social security:

(a) There was reasonable justification for the action;
(b) Alternatives were comprehensively examined;
(c) There was genuine participation of affected groups in examining the proposed measures and alternatives;
(d) The measures were not directly or indirectly discriminatory;
(e) The measures will not have a sustained impact on the realization of the right or an unreasonable impact on acquired rights and will not deprive an individual or group access to the minimum essential level;
(f) There was an independent review of the measures at the national level.[82]

One could question the general nature of the requirements set out by General Comment No. 19. They could be considered to be only relevant for the right to social security in particular, certainly considering the aforementioned variations between the different General Comments. In the same vein, the presumption of impermissibility might only pertain to the specific right discussed in each of those later General Comments (and, in other words, not to the right to housing). In General Comment No. 18, however, the Committee adds the short but significant phrase "as with all other rights",[83] which suggests a more general application of this presumption.

80 LANGFORD (n 53) 493.
81 M. DOWELL-JONES, *Contextualising the International Covenant on Economic, Social and Cultural Rights: assessing the economic deficit*, Leiden, Martinus Nijhoff Publishers, 2004, 52.
82 CESCR, *General Comment No. 19*, par. 42.
83 CESCR, *General Comment No. 18*, par. 34.

2) More Leeway for Budgetary Concerns?

Regardless of the above, the Committee seems to have taken a step back in recent years. In General Comment No. 21, but especially Nos. 22 and 23, the CESCR no longer mentions impermissibility as the starting point.[84] Equally remarkable is how these General Comments have been adopted since the beginning of the economic crisis.[85] Is it a coincidental diversion of its previous General Comments[86] or did the Committee very consciously aim to leave more normative and policy wiggle room in tackling the crisis? It is difficult to say. General Comment No. 23 still proclaims that State parties "should avoid taking any deliberately retrogressive measure without careful consideration and justification", but at the same time it does refer to the economic crisis as a reason for introducing retrogressive measures. The requirements the document cites next stem directly from a letter about austerity measures from the CESCR Chairperson as well:[87] states have to demonstrate that the measures are temporary, necessary and proportionate, non-discriminatory and respect the core obligations.[88]

This was not the first time the Committee addressed the scenario in which a state party uses resource constraints as an explanation for retrogressive measures. An earlier statement had already provided some limited guidance in the form of objective criteria that have to be taken into consideration in such scenarios.[89] Of course, all of this specifically relates to measures adopted out of budgetary concerns, not to non-resource-related normative or policy choices

84 CESCR, *General Comment No. 21: Right of everyone to take part in cultural life (art. 15, para. 1(a), of the International Covenant on Economic, Social and Cultural Rights)*, 21 December 2009, par. 65; CESCR, *General Comment No. 22 on the right to sexual and reproductive health (art. 12 of the International Covenant on Economic, Social and Cultural Rights)*, 2 May 2016, par. 38; CESCR, *General Comment No. 23 on the right to just and favourable conditions of work (art. 7 International Covenant on Economic, Social and Cultural Rights)*, 27 April 2006, par. 52.

85 The adoption of General Comment No. 19 on the right to social security also dates from after the beginning of the crisis, but was developed and discussed earlier.

86 After all, the General Comment merely concerns the right to take part in cultural life, not one of the more discussed ones in times of economic crisis compared with the right to work or social security that do raise more significant budget-related questions.

87 Chairperson of the CESCR, *Open letter to states parties regarding the protection of rights in the context of economic crisis*, 16 May 2012.

88 CESCR, *General Comment No. 23*, par. 52; See also: CESCR, *Right to just and favourable conditions of work (art. 7 of the Covenant)*, Draft prepared by Virginia Bras Gomes and Renato Ribeiro Leao, 20 January 2015, par. 52.

89 CESCR, *An evaluation of the obligation to take steps to the 'maximum of available resources' under an Optional Protocol to the Covenant*, E/C.12/2007/1, 10 May 2007, par. 10: "(a) the country's level of development; (b) the severity of the alleged breach, in particular whether the situation concerned the enjoyment of the minimum core content of the Covenant; (c) the country's current economic situation, in particular whether the country was undergoing a period of economic recession; (d) the existence of other serious claims on the State party's limited resources [. . .]; (e) whether the State party had sought to

that also negatively impact socio-economic rights protection. The Chairperson's letter from which General Comment No. 23 borrowed its conditions clearly indicates that it envisions austerity measures in particular and does in fact not mention the words "retrogressive measures" once.[90] The inclusion of the condition that these measures should only be temporary also hints at that. So while the economic crisis appears to have made the CESCR reconsider the presumed impermissibility of retrogressive measures due to budgetary considerations, it is far from established that its position on retrogressive measures in general has changed or is changing significantly. First, because the cited documents do obviously not concern non-resource related retrogressive measures, but, second, also because the requirements outlined in the Chairperson's letter are actually still applied by the CESCR in a strict manner in its Concluding Observations.[91]

3) Connection between Article 2(1) and 4 ICESCR

When making a distinction between resource- and non-resource-motivated retrogressive measures, we cannot ignore the relationship between article 2(1) and the limitations clause of article 4 of the Covenant, a problematic relationship the Committee has thus far failed to properly unravel.[92] According to the latter provision, state parties may only subject Covenant rights to limitations "determined by law" and "in so far as this may be compatible with the nature of these rights and solely for the purpose of promoting the general welfare in a democratic society".[93] Since every retrogressive measure limits the enjoyment of one or more socio-economic rights, both Craven and Leckie have argued that every one of those measures should also have to be justified on the basis of article 4 ICESCR.[94] This would obviously further tighten the obligation not to take retrogressive measures.

But there is also a different reasoning, one that assigns each provision to a type of retrogressive measure. Article 4 then refers to formal limitations, while article 2(1) merely concerns resource-motivated reductions in the level of

identify low-cost options; (f) whether the State party had sought cooperation and assistance or rejected offers of resources from the international community [. . .]."

90 NOLAN (n 74) 378.

91 CESCR, *Concluding Observations Iceland*, 11 December 2012, E/C.12/ISL/CO/4, par. 6; CESCR, *Concluding Observations New Zealand*, 31 May 2012, E/C.23/NZL/CO/3, par. 17; CESCR, *Concluding Observations Spain*, 6 June 2012, E/C.12/ESP/CO/5, par. 8.

92 NOLAN (n 74) 375.

93 Cf. article G Revised European Social Charter, which permits limitations that "are prescribed by law and are necessary in a democratic society for the protection of the rights and freedoms of others or for the protection of public interest, national security, public health or morals".

94 CRAVEN (n 10) 132; LECKIE (n 18) 98.

protection.[95] If that is the case, our comparison of the conditions justifying domestic retrogressive measures to international human rights law conditions should also take into account the requirements from article 4 ICESCR. And these conditions point to an even more rigid interpretation, because it can only be justified for the purpose of promoting general welfare.[96] Reasons of, for example, maintaining public order or public morality are, in other words, rejected. The same can even be said with regard to respect for rights and freedoms of others, which would have a considerable impact on any proportionality assessment between the right to housing and the right to property. Consequently, the only justification appears to refer to the socio-economic wellbeing of people,[97] which offers a clearly smaller window of opportunity for retrogressive measures than 'reasons of general interest'.

There are, however, two major issues with having two sets of criteria. First of all, it is difficult "to draw a strict line between retrogressive measures that were taken because of resource constraints and limitations that are not related to scarce resources".[98] But, second, since it would be easier to justify, it would also invite governments to play the resource card more frequently.[99] That would in turn instigate the already regularly used criticism that the economic crisis has been used as a convenient excuse by certain parts of the political spectrum for a policy that it wished to pursue on ideological grounds anyway.[100]

4) Budgetary Concerns: The Position of the European Committee of Social Rights

Before we switch to a translation of the principle at the national level, we should not ignore the position of the European Committee of Social Rights. While the principle of non-retrogression is not explicitly mentioned in the European Social Charter either, the ECSR has referred to the principle twice in the collective complaints mechanism.[101, 102] One of those occasions was in

95 M; VLEMMINX (n 17) 155–156; ALSTON (n 2) 205; M. GOLDMANN, "Human rights and sovereign debt workouts", in J.P. BOHOSLAVSKY and J.L. CERNIC (eds.), *Making sovereign financing and human rights work*, Oxford, Hart Publishing, 2014, (71) 87.

96 MÜLLER (n 74) 587.

97 Ibid., 570–573.

98 Ibid., 590.

99 VLEMMINX (n 17) 157.

100 For a strong voice against the demonization of the austerity crisis as "neo-liberal", see: M. DOWELL-JONES, "The economics of the austerity crisis: unpicking some human rights arguments", *HRLR* 2015, no. 15, (193) 208–212.

101 ECSR 23 May 2012, no. 66/2011, General Federation of employees of the national electric power corporation (GENOP-DEI) and the Confederation of Greek Civil Servants' Trade Unions (ADEDY)/Greece, par. 47.

102 Additionally, the ECSR has implicitly referred to the prohibition to take retrogressive measures in ECSR 7 December 2012, no. 76/2012, Federation of employed pensioners

the aforementioned case of *COHRE v Italy*, where the considerations on progressiveness cited earlier were actually triggered by the argument that the Italian government had taken retrogressive measures.[103] More significant is the reporting procedure which the European Committee has chosen for a more pragmatic approach.[104] In the context of the economic crisis in Greece, the European Committee recognized in 2012 that "it may be necessary to consolidate public finances in times of economic crisis" to guarantee the sustainability of the welfare state, as long as it does not undermine the core framework of social protection.[105] It also declared that a retrogressive measure is permissible if it does not "excessively destabilize the situation of those who enjoy the rights enshrined in the Charter".[106] This is obviously much more reminiscent of the conditions brought forward in domestic case law (i.e. only excessive regression is impermissible, margin of discretion until the core is reached).

Yet the Committee has shown a whole different approach as well. Back in 2009, it clearly stated that the economic crisis provides no excuse for states not to fulfill their obligations.[107] In the context of the right to housing, the Committee has also spoken very clearly against the reduction of socio-economic rights protection during the crisis. It has argued that state parties have to take measures to effectively guarantee the protection of Charter rights at times when beneficiaries need it most. Regardless of the economic situation, a state must, for example, match the increase of persons necessitating shelter or social housing.[108] According to the ECSR, even in harsh economic times the idea of progressiveness apparently prevails over the possibilities for retrogression.

C. *The Application in Belgian Case Law*

Despite the lack of clarity on the part of both the CESCR and ECSR concerning retrogressive measures, the conditions they propose definitely advocate a stringent interpretation of the principle. Their observations and recommendations are, however, not legally binding, which makes it difficult to assess the

of Greece (IKA-ETAM)/Greece, par. 69 and 78; see also I. HACHEZ, "Le Comité Européen des Droits Sociaux confronté à la crise financière Grecque: des decisions osées mais inégalement motivées", *TSR* 2014, no. 3, (243) 257.

103 ECSR 25 June 2010, no. 58/2009, COHRE/Italy, par. 24–27.

104 ECSR, "General consideration on certain areas covered by the Charter: social protection. General Introduction", *Conclusions* XIII-4, 143; ECSR, *Conclusions* XIV-1, Finland; VANDENHOLE (n 11) 29.

105 GOLDMANN (n 95) 89.

106 ECSR 23 May 2012, no. 66/2011, General Federation of employees of the national electric power corporation (GENOP-DEI) and the Confederation of Greek Civil Servants' Trade Unions (ADEDY)/Greece, par. 13.

107 ECSR, *Conclusions* XIX-2 on the repercussions of the economic crisis on social rights.

108 ECSR 2 July 2014, no. 86/2012, Feantsa/the Netherlands, par. 128.

usefulness of retrogressive measures in search of a more result-oriented right to housing. How does this or could this play a role at the national level? While this is still not an immensely popular notion in domestic case law across the world, Belgium is one of the countries where the judicial branch has used it on an occasional basis. It has done so under the term "standstill obligation". As a matter of fact, the preparatory documents for the relevant article 23 of the Constitution explicitly acknowledge a standstill obligation to be applicable, as a compromise for not bestowing the provision with direct effect.[109] The exact interpretation of its content was then left to judges and scholars.[110] This obviously begs the question: what lessons could be drawn and which problems arise from its application with regard to the protection and further realization of socio-economic rights? We distinguish three elements.

1) A Broader Margin of Appreciation: No Presumption of Non-Retrogression

The Belgian case law on the standstill principle has evolved over time. Initially, the Council of State declared that the legally embedded socio-economic guarantees could only be diverted from for compulsory reasons of general interest.[111] This is obviously a stringent interpretation of the obligation, much in line with the international principle. The Constitutional Court, however, broadened that margin of appreciation and the possibilities for taking retrogressive measures.[112] It decided that the obligation is violated only when the competent legislator has reduced the level of socio-economic legal

109 Explanatory Memorandum of the proposal by Mr. Stroobant and Mr. Taminiaux, *Parl.St.* Senaat BZ 1991–92, no. 100–2/3°, 13; Report on behalf of the Commission for the review of the Constitution and the reform of the institutions released by Mr. Arts and Ms. Nelis, *Parl.St.* Senaat BZ 1991–92, no.100–2/4°, 86–88; Explanatory Memorandum of the proposal by Mr. Stroobant and Mr. Taminiaux, *Parl.St.* Senaat BZ 1991–92, no. 100–2/3°, 4 and 9–11.

110 M. STROOBANT, "Sociale en economische grondrechten in de Belgische Grondwet. Wordingsgeschiedenis van artikel 23: het Akkoord van "Le Ry d'Ave" Rochefort", in W. RAUWS and M. STROOBANT (eds.), *Sociale en economische grondrechten. Art. 23 Gw.: een stand van zaken na twee decennia*, Antwerpen, Intersentia, 2010, (19) 44 and 50; G. MAES, *De afdwingbaarheid van sociale grondrechten*, Antwerpen, Intersentia, 2003, 439–444.

111 E.g. Council of State 29 April 1999, no. 80.018; Adv. Council of State 8 October 2003, no. 35.6889/4 on a draft of an Ordinance concerning a couple of provisions regarding spatial *planning, Parl.St. Br. Parl. 2003–2004, 703/1, 49–50; B. STEEN, "Artikel 23 van de Grondwet en de rechtspraak van de Raad van State"*, in W. RAUWS en M. STROOBANT (eds.), *Sociale en economische grondrechten. Art. 23 Gw.: een stand van zaken na twee decennia*, Antwerpen, Intersentia, 2010, (113) 121–123.

112 A. VANDEBURIE, *L'article 23 de la Constitution. Coquille vide ou boîte aux trésors?*, Brussel, La Charte, 2008, 58–59.

protection *considerably* and without a reason of general interest.[113] The Council of State has since followed this approach.[114] It even explicitly renounced its earlier case law by refuting the applicant's argument that compulsory reasons are necessary to justify a reduction of the level of protection on the basis that "this view cannot find support in the case law of the Constitutional Court".[115]

This approach is obviously more lenient than the conditions set out by the CESCR. If we compare it with those formulated in the General Comment on the right to social security, we see that the Belgian governments do not have to illustrate that alternatives were comprehensively examined or that affected groups genuinely participated in the examination of the proposed measures. On the other hand, the condition that the action must be "reasonably justified" does resemble the necessary reason of general interest described by the Belgian Constitutional Court.

Gunther Maes distinguished three categories of reasons of general interest that could justify such measures.[116] The first one concerns having measures in place that can serve as equivalent alternatives for the adopted retrogressive measures. These measures have the ability to absorb restrictions on or even the abrogation of another measure to guarantee an equal degree of socio-economic protection. Take, for example, the decision to increase the maximal rent guarantee to three months of rent. The legislator could make a case for the Public Centers for Social Welfare (OCMW) and the bank guarantee as alternatives that are being used and could expansively be used by socio-economically disadvantaged persons in society to settle increasing problems that might arise in paying the guarantee.[117] This presumes, of course, that an alternative like the bank guarantee works without too many problems and, as we have discussed earlier in this chapter, this remains rather questionable. The question, however, is whether or to what extent this factual knowledge would have to be taken into account to assess the justification of the retrogressive measure. After all, did we not conclude earlier that the legal and not the factual state of affairs is the main focus of the comparison to assess the severity of the regression?

113 E.g. Constitutional Court 14 July 2004, no. 130/2004, B.5; Constitutional Court 14 September 2006, no. 135/2006, B.10.

114 E.g. Adv. Council of State 10 December 2004, no. 37.741/2/4 concerning a draft of the 'décret-programme de reliance économique et de simplification administrative', *Parl.St. W. Parl.* 2004--05, 74/1, 82–89.

115 Council of State 17 November 2008, no. 187.998, Coomans, par. 18.1.

116 G. MAES, "Het standstillbeginsel in verdragsbepalingen en in art. 23 G.W.: progressieve (sociale) grondrechtenbescherming", *RW* 2005–2006, no. 28, (1081) 1090–1093; see also H. VANDERLINDEN, "Effectiviteit van de sociale grondrechten in het Belgische recht, mythe of realiteit", *RW* 2008–09, no.29, (1202) 1212–1213.

117 Anno 2013, 9% of the renting households paid their rent guarantee with a loan from their bank and 3% with an intervention by the OCMW: S. WINTERS et al., *Wonen in Vlaanderen anno 2013. De bevindingen uit het Grote Woononderzoek 2013 gebundeld*, Leuven, Steunpunt Wonen, 2015, 74.

A second category pertains to retrogressive measures that are compensated for in the totality of socio-economic rights protection. This very much resembles the condition that justifies a retrogressive measure "by reference to the totality of the rights" in General Comment No. 3. The regression that has been made can be compensated for either in a different aspect of the same right or with an increase of protection in a different right altogether. It has fittingly been called the "*effet standstill global*" by some authors.[118] The dismantlement of the housing bonus can serve as an example. This decision could have been justified by pointing out the need for a revised budget allocation in the Flemish housing policy. After all, the price tag of the housing bonus for the public authorities has been very high, certainly when compared with other housing-related expenses. It was projected that by 2024 the cost would have amounted to somewhere between €2.5 billion and €2.9 billion.[119] At the same time, it has been proven that the housing bonus does not help those who are most in need of it and that it has increased not only property prices but also rent prices.[120] Consequently, an injection of (part of) those resources into the private housing market could undeniably be seen as a justifiable direct compensation.[121]

The third and last category of reasons of general interest concerns the stability of welfare. It departs from the idea that it must be possible to alter, limit and abolish measures due to a changed economic or budgetary situation. This means that it can be justified to raise public incomes (e.g. tuition fees for education) according to the increasing cost of living, but also to not allow public expenditures (e.g. subsidies) to evolve accordingly.[122] The housing bonus once again offers a useful example. We mentioned earlier the defaults of this fiscal advantage and how its dismantlement can be advocated by investing the saved resources in a more efficient manner by way of compensation. Yet the measure was taken primarily out of budgetary concerns, as an austerity measure.[123] Consequently, the adopted decision actually falls into this third category. But how appropriate is it to adopt a retrogressive measure based on budgetary concerns? Hachez makes the distinction between financial or economic considerations as reasons of general interest (which can be justified) and as legitimate

118 Y. TRILLET, "Vers une nouvelle effectivité des droits économiques, sociaux et culturels?", *Dr.Q.M.* 2000, vol.27, (3) 32–33; J. FIERENS, "L'article 23 de la Constitution. Une arme contre la misère?", *Dr.Q.M.* 1994, no. 3, (3) 9.

119 N. HUYGHEBAERT, *Berekening woonbonus op kruissnelheid*, KU Leuven, 2012, unpublished; P. DE DECKER, "Afbouw woonbonus: nu of nooit", *Samenleving en Politiek* 2014, vol. 21, no. 1, (64) 74.

120 K. HEYLEN and S. WINTERS, *De verdeling van de subsidies op vlak van wonen in Vlaanderen*, Leuven, Steunpunt Ruimte en Wonen, 2012, 36.

121 FLEMISH HOUSING COUNCIL (n 33); DE DECKER (n 119) 64–75.

122 MAES (n 116) 1091.

123 M. HAFFNER and S. WINTERS, "Homeownership taxation in Flanders: moving towards 'optimal taxation'?", *International Journal of Housing Policy* 2015, (1) 15.

purposes in and of itself (which should not be justifiable).[124] Although we agree with this principal standpoint, the example shows that it is not always easy to distinguish the two. One can also disguise a measure as being necessary for different reasons of general interest, while in essence adopting it primarily for austerity reasons. This obviously only further complicates the already difficult question whether or not the standstill obligation has been violated.

Whether or not these reasons of general interest fall under the "reasonable justification" of the CESCR, the main element that renders the interpretation of the standstill obligation in Belgian case law much more lenient is the fact that only considerable regression ought to be examined. In contrast, the CESCR prohibits measures that "will have an impact on the realization of the right or an unreasonable impact on acquired rights". In other words, it does not use considerable regression as only a condition to decide whether or not to investigate a possible violation of the standstill principle. There, an inquiry into, for example, the extent to which an increase of the rent guarantee creates an unfavorable impact on the right to housing would be an inquiry to decide on the permissibility of the measure altogether, not to answer the question of whether or not a reason of general interest should have to be found to explain the existence of the measure.

While adopted to the Belgian context, the above considerations do illustrate a first potential problem with regard to the use of the standstill obligation at the national level. The perception that socio-economic rights require a much broader margin of appreciation for national governments is still very much alive. The obligation is therefore susceptible to a more lenient interpretation by the domestic judicial branch. As the Belgian Constitutional Court and Council of State have said with regard to the right to legal assistance:

> The prohibition to significantly reduce the existing level of protection without reasons of general interest cannot be understood in such a way that every legislator, in the context of its competences, has the obligation not to touch upon the particular rules that exist in the context of the right to legal assistance. [. . .] It does not deny them their competence to assess how that right should be ensured in the most adequate way.[125] [Translated]

2) Practical Problems: Establishing Retrogression

When elaborating on the standstill principle in a more practical context relating to domestic housing-related measures, different difficulties also emerge to the foreground. We will try to clarify them with a couple of illustrations.

124 I. HACHEZ, *Le principe de standstill dans le droit des droits fondamentaux: une irreversibilité relative*, Brussel, Bruylant, 2008, 420–421.

125 Constitutional Court 27 November 2002, no. 169/2002, B.6.6; Adv. Council of State 10 June 2013, no. 53.322/3, 4.2.2.2.

First, it is simply not always clear what constitutes a (considerable) decline in socio-economic rights protection. Judges might not always be well-positioned or in possession of the right tools to assess the exact implications of a measure or policy.[126] A couple of years ago, for example, the Flemish government made the decision to constrain the right of those waiting for social housing to give their preference regarding the type, location and maximum rental price of the social dwelling.[127] The Council of State has annulled this modification because it did not abide by the free choice of the social (prospective) tenant that had been guaranteed by decree (article 93, § 1 of the Flemish Housing Code),[128] but it could also have been argued that it violates the standstill principle because it limits their access to adequate housing.[129] From a different perspective, however, one could also argue that the contested measure would actually reveal those who are most desperately in need of housing, thereby contributing to social housing access. A similar illustration relates to the modernization of the housing market by imposing stricter quality requirements, for example, also with regard to energy efficiency. While it obviously improves housing quality, an upgraded housing stock can also have a damaging effect on the issue of affordability.

Second, a domestic application of the obligation affirms the aforementioned shortcomings of assessing one legal state of affairs against the previous one. In line with the interpretation by the CESCR, the Belgian courts tend not to

126 H. DUMONT, "Conclusions: l'apport des droits fondamentaux au droit de l'environnement, de l'urbanisme et du logement", *Amén.* 1996, (287) 289; J. VANDE LANOTTE and T. DE PELSMAEKER, "Economic, social and cultural rights in the Belgian Constitution", in P. VAN DER AUWERAERT, T. DE PELSMAEKER, J. SARKIN and J. VANDE LANOTTE (eds.), *Social, economic and cultural rights. An appraisal of current European and international developments*, Antwerpen, Maklu, 2002, (263) 276.

127 Art. 3 Decision Flemish Government 30 September 2011 concerning the amendment of various provisions of the decision of the Flemish Government of 12 October 2007 on the regulation of the social renting system in execution of title VII of the Flemish Housing Code and in modification of art. 17 of the decision of the Flemish Government of 12 October 2007 concerning the financing of social rental companies for the realization of social rental housing and the accompanied operating costs, *BS* 25 November 2011: the provision modified art. 10 Framework Decision Social Rent, which was later restored following the annulment judgment by the Council of State.

128 The request for annulment was made by the Flemish Platform for Tenants and the Flemish Network of Associations of People Experiencing Poverty: Council of State 18 February 2013, no. 222.544, par. 5.7–5.8.

129 In fact, the applicants also invoked the standstill argument, but it was not explicitly addressed by the Council. B. HUBEAU and T. VANDROMME, "De beperking van het keuzerecht van kandidaat sociale huurders: beperking van het grondrecht op wonen of net toepassing van het grondrecht op wonen" (note under Council of State 18 February 2013, no. 222.544), *RW* 2013–14, no. 39, (1537) 1539–1540.

compare retrogressive measures to the law in action.[130] While understandable from a pragmatic and legal security point of view, there can obviously be a considerable gap between what law dictates and how it functions in practice. For example, article 134bis of the Flemish New Municipality Act authorizes a mayor to lay claim to any building that has been abandoned for more than six months to place at the disposal of the homeless – an obviously well-intended and result-oriented measure to accommodate those who do not have a roof over their head that is nonetheless only rarely applied. Here, it is obviously beneficial to the right to adequate housing to look at the reference norm in order to judge whether or not a measure on this matter would be retrogressive. But it can also be beneficial to look at those types of practical problems and take them into account as a reference point in order to ultimately improve measures.

Take, for example, the decision to reduce the housing bonus.[131] This undoubtedly falls within the *ratione materiae* of the standstill clause. When we only use the previous norm as the reference point, there is an undeniable decline visible in the legal protection of the affordability of housing (regardless of the question whether this would constitute the necessary *considerable* decline). But if our comparison takes into account the consequences of and numbers behind this fiscal measure, we find out that there are also practical disadvantages attached to the housing bonus (the aforementioned increase in property prices, unfair distribution of benefits among different income groups),[132] resulting in a whole different perspective on the issue, one that might not lead to the same conclusion. If, of course, the spare money is then not recycled into socio-economic rights protection in a different shape or form, one could once again make a strong argument that the standstill clause still applies.

Finally, there is the question whether an assessment of alleged retrogressive measures should be based on a fixed or a mobile point of reference. Should a comparison be made with the legislation in place either when the right to housing was ratified/entered into force or at the moment just before the retrogressive measure was adopted? In our opinion, the first option runs

130 The Constitutional Court has been very explicit on this with regard to free art education: Constitutional Court 19 May 1994, no. 40/94, B.2.6; MAES (n 50) 128; STEEN (n 111) 125.

131 Art. 64–71 Decree 19 December 2014 concerning provisions accompanying the budget estimates, *BS* 30 December 2014; Flemish Government, *Coalition Agreement Flemish Government 2014–2019*, 22 July 2014, 19.

132 DE DECKER (n 121) 64–75; F. VASTMANS and E. BUYST, *Vastgoedprijzen en woningaanbod in de centrumsteden. Deel 1: Woningprijzen en woningkenmerken*, 2011, 12–15; N. BERNARD and V. LEMAIRE, “Regionalisering van de woonbonus: naar een beleid op maat van het Brussels Gewest?”, *Brussels Studies* 2015, no. 83, (1) 1–7; FLEMISH HOUSING COUNCIL, *Advies over de regionalisering van de woonbonus*, 10 December 2012, no. 2012/12.

counter to the basic idea of progressiveness behind the standstill principle.[133] The aim and obligation is to improve the protection level of the right to housing and comparing new measures to the initial protection level enables a government to withdraw the improvements made all the more easily. For these reasons, we definitely support how more recent decisions by the Belgian courts tend to look at the applicable legislation[134] instead of a fixed reference point in the past.[135]

Take, for example, the amount of rent guarantee that can be requested by the landlord. In the summer of 2017, the Flemish government decided that that amount will be raised from two to three months' rent in what was described as an attempt to balance out the rights and duties of both contracting parties. Regardless of whether this retrogressive measure can be justified, it would not even be considered a retrogressive measure altogether when adopting a fixed point of reference since the current rules (maximum of two months' rent for those who choose to deposit the guarantee on a personal bank account) was only adopted back in 2007.

3) *A Different Application of the Principle: The Proportionality Test*

A final potential problem with applying the prohibition of retrogressive measures as a way to improve the realization of socio-economic rights at the domestic level is the inaccurate application of the principle by national judges. In Belgian case law, a very peculiar interpretation arises. When confronted with the standstill argument, the Belgian Constitutional Court and the Council of State usually adopt a proportionality test.[136] This entails that the relevant rules

133 I. HACHEZ, "L'effet de standstill: le pari des droits économiques, sociaux et culturels?", *AP* 2000, (30) 50; MAES (n 116) 1086.

134 E.g. Constitutional Court 16 September 2010, no. 99/2010, B.4.7; Constitutional Court 16 September 2010, no. 99/2010, B.4.7; Constitutional Court 16 March 2005, no. 59/2005, B.7.2; Adv. Council of State 10 June 2013 concerning a draft of Law to amend the Judicial Code with regards to legal aid, no. 53.322/3 4.2.2.2; Adv. Council of State 24 January 2006, advice no. 39563/VR/3 on a draft of Decree concerning the modification of the decree of 15 July 1997 concerning the Flemish Housing Code, *Parl. St.* Vl. Parl. 2005–06, no. 824/1; Council of State 9 January 2007, no. 166439; J. THEUNIS, "De toetsing aan grondrechten door het Grondwettelijk Hof", *TBP* 2012, no.1, (3) 35; VANDEBURIE (n 112) 63–65.

135 E.g. Constitutional Court 27 November 2002, no. 169/2002, B.6.5; Constitutional Court 14 January 2004, no. 5/2004, B.14.6; Constitutional Court 18 December 2008, no. 182/2008, B.7.3.

136 E.g. Constitutional Court 10 July 2008, no. 101/2008; Constitutional Court 5 March 2015, no. 24/2015;Adv. Council of State 9 December 2008, no. 45479 concerning a draft of a Decision of the Flemish Government to modify the regulation on the social rental system and the transfer of immovable property (unpublished); Adv. Council of State 24 January 2006, no. 39563/VR/3 concerning a draft of Decree on the modification of the Decree of 15 July 1997 concerning the Flemish Housing Code, *Parl. St.* Vl. Parl. 2005–06, no. 824/1.

are directly tested against the constitutional right to housing. Similar to other housing-related case law applying a proportionality test, which most commonly concerns conflicts with the right to property,[137] the Court starts the balancing of interests from the principle that the opinion of the legislator regarding the general interest must always be respected, unless it is manifestly unreasonable.[138] This obviously renders the state with a considerable margin of appreciation, said to be restricted only when the measure under scrutiny can cause certain categories of persons to lose their home, using the ECtHR's *McCann* judgment as reference.[139]

Let us elucidate on one example, the advisory opinion by the Council of State concerning the imposition of an obligation for (prospective) tenants of social housing to show willingness to learn the Dutch language.[140] On the question whether this measure was reconcilable with the standstill principle, the Council argued that it did not have to identify a regression of the existing legal protection. It continued that, taking into account the purpose of the measure and the conditions the Council had set out in its proportionality assessment in the previous paragraphs, it had already clarified that the measure could not be considered a significant regression, let alone one that could not be justified for reasons of general interest. As such, the measure under scrutiny was found not to be in conflict with the standstill obligation.[141] The Council of State thus relied entirely on its proportionality assessment to come to that conclusion, which raises a couple of thoughts.

First, we think that it is simply not possible to conclude that there is no regression on the mere basis that the measure is balanced. Those are two entirely different questions. We do, however, agree that the proportionality assessment in this specific case certainly conveys the existence of a general interest, more specifically the improvement of communication between landlord and tenant and thereby also the livability of social residential complexes.[142] As a consequence, no violation of the standstill clause had appeared according to the Council of State. This inevitably leads us to our

137 Constitutional Court 12 February 2015, no. 16/2015; Constitutional Court 29 July 2010, no. 91/2010; Constitutional Court 10 May 2006, no. 75/2006; Constitutional Court 26 June 2008, no. 92/2008; M. DAMBRE, *Bijzondere overeenkomsten*, Brugge, Die Keure, 2014, 248.

138 Constitutional Court 10 July 2008, no. 101/2008, B.23.3.

139 Ibid.: reference to ECtHR13 May 2008, no. 19009/04, McCann/UK, par. 50; Constitutional Court 5 March 2015, no. 24/2015, B.21.2; see also T. VANDROMME, "Ook partner van sociale huurder moet aan voorwaarden sociale huur voldoen", *Juristenkrant* 2015, no. 317, 4.

140 Adv. Council of State 24 January 2006, no. 39563/VR/3 concerning a draft of Decree on the modification of the Decree of 15 July 1997 concerning the Flemish Housing Code, *Parl.St.* Vl. Parl. 2005–06, no. 824/1.

141 Ibid., 5.4.

142 Ibid., 5.2.2.

second remark. How do both tests relate to each other? Do they actually merge into one test or are they two separate tests? And, if so, is there one that we should favor to enhance the protection of the fundamental right to adequate housing?

Proportionality definitely plays a role in the investigation as to whether a retrogressive measure can or cannot be allowed. At the same time, however, we believe that a proportionality assessment that directly tests these measures against the fundamental right itself differs quite significantly from the way in which we described the standstill principle earlier. At first sight, this could be seen as a favorable interpretation from the perspective of socio-economic rights protection because it bestows (more) direct effect on the right to housing, and the first essential step, an inquiry into the regression itself and the extent thereof to establish a comparison between the two legal situations, is no longer necessary.[143] Consequently, Hachez argues that the justification of retrogressive measures should be approached similarly to the way in which the European Court of Human Rights (ECtHR) discusses the justification of limitations to Convention rights – in other words, based on the conditions of legality, legitimate purpose and proportionality.[144]

We argue, however, that, somewhat paradoxically, reducing the prohibition of retrogressive measures to a proportionality test actually provides the government more leeway to decrease the protection level than is accepted on the basis of the traditional theory of the standstill principle.[145] We have said that where a considerable regression has been determined in the context of the standstill principle, the government has to prove that a (pressing) general interest for the challenged measure exists. But we have also seen how the proportionality test is based on the assumption that the government has acted in the general interest, and that this can only be contested in case of manifest unreasonableness. In other words, there is a difference in who carries the burden of proof.

We may conclude that directly testing a retrogressive measure against the right to housing on the basis of proportionality may not create a stronger protection of that right in comparison with an accurate application of the standstill principle. At best, it is able to further concretize the right's content. It is clear that in this context a proportionality test will not create some sort of breakthrough in housing rights protection.

143 STEEN (n 111) 130.

144 HACHEZ (n 124) 424–429.

145 F. VANNESTE, "Over de cruciale rol van (sociale) grondrechten in België", in Vereniging voor de vergelijkende studie van het recht van België en Nederland (ed.), *Preadviezen 2012,* Den Haag, Boom Juridische Uitgevers, 2012, (13) 33; STEEN (n 111) 130.

D. Appropriateness of Retrogressive Measures

In our search for more result-oriented obligations to improve the enjoyment of the right to housing, the narrative has thus far been to pinpoint the possible hurdles for a stringent application of the standstill obligation in domestic case law. But is such a strict prohibition of retrogressive measures also the most appropriate way forward?

A firm opponent of the principle of non-retrogression is Mary Dowell-Jones. She states as follows:

> Not only does it appear to create an incentive for States parties not to implement Covenant rights to their highest ability nor to experiment with various strategies for their realization in case they are then held to be an unsuccessful program, it also fails to capture the complexity and fluidity of the task of realizing socio-economic rights given the ebb and flow of economic and political conditions.[146]

From this passage, we can distinguish two major quarrels she has with the concept.

Her first point of criticism (the part before the comma) relates to how a standstill obligation could limit the commitment of the public authorities to make further strides in socio-economic rights protection, since they would no longer be able to scale the new level down again. While this might depend upon how strictly the judiciary would apply the principle, making retrogressive measures much more conditional or almost absolute does indeed do little to promote or incentivize the progressive realization of socio-economic rights in the long run. It can demobilize states to actively pursue the full enjoyment of these rights, thereby taking the edge of the idea of progressive realization.[147] Instead of focusing on making strides, it directs our attention to what has been done, no matter how ineffective that might be.[148]

We can criticize possible methods to weaken the effect of the standstill obligation, but for the reasons given above we do not oppose the idea that the government must have a certain margin of discretion either. It should keep the possibility to re-evaluate measures and policies and change course drastically if it considers this to be necessary for the effectiveness of socio-economic rights, even if this first entails taking a step back. Let us explain this by using the free share of electricity to which all Flemish households were entitled to up to 2015. Besides the ecological argument used in favor of the abolition of this measure,

146 DOWELL-JONES (n 81) 52.
147 VANDEBURIE (n 112) 66.
148 HACHEZ (n 124) 585–588 and 591–592.

it was also said that it did not attain its social objectives.[149] Since the cost of the measure was compensated for in the other kilowatt-hours, it favored those households with a low energy consumption level. Yet a significant number of poorer households live in isolated dwellings heated with electricity and/or use older energy-wasting equipment. They did not benefit from the measure.[150] Even worse, households with a budgetmeter (i.e. those who already have serious problems paying their energy bills) did not receive the free share at all, since they have to load a pay card in order to receive electricity.[151] In short, there is enough reason to argue in favor of an abolition of the measure. This, of course, requires one big leap of faith: we must assume that these types of measures are indeed taken out of concern for the protection of the right to adequate housing. It is a difficult task to decide whether or not the government has adopted these measures in the general interest.

The second problem (the part after the comma) that can be gathered from the cited passage concerns the flexibility of the principle in light of the affordability of the welfare state. In other words, it relates more specifically to resource-motivated decisions, which find particular relevance in the economic crisis. This is, of course, not the first economic crisis since the adoption of the ICESCR. In response to the economic recession in the 1980s, Tomuschat pessimistically said that "with the collapse of the underlying economic assumptions [. . .], the [ICESCR] itself now seems to have lost its cornerstones".[152] The assumptions Tomuschat refers to were based on the economic optimism of the 1950s and 1960s. But then again, every treaty or piece of legislation is essentially a testament of its time. Just as much as democratic elections or free speech should be upheld and respected in times of political distress or uproar, an economic recession is a litmus test for socio-economic rights.[153] It is specifically at these moments that fundamental rights should rise to the occasion.[154]

At the same time, it is, of course, much easier to proclaim a principled prohibition of retrogressive measures in times of economic prosperity. An important

149 Report on behalf of the Commission for Living Environment, Nature, Spatial Planning, Energy and Animal Welfare on the draft of Decree concerning miscellaneous provisions on energy, *Parl.St.* Vl. Parl. 2015–16, no. 461/6, 5.

150 N. BATIS and H. VAN OOTEGEM, "Eau et énergie: à quand des droits effectifs?", *Echos log.* 2010, no.1, (14) 15; VREG and VEA, *Eindrapport met betrekking tot de evaluatie van de maatregel tot toekenning van gratis elektriciteit*, 2012, 40.

151 M. CLYMANS and M. VANDEN EYNDE, "Leve de liberalisering! Gas en elektriciteit vrij te koop. Of toch niet?", in B. HUBEAU and P. JADOUL (eds.), *Vers un droit fondamental à l'énergie? Naar een grondrecht op energie?*, Brugge, Die Keure, 2006, (183) 187.

152 C. TOMUSCHAT, "Human rights in a world-wide framework – some current issues", *Zeitschrift für Aüslandisches öffentliches Recht und Völkerrecht* 1985, vol.45, (547) 566–567.

153 Simma, E/C.12/1990/SR.15, 3, par. 7.

154 K.D. BEITER, *The protection of the right to education by international law*, Leiden, Martinus Nijhoff Publishers, 2005, 401–402; ALSTON (n 2) 163–164.

question, applicable to Belgium but to a lot of other Western European countries as well, is the following: with a considerable public debt, an economy still recovering from a serious crisis and, most importantly, a population gradually ageing, to what extent will the current level of socio-economic protection remain feasible? Against that background, one might argue that for the survival of the social welfare state in the long run, the standstill principle should not be applied too rigorously so that budgetary cuts can be made. Not addressing deficits now could also lead to a subpar protection of socio-economic rights in the future, potentially worse than what might result from current retrogressive measures. Legal backing for that argument can actually be found in the requirement of article 2(1) ICESCR to use the maximum of available resources. While this phrase is traditionally used to urge state parties to do more, there is no reason why it could not also impose the obligation not to go beyond that maximum, not to financially stretch beyond those limits.[155]

Ultimately, the lasting affordability of socio-economic rights on its own is indeed a legitimate reason to take retrogressive measures. But only this reason should then be able to trigger such action. We argue that such measures can only be justified when they are indeed adopted with serious concern for the protection of socio-economic rights and with the idea of progressive realization still in mind. Part of that entails that disadvantaged groups in society have to be exempted as much as possible.[156] It also means that the aforementioned argument for austerity measures should be clearly differentiated from delaying or reducing the development of socio-economic rights purely for reasons of benefitting economic development. The latter should not suffice as a justification for austerity measures.[157] The so-called trickle-down effect, the idea that benefits from higher growth will ultimately flow to the disadvantaged sectors of society,[158] has generally been dismissed.[159] Moreover, questions have

155 M. DOWELL-JONES, "The sovereign bond markets and socio-economic rights. Understanding the challenge of austerity", in E. RIEDEL, G. GIACCA and C. GOLAY (eds.), *Economic, social, and cultural rights in international law: contemporary issues and challenges*, Oxford, Oxford University Press, 2014, (51) 66.

156 CESCR, *General Comment No. 3*, par. 12; CESCR, *Concluding Observations Spain*, 6 June 2012, E/C.12/ESP/CO/5, par. 8; SEPULVEDA (n 21) 328.

157 MÜLLER (n 74) 574 and 590.

158 E.g. F.A. HAYEK, *The mirage of social justice*, London, Routledge, 1976.

159 E.g. OECD, *Focus on inequality and growth*, 2014, www.oecd.org/els/soc/Focus-Inequality-and-Growth-2014.pdf; E. DABLA-NORRIS, K. KOCHNAR, F. RICKA, N. SUPHAPHIPHAT and E. TSOUNTA, "Causes and consequences of income inequality: a global perspective", *IMF Staff Discussion Note SDN/15/13*, 2015; A. McCHESNEY, "Promoting the general welfare in a democratic society: balancing human rights and development", *NILR* 1980, vol. 27, (283) 319; UN Sub-Commission on Prevention of Discrimination and Protection of Minorities, *The realization of economic, social and cultural rights. Final report submitted by Mr. Danilo Türk, Special Rapporteur*, E/CN.4/Sub.2/1992/16, 3 July 1992, 24–26; P. HUNT, *Reclaiming social rights*, Aldershot, Ashgate, 1999, 197.

also arisen about the effects of austerity measures on the economy in general. It has been said that they can actually create a negative spiral on the economy and could *de facto* materialize what they were originally set out to prevent.[160]

Finally, we should address the uncontested presumption that has underpinned the whole discussion up to now: austerity measures threaten socio-economic rights protection. Since the budget is undeniably a very important instrument in the realization of socio-economic rights, budgetary decisions most definitely play a key role in the realization process.[161] Most of the time these negative measures will manifest themselves in stricter conditions and lower allowances in order to optimize the budget. But do saving measures always have to be at odds with improving socio-economic rights, with adopting result-oriented measures?

Consider, for example, the battle against homelessness. Research has repeatedly shown that prevention of homelessness and providing housing for homeless people is much more cost-effective for a state than solving and financing recurring problems afterwards.[162] In 2015, the Centre for Housing Policy presented new results that once more clarified how homelessness not only has a terrible human cost but is also incredibly expensive for the public purse.[163] With regard to the United Kingdom, it illustrated that differences in public costs between resolving homelessness quickly and allowing it to persist depend severely on the personal stories behind and reasons for homelessness. But there is one recurring element: preventing and rapidly resolving homelessness always costs less public money than allowing it to become sustained or repeated, ranging from little more than £3,000 to almost £19,000 pounds (between €4,000 and €26,500).[164] In 2005, the state of Utah (US) calculated the annual costs for an average homeless person to be $16,670, while providing

160 J. GUAJARDO, D. LEIGH and A. PESCATORI, "Expansionary austerity: new international evidence", *IMF Working Paper WP/11/158*, 2011; Financial Times, "Nobel economist blasts Europe's austerity plans", 14 December 2011; DOWELL-JONES (n 155) 82.

161 OHCHR, *Report of the High Commissioner for Human Rights on Implementation of Economic, Social and Cultural Rights*, E/2009/90, 8 June 2009, par. 46; *Los Angeles Times*, "Utah is winning the war on chronic homelessness with 'housing first' program", 24 May 2015.

162 E.g. D.P. CULHANE, "The Cost of Homelessness: A Perspective from the United States", *European Journal of Homelessness* 2008, vol. 2, no. 1, 97–114; P. FLATAU, K. ZARETKY, M. BRADY, Y. HAIGH and R. MARTIN, *The cost-effectiveness of homelessness programs: a first assessment: Volume 1*, Australian Housing and Urban Research Institute, 2008; P. KENWAY and G. PALMER, *How many, how much? Single homelessness and the question of numbers and cost*, New Policy Institute, 2003; E. DEMAERSCHALK, "Dakloosheid kost handenvol geld. Housing first als goedkoper alternatief", *Alert* 2014, vol. 40, no. 5, 16–24.

163 N. PLEACE, *At what cost? An estimation of the financial costs of single homelessness in the UK*, Centre for Housing Policy, University of York, 2015.

164 Ibid., vi and 10–17.

an apartment and social worker only totaled $11,000. Convinced by those numbers, the state adopted the Housing First program providing permanent supportive housing for targeted individuals and managed to reduce the share of chronically homeless with 91 percent over the last decade.[165] On the basis of this knowledge, we can only support measures taken by the Flemish government at a time of austerity to invest an extra €312,000 into the prevention of evictions.

A last example comes from the Netherlands, where in 2006 the four largest Dutch cities launched an ambitious plan to tackle homelessness. This plan aimed to provide homeless people with a structural form of housing (besides an income and an obligatory care plan) and also to prevent homelessness resulting from eviction.[166] Not only were the effects visible in practice,[167] but research in 2011 illustrated that it was also cheaper. With regard to the factual homeless, the financial benefits of the plan were measured to be double its costs. The benefits of the plan for the potential homeless even totaled €1.3 billion.[168] Of course, this does require a long-term vision, which is not always evident in times of economic crisis. With the beginning of the second phase of the program, resources were no longer assured. Short-term financial gains were chosen over long-term result-oriented governing. Nevertheless, these examples show that sometimes the expenses for protecting the right to housing can indeed be optimized, but that this does not automatically have to entail a decline of the protection level itself.

4. Conclusion

The prohibition of taking retrogressive measures, developed by the CESCR, fits within the broader idea of progressive realization and is therefore an important aspect to analyze in order to improve the protection of the right to housing at the domestic level. Despite some uncertainties about the exact conditions, the international human rights bodies advocate a rather stringent interpretation of the principle. On the basis of Belgian case law concerning the standstill obligation, we have seen how different practical problems as well as a very broad margin of appreciation allowed to the government can temper the

165 Utah Housing and Community Development Division, *Comprehensive report on Homelessness*, 2014, https://jobs.utah.gov/housing/scso/documents/homelessness 2014.pdf.

166 K. HERMANS, "Bouwstenen voor een Vlaams actieplan tegen dak- en thuisloosheid. Inspiratie uit Nederland, Finland en Schotland", Leuven, Steunpunt Beleidsrelevant Onderzoek Armoede, 2012, 7–13.

167 Dutch Ministry of Health, Welfare and Sport, *Plan van aanpak dak- en thuislozen (maatschappelijke opvang). 2e fase*, 2011, 6.

168 Cebeon, *Kosten en baten van maatschappelijke opvang. Bouwstenen voor effectieve inzet van publieke middelen,* Dutch Ministry of Health, Welfare and Sport, 2011, 6, 24 and 30.

effect of the principle at the national level. At the same time, however, we have noted that a stringent approach to the concept might also undercut the value and primary objective of the principle. Whether adopting a broad or a narrow interpretation of the obligation, we conclude that it is intrinsically flawed in pushing the envelope towards the full realization of the right to housing. The last chapter will therefore reflect specifically on possibilities and mechanisms that are ultimately more result-oriented.

Bibliography

ALSTON, P. and QUINN, G., "The nature and scope of states parties' obligations under the International Covenant on Economic, Social and Cultural Rights", *HRQ* 1987, vol. 9, no. 2, 156–229.

ANDREASSEN, B.A, SMITH, A.G. and STOKKE, H. "Compliance with economic and social human rights: realistic evaluations and monitoring in the light of immediate obligations", in EIDE, A. and HAGTVET, B. (eds.), *Human Rights in Perspective: A Global Assessment,* Oxford, Oxford University Press 1992, 252–267.

BADERIN, M.A. and McCORQUODALE, R., "The International Covenant on Economic, Social and Cultural Rights: Forty Years of Development", in BADERIN, M.A. and McCORQUODALE, R. (eds.), *Economic, Social and Cultural Rights in Action*, Oxford, Oxford University Press, 2007, 3–24.

BATIS, N. and VAN OOTEGEM, H., "Eau et énergie: à quand des droits effectifs?", *Echos log.* 2010, no. 1, 14–20.

BEITER, K.D., *The protection of the right to education by international law*, Leiden, Martinus Nijhoff Publishers, 2005, 719 pages.

BERNARD, N. and LEMAIRE, V., "Regionalisering van de woonbonus: naar een beleid op maat van het Brussels Gewest?", *Brussels Studies* 2015, no. 83, (1) 1–7.

BERNARD, N., "Vers un fonds centralisée (mutualisé!) de garanties locatives: balises et suggestions pour une opérationnalisation", *Les Échos du Logement* 2015, no. 3, 3–10.

BILCHITZ, D., *Poverty and Fundamental Rights: The Justification and Enforcement of Socio-Economic Rights*, Oxford, Oxford University Press, 2007, 300 pages.

CEBEON, *Kosten en baten van maatschappelijke opvang. Bouwstenen voor effectieve inzet van publieke middelen,* Dutch Ministry of Health, Welfare and Sport, 2011, 64 pages.

CHAPMAN, A. and RUSSELL, S., *Core obligations: building a framework for economic, social and cultural rights*, Antwerpen, Intersentia, 2002, 351 pages.

CHENWI, L., "Unpacking 'progressive realisation', its relation to resources, minimum core and reasonableness, and some methodological considerations for assessing compliance", *De Jure* 2013, vol. 46, no. 3, 742–769.

CLYMANS, M. and VANDEN EYNDE, M., "Leve de liberalisering! Gas en elektriciteit vrij te koop. Of toch niet?", in HUBEAU, B. and JADOUL, P. (eds.), *Vers un droit fondamental à l'énergie? Naar een grondrecht op energie?*, Brugge, Die Keure, 2006, 183–192.

COOMANS, F., "Reviewing implementation of social and economic rights: an assessment of the 'reasonableness' test as developed by the South African Constitutional Court", *ZaöRV* 2005, vol. 65, 167–196.

CRAVEN, M.C.R., "The International Covenant on Economic, Social and Cultural Rights", in HANSKI, R. and SUKSI, M. (eds.), *An introduction to the international protection of human rights: a textbook*, Turku, Institute for Human Rights, Abo Akademi University, 1999, 101–123.

CRAVEN, M.C.R., *The International Covenant on Economic, Social and Cultural Rights. A perspective on its development*, Oxford, Clarendon Press, 1995, 144 pages.

CULHANE, D.P., "The Cost of Homelessness: A Perspective from the United States", *European Journal of Homelessness* 2008, vol. 2, no. 1, 97–114.

DABLA-NORRIS, E., KOCHNAR, K., RICKA, F., SUPHAPHIPHAT, N. and TSOUNTA, E., "Causes and consequences of income inequality: a global perspective", *IMF Staff Discussion Note SDN/15/13*, 2015, 39 pages.

DAMBRE, M., *Bijzondere overeenkomsten*, Brugge, Die Keure, 2014, 534 pages.

DAMBRE, M., *De huurprijs. Analyse van de financiële verbintenissen van de huurder en onderzoek naar de mogelijkheid tot objectivering van de woninghuurprijzen*, Brugge, Die Keure, 2009, 598 pages.

DE BECO, G., "The interplay between human rights and development the other way round: the emerging use of quantitative tools for measuring the progressive realization of economic, social and cultural rights", *HR&ILD* 2010, No. 2, 265–287.

DE DECKER, P., "Afbouw woonbonus: nu of nooit", *Samenleving en Politiek* 2014, no. 1, 64–75.

DE SCHUTTER, O., "Introduction", in DE SCHUTTER, O. (ed.), *Economic, social and cultural rights as human rights*, Edward Elgar Publishing, Cheltenham, 2013, xiii–xxvii.

DEMAERSCHALK, E., "Dakloosheid kost handenvol geld. Housing first als goedkoper alternatief", *Alert* 2014, vol. 40, no. 5, 16–24.

DOWELL-JONES, M., "The economics of the austerity crisis: unpicking some human rights arguments", *HRLR* 2015, no. 15, 193–223.

DOWELL-JONES, M., "The sovereign bond markets and socio-economic rights. Understanding the challenge of austerity", in E. RIEDEL, G. GIACCA and C. GOLAY (eds.), *Economic, social, and cultural rights in international law: contemporary issues and challenges*, Oxford, Oxford University Press, 2014, 51–85.

DOWELL-JONES, M., *Contextualising the International Covenant on Economic, Social and Cultural Rights: assessing the economic deficit*, Leiden, Martinus Nijhoff Publishers, 2004, 214 pages.

DUMONT, H., "Conclusions: l'apport des droits fondamentaux au droit de l'environnement, de l'urbanisme et du logement", *Amén.* 1996, 287–289.

FELNER, E., "Closing the 'escape hatch': a toolkit to monitor the progressive realization of economic, social and cultural rights", *Journal of Human Rights Practice* 2009, vol. 1, no. 3, 402–435.

FIERENS, J., "L'article 23 de la Constitution. Une arme contre la misère?", *Dr.Q.M.* 1994, no. 3, (3) 9.

FLATAU, P., ZARETKY, K., BRADY, M., HAIGH, Y. and MARTIN, R., *The cost-effectiveness of homelessness programs: a first assessment: Volume 1*, Australian Housing and Urban Research Institute, 2008, 160 pages.

FLEMISH HOUSING COUNCIL, *Advies over de regionalisering van de woonbonus*, 10 December 2012, no. 2012/12.

FLEMISH HOUSING COUNCIL, *Naar een beleid ter ondersteuning van de private huurwoningmarkt*, 30 September 2010, no. 2010/11.

FORMISANO PRADA, M., *Empowering the poor through human rights litigation*, Paris, UNESCO, 2011, 123 pages.

GOLDMANN, M., "Human rights and sovereign debt workouts", in BOHOSLAVSKY, J.P. and CERNIC, J.L. (eds.), *Making sovereign financing and human rights work*, Oxford, Hart Publishing, 2014, 79–100.

GUAJARDO, J., LEIGH, D. and PESCATORI, A., "Expansionary austerity: new international evidence", *IMF Working Paper WP/11/158*, 2011, 41 pages.

HACHEZ, I., "Le Comité Européen des Droits Sociaux confronté à la crise financière Grecque: des decisions osées mais inégalement motivées", *TSR* 2014, no. 3, 243–279.

HACHEZ, I., *Le principe de standstill dans le droit des droits fondamentaux: une irreversibilité relative*, Brussel, Bruylant, 2008, 694 pages.

HACHEZ, I., "L'effet de standstill: le pari des droits économiques, sociaux et culturels?", *AP* 2000, 30–57.

HAFFNER, M. and WINTERS, S., "Homeownership taxation in Flanders: moving towards 'optimal taxation'?", *International Journal of Housing Policy* 2015, 1–18.

HAYEK, F.A., *The mirage of social justice*, London, Routledge, 1976, 195 pages

HERMANS, K., *Bouwstenen voor een Vlaams actieplan tegen dak- en thuisloosheid. Inspiratie uit Nederland, Finland en Schotland*, Leuven, Steunpunt Beleidsrelevant Onderzoek Armoede, 2012, 41 pages.

HEYLEN, K. and WINTERS, S., *De verdeling van subsidies op vlak van wonen in Vlaanderen*, Leuven, Steunpunt Ruimte en Wonen, 2012, 95 pages.

HOHMANN, J., *The right to housing. Law, concepts, possibilities*, Oxford, Hart Publishing, 2013, 75–91.

HUBEAU, B. and VERMEIR, D., *Een evaluatie van het federale woninghuurrecht. Tussentijds rapport inzake duur, opzegging, waarborg en woningkwaliteit*, Leuven, Steunpunt Wonen, 2014, 180 pages.

HUBEAU, B. and VANDROMME, T., "De beperking van het keuzerecht van kandidaat sociale huurders: beperking van het grondrecht op wonen of net toepassing van het grondrecht op wonen" (note under Council of State 18 February 2013, no. 222.544), *RW* 2013–14, no. 39, 1537–1541.

HUNT, P., *Reclaiming social rights*, Aldershot, Ashgate, 1999, 313 pages.

HUYGHEBAERT, N., *Berekening woonbonus op kruissnelheid*, KU Leuven, 2012, unpublished.

KENNA, P., *Housing rights and human rights*, 2005, www.nuigalway.ie/media/housinglawrightsandpolicy/Housing-rights-and-human-rights.pdf, 119 pages.

KENWAY, P. and PALMER, G., *How many, how much? Single homelessness and the question of numbers and cost*, New Policy Institute, 2003, 66 pages.

KHALIQ, U. and CHURCHILL, R., "The European Committee of Social Rights", in LANGFORD, M. (ed.), *Social rights jurisprudence. Emerging trends in international and comparative law*, Cambridge, University Press, 2009, 428–452.

KOCH, I.E., *Human rights as indivisible rights. The protection of socio-economic demands under the European Convention of Human Rights*, Leiden, Martinus Nijhoff Publishers, 2009, 346 pages.

KÜNNEMANN, R., *A human rights textbook*, Heidelberg, FIAN International Secretariat, 1998, 48.

LANGFORD, M. and KING, J.A., "Committee on Economic, Social and Cultural Rights", in LANGFORD, M. (ed.), *Social rights jurisprudence. Emerging trends in international and comparative law*, Cambridge, Cambridge University Press, 2009, 477–516.

LECKIE, S., "Another step towards indivisibility: identifying the key features of violations of ECOSOC rights", *HRQ* 1998, 81–124.

LEIJTEN, I., "Meergelaagdheid en ondeelbare mensenrechten", *TBP* 2013, no. 2–3, 95–113.

LEMAHIEU P. and BUYST, E., *Naar een centraal huurwaarborgfonds*, Leuven, Kenniscentrum voor Duurzaam Woonbeleid, 2007, 15 pages.

MAES, G., "Het standstillbeginsel in verdragsbepalingen en in art. 23 G.W.: progressieve (sociale) grondrechtenbescherming", *RW* 2005–06, no. 28, 1081–094.

MAES, G., *De afdwingbaarheid van sociale grondrechten*, Antwerpen, Intersentia, 2003, 523 pages.

McCHESNEY, A., "Promoting the general welfare in a democratic society: balancing human rights and development", *NILR* 1980, vol. 27, 283–334.

MÜLLER, A., "Limitations and derogations from economic, social and cultural rights", *HRLR* 2009, vol. 9, no. 4, 557–601.

NOLAN, A., "Budget analysis and economic and social rights", in RIEDEL, E., GIACCA, G. and GOLAY, C. (eds.), *Economic, social, and cultural rights in international law: contemporary issues and challenges*, Oxford, Oxford University Press, 2014, 369–390.

ÖRÜCÜ, E., "The core rights and freedoms: the limits of limits", in CAMPBELL, T., GOLDBERG, D., McLEAN, S. and MULLEN, T. (eds.), *Human rights: from rhetoric to reality*, Oxford, Blackwell, 1986, 52.

PLEACE, N., *At what cost? An estimation of the financial costs of single homelessness in the UK*, Centre for Housing Policy, University of York, 2015, 36 pages.

RIEDEL, E., GIACCA, G. and GOLAY, C., "The development of economic, social, and cultural rights in international law", in RIEDEL, E., GIACCA, G., and GOLAY, C. (eds.), *Economic, social, and cultural rights in international law: contemporary issues and challenges*, Oxford, Oxford University Press, 2014, 3–50.

ROBERTSON, R.E., "Measuring state compliance with the obligation to devote the maximum available resources to realizing economic, social and cultural rights", *Human Rights Quarterly* 1994, 693–714.

SEPULVEDA, M., *The nature of the obligations under the International Covenant on Economic, Social and Cultural Rights*, Antwerpen, Intersentia, 2003, 477 pages.

SKOGLY, S., "The requirement of using the 'maximum of available resources' for human rights realization: a question of quality as well as quantity", *HRLR* 2012, vol. 12, no. 3, 393–420.

STEEN, B., "Artikel 23 van de Grondwet en de rechtspraak van de Raad van State", in RAUWS, W. and STROOBANT, M. (eds.), *Sociale en economische grondrechten. Art. 23 Gw.: een stand van zaken na twee decennia*, Antwerpen, Intersentia, 2010, 113–138.

Steunpunt tot bestrijding van armoede, bestaansonzekerheid en sociale uitsluiting, "Huurwaarborg: hoe werkelijk de toegang tot de huisvestingsmarkt verlagen?" in *Verslag Armoedebestrijding 2008–2009. Deel 1: Een bijdrage aan politiek debat en politieke actie*, Brussel, 2009, 222 pages.

STROOBANT, M., "Sociale en economische grondrechten in de Belgische Grondwet. Wordingsgeschiedenis van artikel 23: het Akkoord van 'Le Ry d'Ave' Rochefort", in RAUWS, W. and STROOBANT, M. (eds.), *Sociale en economische grondrechten. Art. 23 Gw.: een stand van zaken na twee decennia*, Antwerpen, Intersentia, 2010, 19–57.

THEUNIS, J., "De toetsing aan grondrechten door het Grondwettelijk Hof", *TBP* 2012, no. 1, 3–37.

TOMUSCHAT, C., "Human rights in a world-wide framework – some current issues", *Zeitschrift für Aüslandisches öffentliches Recht und Völkerrecht* 1985, vol. 45, 547–584.

TRILLET, Y., "Vers une nouvelle effectivité des droits économiques, sociaux et culturels?", *Dr.Q.M.* 2000, vol. 27, 3–10.

VANDEBURIE, A., *L'article 23 de la Constitution. Coquille vide ou boîte aux trésors?*, Brussel, La Charte, 2008, 266 pages.

VANDE LANOTTE J. and DE PELSMAEKER, T., "Economic, social and cultural rights in the Belgian Constitution", in VAN DER AUWERAERT, P., DE PELSMAEKER, T., SARKIN, J. and VANDE LANOTTE, J. (eds.), *Social, economic and cultural rights. An appraisal of current European and international developments*, Antwerpen, Maklu, 2002, 263–285.

VANDENHOLE, W., "Article 26: The right to benefit from social security", in ALEN, A., VANDE LANOTTE, J., VERHELLEN, E., ANG, F., BERGHMANS, E. and VERHEYDE, M. (eds.), *A commentary on the United Nations Convention on the Rights of the Child*, Leiden, Martinus Nijhoff Publishers, 1–45.

VANDERLINDEN, H., "Effectiviteit van de sociale grondrechten in het Belgische recht, mythe of realiteit", *RW* 2008–09, no. 29, 1202–1216.

VANDROMME, T., "Ook partner van sociale huurder moet aan voorwaarden sociale huur voldoen", *Juristenkrant* 2015, no. 317, 4.

VANNESTE, F., "Over de cruciale rol van (sociale) grondrechten in België", in Vereniging voor de vergelijkende studie van het recht van België en Nederland (ed.), *Preadviezen 2012*, Den Haag, Boom Juridische Uitgevers, 2012, 11–60.

VAN OEVELEN, A., "Wijzigingen in het (woning)huurrecht", *RW* 2007, no. 8, 298–306.

VASTMANS, F. and BUYST, E., *Vastgoedprijzen en woningaanbod in de centrumsteden. Deel 1: Woningprijzen en woningkenmerken*, 2011, 89 pages.

VERHAEGHE, P. and VAN DER BRACHT, K., *Is de bankwaarborg wel gewaarborgd? Praktijktesten bij banken*, Gent, University of Gent, 2015, 15 pages.

VLEMMINX, F., *Een nieuw profiel van de grondrechten: een analyse van de prestatieplichten ingevolge klassieke en sociale grondrechten*, Den Haag, Boom Juridische Uitgevers, 2002, 251 pages.

VLEMMINX, F., *Het profiel van sociale grondrechten*, Zwolle, Tjeenk Willink, 1994, 162 pages.

WINTERS, S. et al., *Wonen in Vlaanderen anno 2013. De bevindingen uit het Grote Woononderzoek 2013 gebundeld*, Antwerpen, Garant, 2015, 97 pages.

YOUNG, K.G., "The minimum core of economic and social rights: a concept in search of content", *Yale Journal of International Law* 2008, vol. 33, (113) 126–140.

6 Towards Result-Oriented Obligations

The standstill obligation focuses on the (prohibition of a) significant reduction of the protection of the right to adequate housing. In other words, standstill is applied in a negative sense and fails to give a real positive impulse to make further progress. In search for a more effective approach, it would be an option to investigate the possibility of a positive standstill obligation, which would compel the government to take steps and hold it accountable for not making the constant effort to further realize the right to housing.[1] The problem with this approach is that it merely deals with the question whether there is legislation regarding the different elements of this fundamental right and whether there are no legislative lacunas. While this is important for states that provide hardly

1 While definitely a big encroachment on a government's large margin of appreciation with regard to socio-economic rights, we believe the evolution of state responsibility in the Belgian case law and legal doctrine does at the very least not leave any real major legal stumbling blocks for such an application of the standstill obligation; see: Court of Cassation 28 September 2006, *Pas.* 2006, no. 9–10, 1907; *CDPK* 2007, 218, note M. RIGAUX; *RCJB* 2007, 353, note S. VAN DROOGHENBROECK; *RW* 2006–07, 27, note A. VAN OEVELEN; *TBP* 2007, 546, note E. MAES; J. JACQMAIN, "Droit au travail, droit du travail", in R. ERGEC (ed.), *Les droits économiques, sociaux et culturels dans la constitution*, Brussel, Bruylant, 1995, (163) 188; A. VAN OEVELEN and P. POPELIER, "De aansprakelijkheid van publiekrechtelijke rechtspersonen voor ondeugdelijke wetgeving", in A. ALEN (ed.), *De doorwerking van het publiekrecht in het privaatrecht*, Gent, Mys & Breesch, 1997, (75) 125–126; M. MELCHIOR and C. COURTOY, "Het verzuim van de wetgever of de lacune in de grondwettelijke rechtspraak", *TBP* 2008, no. 10, (587) 589; H. VUYE, "Aansprakelijkheid van de Belgische Staat voor het doen en laten van de wetgever", *TBBR* 2002, no. 8, (526) 538; G. MAES, "Algemene zorgvuldigheidsnorm en aansprakelijkheid voor de wetgevende macht", *NJW* 2004, no. 66, (398) 403–404; G. MAES, *De afdwingbaarheid van sociale grondrechten*, Antwerpen, Intersentia, 2003, 362; E. MAES, "Het Hof van Cassatie over de fout van overheidsorganen: streng, strenger, strengst . . ." (note under Court of Cassation 28 September 2006), *TBP* 2007, no. 9, (547) 549–551; A. ALEN, "De overheidsaansprakelijkheid voor fouten van de wetgever. Over de cassatiearresten van 1 juni 2006 en 28 septemer 2006, in W. PINTENS, A. ALEN, E. DIRIX and P. SENAEVE (eds.), *Vigilantibus ius scriptum: feestbundel voor Hugo Vandenberghe*, Brugge, Die Keure, 2007, (1) 8.

any legal protection regarding the main elements of adequate housing, most countries do have certain housing quality requirements, a public housing market, housing benefits, etc. In our search for a result-oriented right to housing, the more important question that we will ask in this final chapter is therefore whether measures related to housing rights effectively contribute to further progress. But how do we test whether sufficient progress is made and how could this be given any more enforceable meaning in a national context? We will first look into some techniques that have been developed in order to measure progress (1). Then we investigate the possibilities for enforcing progressive realization through court, again based on the international development of that concept (2). With that knowledge, we try to develop a framework that has the potential to create more result-oriented obligations on the domestic level (3).

1. International Monitoring Techniques

On the international plane, attempts to find the most appropriate ways to monitor progress have been made for several decades now. Quantitative tools can certainly provide at least some guidance.[2] An important early source in this respect was the 1990 report by Special Rapporteur Danilo Türk regarding economic and social indicators. These indicators refer to statistical data that provide information for the assessment of progress in the realization of the rights concerned.[3] With a comprehensive publication on human rights indicators by the Office of the High Commissioner for Human Rights 22 years later, it is safe to say that considerable progress has been made in the theoretical development of these indicators.[4]

They are traditionally divided into three categories: structural, process and outcome. The first one relates to the extent to which a state has ratified relevant international instruments, adopted a regulatory framework and set up institutional mechanisms. Process indicators then look at the policy measures and necessary budgetary commitments the state has made or is willing to make in order to give effect to the rights it has accepted. Finally, the outcome indicators measure a state's human rights performance in different specific

2 G. DE BECO, "The interplay between human rights and development the other way round: the emerging use of quantitative tools for measuring the progressive realization of economic, social and cultural rights", *HR&ILD* 2010, no. 2, (265) 276.

3 UN Sub-Commission on Prevention of Discrimination and Protection of Minorities, *The new international economic order and the promotion of human rights. Progress report prepared by Mr. Danilo Türk, Special Rapporteur*, E/CN.4/Sub.2/1990/19, 6 July 1990, 4.

4 OHCHR, *Human rights indicators. A guide to measurement and implementation*, HR/PUB/12/5, 2012.

categories.[5] Indicators have been developed in the context of the right to housing too, for example, in a 2003 working paper by the UN Housing Rights Programme (UNHRP).[6] In retrospect, we can confidently state that this attempt was not overtly convincing. Not only did it not differentiate between the different types of indicators, but it did not classify them under logical categories either. National legal protection and acceptance of international standards were, for example, used as housing rights elements under which indicators were categorized, alongside elements such as housing adequacy and security of tenure. But in contrast to those latter aspects, the former are not components of the right to housing in itself. Rather they belong as structural indicators under each of the more substantive housing dimensions such as housing adequacy.[7] The aforementioned document from the OHCHR is much more useful. It does clearly distinguish between structural, process and outcome indicators and breaks down the indicators into the different dimensions that flow from General Comment No. 4 (habitability, availability, affordability and security of tenure).[8]

While these indicators can help human rights practitioners as well as the Committee on Economic, Social and Cultural Rights (CESCR) in the assessment of progressive realization, they do focus only on the quantitative aspect. This is illustrated in the OHCHR document where all the indicators begin with the words "proportion of" or very similar wording (e.g. proportion of households living with sufficient living space, number/proportion of legal procedures seeking compensation following evictions). These indicators on their own are mere empty figures. They do not tell the entire story or expose the reasons behind certain patterns – why, for example, x number of households live in hazardous conditions. Process and outcome indicators are basically interpreted in a simple cause-and-effect relationship.[9] This is somewhat reminiscent of the perception of law as the ultimate instrument for social change (i.e. legal instrumentalism), which we have criticized in Part I of this

5 O. DE SCHUTTER, *International human rights law*, Cambridge, Cambridge University Press, 2010, 480; OHCHR, *Report on indicators for monitoring compliance with international human rights instruments: a conceptual and methodological framework*, HRI/MC/2006/7, 11 May 2006, 7.

6 United Nations Housing Rights Programme, *Monitoring housing rights. Developing a set of indicators to monitor the full and progressive realisation of the human right to adequate housing*, Nairobi, UN-HABITAT, 2003, 37–38.

7 A. EIDE, "The use of indicators in the practice of the Committee on Economic, Social and Cultural Rights", in A. EIDE, C. KRAUSE and A. ROSAS (eds.), *Economic, social and cultural rights*, Dordrecht, Martinus Nijhoff Publishers, 2001, (545) 550.

8 OHCHR, *Human rights indicators. A guide to measurement and implementation*, HR/PUB/12/5, 2012, 94.

9 OHCHR, *Report on indicators for monitoring compliance with international human rights instruments: a conceptual and methodological framework*, HRI/MC/2006/7, 11 May 2006, 7.

research. There, we highlighted the need to take more socio-legal influences into consideration as well.

The system of indicators can be given more meaning with the establishment of benchmarks, which serve as projected levels of compliance (over a period of time) set at the domestic level. The indicators can then be tested against these benchmarks. Indicators and benchmarks also form part of the four-step approach (IBSA) proposed by the CESCR since General Comment No. 14. It requires the state to use a list of relevant human rights indicators (I) and set concrete benchmarks (B) that should then be suggested to the CESCR. In a third step called scoping (S), the latter will then discuss these proposals with the state party. Finally, an assessment (A) takes place of the state party report.[10]

In practice, however, the use of indicators and benchmarks in general has up to now not appeared to have been very successful.[11] Even with sufficient data it is very difficult to pin down benchmarks that are both sufficiently ambitious and realistic at the same time. No matter whether or not the concerned benchmark is reached, that information does not give a conclusive answer to the question whether the state has done everything it could have done according to the maximum of its available resources.[12] In order to evaluate a state's capacity and willingness to use its resources, but also even to determine benchmarks, the need for an analysis of the public budget allocation arises. Such an analysis can look at the public expenditure ratio, the social allocation ratio and the social priority ratio (i.e. how much of the social allocation ratio goes to each social component). With the information provided by the human rights indicators, a budget analysis can assist in identifying whether the government's priorities coincide with those that ought to be made.[13] As with housing rights indicators and benchmarks, however, a certain reticence is appropriate with regard to the causality between ratios and the enjoyment of the right to housing.[14] A budget analysis should not be used in isolation because the bare data and ratios neglect to a certain extent the more complex

10 E. RIEDEL, G. GIACCA and C. GOLAY, "The development of economic, social and cultural rights in international law", in E. RIEDEL, G. GIACCA and C. GOLAY (eds.), *Economic, social, and cultural rights in international law: contemporary issues and challenges*, Oxford, Oxford University Press, 2014, (3) 24–26.

11 L. CHENWI, "Unpacking 'progressive realisation', its relation to resources, minimum core and reasonableness, and some methodological considerations for assessing compliance", *De Jure* 2013, vol. 46, no. 3, (742) 759; E. FELNER, "Closing the 'escape hatch': a toolkit to monitor the progressive realization of economic, social and cultural rights", *Journal of Human Rights Practice* 2009, vol. 1, no. 3, (402) 410; M. SEPULVEDA, *The nature of the obligations under the International Covenant on Economic, Social and Cultural Rights*, Antwerpen, Intersentia, 2003, 317.

12 S. OSMANI, "Human rights to food, health and education", *Journal of Human Development* 2000, vol. 1, no. 2, (273) 291.

13 Fundar Center for Research and Analysis, *Dignity counts. A guide to use budget analysis to advance human rights*, 2004, www.iie.org/Programs/IHRIP/Publications, 30.

14 DE BECO (n 2) 284.

and subjective societal reality that affects budget expenditures and their efficiency.[15] With regard to Flanders, for example, the relatively limited resources allocated to housing cannot be analyzed separately from the high home ownership rate.

A specific approach that makes use of all these types of information to evaluate a state's compliance with its economic and social rights obligations is the International Social and Economic Rights Fulfillment Index.[16] This SERF index, as it is abbreviated, is built on the information provided by outcome indicators as to how well aspects of socio-economic rights are enjoyed. From there the approach works with so-called Achievement Possibility Frontiers or APFs. On the basis of a comparison between the selected indicators and the concerned state's GDP per capita, APFs reveal what is feasible for a state to achieve if it were to allocate the maximum of available resources to realizing socio-economic rights. They benchmark the obligations a state should be required to meet according to best practice. In other words, this approach tries to quantify the intricate meaning of "maximum of its available resources", reconciling for practical purposes the idealism of human rights rhetoric ("maximum") with the policy space states have at their disposal ("available").[17] It is a very technical approach firmly rooted in economics and therefore a good illustration of how the monitoring of socio-economic rights is very much dependent on interdisciplinary collaboration.

As is the case with all aforementioned techniques that may monitor progress in the field of the right to housing, the SERF index is part of a quantitative assessment, primarily based on statistical data. All these approaches have a tendency to focus merely on the results without answering the many critical questions that arise between the existence of a right and its outcome. To what extent is the outcome actually the consequence of the adopted measure? We do not in any way contend that quantitative analysis cannot contribute to the assessment of progressive realization. On the contrary, it is a necessary element to assess a state's compliance, but it does give only an incomplete picture.[18]

15 FELNER (n 11) 412.

16 S. FUKUDA-PARR, T. LAWSON-REMER and S. RANDOLPH, "Measuring the progressive realization of human rights obligations: an index of economic and social rights fulfillment", *Economics Working Papers* 2008; S. FUKUDA-PARR, T. LAWSON-REMER and S. RANDOLPH, "Making the principle of progressive realization operational – The SERF Index. An index for monitoring state fulfillment of economic and social rights obligations", in L. HAGLUND and R. STRYKER (eds.), *Closing the Rights Gap. From Human Rights to Social Transformation*, Oakland, University of California Press, 2015, 239–264.

17 A paradox described by: R.E. ROBERTSON, "Measuring state compliance with the obligation to devote the maximum available resources to realizing economic, social and cultural rights", *Human Rights Quarterly* 1994, (693) 694.

18 For more downsides of mere quantitative analysis, see Center for Economic and Social Rights, "The OPERA Framework. Assessing compliance with the obligation to fulfill economic, social and cultural rights", 11–12.

Additionally, given the main research question of this chapter, a more qualitative perspective is appropriate. Our primary aim is to look for ways to make the right to housing and the obligations that derive from it more result-oriented on the domestic level, not only to answer the question whether sufficient progress has been made in certain aspects of this right, which is the purpose of the CESCR reporting procedure and the main impetus for the use of indicators.

More useful for our purposes, then, is the OPERA framework. This approach contains both a quantitative and a qualitative analysis. It assesses both the outcome of a socio-economic right and the efforts taken to improve its realization, both obligations of result as well as obligations of conduct and the link between them.[19] OPERA is an acronym depicting the four steps of the approach: outcomes, policy efforts, resources and assessment. The first step is pretty much self-explanatory in that it looks at indicators to measure the level of rights enjoyment. It does so with regard to minimum core obligations, non-discrimination and progressive realization. Since OPERA departs from the idea that outcomes alone cannot give a full understanding of a state's compliance, the second step looks at the policy efforts and seeks to determine to what extent laws and policies have translated into goods and services on the ground that are available, accessible, acceptable and of adequate quality (AAAAQ criteria). This step not only tries to answer the question whether law in the books has transformed into law in action; it also considers whether this has happened while upholding the principles of participation, accountability and transparency, principles that are certainly related to the value of autonomy as part of social dignity (supra). The third step (resources) then draws on the well-known tools of budget and economic policy analysis, but also explores the priorities of the state's resource policy and whether expenditures are equitable and effective (e.g. which income groups benefit from the expenditures?). In its final step (assessment) the frameworks provides a broader analysis of the contextual factors, both bottom-up (e.g. knowledge of law) as well as top-down influences (e.g. state structure, conduct of third parties), to ultimately synthesize with the findings of the first three steps to make a final assessment.[20]

Very similar to OPERA but slightly more compact is Felner's causality analysis.[21] Felner too tries to remedy the idea that the main focus should be on the attainment of indicators, promoting both a quantitative and a qualitative perspective in a three-step approach. The first step once more uses quantitative data to identify deprivation and disparities in the enjoyment of socio-economic rights. Second, the direct and indirect determinants of these outcomes need

19 CHENWI (n 11) 765.

20 Center for Economic and Social Right (n 18) 13–29.

21 E. FELNER, "A new frontier in economic and social rights advocacy? Turning quantitative data into a tool for human rights accountability", *Sur-International Journal on Human Rights* 2008, vol. 5, no. 9, (109) 116–126.

to be analyzed to identify what can reasonably be expected of the state. These influencing factors are present both on the supply-side (where the AAAAQ criteria ought to be taken into account) and on the demand-side. A third and final phase of the causality analysis assesses the adequacy of the policy efforts taken to address these different determinants, which includes an analysis of the budget allocation.

For the purposes of this chapter, approaches like the OPERA framework and Felner's causality analysis are certainly useful, but indicators, benchmarks and other techniques alone enable only the monitoring of the fulfillment of the right to housing. A next step is to see what we can take away from the judicially imposed obligations that stem from the concept of progressive realization.

2. Enforceability of Progressive Realization

A. A Review Criterion

We know from the decisions by the European Committee of Social Rights (ECSR) as referenced throughout this research that this Committee has applied the idea of progressive realization in its decision-making. It is able to put its finger on the existing problems and shortcomings of a state party (and thereby point to what should be done), but the ECSR is, of course, not part of a system of separation of powers and checks and balances similar to that within states.[22] It can therefore take a stance that stretches beyond the jurisprudence of the domestic judicial branch.[23] This is only enhanced by the fact that progressive realization is neither explicitly concretized as one of the provisions of the Charter (a similar wording is used only in the preamble) nor developed elsewhere than in the complaints procedure and the reporting system by the Committee itself. There is, in other words, no politically agreed-upon content that might serve as a viable criterion for application at the domestic level.

In contrast, the Optional Protocol to the International Covenant on Economic, Social and Cultural Rights (OP-ICESCR),[24] which entered into force in 2013, does provide such a review criterion that states have agreed upon: reasonableness. On the basis of the OP, individuals and groups of individuals can now submit communications to the CESCR concerning alleged violations of any of the Covenant rights. Article 8(4) OP-ICESCR provides the CESCR with the review criteria to assess these complaints:

22 F. COOMANS, "Reviewing implementation of social and economic rights: an assessment of the 'reasonableness' test as developed by the South African Constitutional Court", *ZaöRV* 2005, vol. 65, (167) 185.

23 DE BECO (n 2) 274.

24 Art. 18 Optional Protocol to the ICESCR: the OP required ten ratifications to come into force.

> When examining communications under the present Protocol, the Committee shall consider the reasonableness of the steps taken by the State Party in accordance with Part II of the Covenant. In doing so, the Committee shall bear in mind that the State Party may adopt a range of possible policy measures for the implementation of the rights set forth in the Covenant.

Such a reasonableness review cannot, of course, be entirely separated from the aforementioned methods such as Felner's causality approach. The third step of his analysis also requires a clarification of what may reasonably be expected from the concerned state.[25] What is different is the way in which it is applied. Here it serves as the criterion for the CESCR acting as a quasi-judicial mechanism to assess an alleged violation of a specific Convention right. It is no surprise, then, that the incorporation of the reasonableness test and the exact wording of it is the outcome of fierce political debates.

Important voices against the adjudication of the rights in the ICESCR were the USA, China, Canada and the UK. They first opposed the idea of a complaints procedure altogether and later advocated for a reduced level of scrutiny and a general deference to states' policy choices.[26] Several delegations also expressed concerns about possible interference with budget decisions and social policymaking.[27] It was Louise Arbour, then High Commissioner for Human Rights, who made an appeal to the concept of reasonableness as a potential solution to the stalemate:

> As for normal judicial review functions, the key is often in examining the "reasonableness" of measures adopted by each state – given its specific resources and circumstances – by reference to objective criteria that are developed in accordance with standard judicial experience and with the accumulation of jurisprudence. [. . .] In many cases, it can also serve to establish if there is already the effective or appropriate implementation

25 DE SCHUTTER (n 5) 509.

26 C. MAHON, "Progress at the front: the draft Optional Protocol to the International Covenant on Economic, Social and Cultural Rights", *HRLR* 2008, vol. 8, no. 4, (617) 620–626; B. PORTER, "Reasonableness and article 8(4)", in R. BROWN, M. LANGFORD, B. PORTER and J. ROSSI, *The Optional Protocol to the International Covenant on Economic, Social and Cultural Rights: a commentary*, Capetown, Pretoria University Law Press, 2016 (194) 198–199.

27 E.g. UN Commission on Human Rights, *Report of the open-ended working group to consider options regarding the elaboration of an optional protocol to the International Covenant on Economic, Social and Cultural Rights on its first session*, E/CN.4/2004/44, 15 March 2004, par. 22 and 57–66; UN Commission on Human Rights, *Report of the open-ended working group to consider options regarding the elaboration of an optional protocol to the International Covenant on Economic, Social and Cultural Rights on its second session*, E/CN.4/2005/52, 10 February 2005, par. 32.

> of existing laws and policies, rather than to determine the reasonableness of such laws and policies.[28]

That did not immediately persuade the most ardent opponents, who argued for a long time in favor of the inclusion of a reference to a state's broad margin of appreciation and proposed to include a standard of unreasonableness rather than one of reasonableness.[29] It is in this negative sense that reasonableness is best known in common law countries. Giving in to such proposals, however, would have illustrated once more how human rights generations have to be treated differently. But not adequately addressing these political obstacles could have threatened the creation of a complaints procedure altogether.

The solution would ultimately come from the South African Constitutional Court and its judgment in the *Grootboom* case. Considering that the socio-economic rights sections 26 and 27 of the South African Constitution were drafted with article 2(1) ICESCR firmly in mind,[30] it is not that surprising to see the negotiations now reverting back to South African practice in order to give shape to the justiciability of the concept of progressive realization. The relevant passage reads as follows:

> The measures must [be] directed towards the progressive realization of the right of access to adequate housing [. . .] The question would be whether the measures that have been adopted are reasonable. It is necessary to recognise that a wide range of possible measures could be adopted by the state to meet its obligations. Many of these would meet the requirement of reasonableness.[31]

28 UN High Commissioner for Human Rights, *Statement by Ms. Louise Arbour to the open-ended working group established by the Commission on Human Rights to consider options regarding the elaboration of an optional protocol to the International Covenant on Economic, Social and Cultural Rights*, 2005.

29 B. GRIFFEY, "Reasonableness test: assessing violations of state obligations under the Optional Protocol to the International Covenant on Economic, Social and Cultural Rights", *HRLR* 2011, vol. 11, no. 2, (275) 295; Human Rights Council, *Promotion and protection of all human rights, civil, political, economic, social and cultural rights including the right to development. Report of the open-ended working group to consider options regarding the elaboration of an optional protocol to the International Covenant on Economic, Social and Cultural Rights on its fourth session*, A/HRC/6/8, 30 August 2007, par. 37, 95, 97 and 153; Human Rights Council, *Promotion and protection of all human rights, civil, political, economic, social and cultural rights including the right to development. Report of the open-ended working group to consider options regarding the elaboration of an optional protocol to the International Covenant on Economic, Social and Cultural Rights on its fifth session*, A/HRC/8/7, 23 May 2008, par. 10–11.

30 COOMANS (n 22) 170–171.

31 Constitutional Court (South Africa) 4 October 2000, CCT 11/00, Government of the Republic of South Africa et al./Grootboom et al., par. 41.

With this declaration the court recognized the important role of the government in exercising policy choices without deferring to the state with regard to the assessment of the reasonableness itself.[32] The excerpt served as a blueprint for a revised version of article 8(4) OP-ICESCR with the criterion of reasonableness but without the explicit words "margin of appreciation", a draft that could finally be agreed upon by all delegates.[33]

Through this difficult drafting process, it became clear that the CESCR would not be able to impose its own policy choices as part of the reasonableness review. The state was considered to be better placed to adopt effective measures and design adequate policies.[34] Additionally and to reassure states during the negotiations, the Committee listed a number of possible factors that would come into play when assessing reasonableness:

(a) the extent to which the measures taken were deliberate, concrete and targeted towards the fulfillment of economic, social and cultural rights;
(b) whether the State party exercised its discretion in a non-discriminatory and non-arbitrary manner;
(c) whether the State party's decision (not) to allocate available resources is in accordance with international human rights standards;
(d) where several policy options are available, whether the State party adopts the option that least restricts Covenant rights;
(e) the time frame in which the steps were taken;
(f) whether the steps had taken into account the precarious situation of disadvantaged and marginalized individuals or groups and, whether they were non-discriminatory, and whether they prioritized grave situations or situations of risk.[35]

These criteria do not bring a lot of new elements to the table compared with the interpretations given in the context of article 2(1) ICESCR.[36] For practical (quasi-)judicial purposes, they still leave an awful lot of middle ground. The Committee has plenty of space to elaborate on, to choose the direction it will ultimately go in with the concept of reasonableness. We opt very consciously for a future tense here because the complaints mechanism is still in its infancy and therefore difficult to draw any definitive conclusions from regarding the Committee's take on the reasonableness review. Even though one of the communications thus far dealt with an alleged violation of the right to housing,

32 PORTER (n 26) 208–209.
33 MAHON (n 26) 638; GRIFFEY (n 29) 302.
34 PORTER (n 26) 40–41.
35 CESCR, *An evaluation of the obligation to take steps to the 'maximum of available resources' under an Optional Protocol to the Covenant*, E/C.12/2007/1, 10 May 2007, par. 8.
36 They also resemble the obligations set out in *ATD Fourth World*, par. 58–60.

the decision does not add a whole lot to the current discussion. That has more to do with the facts of the case than with the CESCR. The Committee held that Spain had failed to take all reasonable measures to adequately notify the applicant that the lending institution from which she had received a mortgage loan had filed a mortgage foreclosure against her. She was deprived of the opportunity to adequately defend her right to housing in judicial proceedings. Consequently, the CESCR concluded that Spain had violated the right to housing.[37] The findings in this case are clearly not all that different from what the European Court of Human Rights would be able to judge on the basis of article 6 ECHR applied in a socio-economic rights context. The explicit reference to the judgment of the European Court of Justice in *Aziz* also illustrates how this could well be decided by a court not particularly known for socio-economic rights adjudication.[38] Because of all this, the Committee's reasonableness review did not have to delve into sensitive questions concerning the adequacy of socio-economic rights policy *in se*, unveiling very little on the future potential of the reasonableness assessment.

B. Reasonableness

1) Different Scopes of Reasonableness

There are some unclear elements about the concept of reasonableness in the context of progressive realization that need to be clarified before we can properly judge the potential and desirability of this internationally adopted approach for application at a national level. On the one hand, it can be used to assess whether the government has acted reasonably. This way, the reasonableness question is still primarily concerned with state conduct, with abiding by a formal obligation rather than reaching for the full realization of a right. On the other hand, however, it can serve as an appropriateness or even ability review, where the government's actions are submitted to a substantive analysis of rights claims that go to the systemic causes of social problems. As a legal standard, appropriateness clearly sets a higher bar than reasonableness.[39] Unsurprisingly, there was little support for a text proposal for article 8(4) OP-ICESCR stating that the Committee should not only consider the reasonableness but also the appropriateness of the steps taken.[40]

37 CESCR 13 October 2015, no. 2/2014, I.D.G/Spain, par. 15.

38 Ibid., par. 13.6.

39 V. ABRAMOVIC, "Fostering dialogue: the role of the judiciary and litigation", in J. SQUIRES, M. LANGFORD and B. THIELE (eds.), *The road to a remedy: current issues in the litigation of economic, social and cultural rights*, Sydney, University of New South Wales Press 2006, (167) 171.

40 PORTER (n 26) 49; see also A. VANDENBOGAERDE and W. VANDENHOLE, "The optional Protocol to the International Covenant on Economic, Social and Cultural

In this regard we may want to look back at the *Grootboom* judgment, which inspired the adoption of the reasonableness review in the first place and is a good illustration of what it can and cannot entail. In this case, Mrs. Grootboom challenged the forced eviction of her community from their informal settlements. Their homes were destroyed in a bid to clear the land for a regularized housing development for other informal settlers. More important than the facts of this specific case here is how the South African Constitutional Court conceptualized progressive realization and reasonableness (in the context of the public housing program).

While some welcomed the interpretation as a realistic standard of review and a flexible tool,[41] others have described this flexibility as "a double-edged sword"[42] and applicable "as though on a sliding scale".[43] The *Grootboom* judgment definitely sends out mixed signals as to what interpretation the court adheres to most. Judge Yacoob J (with whose judgment all the justices concurred) clarified how the government is not obliged to take appropriate steps, only reasonable steps.[44] And we already know from the negotiations on article 8(4) OP-ICESCR that it was also said that many of the wide range of measures open for the state would meet the requirement of reasonableness.[45] Ultimately, however, and in spite of these excerpts, reasonableness is certainly not interpreted in such a restrictive way that it can justify a virtually unlimited margin of discretion. The same paragraph of the *Grootboom* judgment actually states that the housing program must be capable of facilitating the realization of the right. It continues that it may not even be sufficient "to meet the test of reasonableness to show that the measures are capable of achieving a statistical advance in the realisation of the right".[46] Yacoob J ultimately concluded that the state had instituted an integrated housing development policy whose "medium and long term objectives cannot be criticised".[47] To be reasonable, he added that measures cannot exclude a significant segment of society.

Rights: An *Ex Ante* assessment of its Effectiveness in Light of the Drafting Process", *HRLR* 2010, vol. 10, no. 2, 207–237.

41 E.g. C.R. SUNSTEIN, "Social and economic rights? Lessons from South Africa", *Constitutional Forum* 2001, vol. 11, no. 4, 123–131; J.M. WOODS, "Justiciable social rights as a critique of the liberal paradigm", *Texas International Law Journal* 2003, vol. 38, (763) 785; P. DE VOS, "Grootboom, the right of access to housing and substantive equality as contextual fairness", *SAJHR* 2001, vol. 17, (258) 260–263; COOMANS (n 22) 186.

42 PORTER (n 26) 40.

43 D. BRAND, "Socio-economic rights and courts in South Africa: justiciability on a sliding scale", in F. COOMANS (ed.), *Justiciability of economic and social rights. Experiences from domestic systems*, Antwerpen, Intersentia, 2006, (207) 227.

44 Constitutional Court (South Africa) 7 June 2000, CCT 35/99, Dawood et al./Minister of Home Affairs et al., par. 28.

45 Ibid., par. 41.

46 Ibid., par. 44.

47 Ibid., par. 64

A housing program like the one under scrutiny cannot ignore “those whose needs are most urgent and whose ability to enjoy the right is therefore most in peril”.[48] It is exactly here that the programme was found to fall short of the obligations imposed on the government. It had failed “to recognise that the state must provide for relief for those in desperate need”.[49]

By imposing priorities for the socio-economically disadvantaged, it is fair to say that the court’s assessment definitely surpasses a mere review of unreasonableness of conduct.[50] Moreover, it has been asserted that this assessment of reasonableness is indeed result-based and not merely focused on intent.[51] Arosemena has argued that “even as duties of results are replaced by duties of conduct, the whole approach remains goal-oriented”.[52] A government might not be able to provide shelter for every homeless person, but it needs to take measures that are adequate to contribute to the eventual achievement of this goal.

But there has also been criticism of the formal way in which the reasonableness review has been applied. By arguing that the government had excluded the more vulnerable groups in society but not elaborating further on whether the government is required to do anything more substantial than just be inclusive,[53] the court had reached its decision on the basis of the more structural rather than concrete elements of the test.[54] Accordingly, some commentators consider the application of the reasonableness review strongly proceduralized and largely divorced from the substantive content of the fundamental rights, raising doubts about the suitability of the approach to meet the transformative aims of the South African Constitution.[55] In their opinion, deference owed to the government in defining reasonable action appears to extend to an undue deference to the state in defining the content of the right itself.[56] They therefore call for a more substantive judicial approach to reasonableness, which

48 Ibid., par. 44.

49 Ibid., par. 66.

50 GRIFFEY (n 29) 312.

51 G. AROSEMENA, *Rights, scarcity and justice. An analytical inquiry into the adjudication of the welfare aspects of human rights*, Cambridge, Intersentia, 2014, 105; PORTER (n 62) 51.

52 AROSEMENA (n 51) 94.

53 T. ROUX, “Understanding Grootboom – A response to Cass R Sunstein”, *Constitutional Forum* 2002, vol. 12, no. 2, (41) 43; S. LIEBENBERG, *Socio-economic rights. Adjudication under a transformative constitution*, Claremont, Juta, 2010, 177.

54 D. BRAND, “The proceduralisation of South African socio-economic rights jurisprudence, or ‘What are socio-economic rights for?’ ”, in H. BOTHA, A. VAN DER WALT and J. VAN DER WALT (eds.), *Rights and democracy in a transformative constitution*, Stellenbosch, SUN Press, 2003, (33) 49–50.

55 M. PIETERSE, “Coming to terms with the judicial enforcement of socio-economic rights”, *SAJHR* 2004, vol. 20, (383) 410–411; LIEBENBERG (53) 173.

56 J. HOHMANN, *The right to housing. Law, concepts, possibilities*, Oxford, Hart Publishing, 2013, 100.

includes an assessment of what the right in question requires.[57] Until some understanding of this content has been developed, the assessment of whether the measures adopted by the state are reasonably capable of facilitating its realization takes place in a normative vacuum.[58]

2) *Reasonableness as Appropriateness*

A. A PRELIMINARY PROPOSAL

Our aim is not, of course, to evaluate the factual outcome of the relevant South African case law. We look for legal possibilities to assess the contribution of national housing measures, programs, etc. to the realization of the right to housing. Such an assessment does indeed require a substantive assessment. As we have seen earlier in housing rights examples regarding the standstill principle, it is not always straightforward to determine whether a measure or policy signifies progress or regression. To properly do so, it is indispensable that a judge assesses the situation by reference to the substantive requirements of the right and the real-life influences on the effectiveness of that right.[59]

Moreover, we argue that for a reasonableness review to be useful as an instigator for result-oriented obligations, it is definitely necessary that it is interpreted as an appropriateness or even an ability review. Only when a judge is able to substantively assess whether an adopted measure or initiative has the ability to achieve improvement of the right to housing would a reasonableness approach take the socio-economic rights realization to another level, beyond the implications of a mere obligation of means. It is important to emphasize that this scenario is still significantly different from a court imposing certain measures or policies on the government. But at the same time this interpretation does try to bridge the earlier discussed gap between an effective right and the effective realization of a right. This corresponds to a distinction made by Amartya Sen.[60] Circumstances might impede a subjective right to be adequately housed immediately, but there is a meta-right to housing, a right to have measures and policies that genuinely pursue this goal and are able to do so.[61]

57 S. LIEBENBERG, "Socio-economic rights: evaluating reasonableness review and minimum core obligations", in S. WOOLMAN and M. BISHOP (eds.), *Constitutional conversations*, Cape Town, Pretoria University Law Press, 2008, (303) 324; M. PIETERSE, "On 'dialogue', 'translation' and 'voice': reply to Sandra Liebenberg", in S. WOOLMAN and M. BISHOP (eds.), *Constitutional conversations*, Cape Town, Pretoria University Law Press, 2008, (331) 333.

58 D. BILCHITZ, *Poverty and fundamental rights: the justification and enforcement of socio-economic rights*, Oxford, Oxford University Press, 2007, 143.

59 AROSEMENA (n 51) 114–115.

60 A. SEN, "The right not to be hungry", in P. ALSTON and K. TOMASEVSKI (eds.), *The right to food*, Leiden, Martinus Nijhoff, 1984, (69) 70–71.

61 BILCHITZ (n 58) 218–219.

In order to make the right to housing more of a result-oriented obligation, our preliminary proposal is that housing measures should be able to be examined by court on the question whether they can contribute to progressively realizing the right to housing. We do apply the term "preliminary proposal" because important questions and practical counterarguments that arise concerning the practical application of this approach are yet to be properly addressed, not in the least because, as sketched here, the assessment would be entirely outsourced to the judicial branch.

B. POSSIBLE CRITICISM AND IMPERFECTIONS

There are a couple of aspects that deserve attention in the context of our preliminary proposal. First, it could be questioned whether such a reasonableness review sufficiently protects vulnerable persons and groups from the perspective of individualized relief. It is indeed true that the focus of the approach is not as much on how to help a claimant in particular than it is on the bigger picture of an effective right to housing and result-oriented obligations.[62] That is the route we chose to take. Neither should we forget that a considerable amount of relevant housing legislation already enables subjective claim-rights as well. And if our proposal would incentivize more result-oriented obligations, this might obviously benefit individual protection in the longer run too.

Additionally, emphasizing primarily individualized relief would prioritize only those who are able and willing to bring their claims to court, which could lead to greater inequalities. It forces a government to address instant problems in a way that does not necessarily expose and remedy the underlying reasons for those problems. Instead of focusing on long-term solutions and investments, the government would be forced to divert valuable resources to meeting specific court-enforced claims which might hinder it to effectively realize the right to housing for every one of its citizens.[63] In contrast to such one-dimensional rule-based jurisprudence, our account of reasonableness is normatively more open and therefore not only a better and more comprehensive facilitator for structural improvement, but also a more realistic one since it still respects the effective functioning of the legislative and executive branches of government.[64]

62 COOMANS (n 22) 188.

63 M. WESSON, "Grootboom and beyond: reassessing the socio-economic rights jurisprudence of the South African Constitutional Court", *SAJHR* 2004, vol. 20, (284) 303–305; A. NOLAN, *Children's socio-economic rights, democracy and the courts*, Oxford, Hart Publishing, 2011, 237; BILCHITZ (n 58) 203.

64 C. STEINBERG, "Can reasonableness protect the poor? A review of South Africa's socio-economic rights jurisprudence", *South African Law Journal* 2006, vol. 123, (264) 274–276; K. YOUNG, "The minimum core of economic, social and cultural rights: a concept in search of content", *Yale International Law Journal* 2008, vol. 33, (113) 140.

A second point of discussion concerns the use of the term "reasonableness". Some commentators argue that a proportionality review is a more appropriate standard for (socio-economic rights) jurisprudence than a reasonableness test.[65] In traditional civil and political rights adjudication, proportionality is primarily used as a method to evaluate limitations to fundamental rights. After looking at the questions whether the measure/policy pursues a legitimate aim and whether the means to do so are rationally connected to it, benefits resulting from the measure/policy are finally weighed against the harm inflicted to the fundamental right. The aforementioned proponents prefer such a proportionality review to a reasonableness assessment because it has a more structured, transparent and substantive nature and because it provides a more demanding examination of state policy.[66] According to Rivers, this is the reason why the European Court of Human Rights rejected the reasonableness review.[67]

The validity of this argument strongly depends, though, on what interpretation of reasonableness one compares the proportionality review with. The more substantive approach to reasonableness that we have put forward surely also addresses the advantages that were deemed exclusive properties of the proportionality review. In our interpretation, reasonableness is connected to the measure or policy itself; it does not only refer to the conduct the government has to adopt.[68] As a matter of fact, O'Connell stated that for the application of a proportionality review in the context of socio-economic rights adjudication, courts should adopt a "consequential" approach to proportionality, asking whether the state action is likely to achieve a mandated measure or policy.[69] Likewise, Hershkoff argues that the key "judicial question should be whether a challenged law (or policy) achieves, or is at least likely to achieve, the constitutionally prescribed end".[70] Those interpretations of what a proportionality review should entail in a socio-economic rights context are strikingly similar to the interpretation that we have deduced from the concept of reasonableness.

65 A. STONE SWEET and J. MATHEWS, "Proportionality balancing and global constitutionalism", *Columbia Journal of Transnational Law* 2008, vol. 47, (68) 73–74; S. FREDMAN, "New horizons: incorporating socio-economic rights in a British Bill of Rights", *Public Law* 2010, April issue, (297) 318.

66 D. DYZENHAUS, M. HUNT and M. TAGGART, "The principle of legality in administrative law: internationalisation as constitutionalisation", *Oxford University Commonwealth Law Journal* 2001, vol. 1, (5) 20; M. NOVAK, "Three models of balancing (in constitutional review)", *Ratio Juris* 2010, vol. 23, (101) 108; STONE SWEET (n 65) 79.

67 J. RIVERS, "Proportionality and variable intensity of review", *Cambridge Law Journal* 2006, vol. 65, no. 1, (174) 191.

68 BILCHITZ (n 58) 143.

69 P. O'CONNELL, *Vindicating socio-economic rights. International standards and comparative experiences*, London, Routledge, 2012, 189.

70 H. HERSHKOFF, "Positive rights and state constitutions: the limits of federal rationality review", *Harvard Law Review* 1999, vol. 112, (1131) 1137.

Considering how similarly legal literature has interpreted both concepts in a socio-economic rights context, we do not believe this choice would make any large substantive differences, let alone create a problem regarding the interpretation in itself.

A more valuable point of criticism against our reasonableness approach is the principle of the separation of state powers. The hardliners in this debate reject the possibility that a court can compel the government to take a certain action because it would discuss utterly political questions and turn the judiciary into a political organ.[71] It has been argued that it is democratically inappropriate to allow courts a more robust role because it would erode vibrant democratic action.[72] It is true that "the blurring of the limits between interpretation and normative jurisdiction could transform the guardian of the constitution into the sovereign".[73] On the other hand, it must be said that the principle of the separation of powers has evolved. Courts are already involved in a considerable range of matters which have important resource and political implications. In Belgium, both jurisprudence and legal doctrine have interpreted the principle as aiming to establish a balance between the different powers, thereby refining rather than rigorously demarcating the basic principle of the constitutional order.[74] A court should obviously not dispose of a freedom of discretion comparable to that of the legislative branch,[75] but our result-oriented approach does not prescribe what specific measures the government should take. In fact, in response to the eroding democracy argument we are tempted to say that its focus on progressive realization would actually increase (the need for more) qualitative and evidence-based democratic deliberation more than anything else.

Notwithstanding the valid counterarguments to the argument of the separation of powers, we cannot deny that a court competent to judge the contribution of housing measures to the improvement of the right to adequate housing would be a major step into unchartered territories. The current assessments of the standstill obligation in Belgium already illustrate how a court, even with regard to the protection against negative impacts on the right

71 E.W. VIERDAG, "The legal nature of the rights granted by the International Covenant on Economic, Social and Cultural Rights", *Netherlands Yearbook of International Law* 1978, vol. 9, (69) 92–93.

72 D.M. DAVIS, "The case against the inclusion of socio-economic demands in a Bill of Rights except as directive principles", *SAJHR* 1992, vol. 8, (475) 488–490.

73 A.R. BREWER-CARIAS, *Constitutional courts as positive legislators: a comparative law study*, Cambridge, Cambridge University Press, 2011, 40.

74 Court of Cassation 28 September 2006, *Pas.* 2006, no. 9–10, (1870) 1907; MAES (n 1) 548; A. ALEN, "'Scheiding' of 'samenwerking' der machten?", *Academiae analecta. Klasse der Letteren* 1990, vol. 52, no. 1, 1–73.

75 E.g. Constitutional Court 3 June 1993, no. 41/93; Constitutional Court 7 February 2001, no. 10/2001; Constitutional Court 20 October 2005, no. 157/2005.

to housing, acts very cautiously to avoid being considered a "*gouvernement des juges*".[76]

An equally important impediment to the adoption of our proposal is of a practical nature. Not only could it potentially lead to a floodgate of cases, but the review in itself is a serious obstacle too. Even when a court takes different perspectives into account in comprehensively assessing proportionality,[77] this is still far removed from the substantive assessment a court would have to make when adopting this approach. To answer the extremely difficult question whether a measure or policy is appropriate to lead to an improvement of the right to housing, courts are ineffective agents. Their longstanding experience does not provide them with the technical knowledge or data to make such an assessment.[78] Moreover, the Belgian experience illustrates that even if a constitutional court disposes of the most extensive research possibilities,[79] it might not be tempted to utilize them on a regular basis, rendering judges dependent on the information provided by the parties.[80]

Ultimately, we think this preliminary proposal is defendable on a theoretical level, but for the reasons set out it may be a more viable and realistic approach if we take some of that burden away from the judicial branch.

3. Combining Monitoring and Reasonableness

A. Overview of the Proposal

In order to address the most poignant counterarguments, the focal point of our result-oriented approach should be moved from the judicial branch to the legislative process. Not only is this necessary for the reasons given above, but it also has the advantage that the improvement of the right to housing would no longer be protected only reactively by a court, but also proactively.[81] For an optimal chance of assuring measures that effectively improve adequate housing in all its elements, we therefore propose the adoption of a strongly equipped

76 P. POPELIER, "Het evenredigheidsbeginsel in de rechtspraak van Grondwettelijk Hof: tussen grondrechtenbescherming en scheiding der machten", in P. MARTENS et al. (eds.), *Liège, Strasbourg, Bruxelles: parcours des droits de l'homme*, Limal, Anthemis, 2010, 189–196.

77 E.g. In the context of a proportionality test concerning the infringement of the right to property due to a 'social obligation' for building operators according to the Flemish Decree on Land and Real Estate Policy, the Constitutional Court referred to a couple of analyses from strategic advice councils: Constitutional Court 6 April 2011, no. 50/2011, B.40.2.

78 BRAND (n 43) 225.

79 Art. 91 Special Law 6 January 1989 concerning the Constitutional Court.

80 J. DE JAEGERE, "Inclusiviteit als deliberatieve bouwsteen van legitimiteit", *TBP* 2015, no. 4–5, (194) 197.

81 NOLAN (n 63) 232–233.

monitoring mechanism for the right to housing.[82] This monitoring instance would first be competent to investigate early in the legislative process whether a new legislative or executive act will be able (i.e. reasonable) to work towards the further realization of the right to housing (analysis ex ante). Second, and on the basis of its earlier findings, it would also conduct a causality analysis on the basis of the effects afterwards (ex post). The third and final aspect of our proposal aims to provide an enforceable capstone for a result-oriented right to housing. On the basis of the monitoring body's extensive research and assessment ex post, it could be possible to request the annulment of the measure before court. Let us first elaborate on the intricacies of this proposal before addressing its requirements and difficulties one step at a time.

In theory, any preliminary proposal or draft of a measure related to (the right to) housing would have to be scrutinized by the monitoring mechanism on the basis of the question whether the measure at hand would have the potential to improve the right to housing. It is, in other words, subjected to the sort of reasonableness review that we have discussed earlier. Improvement can be interpreted as relating to one of the main elements of adequate housing: accessibility, affordability, quality and security of tenure. It is also important to stress that the assessment should be approached from a practical perspective, not only a mere legal one as is the case with the prohibition of retrogressive measures. In that context we would like to refer back to the illustration used earlier of the increase of the rental guarantee from two months to three. As we have seen, legal alternatives are in place to help those who have trouble collecting the necessary deposit. The mere existence of such alternatives to ensure the affordability of housing (e.g. the bank guarantee) is, however, not sufficient, since its functioning in practice leaves much to be desired.

The conclusion of this monitoring mechanism cannot, however, contain any binding consequences for the legislator. This would undermine the principles of the democratic process. While it aims to persuade the legislator in case of a negative evaluation, the legislator can obviously choose to be persistent on the matter and stick to its original proposal.[83] Moreover, an assessment like this requires a great deal of expertise, knowledge and data. No matter how much data is available, it will be nearly impossible for the vast majority of analyzed proposals to answer our reasonableness question with a probability bordering on certainty. No matter how valuable it might be to take the capability analysis

82 The monitoring mechanism is at its core inspired by: M. STROOBANT, "Algemeen besluit", in W. RAUWS and M. STROOBANT (eds.), *Sociale en economische grondrechten. Art.23 Gw.: een stand van zaken na twee decennia*, Antwerpen, Intersentia, 2010, (201) 206.

83 That is, of course, based on the assumption that the ex-ante analysis has been carried out appropriately. If not, it should be possible to invoke a violation of the due diligence principle before the Constitutional Court.

ex ante into consideration in the law and decision-making process, the lack of scientific certainty should temper any possible expectations regarding its enforceability. Not only from a theoretical but also from a practical viewpoint it is therefore undesirable to question the political primacy at this point in the legislative process. Policy makers will obviously remain able (and be necessitated) to make ideological choices.[84]

It is important, though, that the monitoring mechanism would not develop into a mere obligatory formality. In addition to the ex-ante analysis of the potential to improve the right to housing, the assessed measures would therefore need to be monitored afterwards as well. We could say that such an assessment will be reminiscent of Felner's causality analysis discussed in the previous section.[85] The results will be compared with the scientific projections/assessments of the ex-ante analysis and the question remains virtually the same: do the adopted measures take steps in progressively realizing the right to housing? And, if not, is this due to the measure itself or are there other reasons that might hamper its impact? Again, neither the legislator nor the government can be immediately bound by the recommendations following the analysis, even though it would attest to rational policy making if these were taken into account.

The difference at this point is that because of the more tangible indicators and the knowledge of the law in action, the quality of the analysis should be far superior to that of the ex-ante analysis. In anticipation of the ex-post analysis, research can be very issue-specific and useful indicators could be set up when possible. When a measure based on all this gathered scientific information does not contribute to the progressive realization of the right to housing and no steps are taken by the legislator to address the obstacles and make the necessary modifications, we come to a point at which we argue that a more result-oriented measure could be enforced. The most appropriate judicial body will usually be the Constitutional Court. In the case of an appeal for annulment of the measure under scrutiny, the court could then rely on the scientific analysis to assess the evidence-based character of the legislation and decide on a violation of the constitutional right. This in turn aims to incentivize the legislator to take the assessments of the monitoring body to heart more seriously and trigger effective progress.

From a more practical perspective, one should be aware that in order to conduct a proper and representative ex-post analysis, a couple of years should ideally pass. Depending on the state, however, a Constitutional Court can be competent to consider only appeals for annulment that have been lodged within a certain period of time since the adoption of the measure under

84 P. POPELIER, "De (ir)rationele wetgever vroeger, vandaag en in de toekomst", in B. PEETERS and J. VELAERS (eds.), *De Grondwet in grootboekperspectief*, Antwerpen, Intersentia, 2007, (57) 63 and 91.

85 We do acknowledge that Felner laid more emphasis on the resource question.

scrutiny. In Belgium such appeals can be lodged only within six months of the publication of the legislation.[86] This might therefore also have to be modified in order for the proposal to be viable, even though we acknowledge that this would decrease legal security to a certain extent.

B. Requirements and Areas of Concern

1) The Monitoring Body

A first requirement is, of course, the installment of a mechanism that would hold measures up against a result-oriented perception of the right to housing. In order to develop an effective, well-functioning mechanism, lessons can be drawn from other, already existing forms of law evaluation. In Flanders, a so-called regulation impact analysis or RIA has been in place since 2005. In principle, such an RIA has to be made for all drafts of decrees and decisions by the Flemish government, notwithstanding a list of exceptions for specific types of decrees and decisions. This is conducted by the person or team that prepares this legislative act. A RIA looks at the intended purpose of the proposed piece of legislation and makes an estimated assessment of its positive and negative effects. Additionally, it needs to include an analysis of at least two other scenarios, including the zero option and one other alternative and relevant option. For both, the benefits and disadvantages will also have to be scrutinized.[87] In the end, a RIA should help in making thoughtful, well-informed legislative choices that take underlying societal problems more into consideration and at the same time increase transparency between government and citizen.

Obviously, our approach to the ex-ante analysis is significantly different to that in the RIA. The latter is merely concerned with the question of what the positive and negative effects of a certain measure would be and which option is in that respect the most favorable one to adopt. The question relevant to the form of monitoring we propose, on the other hand, concerns whether the proposed measure is result-oriented in the context of the right to housing. The cost–benefit analysis is important but subordinate to that primary question. Despite the different approach, the inclusion of other scenarios might be a good addition to the concept of a housing rights monitoring instance.

The legal literature and the Socio-Economic Council of Flanders (SERV) have identified several problems that prevent current law evaluation from having a more tangible effect on the eventual legislative act. These problems

86 Art. 3, § 1 Special Law 6 January 1989 concerning the Constitutional Court, *BS* 7 January 1989.

87 K. POEL and W. MARNEFFE, "De federale regelgevingsimpactanalyse: een stand van zaken na zes maanden", *TVW* 2014, no. 3, (185) 189.

should be addressed to have a fully functioning monitoring mechanism in the context of the right to housing. A very important factor in the impediment of a better application of the RIA is the lack of political will. This relies on the idea that policy makers are most of all concerned about getting re-elected. If largely symbolic law-making is necessary to please the voting public, they will not hesitate to do so. From this perspective, policy makers wish to avoid the transparency that law evaluation brings along with it.[88] It is in part due to this (but also because of the difficulty of disposing of all relevant data) that the quality of the RIA is often questionable too. In addition to that, RIAs are usually made only at a moment when the important political choices have already been made. Consequently, they do not serve as a way to reasonably underpin a legislative decision, nor do they have a tangible impact on the whole law-making process. Too often it becomes an administrative formality that only aims at legitimizing a decision that has been determined earlier.[89] These are without doubt serious pitfalls to which a weak housing monitoring mechanism for the right to housing might succumb as well.

The same core deficiencies occur in the context of two more specific ex-ante impact analyses, the Flemish poverty test and the Child and Youth Impact Report (JoKER). They are occasionally added to the RIA, but evaluate in particular the effect of new measures on poverty and on persons under the age of 25 respectively. An evaluation report of the JoKER documents how the evaluation is made at a point in time when all political decisions have been taken,[90] rendering the evaluation process an obligatory formality rather than an influencing mechanism contributing to legislation of a higher quality.[91] Since proposals of decree by the Flemish Parliament are exempted from the JoKER (and RIA) methodology, the evaluation report reveals that the Flemish government can bypass the evaluation process by having a draft decree formally introduced by a member of parliament (thus becoming a proposal of decree).[92] This is obviously another tricky characteristic that might have to be addressed for the best possible application of our housing rights monitoring body.

At the Flemish level, an important independent strategic advisory body analyzing housing legislation ex ante actually already exists: the Flemish Housing Council. While our assessment body would approach housing measures very specifically from the perspective of progressive realization, it is only logical that the Flemish Housing Council would be involved in the new

88 M. DIERICKX VISSCHERS, "De Vlaamse reguleringsimpactanalyse, gewikt en gewogen", in J. DE MOT (ed.), *Liber amicorum Boudewijn Bouckaert. Vrank en vrij*, 2012, (243) 244.

89 SERV, *Wetgevingsprocedures, -structuren en –instrumenten in Vlaanderen: een evaluatie van 10 jaar wetgevingsbeleid in Vlaanderen*, 2009, 46.

90 E. DESMET, H. OP DE BEECK and W. VANDENHOLE, *Evaluatie van de kind- en jongereneffectrapportage (JoKER)*, Gent, KEKI, 2012, 60

91 Ibid., 70 and 85–87.

92 Ibid., 30.

institutional structure due to the expertise it has built up over the years. Unlike the Housing Council, however, the assessment should not be conducted at the end of the law-making process, long after the RIAs are made.

Our proposal installs both an ex-ante as well as an ex-post analysis with regard to measures related to the right to housing. This is in line with the general perception that sound law-making requires both types of analysis.[93] Ex-post evaluations, however, are usually limited to providing an answer to the question whether the adopted measure attains the intended effects and which difficulties have arisen in the process.[94] As such, an ex-post evaluation of a piece of housing legislation would not (necessarily) investigate whether and to what extent this measure has shown to be able to improve the realization of the right to housing. This assessment, either in line or at odds with the ex-ante reasonableness assessment, is what we would expect our ex-post monitoring mechanism to have to do in order to make a tangible impact.

Current forms of ex-post law evaluation share similar problems with the RIAs. Representatives that reside in the Parliamentary Committee in charge of law evaluation at the federal level (ex-post law evaluation is not yet an established component of the legislative process in Flanders) do not have any real stake in investing a considerable amount of their time in law evaluation. It will not pay off in votes, especially not when the results of an evaluation turn out to be disappointing. As a result, an ex-post monitoring mechanism composed of politicians and largely dependent upon political goodwill will certainly be questionable in terms of objectivity and quality, certainly when considering that legislation is not reviewed on the basis of empirical research data.[95]

In order to establish an effective housing rights monitoring mechanism that aims to conduct the type of analysis we have set out and have an impact at the same time, we can conclude that hindrances of a more political nature would need to be avoided. That means, for example, that the reasonableness analysis ex ante should be held early enough in the legislative process so that political opinions are still open for review and adjustments are still very much possible when desirable. Avoiding political maneuvering will also be achieved by making the assessment applicable for all types of proposed housing measures

93 P. VAN HUMBEECK, "Best practices in regulatory impact analysis: a review of the Flemish region in Belgium", *SERV Working Paper* 2007, 38; K. VAN AEKEN, "Een kroon van klatergoud? De wet van 25 april 2007 over de oprichting van een Parlementair Comité belast met wetsevaluatie", *TVW* 2009, no. 3, (204) 210; V. VERLINDEN, "Wie hoedt de wet? Op zoek naar een nieuwe invulling van de wetgevingsprocedure", *RW* 2010–11, no. 20, (818) 823.

94 SERV, *Tien denksporen voor ex post decreetsevaluatie in en door het Vlaams Parlement*, 21 September 2015, available at https://docs.vlaamsparlement.be/docs/stukken/2014-2015/g61-1.pdf, 12.

95 VERLINDEN (n 93) 824–825; J. VAN NIEUWENHOVE, "Een aantal kanttekeningen bij het wetsvoorstel tot oprichting van een Parlementair Comité belast met de wetsevaluatie", *TVW* 2004, no. 8, (275) 275–276; VAN AEKEN (n 93) 205, 208 and 214.

(i.e. legislative and executive). While it can be argued that a political composition of the proposed monitoring body might give better guarantees for later modifications on the basis of the analysis,[96] the nature of this mechanism and the task it should perform definitely demands it to be an expert (predominantly non-political) body (that should nonetheless remain in close contact with the relevant administrations).

2) Ex-Ante and Ex-Post Analysis: Practical Difficulties

Besides the institutional requirements, there are also some more practical questions to discuss. The ex-post evaluation will depart from the outcomes of the measure over the last two to three years. These outcomes are ideally given shape in relevant indicators. In Flanders, the Policy Research Centre for Housing has developed an interesting list of such housing indicators that could be used at the Flemish level.[97] But even with a good amount of scientific knowledge on housing and housing rights already available, not every measure will have its own very specific indicator. If, for example, general indicators on affordability are the only data available for the quantitative assessment of a particular measure concerning housing affordability, the qualitative analysis becomes even more important. To what extent does the measure contribute to the outcomes and what are the reasons for it? While essential in the assessment of what the measure can signify for the realization of the right to housing, there is no point in denying the difficulty of isolating the influence of legislation from the many different influencing factors.[98] If housing has become less affordable for the poorer segments of society, this, on its own merits, should not be regarded as indisputable evidence that a certain measure has negatively affected a vital aspect of the right to housing. Other factors could thwart the potential of a measure that is otherwise result-oriented. The same is obviously true the other way around.

Complications do not only arise in the context of illustrating causality. For some proposed measures it is simply very difficult to assess whether or not they are reasonable to improve the right to housing. We have already touched upon this issue shortly in the context of the standstill principle when discussing the preferences of prospective tenants for social housing. The example illustrates how this is particularly evident in discussions whether to adopt a more universal/maximalist or a more selective/minimalist approach to the improvement of fundamental rights.[99]

96 J. VAN NIEUWENHOVE, *Wetsevaluatie in België*, Deventer, Kluwer, 2002, 15–17.

97 S. WINTERS et al., *Voorstel tot indicatoren voor het Vlaamse woonbeleid*, Leuven, Steunpunt Wonen, 2013, 58–63.

98 VAN AEKEN (n 93) 211–212.

99 For an overview of the accessibility system used in some European countries, see: K. SCANLON and C. WHITEHEAD, “Le logement social en Europe: tendances

Take, for example, the waiting list for social housing in Flanders. By the end of 2014 that list contained 120,436 prospective tenants, an increase of 30,000 compared with a year earlier. This has been attributed largely to the expansion of the income requirements back in 2013.[100] That measure aimed at providing many more people who are in need of social housing, especially one-person households, with the opportunity of eventually obtaining such accommodation. Theoretically, it can also contribute to the prevention of social segregation, in achieving more of a social mix, as we discussed in the chapter on social dignity.[101] Other Flemish representatives disagreed because of what is basically the same argument: access to housing. The argument was raised that it would become more difficult to obtain social housing in practice, that the shortage would just be redistributed and that accordingly the focus should be on the most disadvantaged people in society.

What it boils down to is the question of how selective housing measures should be to have optimal effect. While the figures clearly indicate that the waiting lists have grown in the aftermath of the expansion of the income requirements, it is difficult to say that in principle the expansion of the income conditions is not able to contribute to the realization of the right to housing. An expansion of income requirements both expands and restricts the accessibility of housing, one of the main pillars of the right to housing, at the same time.[102] This definitely presents an extra difficulty to make a convincing case either for or against such a measure. Regardless of the question of what

communes et diversités persistantes", in C. LÉVY-VROELANT and C. TUTIN (eds.), *Le logement social en Europe au début du XXI*[e] *Siècle: la révision générale*, Rennes, Presses Universitaires de Rennes, 2010, (17) 29–31; D. DIERCKX, and T. GHYS, "Solidariteit en herverdeling in structurele armoedbestrijding" in D. DIERCKX, J. COENE, A. VAN HAARLEM and P. RAEYMAECKERS (eds.), *Armoede en sociale uitsluiting. Jaarboek 2013*, Leuven, Acco, 2013, (175) 185; W. KORPI and J. PALME, "The paradox of redistribution and strategies of equality: welfare state institutions, inequality, and poverty in the Western countries", *American Sociological Review* 1998, vol. 63, no. 5, (661) 683.

100 Art. 3, § 2 Framework Decision Social Rent; As Hubeau said a decade ago, income requirements have been on a sliding scale for decades, see: B. HUBEAU, "Zijn het sociaal woonbeleid en de huisvestingssector mee met de onderkant?", in P. DE DECKER, L. GOOSSENS and I. PANNECOUCKE (eds.), *Wonen aan de onderkant*, Antwerpen, Garant, 2005, (353) 356.

101 An additional argument in favor of higher income limits is the higher revenue it provides for the social housing sector, which could enable them to help more prospective tenants in the long run. The additional revenue should, however, be considerably higher to make a tangible impact on the housing stock; cf. B. HUBEAU, "Het kooprecht van de zittende sociale huurder: juridisch en/of maatschappelijk een maat voor niets?" (note under Constitutional Court 30 June 2004, no. 115/2004) *RW* 2004–05, (891) 894.

102 FLEMISH HOUSING COUNCIL, *Advies over het ontwerp van besluit van de Vlaamse Regering tot wijziging van diverse bepalingen betreffende het woonbeleid*, 7 June 2013, no. 2013/08, 3–5.

segment of society should be eligible for social housing,[103] we do argue that the focus of the allocation should first and foremost be on those with an urgent housing need. The issue of raising or lowering income requirements would thus lose some of its practical relevance if housing need became be the main criterion. The ETHOS-typology, which awards points depending on the factual severity of a person's housing need, can therefore serve as a framework.[104]

Discussions on housing measures regularly revolve around an interpretation of categorical selectivity. Another topic that fits this context is the introduction of temporary rental agreements in social housing.[105] New contracts will no longer be of an indefinite duration, but initially limited to a nine- year period, in accordance with private rental agreements.[106] Instead of having two approaches to one aspect of the right to housing as in the previous example, the accessibility element is pitted here against housing security. The nine-year contracts would make it possible to terminate the agreement when a certain income level has been exceeded at the end of the initial nine-year period. If the social tenant still meets the requirements, the rent agreement would be extended for another three years.

This measure aims to create a better flow of people from the social to the private housing market which could increase access to social housing. At the same time, however, it also reduces the housing security of social tenants, which makes for a very difficult reasonableness assessment as to whether it would improve the right to housing.[107] Proponents of the reform interpret moving to the private market as part of a person's regained autonomy,[108] creating space for those who have even fewer resources in the process. On the other hand, a more maximalist view encourages a system that aims to develop more of a sustainable basis from which it becomes possible for a person to improve his/her socio-economic position.[109] With regard to the first perspective it is doubtful whether the measure actually encourages self-development at all.

103 For more information on this issue, see: S. WINTERS, M. ELSINGA, M. HAFFNER, K. HEYLEN, K. TRATSAERT, G. VAN DAALEN and B. VAN DAMME, *Op weg naar een nieuw Vlaams sociaal huurstelsel?*, Brussel, Departement RWO, 2007, 79–98.

104 FLEMISH HOUSING COUNCIL, *Sociale huur in Vlaanderen. Een aanzet tot toekomstoriëntatie*, 17 October 2014, no. 2014/08, 10; FEANTSA, *European Typology of Homelessness and housing exclusion (ETHOS)*, available at www.feantsa.org/download/en-16822651433655843804.pdf.

105 This excludes housing provided by social rental agencies, since they dispose of the accommodation for only a limited period.

106 Art. 97bis Flemish Housing Code.

107 For an overview of some of the arguments pro and contra, see: Report on behalf of the Commission for Housing, Poverty Policy and Equal Opportunities concerning the policy letter on Housing 2015–2016, *Parl.St.* Vl. Parl. 2015–16, no. 524/4, 19, 28–29 and 40–44.

108 Ibid., 29.

109 T. VANDROMME and B. HUBEAU, *De sociale huur als instrument ter verwezenlijking van het grondrecht op wonen*, Antwerpen, Universiteit Antwerpen, 2015, 56.

It could very well undermine a tenant's incentive to find a (better) job because it might lead to the loss of his or her home, the so-called unemployment trap. In order to prevent such a scenario unfolding, the income limit after nine years is placed 25 per cent above the income conditions to register initially for social housing. We nonetheless agree with the advice of the Flemish Housing Council that this may not be sufficient to ascertain that tenants leaving the social housing market will find an adequate dwelling on the private market, especially in the case of single-person households.[110]

From an ex-ante analysis perspective, it is hard to argue in advance that adopting a measure that prioritizes prospective tenants and has their interests prevail over those of the present tenants is unreasonable – that is, it would not be able to improve the right to housing.[111] That, of course, does not mean that the specific conditions of the initiative itself cannot be in conflict with the right to housing. It exemplifies the need for a proper ex-post analysis, especially in scenarios where the impact of a measure is particularly unclear or unpredictable. In that regard it will have to be examined whether the amendment has created enough access to social housing to justify the infringement of the element of housing security. Conducting follow-ups of households whose social rental contracts have been terminated could, for example, indicate whether their forced departure from social housing has proven to be socio-economically sustainable or whether they were back on that waiting list within a considerable period of time. And if the system turns out to have the tendency to take the form of a revolving door, could that perhaps be due to the way in or period over which the decisive increase in income has been evaluated?

In contrast to the previous examples, the potential of a measure is sometimes much more obvious at first glance, but only when the assessment is limited to a short-term perspective. Take, for example, the rental premium.[112] There is no doubt that the affordability of housing has improved with the adoption of an allowance for those who have been on the waiting list for social housing for four years.[113] At the same time, however, it could be regarded as a largely

110 FLEMISH HOUSING COUNCIL, *Advice concerning the modifications on social rent in the draft decree on the amendment of various decrees on housing and concerning the draft decision by the Flemish Government to amend the Framework Decision Social Rent*, 28 January 2016, no. 2016/03, 7–8.

111 VANDROMME (n 109) 56–57.

112 Art. 81–82 Flemish Housing Code; Decision Flemish Government 21 March 2014 on the amendment of the decision by the Flemish Government from 2 February 2007 concerning the installation of a rental price compensation for tenants in housing need and the decision of the Flemish Government from 4 May 2012 concerning the installation of a compensation for prospective tenants, *BS* 5 May 2014.

113 J. VANDENBERGHE, "De huurpremie voor kandidaat-huurders voor een sociale woning", in M. DAMBRE, B. HUBEAU, A. KIEKENS, T. VANDROMME and K. VANNESTE (eds.), *Huurzakboekje 2015*, Mechelen, Wolters Kluwer, 2015, 255–259; V. VAN DE KEERE, "Vlaamse huurpremie voor huurders die wachten op een sociale woning", *NNK* 2013, no. 1, 6–12.

cosmetic measure, a patchwork solution to a failing social housing policy rather than a structural one. Considering the average waiting time of little over three years, it does not create any considerable financial pressure on the government either to make additional efforts in optimizing and expanding the social housing stock,[114] even despite the fact that the rental premium has been expanded to tenants waiting only four instead of five years.[115]

The same can be said about the decision of the Flemish government that social housing organizations can use their housing stock outside the social rental regulations to provide temporary shelter for homeless people during the winter period.[116] The dwellings can only be provided for a period of six months and do not have to fully comply with all housing quality norms as long as they do not exhibit any safety or health risks. Besides some practical questions concerning the specific organization of the initiative, it is difficult to oppose this more pragmatic short-term solution on its own merits.[117] At the same time it only offers a temporary solution. Our reasonableness approach also requires an answer to the question whether it can improve the right to housing in the long run, in a more structural manner. When the proposed monitoring body is in such a position, it should therefore take a quick look at other relevant

114 In accordance with the Flemish Coalition Agreement 2014–2019, the deadline to obtain the social objective will be postponed to 2025 (instead of 2023) with an amendment to the Flemish Housing Code. The amendment also updates the objective of social rental housing itself from 43,440 to 50,000. There are, however, serious questions about the growth path. Between 2009 and 2014 the waiting list for social housing increased by 46 percent. Even if the objective of 50,000 extra social rental houses is reached by 2025, the increase since the baseline measurement in 2008 will not even cancel out the increase of eligible prospective tenants (FLEMISH HOUSING COUNCIL, *Advice concerning the draft decree on the amendment of various decrees on housing*, 28 January 2016, no. 2016/02, 5). Of course, this is only a preliminary prediction. Over the following years, the waiting list could become even longer (e.g. due to the refugee crisis), but also decrease (e.g. due to the introduction of temporary contracts). Regardless, the social housing stock will probably not reach the minimum of 9 percent of the entire housing stock as recommended by the Flemish Housing Council (FLEMISH HOUSING COUNCIL, *Sociale huur in Vlaanderen. Een aanzet tot toekomstoriëntatie*, 17 October 2014, no. 2014/08, 9); S. ZWART, "Maintaining an efficient and equitable housing market in Belgium", *OECD Economics Department Working Papers, no. 1208*, Paris, OECD Publishing, 2015, 22.

115 Less than 0.5 percent of Flemish private tenants receive a rental premium or a rent subsidy; see: S. WINTERS and D. VERMEIR, *The evolution of the private rental market in Flanders*, Leuven, Steunpunt Wonen, 2013, 4.

116 Decision of the Flemish Government 27 November 2015 to amend article 55quinquies of the decision by the Flemish Government from 12 October 2007 concerning the regulation of the social rental system in execution of title VII of the Flemish Housing Code and to amend article 1 and 2 and annex 1, 2 and 3 of the decision of the Flemish Government from 12 July 2013 concerning the housing quality and safety norms, *BS* 12 January 2016.

117 FLEMISH HOUSING COUNCIL, *Advice concerning the organization of the winter shelter of homeless people in social housing*, 9 October 2015, no. 2015/08.

measures in force, possibly on the basis of its own earlier assessments. Do they combat homelessness on a more structural level? Are they geared towards housing rather than just shelter? When that is not the case, the monitoring body should make a clear mention of it. Otherwise, the assessment would be comparable to a regular regulation impact analysis or evaluation, where the outcome is tested only against the objective of the measure itself.

By conducting both ex-ante and ex-post analyses of housing measures, all the necessary expertise on what does and does not work, attested by quantitative and qualitative research, would be centralized in one authoritative voice. This voice could perhaps convince the legislator of the need for a more structural approach when necessary, especially when the monitoring body would have to resort to that argumentation repeatedly with regard to different patchwork measures. In very progressive fashion, one could even make the argument that such repeated statements could support a claim against the inaction of the legislator in the context of an aforementioned positive application of the standstill obligation.

A final aspect that deserves at least some attention in this section concerns the relationship of the right to housing with the right to property. We have seen earlier how in European and domestic jurisprudence both fundamental rights are regularly considered to be at odds with each other. With a strong(er) legislative focus on the realization of the right to housing, concerns could be raised that the right to property might be interfered with more frequently. There is, however, little credence in a possible devaluation of the right to property. First of all, a proper analysis of what might improve the right to housing should take the interests of owners into account as well. As we have seen earlier, this might very well have an impact on a housing measure's chances for success. In addition to that, the mechanism does obviously not delegitimize the right to property either. It does not hinder owners to appeal to court on the basis of an alleged infringement of their right to property whatsoever.

3) Enforceability of Progress

That brings us to the third and final (potential) step of the proposal: the possibility of appealing for the annulment of the measure before court. It speaks for itself that this is the most controversial and progressive element too. In contrast to other considerations and recommendations made throughout this book, which we believe to be widely relevant and/or applicable to different domestic contexts, we approach this option from a Belgian/Flemish perspective not just as an illustration but because the Belgian jurisprudence and legal doctrine offers at least a theoretical plausibility for such a development over time. Whether this would be viable in other countries will largely depend on whether that country recognizes a constitutional right to housing, provides the Constitutional Court with a large margin of appreciation to assess acts and conduct by the legislative power and bestows direct effect on at least the main principles of the ICESCR. Even with these conditions in place and the knowledge that the principle of the separation of state powers has evolved in Belgian case law and legal doctrine to more of a balance between powers, it should be clear that this very progressive approach is still far from a reality in Belgium.

The Belgian Constitutional Court has stated in explicit terms that no constitutional provision renders the legislator dependent upon the existence of statistical data.[118] Yet, at the same time, it regularly refers to scientific studies, statistics and advices to base its judgment on.[119] When, for example, the Flemish Decree on Land and Real Estate Policy was under scrutiny for obliging building operators to reserve a certain quota of houses for social housing purposes, the court used a couple of analyses from independent strategic advice councils to reach its conclusion concerning the infringement of the right to property.[120] This is also the big difference with the preliminary proposal set out at the beginning of this chapter, where the court would have to investigate on its own whether a measure could make progress. One could as a matter of fact argue that when the Constitutional Court is able to rely on such evidence, it should be encouraged to be more audacious in its protection of constitutional rights.[121] Backed by an authoritative housing rights monitoring body that operates both ex ante and ex post, it will find itself in a stronger position to assess the adopted housing measure. Popelier argues that considering the undeniable evolution towards more evidence-based legislation, such a so-called procedural rationality test most likely will gain further importance.[122] A monitoring mechanism with a strong scientific component like the one we propose would certainly enhance this opportunity.[123]

At the same time, however, it must first be mentioned that the court still adheres to the presumption that the assessment of the legislator is based on adequate information. Second and also more important is the need to stress that despite resemblances with the emerging procedural rationality test, our result-oriented approach would most definitely still go beyond any currently emerging evolution. Accordingly, the court would no longer only judge whether the legislator has adopted a measure that directly infringes a

118 Constitutional Court 31 July 2008, no. 110/2008, B.8.4.

119 E.g. Constitutional Court 30 April 2003, no. 51/2003; Constitutional Court 11 January 2007, no. 9/2007; Constitutional Court 7 January 1993, no. 1/93.

120 Constitutional Court 6 April 2011, no. 50/2011, B.40.2.

121 P. POPELIER and C. VAN DE HEYNING, "Procedural rationality: giving teeth to the proportionality analysis", *European Constitutional Law Review* 2013, (230) 254–256 and 260.

122 This test can be called a procedural rationality test; see: P. POPELIER and W. MARNEFFE, "De reguleringsimpactanalyse en de bescherming van grondrechten: een verantwoordelijkheid van wetgever en rechter. Een toepassing op het huisonderwijs", *TVW* 2014, no. 3, (202) 205.

123 This has been argued in the context of the RIA-methodology (regulation impact analysis); see: ibid., 224.

constitutional provision on the basis of the proportionality test, but rather whether it has adopted one that infringes the right to housing because it cannot improve this fundamental right. It would, in other words, be concerned more about the positive (instead of only negative) obligation to fully realize the right to housing. For both these reasons, the quality of the analysis of the monitoring mechanism as well as data on which it relies is of vital importance. The more this is the case, the more the Constitutional Court will feel confident to be the legal capstone of our result-oriented proposal, and the less its assessment will be regarded as a "*gouvernement des juges*".[124]

A final argument for the extended application of the concept of progressive realization on the domestic level comes from the interpretation of the ICESCR by the Council of State. The Council has said that while the rights of the Covenant do not have direct effect in the Belgian legal order, the government does have the obligation to act in accordance with the principles of the ICESCR.[125] While usually cited as an argument in favor of the standstill obligation, one should then question why the government should not have to act in accordance with and be held accountable to the most elementary principle of the ICESCR, the principle of progressive realization.

5. Conclusion

In order to attain an enforceable reasonableness approach to the right to housing that incentivizes result-oriented obligations, we have advocated the need for both an ex-ante and an ex-post analysis for each measure related to this fundamental right. The ex-ante assessment should be held at a time when it can still have a substantive impact on the development of the policy measure, while the evaluation afterwards can rely on the issue-specific research (qualitative and/or quantitative) organized on the basis of the ex-ante analysis to decide whether the measure is indeed result-oriented. We argue that only in the event of a more coordinated assessment process will it become more likely that a Constitutional Court will feel confident enough to rely on this analysis in the context of annulment proceedings.

We should not be naive about the plausibility of this three-step approach materializing. Besides the institutional stumbling blocks that currently impede better law evaluation, it is also costly and time-consuming. While we have taken into account that such a complex assessment of the potential to improve the realization of the right to housing cannot be left exclusively to a judge, the judiciary would still have to go well beyond its current assessment criteria

124 DIERICKX VISSCHERS (n 88) 252–253.

125 Council of State 30 December 1993, no. 45.552, De Wispelaere, Soc.Kron.1994, 244, note J. JACQMAIN; K. DE FEYTER, "De juridische gevolgen van de internationale en nationale erkenning van economische, sociale en culturele rechten", *Jaarboek Mensenrechten* 1994, (161) 169.

as well. The plausibility of such a measure obviously varies from state to state, depending on their recognition of the right to housing, their attitude towards socio-economic rights as being equally enforceable as civil and political rights and their willingness to limit a government's large margin of appreciation in the context of human rights law.

For Belgium, we would argue that the proposal fits within this result-oriented idea of progressive realization. The constitutional provision expects the government to take positive steps to try to achieve the principled perspectives of the right to housing.[126] Since the Constitutional Court has illustrated that it can assess infringements of a legislative act with a constitutional right on the basis of scientific knowledge, can we not hope for a similar approach with respect to a fundamental right that has been described as having to be progressively realized? The approach does not hamper democratic law-making nor does it exclude ideological choices. It only requires that these choices are backed by an evidence-based rationale that fits within the boundaries of progressively realizing the right to housing.

Bibliography

ABRAMOVIC, V., "Fostering dialogue: the role of the judiciary and litigation", in J. SQUIRES, M. LANGFORD and B. THIELE (eds.), *The road to a remedy: current issues in the litigation of economic, social and cultural rights*, Sydney, University of New South Wales Press 2006, 167–176.

ALEN, A., "De overheidsaansprakelijkheid voor fouten van de wetgever. Over de cassatiearresten van 1 juni 2006 en 28 septemer 2006", in W. PINTENS, A. ALEN, E. DIRIX and P. SENAEVE (eds.), *Vigilantibus ius scriptum: feestbundel voor Hugo Vandenberghe*, Brugge, Die Keure, 2007, 1–14.

ALEN, A., "'Scheiding' of 'samenwerking' der machten?", *Academiae analecta. Klasse der Letteren* 1990, vol. 52, no. 1, 1–73.

AROSEMENA, G., *Rights, scarcity and justice. An analytical inquiry into the adjudication of the welfare aspects of human rights*, Cambridge, Intersentia, 2014, 214 pages.

BILCHITZ, D., *Poverty and Fundamental Rights: The Justification and Enforcement of Socio-Economic Rights*, Oxford, Oxford University Press, 2007, 300 pages.

BRAND, D., "Socio-economic rights and courts in South Africa: justiciability on a sliding scale", in COOMANS, F. (ed.), *Justiciability of economic and social rights. Experiences from domestic systems*, Antwerpen, Intersentia, 2006, 207–236.

BRAND, D., "The proceduralisation of South African socio-economic rights jurisprudence, or 'What are socio-economic rights for?'", in BOTHA, H., VAN DER WALT, A. and VAN DER WALT, J. (eds.), *Rights and democracy in a transformative constitution*, Stellenbosch, SUN Press, 2003, 33–56.

126 A. VAN OEVELEN, "De burgerrechtelijke en bestuursrechtelijke regeling van de woningkwaliteit in de federale en Vlaamse regelgeving", *RW* 2002–2003, (1401) 1402–1403 VANDROMME (n 109) 19–20.

BREWER-CARIAS, A.R., *Constitutional courts as positive legislators: a comparative law study*, Cambridge, Cambridge University Press, 2011, 962 pages.

Center for Economic and Social Rights, "The OPERA Framework. Assessing compliance with the obligation to fulfill economic, social and cultural rights", http://www.cesr.org/sites/default/files/the.opera_.framework.pdf, 48 pages.

CHENWI, L., "Unpacking 'progressive realisation', its relation to resources, minimum core and reasonableness, and some methodological considerations for assessing compliance", *De Jure* 2013, vol. 46, no. 3, 742–769.

COOMANS, F., "Reviewing implementation of social and economic rights: an assessment of the 'reasonableness' test as developed by the South African Constitutional Court", *ZaöRV* 2005, vol. 65, 167–196.

DAVIS, D.M., "The case against the inclusion of socio-economic demands in a Bill of Rights except as directive principles", *SAJHR* 1992, vol. 8, 475–490.

DE BECO, G., "The interplay between human rights and development the other way round: the emerging use of quantitative tools for measuring the progressive realization of economic, social and cultural rights", *HR&ILD* 2010, No. 2, 265–287.

DE FEYTER, K., "De juridische gevolgen van de internationale en nationale erkenning van economische, sociale en culturele rechten", *Jaarboek Mensenrechten* 1994, 161–178.

DE JAEGERE, J., "Inclusiviteit als deliberatieve bouwsteen van legitimiteit", *TBP* 2015, no. 4–5, 194–215.

DE SCHUTTER, O., *International human rights law*, Cambridge, Cambridge University Press, 2010, 1052 pages.

DESMET, E., OP DE BEECK, H. and VANDENHOLE, W., *Evaluatie van de kind- en jongereneffectrapportage (JoKER)*, Gent, KEKI, 2012, 123 pages.

DE VOS, P., "Grootboom, the right of access to housing and substantive equality as contextual fairness", *SAJHR* 2001, vol. 17, 258–276.

DIERCKX, D. and GHYS, T., "Solidariteit en herverdeling in structurele armoedbestrijding" in DIERCKX, D., COENE, J., VAN HAARLEM, A. and RAEYMAECKERS, P. (eds.), *Armoede en sociale uitsluiting. Jaarboek 2013*, Leuven, Acco, 2013, 175–188.

DIERICKX VISSCHERS, M., "De Vlaamse reguleringsimpactanalyse, gewikt en gewogen", in DE MOT, J. (ed.), *Liber amicorum Boudewijn Bouckaert. Vrank en vrij*, 2012, 243–260.

DYZENHAUS, D., HUNT, M. and TAGGART, M., "The principle of legality in administrative law: internationalisation as constitutionalisation", *Oxford University Commonwealth Law Journal* 2001, vol. 1, 5–34.

EIDE, A., "The use of indicators in the practice of the Committee on Economic, Social and Cultural Rights", in EIDE, A., KRAUSE, C. and ROSAS, A. (eds.), *Economic, social and cultural rights*, Dordrecht, Martinus Nijhoff Publishers, 2001, 545–552.

FELNER, E., "Closing the 'escape hatch': a toolkit to monitor the progressive realization of economic, social and cultural rights", *Journal of Human Rights Practice* 2009, vol. 1, no. 3, 402–435.

FELNER, E., "A new frontier in economic and social rights advocacy? Turning quantitative data into a tool for human rights accountability", *Sur-International Journal on Human Rights* 2008, vol. 5, no. 9, 109–154.

FREDMAN, S., "New horizons: incorporating socio-economic rights in a British Bill of Rights", *Public Law* 2010, April issue, 297–330.

FUKUDA-PARR, S., LAWSON-REMER, T. and RANDOLPH, S., "Making the principle of progressive realization operational – The SERF Index. An index for monitoring state fulfillment of economic and social rights obligations", in HAGLUND, L. and STRYKER, R. (eds.), *Closing the Rights Gap. From Human Rights to Social Transformation*, Oakland, University of California Press, 2015, 239–264.

FUKUDA-PARR, S., LAWSON-REMER, T. and RANDOLPH, S., "Measuring the progressive realization of human rights obligations: an index of economic and social rights fulfillment", *Economics Working Papers* 2008, 40 pages.

GRIFFEY, B., "Reasonableness test: assessing violations of state obligations under the Optional Protocol to the International Covenant on Economic, Social and Cultural Rights", *HRLR* 2011, vol. 11, no. 2, 275–325.

HERSHKOFF, H., "Positive rights and state constitutions: the limits of federal rationality review", *Harvard Law Review* 1999, vol. 112, 1131–1194.

HOHMANN, J., *The right to housing. Law, concepts, possibilities*, Oxford, Hart Publishing, 2013, 75–91.

HUBEAU, B., "Zijn het sociaal woonbeleid en de huisvestingssector mee met de onderkant?", in DE DECKER, P., GOOSSENS, L. and PANNECOUCKE, I. (eds.), *Wonen aan de onderkant*, Leuven, Garant, 2005, 353–370.

JACQMAIN, J., "Droit au travail, droit du travail", in ERGEC, R. (ed.), *Les droits économiques, sociaux et culturels dans la constitution*, Brussel, Bruylant, 1995, 163–192.

KORPI, W. and PALME, J., "The paradox of redistribution and strategies of equality: welfare state institutions, inequality, and poverty in the Western countries", *American Sociological Review* 1998, vol. 63, no. 5, 661–687.

LIEBENBERG, S., *Socio-economic rights. Adjudication under a transformative constitution*, Claremont, Juta, 2010, 541 pages.

LIEBENBERG, S., "Socio-economic rights: evaluating reasonableness review and minimum core obligations", in WOOLMAN, S. and BISHOP, M. (eds.), *Constitutional conversations*, Cape Town, Pretoria University Law Press, 2008, 303–329.

MAES, E., "Het Hof van Cassatie over de fout van overheidsorganen: streng, strenger, strengst . . ." (note under Court of Cassation 28 September 2006), *TBP* 2007, no. 9, 547–553.

MAES, G., "Algemene zorgvuldigheidsnorm en aansprakelijkheid voor de wetgevende macht", *NJW* 2004, no. 66, 398–404.

MAES, G., *De afdwingbaarheid van sociale grondrechten*, Antwerpen, Intersentia, 2003, 523 pages.

MAHON, C., "Progress at the front: the draft Optional Protocol to the International Covenant on Economic, Social and Cultural Rights", *HRLR* 2008, vol. 8, no. 4, 617–646.

MELCHIOR, M. and COURTOY, C., "Het verzuim van de wetgever of de lacune in de grondwettelijke rechtspraak", *TBP* 2008, no. 10, 587–603.

NOLAN, A., *Children's socio-economic rights, democracy and the courts*, Oxford, Hart Publishing, 2011, 300 pages.

NOVAK, M., "Three models of balancing (in constitutional review)", *Ratio Juris* 2010, vol. 23, 101–112.

O'CONNELL, P., *Vindicating socio-economic rights. International standards and comparative experiences*, London, Routledge, 2012, 248 pages.

OSMANI, S., "Human rights to food, health and education", *Journal of Human Development* 2000, vol. 1, no. 2, 273–298.

PIETERSE, M., "On 'dialogue', 'translation' and 'voice': reply to Sandra Liebenberg", in WOOLMAN, S. and BISHOP, M. (eds.), *Constitutional conversations*, Cape Town, Pretoria University Law Press, 2008, 331–347.

PIETERSE, M., "Coming to terms with the judicial enforcement of socio-economic rights", *SAJHR* 2004, vol. 20, 383–417.

POEL, K. and MARNEFFE, W., "De federale regelgevingsimpactanalyse: een stand van zaken na zes maanden", *TVW* 2014, no. 3, 185–201.

POPELIER, P. and MARNEFFE, W., "De reguleringsimpactanalyse en de bescherming van grondrechten: een verantwoordelijkheid van wetgever en rechter. Een toepassing op het huisonderwijs", *TVW* 2014, no. 3, 202–224.

POPELIER, P. and VAN DE HEYNING, C., "Procedural rationality: giving teeth to the proportionality analysis", *European Constitutional Law Review* 2013, 230–262.

POPELIER, P., "Het evenredigheidsbeginsel in de rechtspraak van Grondwettelijk Hof: tussen grondrechtenbescherming en scheiding der machten", in MARTENS, P. et al. (eds.), *Liège, Strasbourg, Bruxelles: parcours des droits de l'homme*, Limal, Anthemis, 2010, 189–196.

POPELIER, P., "De (ir)rationele wetgever vroeger, vandaag en in de toekomst", in PEETERS, B. and VELAERS, J. (eds.), *De Grondwet in groothoekperspectief*, Antwerpen, Intersentia, 2007, 57–98.

PORTER, B., "The reasonableness of article 8(4) – adjudicating claims from the margins", *NJHR* 2009, vol. 27, no. 1, 39–53.

PORTER, B., "Reasonableness and article 8(4)", in BROWN, R., LANGFORD, M., PORTER, B. and ROSSI, J., *The Optional Protocol to the International Covenant on Economic, Social and Cultural Rights: a commentary*, Capetown, Pretoria University Law Press, 2016, 194–226.

RIEDEL, E., GIACCA G. and GOLAY, C., "The development of economic, social, and cultural rights in international law", in RIEDEL, E., GIACCA, G., and GOLAY, C. (eds.), *Economic, social, and cultural rights in international law: contemporary issues and challenges*, Oxford, Oxford University Press, 2014, 3–50.

RIVERS, J., "Proportionality and variable intensity of review", *Cambridge Law Journal* 2006, vol. 65, no. 1, 174–207.

ROBERTSON, R.E., "Measuring state compliance with the obligation to devote the maximum available resources to realizing economic, social and cultural rights", *Human Rights Quarterly* 1994, 693–714.

ROUX, T., "Understanding Grootboom – A response to Cass R Sunstein", *Constitutional Forum* 2002, vol. 12, no. 2, 41–49.

SCANLON, K. and WHITEHEAD, C., "Le logement social en Europe: tendances communes et diversités persistantes", in LÉVY-VROELANT, C. and TUTIN, C. (eds.), *Le logement social en Europe au début du XXIe Siècle: la révision générale*, Rennes, Presses Universitaires de Rennes, 2010, 17–49.

SEN, A., "The right not to be hungry", in ALSTON, P. and TOMASEVSKI, K. (eds.), *The right to food*, Leiden, Martinus Nijhoff, 1984, 69–81.

SEPULVEDA, M., *The nature of the obligations under the International Covenant on Economic, Social and Cultural Rights*, Antwerpen, Intersentia, 2003, 477 pages.

STEINBERG, C., "Can reasonableness protect the poor? A review of South Africa's socio-economic rights jurisprudence", *South African Law Journal* 2006, vol. 123, 264–284.

STONE SWEET, A. and MATHEWS, J., "Proportionality balancing and global constitutionalism", *Columbia Journal of Transnational Law* 2008, vol. 47, 68–122.

STROOBANT, M. "Algemeen besluit", in RAUWS, W. and STROOBANT, M. (eds.), *Sociale en economische grondrechten. Art.23 Gw.: een stand van zaken na twee decennia*, Antwerpen, Intersentia, 2010, (201) 206.

SUNSTEIN, C.R., "Social and economic rights? Lessons from South Africa", *Constitutional Forum* 2001, vol. 11, no. 4, 123–131.

VAN AEKEN, K., "Een kroon van klatergoud? De wet van 25 april 2007 over de oprichting van een Parlementair Comité belast met wetsevaluatie", *TVW* 2009, no. 3, (204) 210.

VAN DE KEERE, V., "Vlaamse huurpremie voor huurders die wachten op een sociale woning", *NNK* 2013, no. 1, 6–12.

VANDENBERGHE, J., "De huurpremie voor kandidaat-huurders voor een sociale woning", in DAMBRE, M., HUBEAU, B., KIEKENS, A., VANDROMME T. and VANNESTE, K. (eds.), *Huurzakboekje 2015*, Mechelen, Wolters Kluwer, 2015, 255–259.

VANDENBOGAERDE, A. and VANDENHOLE, W., "The Optional Protocol to the International Covenant on Economic, Social and Cultural Rights: An *Ex Ante* Assessment of its Effectiveness in Light of the Drafting Process", *HRLR* 2010, vol. 10, no. 2, 207–237.

VANDROMME, T. and HUBEAU, B., *De sociale huur als instrument ter verwezenlijking van het grondrecht op wonen*, Antwerpen, Universiteit Antwerpen, 2015, 273 pages.

VAN HUMBEECK, P., "Best practices in regulatory impact analysis: a review of the Flemish region in Belgium", *SERV Working Paper* 2007, 50 pages.

VAN NIEUWENHOVE, J., "Een aantal kanttekeningen bij het wetsvoorstel tot oprichting van een Parlementair Comité belast met de wetsevaluatie", *TVW* 2004, no. 8, 275–278.

VAN NIEUWENHOVE, J., *Wetsevaluatie in België*, Deventer, Kluwer, 2002, 70 pages.

VAN OEVELEN, A., "De burgerrechtelijke en bestuursrechtelijke regeling van de woningkwaliteit in de federale en Vlaamse regelgeving", *RW* 2002–2003, (1401) 1402–1403.

VAN OEVELEN, A. and POPELIER, P., "De aansprakelijkheid van publiekrechtelijke rechtspersonen voor ondeugdelijke wetgeving", in ALEN, A. (ed.), *De doorwerking van het publiekrecht in het privaatrecht*, Gent, Mys & Breesch, 1997, 75–127.

VERLINDEN, V., "Wie hoedt de wet? Op zoek naar een nieuwe invulling van de wetgevingsprocedure", *RW* 2010–11, no. 20, 818–828.

VIERDAG, E.W., "The legal nature of the rights granted by the International Covenant on Economic, Social and Cultural Rights", *Netherlands Yearbook of International Law* 1978, vol. 9, 69–105.

VUYE, H., "Aansprakelijkheid van de Belgische Staat voor het doen en laten van de wetgever", *TBBR* 2002, no. 8, 526–540.

WESSON, M., "Grootboom and beyond: reassessing the socio-economic rights jurisprudence of the South African Constitutional Court", *SAJHR* 2004, vol. 20, 284–308.

WINTERS, S. et al., *Voorstel tot indicatoren voor het Vlaamse woonbeleid,* Leuven, Steunpunt Wonen, 2013, 74 pages.

WINTERS, S. and VERMEIR, D., *The evolution of the private rental market in Flanders*, Leuven, Steunpunt Wonen, 2013, 9 pages.

WINTERS, S. et al., *Op weg naar een nieuw Vlaams sociaal huurstelsel?*, Brussel, Departement RWO, 2007, 79–98.

WOODS, J.M., "Justiciable social rights as a critique of the liberal paradigm", *Texas International Law Journal* 2003, vol. 38, 763–793.

YOUNG, K.G., "The minimum core of economic and social rights: a concept in search of content", *Yale Journal of International Law* 2008, vol. 33, (113) 126–140.

ZWART, S., "Maintaining an efficient and equitable housing market in Belgium", *OECD Economics Department Working Papers, no. 1208*, Paris, OECD Publishing, 2015, 22.

Conclusions

There can be no argument about the importance of adequate housing for everyday life. Not only does it provide shelter against the elements, but our home – a personal and broad concept – is the central operating base of our existence. It allows us to enjoy other (human) rights to their full potential. This has translated itself into the widespread recognition of the right to adequate housing. From UN Covenants through regional Charters to national Constitutions or other domestic legislation, the right to housing has acquired its own place.

Despite this recognition *de iure*, serious shortcomings regarding accessibility and availability, affordability, housing quality and housing security are often still very much a reality. While we have discussed some specific legislative and policy choices to address these problems in particular, the book has primarily focused on how, from a more general perspective, necessary progress with regard to the right to housing at the national level can be triggered or even enforced. In order to do so, we have relied and built on a couple of concepts that have often been used in either socio-economic rights talk in general or the housing rights debate, but which have not yet/always been given due attention with regard to their potential in improving the realization of the right to housing in practice (e.g. human dignity, obligations of result, standstill, progressive realization). The Belgian/Flemish context was used as a convenient starting point and as an illustration throughout the book, but the theoretical findings definitely resonate beyond the jurisdiction of just this one state.

In Part I, we first explored a couple of aspects that should be taken into account when aspiring to a (more) effective right to housing. We did so by expounding the notion of human dignity. While often a source for human rights, it is just as often regarded as a protectable good within the realm of more concrete international and national socio-economic rights. We have investigated what it contributes in a legal context and what it means from the perspective of an effective right to housing.

We have argued that its open-ended nature is problematic for a consistent application in jurisprudence. A justification for human rights or a fundamental right in itself, a minimum core, a synonym for adequate housing or a platform for other rights, etc., a court can interpret human dignity in any of these ways.

In order not to dismiss the important value endowed upon the concept, we have elaborated further on what it signifies as the purpose of the right to adequate housing. In our take on what we have called social dignity, we take into account both the main elements of wellbeing and autonomy/freedom. The latter was constructed as pertaining to both being factually able to exercise one's right to adequate housing and the autonomy that derives from living in an adequate dwelling. We deem a person's perception of this autonomy an important factor as well. On the basis of this double-edged autonomy concept, we have taken a look at social legal aid and Housing First and investigated whether and how social housing meets these criteria of social dignity. We also concluded that while owning property does have its advantages in the context of autonomy (even though these are sometimes overestimated), we do not think it justifies in particular a property-driven housing policy (in favor of a more tenure-neutral one).

When dignity is regarded as an integral part of human rights protection, it has an influence on what an effective right to housing is. But law- and policy-making efforts to improve this fundamental right are subjected to many more sociological elements that (can) have an impact on whether or not they are able to achieve what they set out to. We have discussed how tenants are often in a disadvantaged position in comparison with their landlords. This relates to both access to justice and the position of dependency in which they find themselves. The dependency is, of course, also present when it comes to choosing the appropriate tenant, where a thin line exists between personal preferences, valid financial considerations and discrimination. Housing rights law can be impacted as well by semi-autonomous social fields creating their own inner norms, sometimes opposite to legal norms, or a simple lack of knowledge among the beneficiaries of a right. It is possible, though, that the quality and clarity of legislation, as we have illustrated with the different housing quality norms (federal and regional), has a hand in thwarting the potential of certain measures. Finally, effectiveness can be influenced by the costs and benefits of complying with or breaching certain obligations. In this context, we are in favor of measures that can benefit both tenants as well as landlords, but we stress at the same time that little bargaining room should be available with regard to elementary requirements of adequate housing. This selection of influencing elements must be taken into account for law to be a successful mechanism in the realization of the right to housing, for assuring that housing rights legislation is indeed effective in practice.

As the first of two parts discussing the (potential) scope of state obligations with regard to the right to housing, Part II focused on judgments and decisions by the European Court of Human Rights, the European Committee of Social Rights (ECSR) and to a lesser extent the European Court of Justice. Of these three, the ECSR is unsurprisingly the most straightforward protector of the right to housing. This fundamental right is after all explicitly established in article 31 of the European Social Charter. Unfortunately, most state parties including Belgium have not ratified this particular provision. Considering, though, the other relevant provisions of the Charter from which a right to housing can be derived, a successful collective complaint with regard to a state's housing policy in general seems plausible anyway. In order to counter the legally non-binding nature of the decisions by the Committee carry (regardless of any possible institutional changes), we deem it important to give them as much symbolic and politically authoritative weight as possible. For those purposes it could be useful to authorize national NGOs to lodge complaints as well and to display the Committee's important place in human rights jurisprudence by cross-referencing the European Court of Human Rights. It would be welcomed if the latter would do the same in turn with regard to vital elements of the Committee's decisions. The same can be said with regard to the European Court of Justice, especially since the right to housing assistance in the EU Charter of Fundamental Rights is significantly based on article 31 RESC.

With regard to the European Court of Justice, it is fair to say that while the potential for the right to housing has not yet been fully explored, limitations to the relevant provisions in the EU Charter will remain. Housing as a competence by itself will not become a supranational competence anytime soon. Aside from some decisions on accommodation for asylum seekers and modest attempts to stress the importance of the home, housing-related case law will probably remain very much rooted in legal concerns for free movement. In contrast, the ECtHR has interpreted housing as an important protectable interest in the broader context of several different Convention rights. Confined by the lack of a substantive right to housing, though, the Court imposes states primarily to comply with certain procedural safeguards. It does require the state to take specific circumstances and the disadvantaged position of people into account, but it is obviously not in a position to assess the effectiveness of a housing measure in itself or dictate what measures should be adopted in that context. That also means that a large margin of appreciation is left to the states. In connection to the right to property, the Court does provide some insight in how much a housing policy can or cannot interfere with the right to property. As such, the Court does not remain entirely silent on the admissibility of tenant protecting measures, such as the adoption of rental price control. As we have seen, though, a case could be made that the Court sides more easily with the owner's interests and thereby somewhat limits the possibility for stronger tenant protection.

The third and final part of this research continued exploring the housing rights obligations that are or could be imposed upon the state. Here, however, we searched for a more structural way to strengthen these obligations. Against that background, we embarked upon the idea of developing the right to housing into an obligation of result. Currently, socio-economic rights are often still regarded as the weaker brother to civil and political rights in terms of enforceability. By exploring this concept further, though, unclarities started to arise. Originally a private law concept, the obligation of result and its counterpart, the obligation of means or conduct, were given a secondary and to a certain extent opposite meaning in public international law. With regard to human rights law and socio-economic rights in particular, this has raised serious questions about the exact scope of the obligation. Moreover, it became clear that circumstances could render an obligation of result ineffective as well and that other obligations, maybe not of result in a strict sense, do effectively work towards attaining that result. It is here that we developed the term "result-oriented obligation" as the focal point for a strengthened right to housing.

What followed was an investigation into the meaning and ultimately potential enforceability of result-oriented obligations. We found inspiration in the international human rights concept of progressive realization. Both are, after all, concerned with making progress and working towards – in this case – the full realization of the right to adequate housing. An important element of progressive realization on which we have elaborated extensively is the (principled) prohibition to take retrogressive measures. Since Belgian case law on article 23 of the Constitution has used a similar standstill obligation, it provided a good starting point to investigate how strict retrogressive measures could and should ideally be applied at a national level.

In the end, though, the primary focus should not be on whether measures are retrogressive in the first place. We believe that this can hinder creativity and long-term solution making. The main question should rather be whether progress is actually made or whether a measure is able to do so. With that question firmly in mind, we have looked at monitoring techniques and the possibility of enforcing progressive realization through court. Ultimately, based on practical concerns and with the aim of providing a viable and realistic approach to incentivize result-oriented obligations, we have adopted a proposal that still gives clear precedence to the legislative branch. We argue for an independent monitoring body that conducts both an ex-ante and an ex-post analysis for each measure related to this fundamental right. Rather than assessing whether a rule's objective has been attained, it looks at whether it is/was able to improve the right to housing. The ex-ante assessment should be held at a time when it can still have a substantive impact on the development of the measure, while the evaluation afterwards can rely on the issue-specific research (qualitative and/or quantitative) organized on the basis of the ex-ante analysis to decide whether the measure is indeed result-oriented. As such, this structured assessment process aims to trigger the government *sensu lato* to adopt such measures and make further progress. As the enforceable capstone of the proposal, we have argued in favor of the opportunity to lodge an appeal for annulment of the concerned measure. The Constitutional Court would then be able to support its judgment on the evidence-based character of the assessment(s) by the monitoring mechanism.

Evidently, these three parts have their own perspective. Part I establishes from a broader point of view what an effective right to housing entails, the second part is preoccupied with European (quasi-)jurisprudence and Part III focuses on how to acquire result-oriented obligations at the national level.

But even though each part focuses on its own pathway to strengthen the right to housing, each also contributes to the idea that progress must be made. As such, they should not be perceived as being disengaged from one another.

Take, for example, the practical influences on the effective functioning of housing rights as well as our conception of social dignity from Part I. They should be taken into account when making the assessments *ex ante* and *ex post* in accordance with our proposal in Part III. Social dignity basically provides an explanation of what progress in the context of housing entails, while the more sociological influences on effectiveness play a role in assessing whether a housing measure or policy is able to establish progress "in action". Part II on European (quasi-)jurisprudence also contributes to this bigger picture. The European Committee of Social Rights, for example, pays attention to progressive and effective realization in practice too. Lodging a collective complaint concerning a state's housing policy could confirm or reveal shortcomings and trigger more result-oriented improvements on the national level. With our proposal from Part III in force, this type of decision could also serve as an extra authoritative statement for ex-post law evaluation or even annulment judgments.

In conclusion, we have purposefully chosen, among the bulk of existing housing rights research and publications, to focus and elaborate on just a selection of concepts and options borrowed from human rights law that are in our opinion able to contribute as stepping stones for a more effective right to housing, in Belgium and Flanders but also elsewhere. With housing protected as a fundamental right across the globe and as a protectable interest in jurisprudence, time has come to search for ways to incentivize and to a certain extent even compel progress rather than non-retrogression, in practice rather than only in law. This book has been an attempt to take a step in that direction.

Index

For Product Safety Concerns and Information please contact our EU representative GPSR@taylorandfrancis.com
Taylor & Francis Verlag GmbH, Kaufingerstraße 24, 80331 München, Germany

www.ingramcontent.com/pod-product-compliance
Ingram Content Group UK Ltd.
Pitfield, Milton Keynes, MK11 3LW, UK
UKHW022001180926
475701UK00003B/133
9780367590437